CONSCIOUS ACTION THEORY

Conscious Action Theory provides a logical unification between the spirit and the material, by identifying reality as an event that processes personal experiences into explanatory memories, from which personal experiences are regenerated in a never-ending cycle of activity. Baer explores the idea that our personal feelings are undeniable facts that have been systematically excluded from the basic sciences, thereby leaving us with a schizophrenic division between objective materialism and spiritual idealism.

Conscious Action Theory (CAT) achieves this unification by recognizing that the observer's existence is the foundational premise underlying all scientific inquiry. It develops an event-oriented physical theory in which the first-person observer is central. By analyzing the methods through which we human observers gain knowledge and create the belief systems within which our experiences are explained, we discover a fundamental truth: all systems are observers and exhibit some form of internal awareness. Events, not the objects appearing in them, are the fundamental building blocks of reality. The book is comprised of three parts: the first addresses the paradigm shift from an object to an event-oriented world view, the second develops the foundations of action physics for an event-oriented world view and the third provides examples of how these new ideas can be applied to move our knowledge up the next evolutionary step of human development.

This book will benefit anyone questioning their role in our universe, especially those in interdisciplinary fields of philosophy, psychology, neuroscience and medicine, who seek understanding of quantum theory as the physics of conscious systems that know the world.

Wolfgang Baer received his PhD in physics from the University of California at Berkeley. He held a research professor position at the Naval Postgraduate School in Monterey, California. Dr. Baer now directs research at Nascent Systems Inc. in cognitive systems development and macroscopic quantum effects leading toward theories integrating subjective and objective experiences.

CONSCIOUS ACTION THEORY

An Introduction to the Event-Oriented World View

Wolfgang Baer

Routledge
Taylor & Francis Group
LONDON AND NEW YORK

First published 2020
by Routledge
2 Park Square, Milton Park, Abingdon, Oxon OX14 4RN

and by Routledge
52 Vanderbilt Avenue, New York, NY 10017

Routledge is an imprint of the Taylor & Francis Group, an informa business

British Library Cataloguing-in-Publication Data
A catalogue record for this book is available from the British Library

Library of Congress Cataloging-in-Publication Data
A catalog record for this book has been requested

ISBN: 978-1-138-66746-4 (hbk)
ISBN: 978-1-138-66747-1 (pbk)
ISBN: 978-1-315-61888-3 (ebk)

Typeset in Bembo
by Apex CoVantage, LLC

FSC www.fsc.org MIX Paper from responsible sources FSC™ C013985

Printed in the United Kingdom
by Henry Ling Limited

With great appreciation to my wife
Kathleen
and those who had the courage to read this book before
it was readable
Roland Aldridge, Nikolaus Baer, Eugene Bourakov, Tom Housel,
Harry Jabs, Sandy Leader, Rita Pizzi, and Sharon Runde

CONTENTS

Prologue xv

PART I
The event-oriented world view 1

1 Introduction to the event-oriented world view 3

1.1 The paradigm shift in our concept of reality 5
1.2 The evolution of alternative models of reality 10
1.2.0 Classic and neo-classic models 11
1.2.1 The quantum model 13
1.2.1.1 Quantum scientists execute an action cycle 16
1.2.2 Automating the scientists' action cycle execution 18
1.2.3 The pan-psychic process model 20
1.3 Why and how a quantum physicist sees what he or she believes 22
1.3.1 How normal people experience what they believe 26
1.4 Including consciousness in the model of matter 27
1.4.1 Metaphysical underpinnings of event-oriented physics 28
1.4.2 The inside and outside of matter explained 30
1.4.3 Separating matter to show interior and exterior aspects 31
1.5 Physical implications of the mass-charge interaction 35
1.5.1 Space is a field of events 36
1.5.2 Event interpretation of quantum theory 38

1.6 Event universe examples 41
1.6.1 Division of the whole 41
1.6.2 The three-person division 43
1.6.3 Cosmologic limits and the isolated systems approximation 45
1.6.4 The multiverse model 47
1.7 Conclusion and summary 49

2 Conscious operations in the 1st-person perspective 51

2.1 The 1st-Person Laboratory 53
2.1.1 The feeling of reality 55
2.1.2 The search for the feeling of reality 57
2.2 Symbolic transcendence 58
2.2.1 The meaning assignment operations 60
2.2.2 Nested book meaning references 61
2.2.3 Action type nomenclature 64
2.2.4 Operational and referential symbols 66
2.3 The basic symbolic operations 67
2.3.1 The self-contained Model of Reality 70
2.4 The action-flow model of reality 72
2.5 Examples of simple conscious action cycles 73
2.6 Example of an objective model in the 1st-Person Laboratory 75
2.7 Controlling one's experience 77
2.7.1 Will and desire 79

PART II
Modeling reality 83

3 How to build a conscious action model 85

3.1 Characteristics and requirements of reality model building 86
3.1.1 Book coordinates and symbolic material 86
3.1.1.1 Book space as absolute nothingness 87
3.1.1.2 Using ink as the material of change 88
3.1.1.3 Using ink as the record of change 88
3.1.2 Operations in book coordinates 89
3.1.2.1 Placement and removal of ink 90
3.1.2.2 The turn-page operation 90
3.1.2.3 Representing physical space and format operations 91
3.1.2.4 Representing the content of physical space 93

3.2 Experiencing the model of an isolated system 94
3.2.1 Conscious experience in the playback of a prerecorded record 95
3.2.2 Imagining what the external world does during playback 96
3.2.3 Encoding the operator's subjective role into book symbols 97
3.2.4 A conscious system in a traditional space-time diagram 100
3.2.5 The basic building block 102
3.3 Modeling interacting systems 104
3.3.1 Modeling interactions between parts of a whole 104
3.3.2 Modeling interactions between independent parts 107
3.4 Visualization techniques for human systems 110
3.4.1 The path of the model operator through the book 110
3.4.1.1 Visualization of action cycles in book space 112
3.4.1.2 Visualizing action flow straight through book pages 114
3.4.2 Eliminating the model support structure 115
3.4.2.1 Taking the model off the page 116

4 The action model 118

4.1 The concept of action in classic physics 119
4.1.1 History of action in physics 121
4.1.1.1 The elimination of change in calculus 122
4.1.2 Examples of action in events 122
4.1.2.1 Falling domino example 123
4.1.2.2 Wave motion example 124
4.1.3 The 1st- and 3rd-person perspectives 126
4.2 Characteristics of action structures 127
4.2.1 Characteristics of the medium 127
4.2.2 Reversible and irreversible changes 128
4.2.2.1 Entropy and our fundamental desire 129
4.2.3 The action flows in classic physics models 129
4.2.3.1 The block universe model 130
4.2.4 Action-flow structures in a classic block universe model 131
4.3 The CAT block universe model 133
4.3.1 Adding the subjective phase to classic action theory 133

4.3.1.1 *Identifying the subjective phase as the inside of matter* 134
4.3.1.2 *Force lines and fields stay in their domains* 137
4.3.2 *The nature of material* 137
4.3.2.1 *Grounding abstract action with mass-charge visualizations* 137
4.3.2.2 *The extension of matter* 140
4.3.2.3 *Material degrees of freedom* 141
4.3.3 *Characteristics of empty material space* 142
4.3.3.1 *The volume of action in equilibrium states* 142
4.3.3.2 *Volume of empty-space equilibrium states* 143
4.3.3.3 *The topology of an isolated system* 146
4.3.3.4 *1st-person experience in an isolated universe* 148
4.3.4 *Time, phase and distance* 150
4.3.4.1 *Path selection and the Least Action Principle* 152
4.3.4.2 *Definition of time* 153
4.3.4.3 *The phase of an action cycle* 155
4.3.4.4 *Measuring time in an isolated system* 156
4.3.4.5 *The ultimate ambiguity of time* 159
4.4 *Translating the graphic action model to physics nomenclature* 160
4.4.1 *Parameterization of the action model* 161
4.4.1.1 *The action model in classic physics parameters* 161
4.4.1.2 *The action model in CAT parameters* 163
4.4.2 *Insights provided by mathematical notation* 165
4.4.2.1 *The fundamental desire behind event interaction* 166
4.4.2.2 *The relationship between action flow and forces* 168
4.5 *Examples of action model analysis* 170
4.5.1 *Stationary particle example in CAT* 170
4.5.2 *Harmonic oscillator example* 172
4.5.3 *Oscillator loop closed through the universe* 175

5 The quantum and classic approximation 178

5.1 Classic and quantum theory 178
5.2 The CAT context for quantum theory 179
5.2.1 The action cycle in Conscious Action Theory 179
5.2.1.1 The quantum approximation 181
5.2.2 The CAT action cycle for a human observer 182
5.2.3 Externalization of the von Neumann Cut 185
5.2.3.1 Action flow through an externalized von Neumann Cut 186
5.3 Hilbert space 189
5.3.1 Analysis of a Hilbert space array 190
5.3.1.1 Interpretation of Hilbert space measurement reports 191
5.3.1.2 Small displacement oscillations 193
5.3.2 Motion in coupled Hilbert space cells 195
5.3.2.1 Derivation of the wave function ψ from the CAT model 197
5.3.2.2 What is a quantum particle? 197
5.4 The quantum model of a conscious being 198

PART III
Implications and applications 203

6 Model of a conscious being 205

6.1 Interactions between two almost isolated beings 205
6.2 Building an action-flow model of a conscious being 208
6.2.1 I's general interaction with unknowable reality 208
6.2.2 Limiting external interactions to gravito-electric influences 210
6.2.3 The CAT model of a conscious being 212
6.2.4 A functional description of the action flow in a conscious being 213
6.3 Breakout of internally generated sensation channels 216
6.4 The fundamental algorithm of the reality model 218
6.4.1 Book model implementation of the fundamental algorithm 222
6.5 Registration of model observables with the 1st-person perspective 223
6.6 Projecting the CAT model into observable sensations 225
6.6.1 Visualizing the connection with the observer 227

6.7 Higher-level characteristics of consciousness 229
6.7.1 Hierarchy of action-flow structures 229
6.7.2 Externalization of brain processing 230
6.7.3 Possibility calculation in reversible action flow 230
6.8 Summary of human-level consciousness 233

7 Applications in artificial intelligence and neuroscience 235

7.1 Impact of Conscious Action Theory on science in general 235
7.2 Consciousness in the physical sciences 236
7.2.1 Mapping the CAT model to a 2nd-person's brain 238
7.3 Artificial intelligence and computer consciousness 241
7.3.1 The computer science analogy 241
7.3.2 The CAT analysis of computer consciousness 243
7.4 The extent of computer consciousness 244
7.5 The quantum brain 245
7.5.1 Why should the brain be like a quantum computer? 246
7.5.2 What are quantum computers? 247
7.5.2.1 The quantum bit as two states of motion 250
7.5.2.2 Example of macroscopic parallelism 251
7.5.2.3 The difference between macroscopic and microscopic parallelism 251
7.5.2.4 Measuring a signal containing parallel information 252
7.5.3 From macroscopic to quantum computer architectures 252
7.5.4 The fundamental CAT algorithm in a quantum brain 256
7.6 Neuroscience and the explanations of consciousness 257
7.6.1 The easy problem of consciousness 258
7.6.1.1 A brief review of objective neuroscience 258
7.6.2 Brain hierarchy to quantum scale 259
7.6.3 Physical brain state transforms at different hierarchical levels 261
7.6.4 Macroscopic neurophysiologic mechanisms of consciousness 262
7.6.4.1 Feed-forward loops 262
7.6.4.2 Consciousness from microtubules 263

7.6.4.3 The role of DNA 265
7.6.4.4 The double inside 266
7.7 The CAT model and the glial network 266

8 Philosophy, psychology and religion 271

8.1 Philosophy 271
8.1.1 Plato vs. Aristotle 272
8.1.1.1 Modern Plato's cave 275
8.1.2 Descartes and dual-aspect monism 276
8.1.3 Kant and Wittgenstein 278
8.1.4 Ontology and epistemology 280
8.1.5 Cosmology of our memory structure 280
8.2 Religion 282
8.2.1 The God illusion 283
8.2.2 I am God and so are you 286
8.2.3 Body, mind and soul 287
8.2.4 What happens when we die? 290
8.3 Psychology 293
8.3.1 Illusions, dreams and hallucinations 295
8.3.2 The feeling of oneness vs. separation from the universe 297
8.3.3 Out-of-body experience 298
8.3.4 Near-death experience 299
8.3.4.1 The physiology of engagement and disengagement 301

9 Future development 303

9.1 Dual-eye and bi-scopic perception 305
9.2 Process-oriented economic theory 309
9.3 Gravity and parapsychology 312
9.4 Concluding remarks 313

APPENDICES **315**

A3.1 Definition of terms 317

A4.1 Applicability of mathematical idealizations in physics 321

A4.2 Action theory in isolated systems 323

A4.3 Mach's Principle and gravito-inertial and electromagnetic equation analogy 327

A5.1 Simple derivation of the wave equation 329

A5.2 Action-flow diagrams in quantum nomenclature 332

References and notes *335*
Index *341*

PROLOGUE

The tree of life is dying. Our soul has been banished from our world view. We are expected to be mechanical beings – robots, trained cogs in the wheel of a machine that has hijacked our science and turned its truths into chains. It has obscured our own purpose by bribing us with immediate pleasures while hiding our rightful destiny. It has imprisoned our feelings into a brain of our own making (Lehar, 2003). We have forgotten that it is our feelings that surround us in every direction, that we are our own universe (Chopra and Kafatos, 2017) and that we are a strange loop in time (Hofstadter, 2007), which exists forever (Baer, 2010a).

To recapture control of our destiny we need a new world view and a science that supports our conscious existence in it. My first glimmer of such a view happened in the late 1960s at the University of California at Berkeley. I had proposed a PhD thesis that would include myself as 1st-person conscious observer and active component in a physics experiment (Baer, 1972). Since one of the foundational principles of quantum theory is that the observer could not be taken out of the phenomena being observed, I argued that the explicit inclusion of the physicist in the experiment was the next logical step for science and the future of physics. The thesis committee was not impressed. I was prepared for a discussion on foundational principles. However, the main difficulty centered on the fact that there was no accredited methodology for evaluating a thesis that was outside the standards of acceptable physics. The department chair rejected my proposal outright, while Charles Townes, Nobel Laureate for the discovery of the laser, was more supportive. A compromise was reached. My standard thesis on the spectral classification of Promethium was accepted, and my expanded physics, which would include a conscious observer, was to be relegated to an un-graded appendix.

The spectrum of Promethium was of interest at the time because this element is only found in nature as a product of nuclear fusion, hence if found in starlight its spectrum would indicate the presence of civilizations that had advanced atomic technologies and possibly an atomic war. As an extra-terrestrial civilization tracer

FIGURE P.1 Thesis registration mug shot

my standard thesis was of considerable interest. I should have been happy. I had passed. However, I was deeply disappointed. The milieu at UC Berkeley in the late '60s had challenged my sense of reality. My personal experiences could not be explained by the theories we were being taught in school. Something was missing and I felt strongly that the systematic elimination of the 1st-person observer from physical theory was a fundamental cause of the gap between what I was feeling and the science I was told to believe.

Could my mentors not understand the importance of adding the subjective 1st-person experience to the physical underpinnings of our scientific world view? A moment's reflection tells us we are more than the body and things we see around it. Materialism is not grasping our actual situation. Its objective 3rd-person methodology only tells half the story. The neglected other half includes the subjective 1st-person experience. Sadly I resigned myself. If I believed that *You and I are bigger and more fundamental than the things we experience* and sought to reformulate science to include our conscious selves, I would have to work outside the sacred halls of our secular institutions. If I believed the first law of physics should be "That the physicist made the law", I would have to prove it by deriving a better theory than currently available and also include the physics of the 1st-person perspective with which we are endowed. Thus contemporary physics became my day job.

I finished my thesis work in record time and found employment as a computer systems engineer in Silicon Valley where making things work was more important than academic peer approval of consensus theories. It was a heady time, when all aspects of engineering work were being computerized. I worked on exciting projects like the early GPS system, flew weather satellites and started a company that developed the graphics system that showed the Mount St. Helens blow-up to Congress. My greatest luck was to land a contract to insert virtual smart weapons effects into war-game maneuvers at Ft. Hunter Liggett, California. This required real-world terrain updates and parallel sensor-to-memory feedback loops, which caused me to realize such architectures would mimic consciousness if they were miniaturized in the human brain. I began doing experiments after hours and started publishing papers on the physics of consciousness. I attended conferences, which gave me an opportunity to discuss how our personal subjective experience could be integrated into the objective sciences.

I quickly realized that the problem I had set out to tackle was substantially larger than including the experimenter's motivations and interpretations in a physics experiment. No one knows how the mind works (Pinker, 1997, 146). To address this question would require a fundamental shift in how we perceive ourselves and the objects in our environment. A shift of our operational frame of mind was required. But how was I to describe such a shift in a clear and convincing way when most readers and even quantum theorists believe reality is "out there" in front of their noses independent of their own existence? This "objective reality" assumption is still a cornerstone of Western thought and it is the main challenge and goal of this book to replace it with one that allows the feelings and desires of perceived objects to be included in a consistent physical framework.

New habits are hard to learn. Every time I look up at the night sky and watch the moon and stars twinkle in the heavens, I struggle to remember that I am experiencing sensations created in my own self. The firmament of dots I see above me are my own perceptions, which are quite different from whatever caused them. But expressing this reality is difficult. The very words "watch the moon and stars" already contain a theoretical conclusion built into our language that moons and stars actually cause our sensations. Right or wrong, this conclusion skips over the fact that we are actually interpreting a flow of stimulation. We do not notice that this flow is being continuingly processed *into* the experience of objects we have programmed ourselves to accept as our reality. Science and the subject-verb-predicate sentence structure taught in English classes have teamed up to eliminate our real selves simply by not mentioning what we do to see what we see. We believe we see objects because they are really there and no conscious awareness of how we interpret our sensations is necessary for making good lifetime decisions. How stimulation to our sensors become those objects out there is the grandest of challenges facing science today. Until it is solved we will steadily slide into the persona of the robots created by statistical accidents that contemporary science claims we are.

The book you are about to read meets the challenge by adding subjective phenomena to the very foundations of science rather than as an emergent end product of random luck. In doing so we will not dwell on the failures of current theories. Objective science has value. It allows us to build things because it *limits* itself to the actionable information display honed by our primate ancestry. It does not address the larger human situation. What is this 1st-person experience? How does it evolve? What happens when we die? A myriad of books point out that material science has no answers to such questions. We no longer need to be reminded of this deficiency. Instead, what we need now is workable answers. Stepping outside our own framework is not easy. The invention of symbols makes it possible. With them we developed technology, not the other way around, and it is time to reclaim our identity as masters of our symbol-making endeavor. We have the power to take the next step along the road of evolution. We can learn to recognize our larger selves as events that contain their own time and space rather than as objects that are controlled in someone else's time and space. But as mentioned previously, these ideas are difficult to express within the subject-verb-predicate paradigm our language enforces. Therefore this volume uses process-flow diagrams as heuristic aids to explain the "Reality" we actually live in.

It is recommended that readers flip through all the figures to get the gist of the content. After that most readers will and should skip over the mathematical formulas and concentrate on the story told by the text and figures. Equations and mathematical terms are used to show that our expansion of science is based upon a foundation of well-established physical theories. Understanding this book does not require detailed knowledge of such theories or their mathematical formulations. The reader will be given a new, expanded, self-centered interpretation of science as he or she moves through the pages. Though we are advancing physics, the goal for most readers will be to achieve a new event-oriented vantage point from which to understand their existence, not to become a physicist. Thus, this book helps the reader to transfer the framework holding his or her knowledge to a new action paradigm that will only make sense after all the pieces have been assimilated. To help with this assimilation, this book is organized into three main parts.

Part I introduces the paradigm shift from an object to an event-oriented world view. It summarizes how our concept of matter must be expanded to incorporate subjective experiences. It proposes we are actually events rather than objects and gives examples of how to build and operate event models that incorporate the mind in a physical framework. This first part includes two chapters.

Chapter 1 provides a complete overview of the Conscious Action Theory (CAT) and the role of the 1st-person experience in it. It traces the origins of our evolving reality concepts from early Greeks to modern science. It discovers the processes we have always executed. These merge our direct 1st-person sensations with our 3rd-person belief projections, which allows conscious experiences to happen. It shows how we visualize these processes by adding a subjective phase to our theory of objective material. This identifies conscious forces happening in a physical system. The chapter concludes with a vision of ourselves as interacting activities in a multiverse of events that replaces our current world view of objects or probabilities in empty space.

Chapter 2 analyzes the thought process we actually execute when constructing the actionable information display we normally act upon. This chapter shows how our mental concepts of reality are externalized in symbolic models that are adjusted to match our measured sensation display. Once our models are updated this chapter shows how the knowledge stored in them is projected back into sensations to produce the fused feeling of the real world we believe to be living in. These first two chapters will suffice to introduce the new mental framework.

For readers wishing to know the benefits of learning the event-oriented way of thinking, skipping directly to the application chapters in Part III is recommended. For those who want learn more about the physics of interacting events, Part II develops the foundations of action physics for an event-oriented world view using nomenclature familiar to readers who have taken some physics or engineering courses. Such terminology is necessary to ground our development in known physical facts. The material concepts of space, time and the architecture of stable events discussed in Chapter 4 will be of interest to all and can be qualitatively understood without specialized knowledge. However the mathematical nomenclature will not be familiar to all readers and passing over equations is recommended for readers who are only interested in grasping the gist of the action-flow physics which quantitatively supports event-oriented thinking.

Chapter 3 presents the characteristics and methods for building an action model of reality that can hold our explanatory memories in the form of a book. Here we address the limitations of the medium which carries the message of a new paradigm to the reader, how a book is used to store the new found knowledge, and how reading and projecting meaning into its symbols is the activity which models Reality.

Chapter 4 provides an introduction to the technical development of event physics in which the flow of stable action forms replaces particles and fields as the fundamental building blocks of "Reality". Here we will show how changes in stable action-flow architectures can produce the appearance of the solid objects we see. We will learn how the functional flow diagrams describing our thought processes are converted into a physical formalism that describes the behavior of all material, whether dead or alive. The flow of activity between our experiences and the memories that explain and control those experiences is proposed as a template for a pan-psychic physics based on interacting events.

Chapter 5 will clarify the counter-intuitive development of quantum theory in the 20th century by reintroducing the processes connecting observable and theoretical experiences. These processes have been eliminated in the statistical fog which hides the mental aspect of physical theories. Replacing particles with small reversible events will make quantum theory more intuitive and understandable. Further understanding of large irreversible events that include our own creation and destruction will open the door to rational management of new phenomena heretofore intractable in current science.

Part III provides examples of how these new ideas can be applied to move our knowledge up the next evolutionary step of human development. Readers unfamiliar with consciousness studies and physical theories are encouraged to start with Chapter 8 and learn what benefits might accrue from this paradigm change, and then return to Chapter 1 to see how it can be done.

Chapter 6 then continues the use of flow diagrams to explain how our action structure contains the 1st-person experience without ad hoc miracles or supernatural intervention. How the architecture of action flow can be grown from the primitive aspects of material to achieve human consciousness is addressed in this chapter.

Chapter 7 shows how artificial intelligence, neuroscience and psychiatry can be advanced by logically grounding the human psyche in the physical activity in which it is imbedded. The change to event-oriented thinking will encourage fundamental progress in these fields of knowledge.

Chapter 8 will be appreciated by individuals leaning toward the humanities. It discusses how Conscious Action Theory will address the big questions of philosophy and religion. Here we will learn how a self-consistent understanding of ourselves as action-seeking events will allow us to conceive of our existence as lifetimes of excitation in transition between timeless states of equilibrium in which force and its associated pain is eliminated.

Lastly Chapter 9 addresses selected topics of future development. Advanced work ranging from performance enhancements, to economics and parapsychology will point to examples that show how a physical-based theory explaining our feelings and thoughts can be used to develop new instruments and procedures. Though speculative these examples suggest how advances in a wide range of disciplines can benefit from an event-oriented frame of mind.

Whatever path You, dear Reader, chose to take through this book, You are encouraged to first become familiar with the definition of terms in Appendix A3.1. Specifically note that the use of nouns has been expanded. The four first letter codes "A, a, **A**, **a**" to respectively represent the cause activities themselves and their three interaction processing phases are required in an observer in order to recognize objects. The unexpected use of capitals referring to You, as well as bold first letters and nonstandard grammar is deliberate.

PART I

The event-oriented world view

1

INTRODUCTION TO THE EVENT-ORIENTED WORLD VIEW

The main objective of this book is to integrate the observer's subjective experiences, feelings, pleasures and pains into a rigorous theory of reality that expands rather than negates technical advances of current science. The first step toward this goal is a description of the 1st-person's conscious experience that is concrete and unambiguous. Figure 1 defines the visual experience of a typical human (Baer, 1972). It shows an individual sitting in an armchair looking out through his left eye into the living room of an apartment. He sees his nose on the right side and his left hand is holding a book. This optical sensory display will be used in this book to represent all subjective experiences. Later parallel sensory channels will be added to include the full spectrum of human experience. For now, it will be used to show how personal sensations are generally connected to the physical world.

Figure 1 was inspired by one published by J. Gibson (1950) to investigate perception, which was in turn derived from a drawing by Ernst Mach (1867). It describes what we actually see but it was originally called "The Visual Ego of Ernst Mach". Ego is a term coined by Sigmund Freud to refer to the control center of the human psyche. It is where actionable information is displayed, and desired intentions expressed. It has also been called "the third eye", Hermann Hesse's "magic theater" or Bernard Baars's "global workspace" (Baars, 1997).

As these names suggest and the drawing implies, our everyday surroundings are actually phenomena happening in a component of the human psyche. It supports the belief that we create our experiences inside a bigger "Self" than the body we see. This bigger Self incorporates a mental display of our environment that includes the appearance of our body. We will show that our "body" can be identified with any appearance that functions as a control lever that moves by will and whose motions modify both our subjective experiences and the external physical reality to which they are connected.

FIGURE 1 The projection into Plato's cave circa 1972 AD

The claim is not new. Long before these drawings were made and named, it was known that what we see is not equal to what there is (Hoffman and Prakash, 2014). The claim goes all the way back to the Plato's cave analogy in which ordinary humans are chained – locked in their bodies – to look only at shadows projected on the walls through an entrance leading to a bright reality of ideals. Since Plato's ideal reality could be identified with God's domain, this division between what we see and what really is was espoused by the Catholic Church throughout the Middle Ages. A change started around 1225 AD when Thomas Aquinas recommended an adoption of Aristotle's natural philosophy. That view rejected Plato's dualistic distinction and proposed that we are not seeing what he called "shadows" of reality in our everyday lives, but instead are looking directly at such a reality through the windows of our senses. Taking what we see for what is, is called the "objective reality assumption" that underpinned the emergence of science and the practical development of classic physics from Newton's time onward.

The belief that "we see what is" dominates popular thinking to this day but it has been challenged by quantum theorists since the beginning of the 20th century. Quantum physicists no longer considered reality to be what we see. Rather, a murky probability amplitude, described by Schrödinger's wave function "ψ", has been resurrected as Plato's ideal reality while measuring instruments have become the entrance to our cave. Figure 1 should therefore be interpreted as a modern-day version of Plato's cave. We are the little men or women chained inside our skull. Plato's shadows are the configuration of objects and sensations we normally experience around us (Pinker, 1997, 84).

Unfortunately, the paradigm switchback to Plato's world view has not led to a quantum theory applicable to the macroscopic world of everyday experience until now. This book provides such a theory. It does so by first reasserting the Platonic distinction between what we see and what is physically real, and second by quantifying the physical connections between what-is and how-it-is-perceived. This book claims:

1 reality is a process that connects what-is with what-is-perceived in a cyclic event, and
2 such events rather than particles are the building blocks of a universe, as well as ourselves.

I understand that this assertion requires a fundamental change in scientific thinking. It implies that we are more than the body, which we obviously observe. I know many readers will reject this premise outright. I ask those readers to peer past their noses with the right eye closed as shown in Figure 1 and note that we are seeing the *result* of a measurement process that transforms sensory stimulation into an actionable "Now" information displayed in what has been called our mind. This "Now" is all we experience. We cannot directly see our physical sensors since they always happened one process step ahead of what is actually presented to us. Nor can we directly see the muscle actuators affecting the physical world until their activations propagate signals back to our sensors and then processed into our next Now display again.

When we first opened our eyes after birth, we practiced exploring our sensations and built a reasonably consistent display of our experiences. Reinforced by parents and teachers, we were taught to operate under the assumption that external reality is exactly identical to what our mental display shows us. This works well for the rest of our lives so long as all we want to do is optimize our material existence based upon the tools our ancestors have evolved so far. For those who want to know what we really are, how we work, how to fix us when we break or how to climb the next step in the ladder of evolution, a larger view of ourselves becomes necessary. We must integrate our subjective conscious experiences with the physical world and conceive of both as a single existence. This book shows why and how to achieve that goal, and its success will justify the change in thinking I am asking the "Reader" to make.

1.1 The paradigm shift in our concept of reality

The early-life process just described is a learning activity that builds a concept of the environment we believe to live in and the actions we can take to make our living experience more satisfying. The result of that activity grows our current classic objective model of reality shown in Figure 1.1-1.

The optical mental experience is surrounded by a thought bubble, which represents the Now experience when one's eyes are closed. This space contains sensations of thoughts, dreams and displays of other sensory modalities.

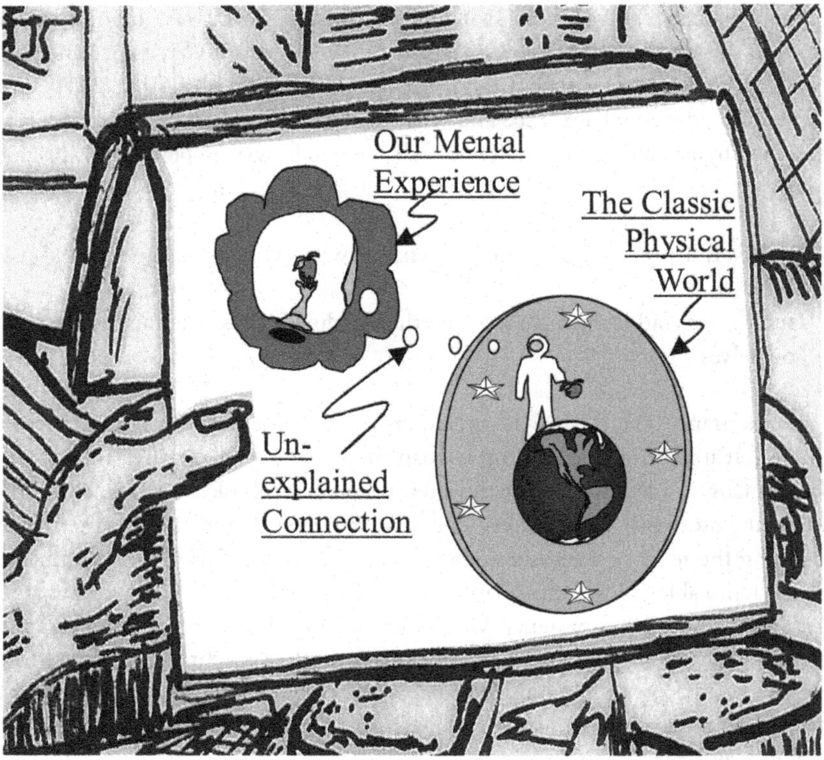

FIGURE 1.1-1 The classic objective reality model

We currently assume the cause of our 1st-person experience is a classic physical objective world represented by the icon on the bottom of Figure 1.1-1. The body of the observer is standing on the earth surrounded by space and stars. This is the Kantian "thing-in-itself", i.e. a permanent physical reality that is supposed to exist whether our body in it is alive or not. The objective scientific world view tells us that when we are alive and conscious, our physical brain generates our 1st-person sensations. This brain is represented by the small oval inside the head of the individual in Figure 1.1-1. The standard view nicely documented by Velmans (2000) states that physical signals emanating from the surface of the apple propagate to sensors attached to our head. The resulting stimulation is processed by the brain and projected into the sensation of the apple represented in the upper 1st-person's perspective. Velmans assumes these projections collocate sensations and their physical causes at the same point in objective space. In Figure 1.1-1, projections into the thought bubble are outside the physical universe in conformance to Descartes's dualism, which assumes that mental experiences are not made of the same material and are not located in the space of real things. Whether mental sensations can also stimulate effecter cells that produce changes in objective bodies or whether such experiences are purely epiphenomenal is controversial. In any case, the mechanism for this projection or the sensation projected is not part of objective physical reality and is not explainable within current science (Stapp, 1993).

This fact is known as Chalmers's (1997) "hard problem of consciousness" and is exemplified by Levine's (1983) "explanatory gap". The gap implies science has no explanation for how a physical activity of any kind in the brain can produce the sensation of an object several feet in front of that brain. For this reason, our Figure 1.1-1 follows the conventional practice of cartoon literature in depicting the connection between the physical world and our mental sensations with a sequence of bubbles. These indicate what we all believe, i.e. that such a connection must exist, but we are not sure how it happens. Solving this problem requires nothing less than a new world view in which events containing conscious sensations replace objects as the fundamental building blocks of reality. It is the goal of this book to present such a world view along with a new physical science that underpins its practical applications in the future.

The next step toward achieving this goal is to recognize that the description provided by the classic-reality model shown in Figure 1.1-1 is flawed and incomplete. The representation of reality as a three-dimensional instance of space surrounding objects is not accurate. A careful examination of the facts (see Chapter 2) will show that the processing steps required to explain our 1st-person experience involves a flow of action between those sensations and our memory holding our model of whatever we believe explains those sensations. In other words, the lower portion of Figure 1.1-1 cannot represent the real physical world, but instead represents *our model* of that world. **S**cience and specifically the physics underpinning our science does not describe Reality, but rather describes our knowledge of Reality in our memory. We wake up every morning by loading the content of that memory into our immediate Now display until we are surrounded by the sensations describing our world and our situation in it. Whether our eyes are open or closed, the Now display of that knowledge fills the mind space, represented by a thought bubble, and guides our actions throughout the day.

Conscious Action Theory (CAT) replaces the mysterious bubbles connecting our sensations and the physical world. The mystery is replaced with a flow of action through measurement sensors and command actuators connecting those same sensations to our internal memory model, which explains those sensations. Following Pinker (1997, 134), consciousness is "building an internal model of the world that contains a [**S**]elf". Our traditional independent physical reality then becomes a physical component of a thought process under our control. This shift makes the process of creating and updating that model the central activity of human intellectual progress.

CAT proposes a processing cycle, shown in Figure 1.1-2, in which our sensations appear during one phase while the explanation of those sensations happens during another phase. An array of sensations occurring in our Now is processed through an explanatory activity into a model of reality, which is concurrently examined by a Measurement Activity that generates a new sensation in a continuous event loop. Werner Heisenberg, a founder of quantum theory, thought quantum theory was

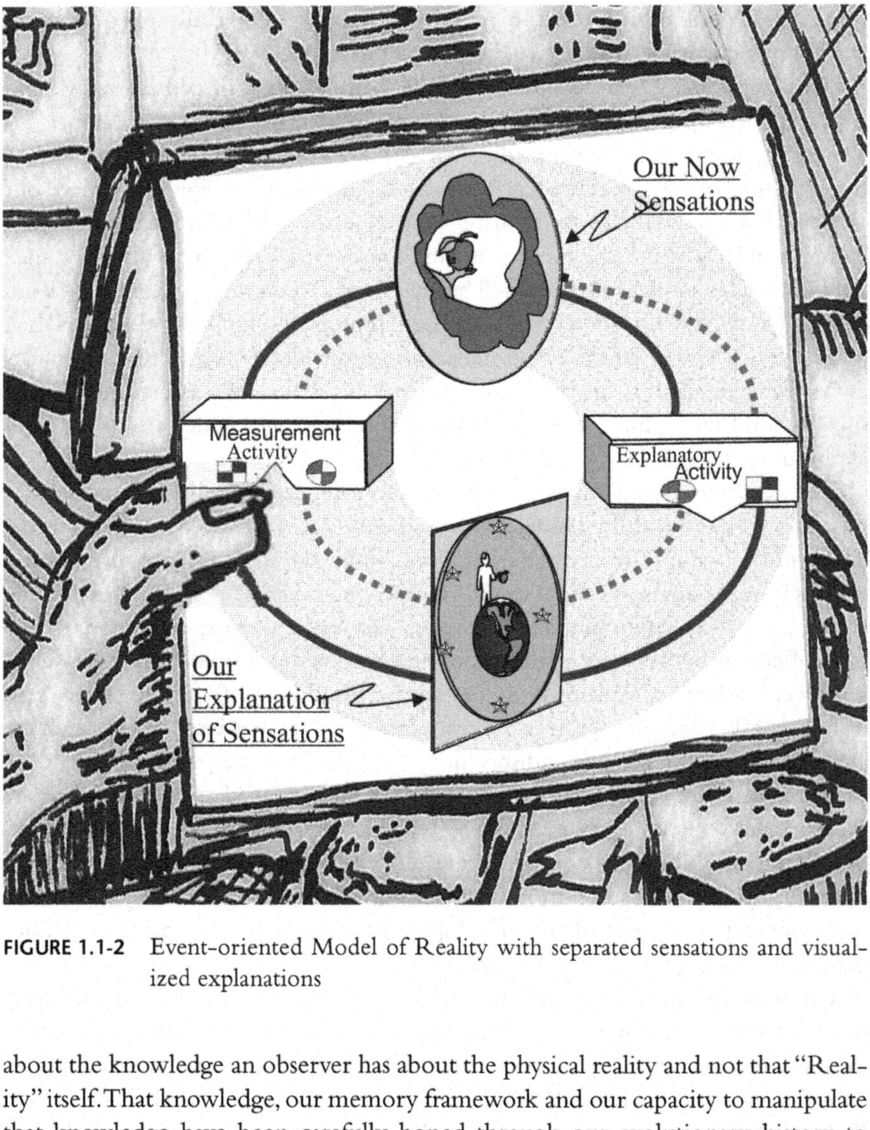

FIGURE 1.1-2 Event-oriented Model of Reality with separated sensations and visualized explanations

about the knowledge an observer has about the physical reality and not that "Reality" itself. That knowledge, our memory framework and our capacity to manipulate that knowledge have been carefully honed through our evolutionary history to present us with an actionable information display we use to control our activities. Accurate or not, it works to a degree, but has always been a component of our thought process, not the totality of what we are.

What we are is a flow of action passing around a sequential time loop. This is the description of our bigger Self. We are Hofstadter's (2007) strange loop. This loop is the event we execute during conscious operations (Walker, 2000). We are the event happening, which provides the context for both the objective thing and the subjective personal experience felt by that thing. It is also the event that replaces the "thing" in Kant's "thing-in-itself". Kant's thing-in-itself is no longer the a priori physical reality that continues to exist as an independent object whether we are alive or not. Kant's reality has now been replaced by the "event-in-itself". Events

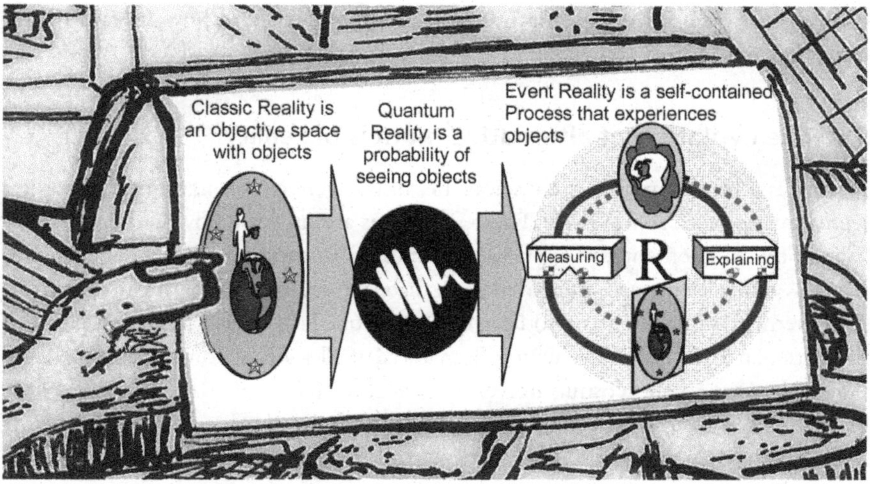

FIGURE 1.1-3 Object to quantum to event-oriented paradigm shift

continue to exist as independent activities whether our objective body appearing in that event is alive or not. The event-oriented world view does not deny the concept of an external independent existence. *It is not solipsism.* It merely replaces the objective visualization of those entities with their visualization as events. "Reality" is no longer a set of objects moving in a three-dimensional space but a set of interacting events that incorporates the appearance of objects and space within those events.

The implications for science are a fundamental paradigm shift from an object to a quantum and on to an event-oriented world view graphically depicted in Figure 1.1-3. What science has been describing in both classic as well as quantum physical theories developed during the last half-millennium is shown on the left. This no longer represents reality itself but rather the knowledge the scientist currently has about that "Reality".

As Sir Arthur Eddington (1938) pointed out with his "Fish Story", as long as we believe that we project our sensations onto an independent objective reality, the search for fundamental answers sought by often large and expensive science experiments will only reveal the methodologies and the construction rules of the systems employed in those investigations. If instead we realize that we transform our experimental results into our own models, as shown in the action cycle on the left of Figure 1.1-3, then we can concentrate on improving those models so we can engineer subjective phenomena we now find intractable in science.

Of course, this path makes no claim that we will ever know "Reality" itself. Even Kant claimed this thing-in-itself is completely unknowable (D'Espagnat, 1989). However, as mentioned previously, the event Model of Reality (MoR) is an operating component of our thought process. It is not accurate knowledge of "Reality", which defines evolutionary success, but rather survival and the ability to efficiently steer one's sensations to more satisfaction that is rewarded. The next section will examine the historic development of physical reality models to show how the evolutionary path of model improvement has progressed and how it leads to the event-oriented world view.

1.2 The evolution of alternative models of reality

Reality is a process which is conscious because it generates sensations in the subjective phase of an action cycle. These sensations are processed by material organizations that implement the explanatory function to produce a Model of Reality (MoR) which is, in turn, measured by a material organization that implements a measurement function to reproduce the sensation. This cyclic architecture is the fundamental form of activity which all material at all scales – from the infinitesimal Planck lengths to the cosmic universe – executes (Baer, 2010a). The top center of Figure 1.2-1 shows a typical action cycle with an apple sensation at the top and a region containing the general explanation of sensations, labeled "Model of

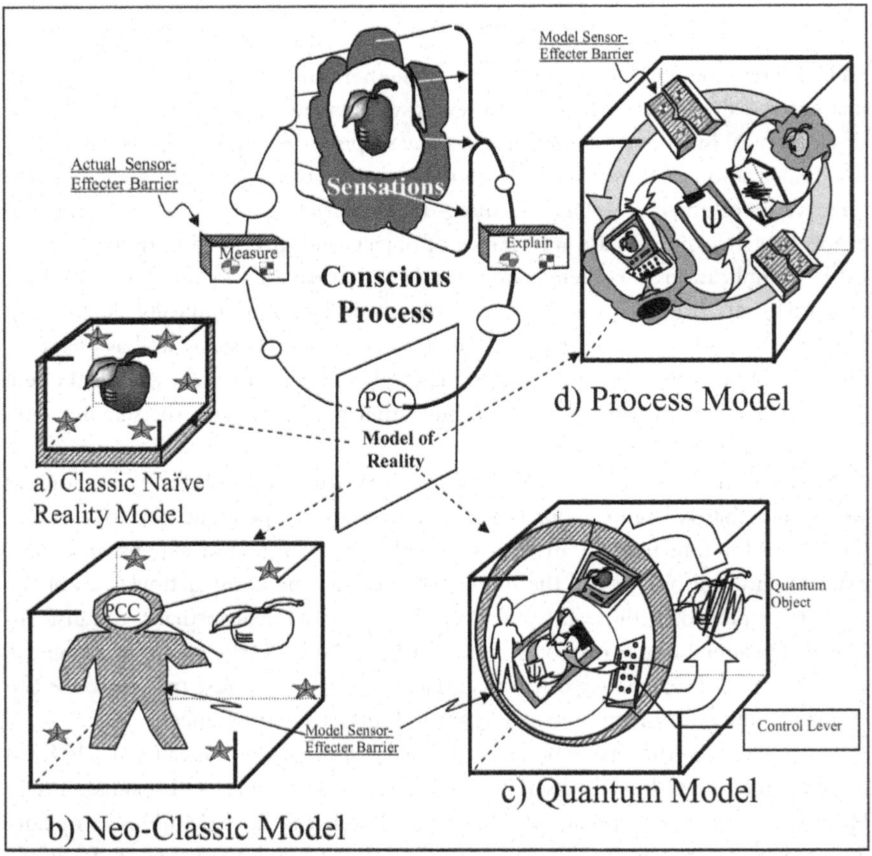

FIGURE 1.2-1 The historic evolution of human Models of Reality that can be installed in the consciousness process cycle

Reality", at the bottom. The symbols defining such models represent the design of incorporated beliefs we hold to explain our experiences. Thus, the meaning of the expression "Model of Reality" is, by definition, whatever entities explain our sensations. We will use drawings inside parallelograms as symbols to represent the belief structures one uses to explain one's sensations.

Given the 1st-person sensation example of an apple, the question addressed in Figure 1.2-1 is, "What theories or models can be used to explain those 1st-person sensations?" To emphasize this point, dashed arrows connect the generic explanation of sensations labeled "Model of Reality" in Figure 1.2-1 with a sequence of alternative models. Different models have been substituted into the explanatory phase of the conscious process by various cultures throughout history. The alternative explanations start on the left with the belief described by philosophers as "objective reality" and lead to an icon intended to represent the "event or process model" on the right. The intent of these drawings is to represent selected examples of reality theories that show a progression of explanations culminating in the process model. I will start by describing "objective reality" and progress counterclockwise through the sequence.

1.2.0 Classic and neo-classic models

Classic objective reality asserts that the experience in front of your nose is the way it is because a real world of physical objects exists the way it appears. An individual asked why he sees an apple would probably say, "Because it is there". The transformations between physical reality and sensory experiences are immediate and direct. Mathematically both the explaining and measuring activities are an identity multiplication operator that makes no changes, since the content of both phases in the action cycle are identical pictures of an apple object. Objective reality underlies classic physics and completely ignores the role of the observer and his or her consciousness. There is no mind in this picture. The primary advantage of this belief is one of speed. The individual using it simply reacts to the configuration of experiences as they appear without the overhead imposed by the awareness of the experience-generating mechanism. The objective reality connections are learned in early childhood and for most of us persist without question throughout adult life. It is by far the most popular and practical reality model used by scientists and athletes alike. It is commonly assumed that this is the way we were built to operate.

If one takes the time to analyze more complex experiences, for example when looking into a mirror, one realizes that not all appearances are physical objects. To accommodate this realization, the objective reality model is modified into what I will call the "neo-classic model" described in Velmans's (2000) works introduced in the last section and shown in Figure 1.2-1b. The neo-classic model includes an observer and his or her brain among the mix of moving objects populating physical reality. In this model, a chain of cause and effect connects the physical apple through a boundary of sensors (shown as diagonal shading lines covering the body's neural network) with the parts of the brain thought to be responsible for generating conscious experiences. Individuals using the "neo-classic model" no longer believe the apple appears because it is there. Rather, the apple appears because some physical phenomena have the ability to project the appearance of objects onto their actual location.

Unfortunately for the neo-classic model, the exact location or the composition of the consciousness-generating mechanism has not yet been identified. It is assumed that the brain, shown as the white oval brain in Figure 1.2-1b, is responsible. It is hoped by most neurophysiologists (Koch and Crick, 1998) that a mind-body correlation will eventually be found in the observable brain and thus provide not a solution to Chalmers's "hard problem", but at least a working control of conscious experiences suitable for medical applications. These sought-after physical activities are known as Neural Correlates of Consciousness because conventional wisdom assumes the neural network is responsible for conscious experiences (Metzinger, 2000). Rather than limit this connecting region to the neural network, this book presents a more general connection between physical and mental experiences called Physical Correlates of Consciousness (PCC) (Chalmers, 1996, 238).

How the PCC are encountered in neurosciences will be discussed in Chapter 7. Here we would like to emphasize that the PCC are a kind of gateway between the physical world and the mental world that had in the past been attributed to the pineal gland by Descartes (Pinker, 1997, 77). In CAT this gateway is conceived as a kind of three-dimensional structure with two aspects. One aspect appears as a set of physical activities explored by neuroscientists when applying reductionism to an analysis of the apparent brain (see Section 4.3.1.1). The second aspect is the inside of material, which looks like the everyday experiences happening to the owner of that brain. We will show it is not a small funnel through which influences squeeze but rather our entire three-dimensional scene surrounding us connected point-for-point to the underlying physical activity. When we peer past our noses, we can imagine our sensations of space and objects are correlated to physical occurrences that happen just before and behind those sensations. These occurrences are not located in the brain one feels behind one's eyes but immediately ahead *in time* to what one sees out there. The physical occurrences and the experiences they produce are two three-dimensional structures separated by temporal processing steps.

The usual diagram of the neo-classic model is often mistakenly interpreted as dividing physical reality into two spatial regions, which are 1) the PCC inside our brain and 2) the rest of the universe outside that apparent brain. Time order is often neglected. Here we note that when installing the neo-classic model as the physical reality model in the central-action cycle of Figure 1.2-1, the PCC are viewed from an external 3rd-person point of view, and the solid-line connecting arcs are attached to the past sides of the PCC region as shown. However, after the Model of Reality (MoR) executes, it outputs its result on the back side, which becomes the future next sensation experienced. The processing arcs represent many parallel channels through which action flows in a clockwise direction, but past-future labeling reverses because the MoR executes a feed-forward loop predicting the next expected sensation.

One can make an analogy to a control room by imagining a conscious homunculus between the past input and future output signal, while the homunculus is looking at an internal display of incoming signals and acting on internal levers to generate outgoing messages. This analogy leads to the architecture of quantum theory to be discussed next.

1.2.1 The quantum model

By moving the sensor-effecter barrier between the PCC and the objective world outside one's body and into external instrumentation, the control-room metaphor becomes more realistic. One can imagine an actual physical body, such as a military commander in a control room, taking the role of Plato's prisoners, sensing internal displays, and moving command levers that work because they are attached to what is real through the communication channels built into the architecture of the control room. The analogy breaks down only because the commander can exit the control room and personally witness events outside the barrier of sensors and effecters and thus witness the difference between symbolic actions inside the control room and their meanings in the external world. This barrier is not penetrable in the case of a scientist investigating the structure of atoms or an astrophysicist investigating the properties of a black hole. By defining an impenetrable barrier surrounding one's objective reality world of sensations, we reach the quantum model represented by the third explanation for sensations in Figure 1.2-1c.

In our diagram we have deliberately pushed the impenetrable sensor-effecter barrier, again shown as a diagonally shaded region, from inside the brain of the scientist into external measuring instruments to emphasize the fact that in the quantum model, the role of the PCC, now the control room, is taken by the ordinary world of naïve realism encountered in the laboratory. Of course, the actual conscious experiences are still thought to happen by the processing flow through the scientist, but the content of the laboratory is treated as the region in which appearances are equated to real objects. In Chapter 2 we will assume the 1st-person view of the scientist to explore how experiments are perceived in what will be called the 1st-Person Laboratory (1st-PL).

Moving the impenetrable barrier in the opposite direction, from laboratory equipment into the brain, is a well-known technique designed to eliminate the classic component in quantum theory. Most discussions of the quantum measurement problem (Wheeler and Zurek, 1983) start with the sensor-effecter barrier (known as the von Neumann Cut) provided by instruments placed in the laboratory between the classic and quantum worlds. A typical experiment treats a quantum system outside the instrumentation barrier as a probability that is actualized into observable object records through the measurement process. This leaves the scientist, the laboratory, the measuring apparatus and its measurement display as classic objects. Quantum theorists would like it if all phenomena could be explained by their theory. However, when the measuring apparatus is also treated as a probabilistic quantum object, the question becomes, "What actualizes the measurement apparatus?"The answer requires a second apparatus that measures the first apparatus combined with the initial quantum system of interest as a combined quantum system. These three systems (the inside measuring system, the outside measuring system and the combined initial quantum system) must now also be actualized by the measurement of a fourth system, etc. The introduction of new measuring instruments continues until the brain of the physicist becomes the final measurement instrument. When this brain is also moved to the quantum side of the barrier, the consciousness mechanism implemented by the PCC of the observer is all that is left to perform the actualization. The theory presumes pure consciousness selects one classic physical state out of the possibilities present in the quantum world and displays that physical state as the objective world of appearances.

Though credit must be given to the quantum theorists who acknowledge the critical role consciousness must play in determining our actual experiences, the treatment has shed little light on the nature of consciousness. How, or even where its supposed actualization is performed remains a mystery. Our treatment differs from the typical analysis by acknowledging that physical reality, whether quantum or classical, is not all there is. Reality must connect physical reality to and from the 1st-person experience. We embrace classic or quantum duality as an architectural feature, not a flaw in our event-oriented world view. Rather than squeeze the brain and its PCC into the mystery of consciousness and thereby eliminate the subjective portion of reality from the physical sciences, we enlarge the PCC and ask, "What process might be happening inside the material realm to achieve conscious experiences?"

To answer this question, we emphasize that when appearances in the laboratory are treated as the things-in-themselves, the entire laboratory becomes a control-room metaphor for the externalized Physical Correlates of Consciousness (PCC). The externalization also emphasizes the flow of signals in time. As some real brain components happen directly prior to what is seen, so the monitor screens in the scientist's laboratory happen prior to signals reaching the scientist. The operations in the laboratory can therefore be treated as externalized versions of what is happening inside the brain of the scientist. The absolute impenetrability of the sensor-effecter barrier makes the quantum physicist, unlike the little-man in a control room, a perfect analogy for the homunculus. *By systematically mapping the physicist's theory onto symbol-manipulation mechanisms performed in the laboratory, we can document the physicist's own role and derive a purely classic physical world representation of the thinking process responsible for his or her personal experiences.*

Note that Figure 1.2-1c, repeated here for convenience, includes an icon of a notepad upon which the scientist's externalized thinking process is mapped. A quantitative description will be provided of this thought process mapping in Part II and only give a brief qualitative overview in the following paragraphs.

The mapping begins by asking the scientist to write a description of the measurement results displayed on the television screen onto the notepad. The screen information is represented by the "a" in the circle, which stands for an action

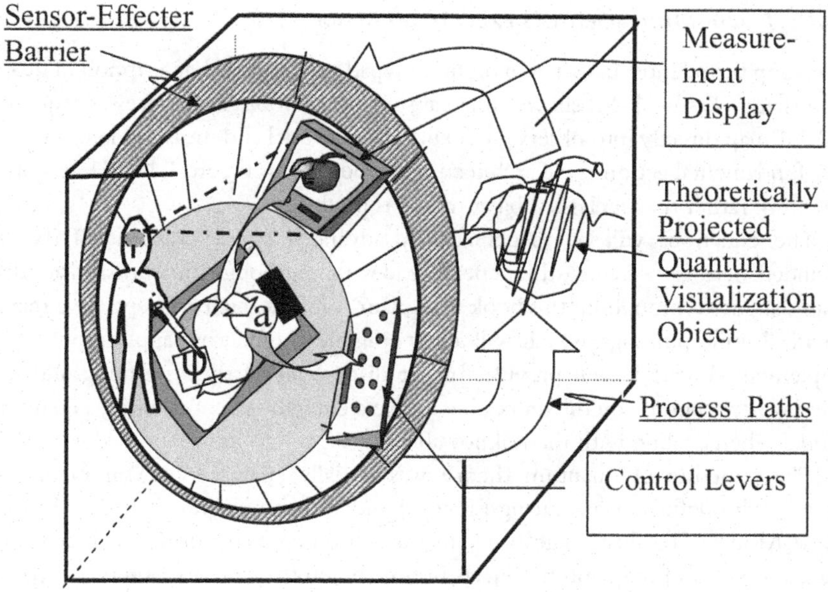

FIGURE 1.2-1C Quantum model: scientist transfers observables to the externalized model inside his or her wall of instruments

pattern "a[q]" recorded during the observation of all the screen points "q". From this basis of observation, the physicist seeks an explanation in the form of a physical-world model. The explanatory activity is represented on the notepad as a curved processing arrow leading from the symbol "a[q]" to the symbol of their explanation as a quantum field "ψ[q]" seen on the notepad. Once a description of the explanation that caused the observable sensation has been formulated, its next state is calculated using the Schrödinger equation. The accuracy of this calculation can be verified by applying a symbolic measurement process represented by the second curved arrow. It recalculates the symbol of sensations a[q] on the monitor screen. If the next "ψ" is the correct explanation for sensations, then the calculated and next measured sensations coincide and reinforce each other. Thus, a resonance between external measurement display available on the TV monitor and the output of the internal processing cycle amplifies the activity. The physicist would say he or she is looking through the monitor and seeing the quantum object described by "ψ". In a very real sense "ψ" defines the entity, i.e. wave contained in an apple form, beyond the sensor-effecter boundary. Any difference between the estimated and measured sensation will lead to error signals that update the ψ-model and/or issue commands to the outside. The arrow from the notepad to the control keys defines the command signals to the world of quantum objects beyond the barrier. The scientist executing the loop operates like a gate in which the sensor input controls the output key states.

1.2.1.1 Quantum scientists execute an action cycle

The loop the scientist has written on his notepad is a truncated description of quantum theory. Figure 1.2-2 shows an expansion of this loop. The processes sequence 0,3,2,1 map directly into observable, explanatory, model and measurement phase of our fundamental action cycle architecture introduced in Figure 1.1-2. Here only a quantum rather than a classic object model is used.

The equations will be recognized by advanced physics students. They are included here to convince the general reader that although functional flow diagrams are used throughout this book to explain concepts, such concepts have mathematical underpinnings, which will allow tangible engineering applications to be implemented. Part II will provide further discussions of their meaning and use. Here we concentrate on the processing loop executed by scientists using a quantum model when dealing with the unknowable.

The structure of quantum theory was initially analyzed by Von Neumann (1955), who defined a measuring Process I and a quantum Process II. The Process II, "ψ-Model of Reality", is governed by the Schrödinger equation, which describes wave propagation of quantum objects in time when they are not observed. Process I converts this description of quantum objects into observable action measurement results. Prof. Stapp (1993) realized that the architecture of quantum theory must be generalized to include additional processes beyond those defined by von Neumann. Here Process 0 is our classic world of observable action distributions "a[q]"

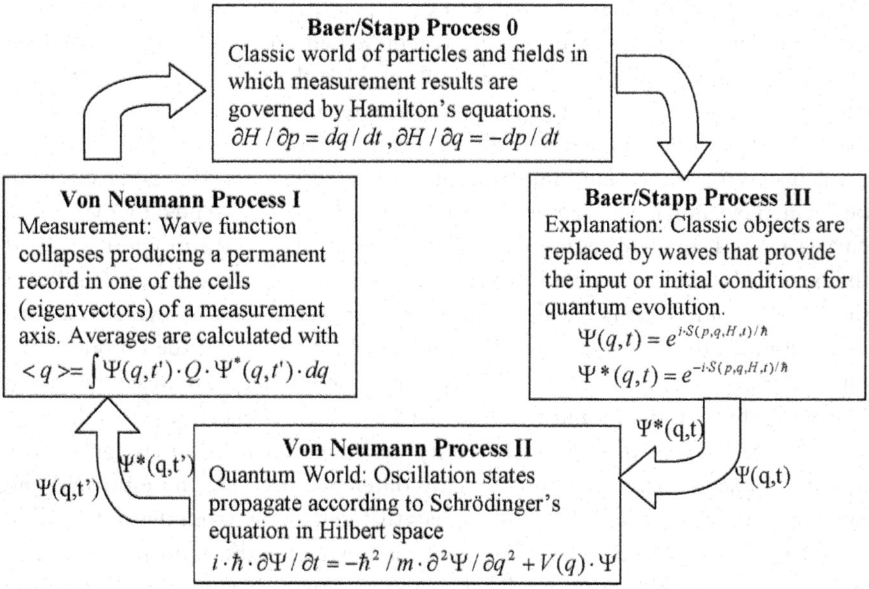

FIGURE 1.2-2 The cyclic architecture of quantum theory processes: oscillation states propagate forward and backward carrying action around a loop in the quantum Reality of Process II

governed by classic Hamilton's equations and Process III as the mechanism by which the action composition "S()" of a classic system is converted into the Louis de Broglie waves. These definitions give quantum theory a suggestive four process architecture shown as a single connected activity in Figure 1.2-2.

Quantum theory and its equations were originally developed by classic physicists who tried to use a "objective reality" philosophy to deal with atomic particles. The fact that atoms could not be seen objectively, even in principle, forced them to include a measurement processes that reached beyond the sensor barrier into a realm that could never be verified directly. To describe this realm a symbolic structure, ψ, which could not be directly connected to objective events, became part of the theory. This lack of objective meaning for the symbols of the quantum realm is crucial to understanding them. The symbols of classic physics point to some past, present or future events in our observable classic universe. The symbols of the quantum realm are information storage structures that hold our belief of the world beyond the sensors and are always connected to the observable world of sensations through measurement and explanation processes in a cyclic architecture.

To what extent the quantum description of physical reality, "ψ", actually represents Kant's unknowable external world is not knowable. Our only criterion for accuracy is that it regenerates the expected measurement result of action hit pattern "a[q]" in instruments designed to measure action hits along a general quantity axis "q". What we do know from the analysis of nervous systems by Maturana (1970) is that a nervous system does *not* operate in response to a *representation* of the environment, but rather accommodates interactions with that environment by modifying its own internal structure. Changes in the internal structure of the loop defining an observer will show up as sensations in his or her mental display. The architecture of this structure, which we have adopted from Maturana, is a kind of processing loop that incorporates a set of self-optimizing configurations. A scientist outfitted with a belief operates a structural implementation of that belief. If that belief is implemented as a quantum model in the processing loop, the scientist can only absorb information if he or she is able to adjust the model so that the action hits actually observed, and those produced by measuring the explanatory model equal each other. Once the scientist's model is accurately adjusted, understanding Reality requires a second interpretation loop, which will be discussed in Section 1.3. That a physicist executes a loop with a quantum model when applying his or her craft is a property of the individual's specifically trained nervous system. CAT proposes such loops are generally executed by all systems, differing only by the models they incorporate. Thus, the theme of this book could equally well be stated as an attempt to generalize Maturana's findings to all physical objects, living or not, and therefore provide a material foundation rather than merely an emergent biological basis for subjective experience.

By extending the scientific method – experimental verification of theoretical claims – the quantum model has provided a systematic mechanism for dealing with the previously unknown interior of matter. However, it stops short of integrating the subjective experience found there. Instead it limits its own domain of applicability by defining the actualization process, which extracts observable measurement results from a spectrum of possibilities, as an intrinsically random process known as the "collapse of the wave function". By elevating the random nature of measurement to a fundamental principle of the theory, quantum physicists cut off debate and exploration of subjective alternatives within their own community. This eliminates mental experience, which must be included in any complete theory of Reality. Most quantum theorists feel they have plenty to do when trying to perfect their theory of physical reality to bother with the expansion required to include subjective experiences. They are comfortable with the fact that physics, as currently practiced, does not deal with reality but only its physical aspect. To complete the story requires the jump to an event Model of Reality (MoR), which will be discussed in the next section.

1.2.2 Automating the scientists' action cycle execution

By recognizing the architecture of quantum theory as the algorithmic steps in Figure 1.2-2, we have already made a conceptual jump. The scientist is treated as a technician whose activities (i.e. reading measuring instrument displays, plugging the readings into formulas of classic or quantum objects, producing calculation results) are the robotic execution of an instrumentalist theory. The scientist need not understand the meaning of theory to perform the prescribed operations. Furthermore, the scientist's personal experience is considered an in-line "Process 0" in a larger flow of change proceeding in the laboratory.

If we replace the scientist by automating the algorithm and incorporate all the laboratory equipment in abstract process boxes, we will arrive at an architecture of the physical reality model shown in Figure 1.2-3.

The model now represents the mental activities of the scientist as an automated physical loop not as a happening inside the brain of a prisoner in Plato's cave. The description of sensations represented by the symbol "a" on the notebook are placed inside the thought bubble as a picture of what he or she actually sees. The scientist's theory, which processes these sensations into the "ψ-model" and back, are now implemented by the inner loop. The symbolic "ψ-model" represents a physical memory activity that names what the scientist believes is outside his or her sensor barrier. How such flow models may be implemented in biological or computer hardware will be discussed in Part III of this book.

The real quantum object, or whatever is thought to cause the sensations of instrument records, is still located beyond the sensor-effecter barrier provided by the scientist's measuring and display mechanism. Only now the scientist's laboratory instruments and the entire processing chain from these instruments, through his or her biological sensor, mental observables and out to the actuator arrays are represented by an outer activity loop. These processing chains are punctuated by the line-filled process boxes that were labeled Explaining and Measuring activities in previous figures. The outer loop represents activity flow through the body, connecting sensations to the external world and the inner smaller processing loop

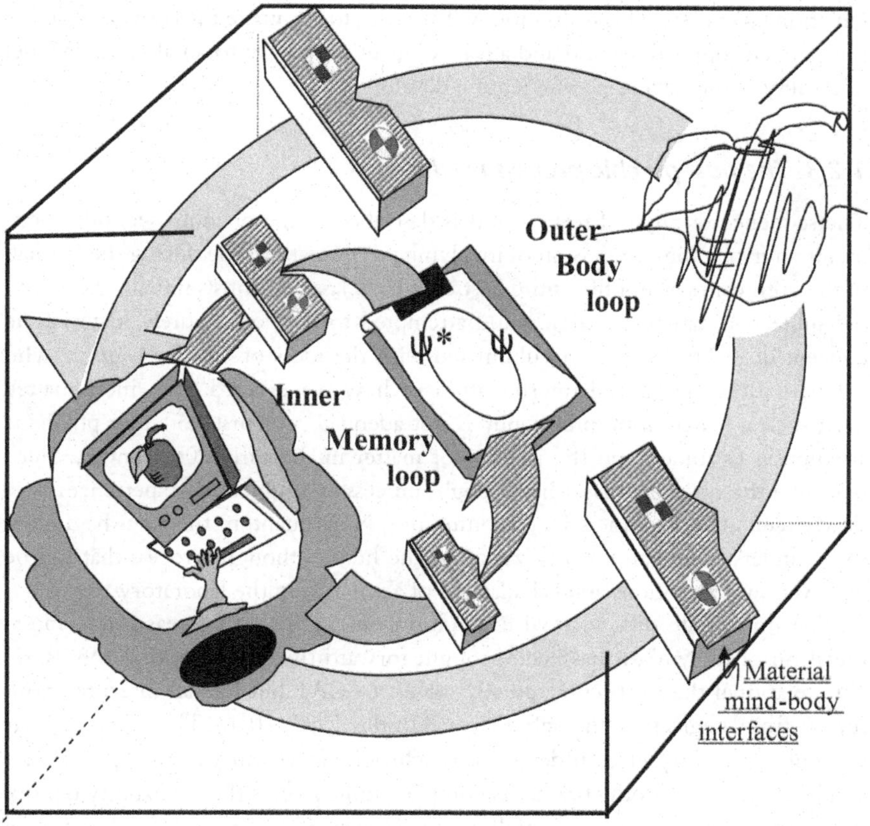

FIGURE 1.2-3 The 1st-person scientist's experience: happening where inner and outer action loops meet

connecting sensations to his or her memory, still shown as an externalized notepad. The scientist, sensations, laboratory instruments and his or her external world have been reduced to a physical process flow that is being executed.

This inner process, which converts actual sensations into explanations and back in a self-measuring feed-forward loop, contains a form of subjective experience whether or not external interaction channels are actually open; i.e. the scientist's eyes could be closed, and he or she could be dreaming. When the inner loop is isolated, it acts as a stand-alone activity which, when applied to reality as a whole, was also labeled "R" in Figure 1.1-3. Such a self-contained action loop is therefore a legitimate candidate for the universal physical cause of conscious experience.

It is no longer a question of some external *thing* causing an internal subjective *thing* to appear. It is not even a question of some internal memory *thing* causing a dream or imagination sensation to appear. Rather the *happening of the activity* is its cause. If it does not happen, conscious experience does not appear. In other words, the explanation of sensation is a model of the process happening when the sensation takes place. This realization will allow us to eliminate the last vestiges of an independent objective world and advance quantum theory to an all-event Model of Reality as the next stage of scientific development.

1.2.3 The pan-psychic process model

The sequence of physical reality models described in the previous sections documents an increasing progression of involving the human psyche during the last half of the 20th century and the entire 21st century. Classic scientists initially exorcized the subjective nature of religion and attempted to develop a purely materialistic concept of reality. This effort culminated with the ideas of Charles Darwin, who left us with a mechanical interpretation of how we evolved from inert matter. That such a materialistic philosophy is not adequate was first noted by physicists attempting to understand the interior of matter in the early 20th century. Since that time the observer, his or her thought process and subjective experiences have slowly reentered the basic science community. Now quantum theory is beginning to be understood as an externalization of the human thought process that can be observed in the motions and calculations of a scientist in the laboratory.

The immediate difficulty with quantum theory is that no reasonable interpretation of its symbols has been brought forward thus far (Blood, 2009). Rovelli's relational theory is conceptually closest to CAT but like all interpretations suffers from neglecting the subjective (Rovelli, 1997, 2016). The most popular Copenhagen interpretation defines the Schrödinger ψ-function as a probability amplitude and the product, with its complex conjugate, as the probability density that a measurement outcome will occur. However, probabilities and statistical averages are not real. Or at least do not correspond to any common expectation of reality. Coins land on heads or tails, not halfway between. Though statistical theories may be useful for large numbers of trials, if we are to develop a theory of reality that includes both the physical and mental aspects of the unique and singular event that we actually are, then neither aspect can be founded in probabilities or statistical averages.

The most straightforward way to overcome this deficiency is to look at the asymmetry between the description of the scientist observer and the rest of the universe as shown in the scientist loop model in Figure 1.2-3. There the observer is shown as an activity flowing through a cyclic-action structure, and the external world is a quantum object described by the symbol "ψ". It must be remembered that we cannot know Reality itself, since all we know is derived from interpretations of our sensory interactions in terms of an objective world vocabulary. However, it is highly likely that if we are processing loops in the inner observable side of our biological sensor-effecter barrier, the most reasonable guess is that the other side of that barrier is also a processing loop. *We therefore make the assumption that the rest of the universe is also described as a processing loop.* The next model of physical reality then becomes a set of interacting processing cycles with interfaces at the fusion between external and internal data flows that make up the 1st-person experiences in both cycles. Figure 1.2-1d shows such a symmetric

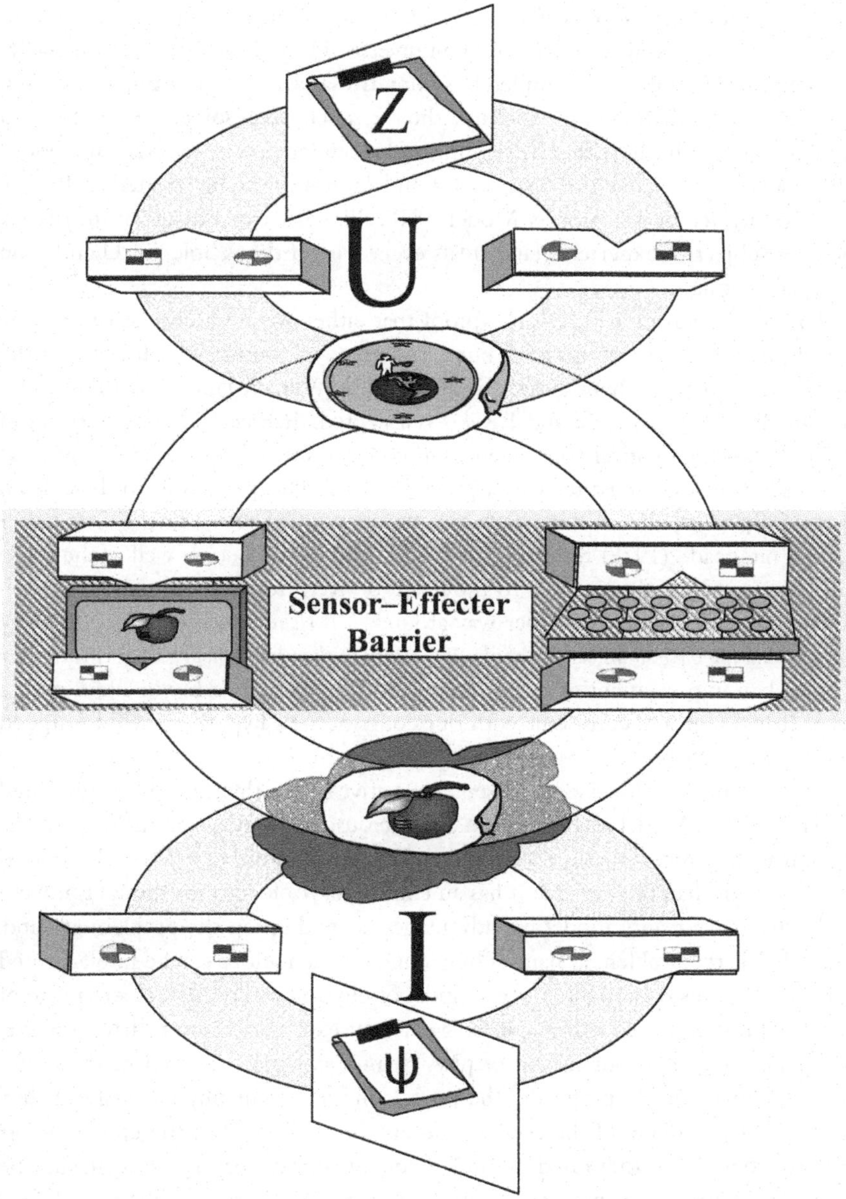

FIGURE 1.2-4 The process Model of Reality showing I's and U's action cycles interacting through their instrument barrier

system of processing loops. An expanded flow diagram of such interacting loops is shown in Figure 1.2-4.

Figure 1.2-4 shows an architecture containing the scientist loop, here labeled "I", along with the scientist's external processing branches terminating at his or her external sensor-effecter barrier. It also shows the rest of the universe, here labeled

"U", as a processing loop with its external branches terminating on its side of the external sensor-effecter barrier. The universe "U" and the conscious being "I" are therefore described as completely symmetric and interacting processes. Each side interacts with the other through their respective sensor-effecter pairs, and these interact with each other by sending and receiving gravito-electric influences. These will be introduced in Section 1.4 and more thoroughly treated in Part II. We have arrived at the process Model of Reality that expands quantum theory, includes subjective experience and treats every part of the Whole, i.e. U and I, on an equal footing.

The previous paragraph is not a proof that either we are a process or that the rest of physical reality is a process, but a statement of consistency. However, if the consciousness process hypothesis – introduced by William James (1890) and diagrammed in Figures 1.2-1d and 1.2-4 – is accepted, then certain characteristics of physical reality are logical consequences. If consciousness is contained in a process, then its explanation must refer to a process as well. This process is not built from moving objects, such as a horse race or a production cycle in a factory, but rather from Whitehead's (1978) fundamental events. Moving objects as well as the space and time in which they appear to move are derived from the properties of such fundamental events, not the other way around. *It is elementary events, not elementary particles that are the building blocks of physical reality in the process model.* That this theory is indeed an improvement of our understanding of physical reality in addition to a belief that is logically consistent with our consciousness hypothesis will be argued in subsequent chapters.

The four models discussed represent alternative beliefs that can all be substituted in place of the "Model of Reality" in a consciousness process that includes sensations. It is the process that is fundamental. The exact nature of a physical model is less important than the fact that it has an explanatory role in one's thought process. Each alternative reality model has advantages depending on the problem at hand. In this book, the problem at hand is how conscious sensations can be implemented in reality. For this reason, the process model of physical reality has the advantage of logical consistency over other beliefs. If personal experiences are to have a physical explanation, then our model of physics must contain a symbol of the entity that implements it. By proposing the process model as our physical reality belief, we have a scale model of the conscious event. It is a symbol of the consciousness process, whereas all other physical models contain an explanatory gap that must be bridged by some ad hoc magic to explain consciousness. In the process model consciousness is – paraphrasing Nagel (1974) – what it is like to be a cycle of activity and all parts of the universe exhibit this characteristic.

1.3 Why and how a quantum physicist sees what he or she believes

The sensations drawn in the observable phase in Figures 1.2-1d, 1.2-3 and 1.2-4 show a fusion of two fundamentally different 1st-person experiences. First, direct experiences resulting from sensors interacting with the external environment are remembered and merged with internally generated expectation sensations. Second, we generate the meaning of those sensations by a 3rd-person interaction with the memory model components holding our beliefs of that environment. We use the visual ego icon to display sensations associated with external interactions and the thought bubble to represent a mind space in which theoretical recognition experiences designed to understand our sensations are displayed. These recognition experiences tell us what our theory says is out there and how to deal with it. These are, however, only the visualization of meanings assigned to the physical-model components that hold the memory of external sensations, not the model components or the external entities-in-themselves. Often this distinction is not fully realized, and we confuse our visualizations with the actual causes of our experiences.

This confusion is a kind of visualization trap, since people who fall into it treat the explanatory visualizations projected into sensations as the real and entire cause of our sensations, when the real cause is actually the unobservable realities behind those sensations. Such individuals will seek to explain consciousness with futile attempts to causally connect two observable images when both are 1st and 3rd aspects of a common action. It is a trap Niels Bohr (1958) warned us about when describing the symbols of quantum theory as calculation tools. This confusion supports objective reality and the outdated classic theory of physics. It also drives the quest for an interpretation of quantum theoretical symbols when, in fact, those symbols are calculation components of our thought process (D'Espagnat, 1989).

To demonstrate how theoretical recognition experiences are implemented let us follow the action flow through a quantum physicist who sees and identifies the cause of a sensation with his or her theory. Figure 1.3-1 shows two processing paths executed by a physicist who sees a light flash in a darkened room and recognizes it as an electron transition from an atom. The upper section, outlined by a dashed oval, represents the physicist's observables. We have separated the physicist's optical sensation field from his or her visualization of the cause of those sensations in the light gray thought bubble below it. We have not shown interaction paths with the outside world for simplicity. Figure 1.3-1, as drawn, assumes the physicist was stimulated but is now isolated and only remembers the light he or she has seen and now wants to explain it. The sequence of events will be listed using numerical references corresponding to the numbers in parenthesis on the drawing:

1 An action flow through the physicist's Now plane is the physical correlate of consciousness (PCC), which the physicist experiences as a light flash in his or her optical field.
2 The physicist processes the action through a series of explanatory-processing operations that symbolically trace the causal chain back to the retina and deposit the result on the internal retina model shown as the right interface material icon at the bottom of the loop.
3 The deposited action pattern "**A**" on the inside of the physicist's simulated sensor-effecter array represents what must have happened in the actual retina

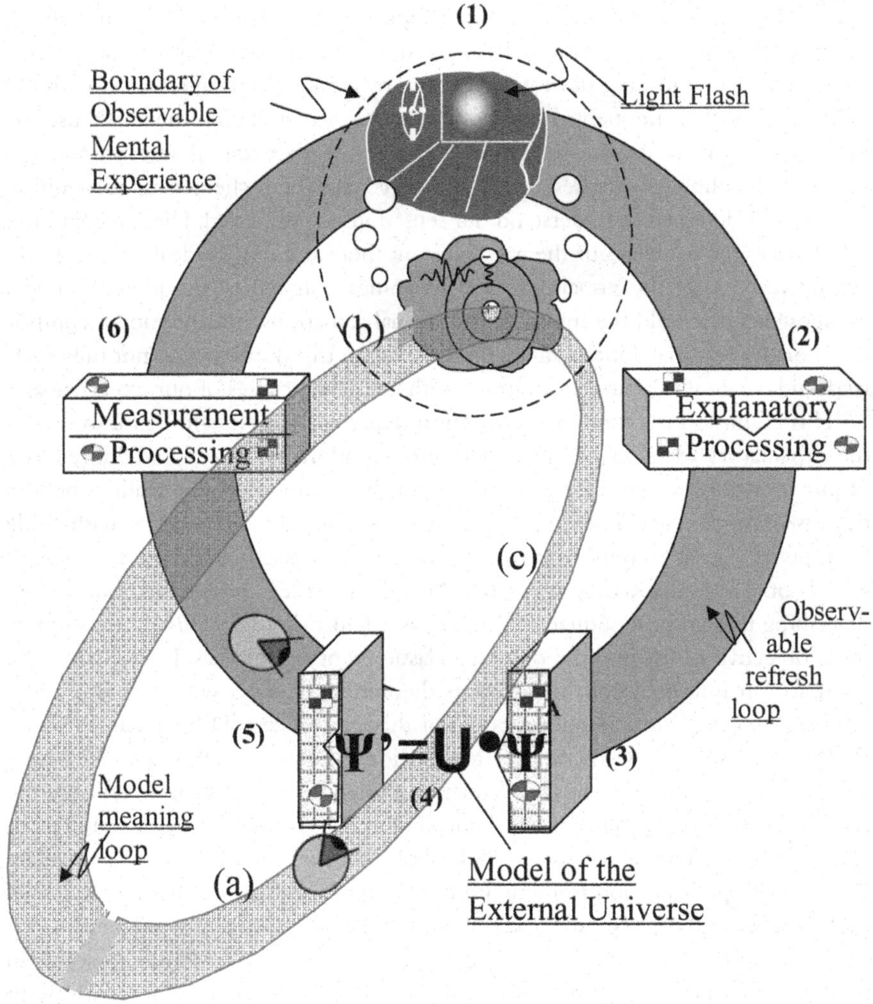

FIGURE 1.3-1 The dual processing paths generate a memory sensation and a visualization of its modeled cause: the two sensations are registered for object recognition

to produce the light. The transition from the classic material to the quantum world is accomplished by assuming, as Schrödinger and later as Feynman did, that reality is described by a ψ-function calculated as $e^{i \cdot 2 \cdot \pi \cdot A/h}$ in the simulated sensor boundary. The ψ-function now describes a quantum pattern on the unseen inside of the right retina model, which faces a quantum-world model.
4 This model is populated by the operational symbol ψ, which is acted upon by an operational symbol "=U•" that represents a unitary transformation in quantum theory, which propagates ψ from what it must have been in the past to the ψ' it becomes in the future.

5 The ψ' pattern in the simulated optical sensor array is processed through a quantum operation implemented in the left (now future material sensor array relative to the next sensation). This operation collapses the ψ-function to one of the possible action patterns A'.
6 The physicist's brain circuitry processes the modeled measurement to produce the next expected sensation of light.

The outer darker processing cycle through the sensation prediction process is now complete. This processing cycle through the quantum physicist's model may continue as an undisturbed measurement-explanatory activity continually refreshing the memory sensation of a light flash in the observable consciousness. In this cycle the "=U•" is an *operational symbol*, implemented in the physicist's "Brain" circuitry as his or her Model of Reality. It represents an *operational component* of his or her mental processing system. Its operational function is determined by its physical structure and how it interacts with the other physical structures in the brain. In this example, its operational function is to remember and reproduce the memory of a light flash. The observer executing this cycle is a detached observer aware of what is but not engaged. There is no understanding of what caused the light in the darker processing cycle, only a calculated reproduction of the light.

In order to understand the light, we need not merely to look at the 1st-person aspect (see eye above the (5)) of the operation executed by the symbol "=U•" but rather to look at its 3rd-person aspect (see eye next to and just above (a)) and understand what it means as a symbol in the context of the scientist's beliefs. Meaning is not intrinsic to a symbol's physical attributes but is assigned by an outside agent, in this case, the physicist or more generally ourselves. A general meaning was already assigned when we stated the symbol "=U•" is the physicist's model of physical reality, but that only replaces a symbol with another symbol, "physical reality". To have a meaning, both of these alternative naming statements must be attached to observable sensations, not simply translated to another symbol. The meaning sensation is attached to "=U•" by executing the light-colored oval loop, which runs perpendicular to the darker colored cycle. This cycle implements projection and learning functions between the model and its meaning display which will be thoroughly discussed in Section 2.3. These operations process the 3rd-person memory look at "=U•" but are not shown in the light-colored loop so as to make the drawing clearer. The reader is asked to assume these operations are included in the processing paths.

The meaning of this quantum mechanical symbol is processed by a projection operation that produces a picture (b) of a Bohr atom. The thought bubble showing the physicist's conscious observable imagination contains a positive nucleus with an electron orbiting at a higher excited energy orbit. The electron transitions to a lower energy orbit emitting a photon, which is shown as a horizontal wavy line in Figure 1.3-1. Something like this observable sensation happened in Niels Bohr's imagination and continues to happen in all following physicists who subscribe to the Copenhagen interpretation of quantum theory. The processing path

(c) represents a series of learned steps. We first learned to imagine an atom as an electron orbiting a proton, then to quantize the angular momentum, from which a Hamiltonian operator is derived and placed into the unitary transformation, implementing the operational structure "=U•". Once the meaning of this symbol was coded into a visualization of an atom as an interpretation of Bohr's working symbol, it would continue to be taught as a Bohr model of the atom. This installs the second closed loop as the explanatory activity of light in the real "Brains" of our population.

In Figure 1.3-1 the light flash and that it means an electron transition in a Bohr atom are shown as separated observable sensations. We must remember this separation was drawn for clarity. In practice, the meaning of the explanatory model is projected onto the sensation it is trying to explain. Often physicists will say they are seeing an atom when, in actuality, they are imagining a visualization of an atom, or whatever other interpretation of their beliefs they subscribe to.

We have now completed our example of how sensations are explained by the processing flow of a conscious being. To explain this conscious phenomenon in physical terms we must recognize that what we have taken to be objective reality in front of our noses, is actually composed of two internal phenomenal experiences – the first being the sensations displayed from merging the signals from our external and simulated sensors and the second being the visualization of the meaning of our explanatory theory projected onto our external sensation display.

1.3.1 How normal people experience what they believe

Projecting the visualized explanation of a sensation onto that sensation using a different sensory modality is a ubiquitous characteristic of human thought processing. If a classic physical reality model is used instead of a quantum model, the same processing architecture would project the meaning of classic physics symbols into the sensation of light discussed earlier. Thus, a conscious being outfitted with a classic model would project a classic object visualization into the light blob he or she actually sees and say, "I am seeing an object". We build a projection loop into our thought process for understanding sensations of all kinds. When hearing the sounds of a language that we understand, we immediately project the meaning of the words into the sound. When hearing a faint ringing, we quickly project the visualization of a bell onto the sound and say, "I hear a bell". When looking at the night sky and say, "I see stars", we project a glowing gas ball onto the dots of light. The critical lesson derived from this example is that *the sensations normally taken to be the real, objective external world are actually a visualization of the theory incorporated in the material of a conscious being, which can be externalized in the symbols of the theory that being believes and uses.*

A second important characteristic demonstrated by Bohr's atomic visualization is that it is a 3rd-person view. One can imagine looking at an atom from above and watching the light wave escape to the side. This characteristic is quite general. Visualizations of theories are memory recall operations. We imagine our memories from a disembodied 3rd-person perspective. Classic and quantum theories imagine an independent world as though seen by an equally independent 3rd-person observer. How the light pulse escapes this perspective and causes the light flash in the 1st-person perspective was not explained by Bohr. It is explained by understanding that physicists identified the experience of light with the operational symbol "photon" and visualized it as a wave. The word "photon" and its visualization were introduced by men creating a theory. It may be a useful theory but the act of creating a name for a phenomenon does not make the name a cause for the phenomena. The physicist made the law, not the other way around.

The data-processing paths in Figure 1.3-1 also show why it is impossible to explain consciousness with our classic or quantum physics theories alone. It is because we normally fall into a visualization trap. We believe and act as though the observable meaning of our theory is actual reality when it is not. The connecting bubbles between the two observable experiences in Figure 1.3-1 indicate our common, but erroneous, belief there is a causal connection between these two experiences. A similar difficulty is encountered when trying to explain the causal connection between two actors seen on a television screen without understanding the parallel flow of electrons that cause both images to appear simultaneously. We now know a processing flow between a model incorporated in the internal structure of our material produces both our sensation and the sensation of its explanation. These two sensations do not cause each other. Our everyday experience combines our direct sensation with our theory visualization channels. It is necessary to grasp the dual-channel-process architecture between our reality model and our observable display in order to find the physical cause of our conscious experience. Since we have identified location of sensations as happening inside our real material "Brain", not our observable "brain", we will now look further into this material to learn how subjective experiences are incorporated there.

1.4 Including consciousness in the model of matter

We have identified both our direct sensory experience and the experience of our reality-model-generated explanatory visualization as the fused experience of objects happening inside our larger material "Selves". The inside of material has been described by quantum theory and applied in atomic and nuclear physics for more than one hundred years. Though quantum theory, as defined by von Neumann, has acknowledged that the observer's consciousness is involved when a human interprets the final result in the last stage of a measurement process chain, the development of this branch of science has largely been driven by particle-accelerator experiments. These efforts answer old questions and generate new questions that are closely tied to the erroneous extension of reductionist methods into the unobservable interior of matter by the mainstream high-energy investigation program. This program ignores the role of the observer performing the experiments yet attempts to discover the mysteries of the universe as though that universe had an independent external existence detached from the experimenter. As a result, the standard model describing the interior of matter has and will continue to find increasingly complex aggregations of material properties and the whole effort is usually ignored by the neurophysiologists, psychologists and other workers dealing with conscious beings.

To overcome this difficulty, this section provides a fresh look at the physics applicable to the interior of matter. The resulting changes to our contemporary physical theories will be further developed in Part II. There we will show how quantum and classic physics theories are given a context within our event-oriented Conscious Action Theory (CAT). Detailed explanations of elementary particles, or the abundance of chemical elements is a specialized study addressing problems pertinent to its specific location along the scale of material complexity. Refinement of advanced theories in nuclear or astrophysics is beyond the scope of this book. Instead we give these disciplines their valid place along the hierarchy of material aggregation (see Section 7.6.2) and focus directly on the changes in the foundations of physics needed to accommodate the existence of conscious observers. Our goal here is to define the simplest physical characteristics necessary to include the experiences and actions of conscious beings in a physical framework.

1.4.1 Metaphysical underpinnings of event-oriented physics

The starting point for our approach is most clearly connected to physics in the *Classical Mechanics* book by Goldstein (1965), itself a classic, which cites the a priori existence of mass, charge, space and time as the metaphysical assumptions underpinning classic physics. Implicitly assumed, but unstated in the *Classical Mechanics* book, is that permanent laws, determining how the intrinsic properties of these four elements interact with each other, exist for all time. Assumptions neither can nor need be proven within a theory. Once the fundamental laws are discovered and the classic physics assumptions are accepted, the location of mass and charge in space at all times and further physical parameters such as velocity, momentum, energy, action, the strength of their force fields and a plethora of material aggregations can be logically derived. Though a good starting point for describing the physical aspect of reality, these assumptions do not include the mental or subjective aspect of our experience and must be upgraded.

Our basic Action Theory will be built on the metaphysical existence assumption that *change* is fundamental. The material of change is the physical quantity of *action*. The form of change is the shape of the action network. Both Action and Form are assumed to exist and therefore *Reality is a Form of Action*. These words are operational symbols that can be inferred from the observable motion of charges and masses much like wind can be inferred from the motion of leaves on a tree. And like the wind, which explains the motion of leaves, so the motion of all material is explained by the flow of action happening between material states. Once this shift from static things to motion is made, the following additional changes in our assumptions are adopted in CAT.

First: CAT accepts that only two material categories are necessary. These generate the gravitation and inertial forces (F_{gi}) attached to the mass (m) of objects and the electric and magnetic forces "F_{em}" attached to the charge "ch" of objects. The configuration of charge and mass happen in a place called a volume of space, "Vol", at a time, "T".

Second: time is no longer accepted as a fundamental element but rather derived from *change* in the evolving pattern of charge and mass that forms an event. A complete event is composed of a sequence of instantaneous changes "ζ()". A total event is summarized by its global dynamic activity state or Zustands function "Z()". A change is composed of an amount of action in the interval between successive states. The length of this interval was measured in seconds and was associated with the flow of time. Since Einstein, time has been called a fourth dimension and is depicted as an axis perpendicular to all spatial dimensions. However, its physical characteristics are distinctly different from those of space. It is therefore best to accept string theorist Graham Green's (1999) definition that, "time is what clocks measure". This means time is derived from the state of a clock which is in turn derived from the mass/charge configuration change of the material from which the clock is built.

Clocks are physical systems. What can be measured are their physical states. The traditional clock is the universe itself whose state is defined by the sequential position of the celestial bodies. The concept of state refers to the configuration of any system while the concept of time refers to the state of a special system through which the flow rate of action, i.e. energy, is constant (see Section 4.3.4). When the universe is identified as one's clock, the rate of gravitational interactions determines the rate of time. The fact that measurements of mechanical and atomic clocks have successfully replaced astronomic observations in modern times implies the gravito-inertial forces that move heavenly bodies are precisely interrelated with the electromagnetic forces that dominate terrestrial phenomena. As we will soon discover, the flow of action passes through both charge and mass and therefore its rate can equally well be measured in both the electromagnetic or gravito-inertial domain.

Third: though the "particle assumption" is not explicitly stated as a foundational assumption in *Classical Mechanics*, it has generally been traditional for physicists to think of elementary particles as the basic organizational units from which the physical universe is built and to treat all *physical* characteristics such as mass, charge and volume as properties of those particles attached to the location of the particle at every point as it moves through space in time. An electron, for example, is visualized as having a charge and mass co-located at one point orbiting a proton in the Bohr model of the atom. Unfortunately points or point particles are idealizations that are not realizable in physical reality (Miller, 2003). CAT eliminates the particle assumption and treats properties of charge and mass as separable densities rather than particles.

Treating mass and charge as separate physical densities immediately raises the question, "What holds charge and mass together?" Due to the particle assumption this question has been ignored in current scientific theories. As we move from atomic to nuclear scales, the answer to this question is buried in the complexity of high-energy physics models, which assume a strong and weak force along with a growing plethora of properties attached to point particle types. Though attempts have been made to formulate string theory in terms of mass/charge shapes (Hara et al., 1968; Hara and Goto, 1970), this work has languished until recently (Sears, 1971). We will therefore bypass the complicated task of aggregating foundational properties of matter into elementary particles by dealing directly with charge and mass, not as point particles, but as extended distributions that constitute the material of space itself. We then assume two force categories are present inside of material that holds charge and mass together. These are the force of charge on mass (F_{cm}) and the force of mass on charge (F_{mc}). Our approach will be to add these two forces to the list of interactions between charge and mass to complete our foundational metaphysical assumptions.

This leaves us with the existence of action as the measure of change along with charge and mass as the components of material doing the changing through four possible interactions as the building blocks of our "Reality". Space and time are then derived from the amount of material and the amount of change respectively (see Section 4.3).

1.4.2 The inside and outside of matter explained

Although we often use references to interior and exterior sides of objects, dividing matter itself into an inside and outside aspect is a new concept that must be carefully explained because what is inside material from a theoretical or 3rd-person perspective is outside material from a 1st-person perspective depending on one's frame of mind.

Observers in the Aristotelian frame of mind (Figure 1.2-1a, b), will believe they are looking at the objects in front of their nose from an outside perspective, i.e. they will say the exterior surfaces of what they see surround their unseen interior volume. This is because realists often fall into the visualization trap and believe they are seeing real objects. To find the interior of these objects, they apply the method of reductionism and break the object into parts in the hope of finding what is inside. Unfortunately, they will then be looking at surfaces that define the outside of each piece. As they break the parts into smaller and smaller pieces, the exterior surfaces of the parts will continue to surround a smaller and smaller interior until the parts get so small that the observer can no longer hope to see any individual pieces. At this point reductionism fails (see Figure 4.3-4), and the observer has reached the Planck's quantum limit since the interior can no longer be defined as being inside the visible surfaces of observable pieces. Beyond this limit, the interior of matter gives way to mental projections that are theoretical conjectures of smaller and smaller pieces that are assumed to be inside. In this frame of mind, the inside of matter is the domain of quantum theory, which is surrounded by a classical world of objective external surfaces.

In contrast, an observer in the Platonic frame of mind (Figure 1.2-1c, d) will recognize those same surfaces as appearances in his or her own internal mind space. For such an observer, exterior is not what he or she sees but what causes these appearances outside of the skull. The observer's reality is outside his or her observable appearances. As shown in Figure 1.3-1, looking at directly experienced light sensations is like looking into the end of a processing pipe through which sensations flow straight at and through the observer. When this process is visualized, one imagines those processing pipes from an external 3rd-person perspective. The processing operations are laid out along external spatial extensions as they transform the flow of action, i.e. the PCC of sensation, from input to output. The observer's experiences are internal to him- or herself and associated mental or theoretical aspects of matter are external to the internal experience.

In summary, the interior and exterior of material is world view dependent. Most physicists are realists who automatically interpret their 1st-person experiences from a 3rd-person perspective. They believe they are seeing the outside of matter while mentally projecting something smaller hidden "inside" the observable exterior as its interior. While idealists interpret their immediate 1st-person experiences, often called "qualia", as the internal view of their own material but, again using a 3rd-person perspective, they project the causes of their internal experience into an external world outside their own material. In this book we usually assume a physicist's perspective and identify our everyday experience as the "outside" aspect of matter and the "inside" of matter as its mental aspect.

1.4.3 Separating matter to show interior and exterior aspects

In CAT, we have separated both matter views by using graphic icons that can be combined to represent material in the Platonic, Aristotelian or in the integrated world-view frame of mind proposed in this book.

Figure 1.4-1 shows an icon depicting an external Now view of a general piece of matter. This is a theoretical side view of influences flowing past the observer. A rectangular volume is shown with the horizontal sides representing an interval of time and the vertical sides representing spatial extensions. The indented long side receives force influences while the protruded side radiates them. Forces appear on both ends of the arrows. Their points indicate the movement of the observer from past to future. The rectangle is filled with a mass density pattern (ρ_m) and a charge density pattern (ρ_{ch}). These are shown as a diagonal line pattern. Densities are fundamental in CAT. However, the charge and mass patterns in the volume are conveniently summarized by the charge and mass centers of mass located by internal coordinates when the volume, named "Vol", is small enough for the densities to be constant.

The diagram shows two temporal sides of material: the past side, onto which gravitation and electric force fields fall from the rest of the universe, and the future side, from which gravito-electric forces radiate out to the rest of the universe. Of course, charge and mass centers can separate when density gradients appear in the volumes but when dealing with elementary particles, physicists traditionally made two assumptions. First, they assumed the mass and charge of elementary particles were always co-located so that the force holding them together was infinite. This allowed them to idealize a particle as a point located at the combined centers of mass and charge. Second, they assumed the reception and radiation of gravito-electric force happened instantly so that no time elapses between the past and future side of gravitational or electromagnetic radiation points. Although challenged by string theory, these assumptions are still made implicitly in atomic and nuclear physics where elementary particles are largely treated as co-located points of charge and mass. These assumptions leave no room for internal activities and no place for the inner sensations and feelings of that material to exist.

That such a simple particle model is not adequate to describe the operations of the brain was suggested by G. Vitiello (2001), who required a doubling of the degrees of freedom in order to analyze brain functions when the brain was analyzed as an open system in continuous interaction with its environment. The author of the book you are reading has suggested that such doubling could be accomplished

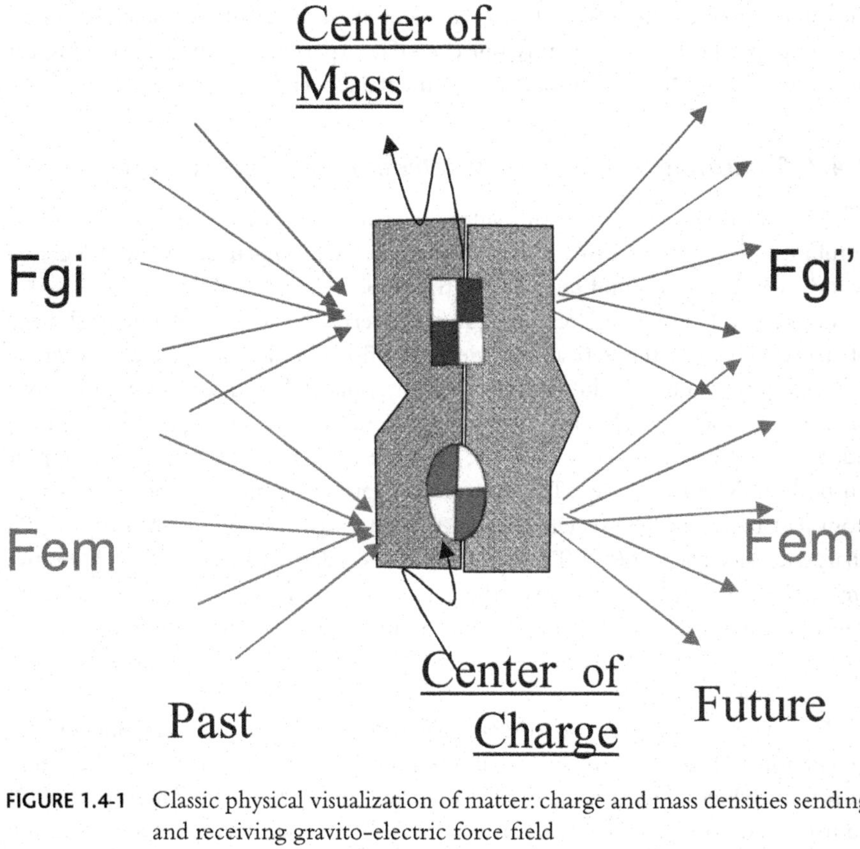

FIGURE 1.4-1 Classic physical visualization of matter: charge and mass densities sending and receiving gravito-electric force field

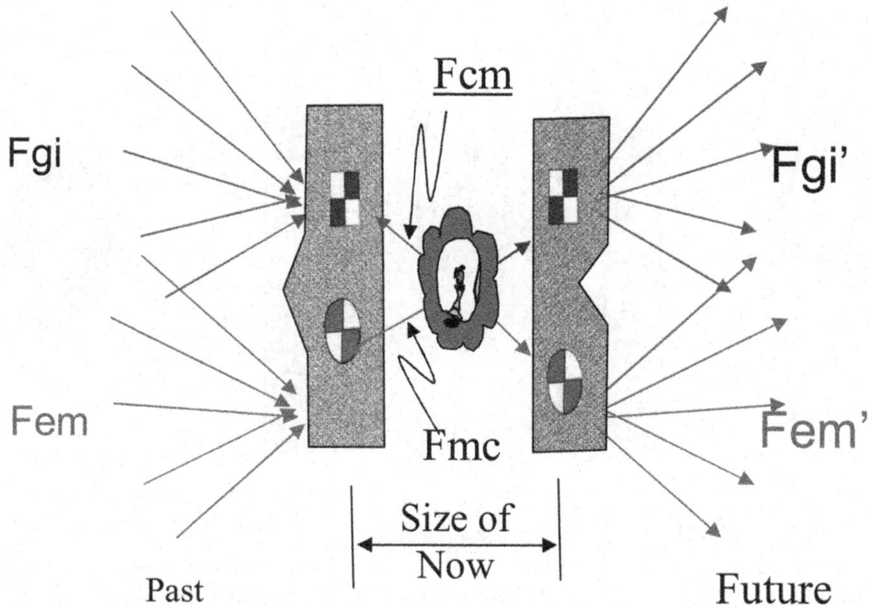

FIGURE 1.4-2 CAT view of matter: conscious experience happening in the interior of matter correlated with mass-charge force fields

if charge and mass were not always located in the same place but were treated as separate entities that are held together by internal forces. By introducing a force of charge on mass (F_{cm}) and the force of mass on charge (F_{mc}), two internal forces were postulated that control the interior of matter. To the extent we project conscious experiences onto the inner structure of brain material, such forces have been identified as the forces of consciousness that determine the behavior of material from the inside (Baer, 2012, 2014a, 2014b).

Figure 1.4-2 shows the updated Conscious Action Theory (CAT) view of matter. Here internal activities are spread out in time. This separation reveals a 1st-person view describing a flow of influence through the observer. The separation shows two icons expressing four sides of material. These are a past-outside, a past-inside, a future-inside and a future-outside. Charges are influenced from the outside past and in turn influence the future-inside mass, which then radiates its influence back into the world. Likewise, masses react to gravitational and inertial forces from the past-outside and influence the future-inside charge, which in turn radiates electromagnetic influences back into classic physical reality.

The complementary, but currently nonscientific, religious or idealistic view holds that physical reality is a manifestation in the mind. Such a view is characterized by an elimination of classic metaphysical underpinnings of physics and treats material as a manifestation inside the 1st-person mental view. It is shown in Figure 1.4-3 from a theoretical perspective. Here the forces of consciousness move the

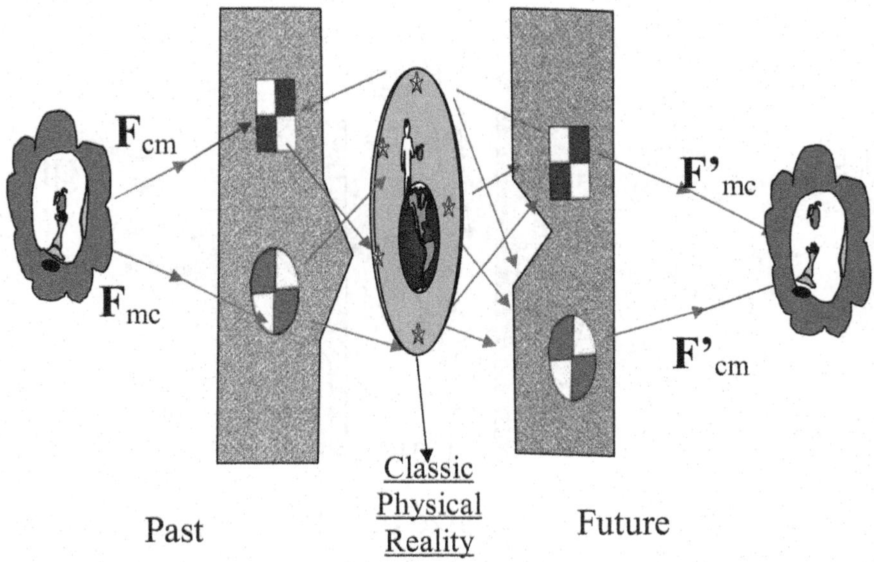

FIGURE 1.4-3 1st-person view of physical matter: classic physical reality visualized outside our sensor/effecter barrier

material from the inside out and in turn receive stimulation from the outside in. This is the view one takes when realizing that the things in front of one's nose are appearances produced by one's sensory process.

Physical reality exists one process step in front of its appearance and is always outside the sensor-effecter boundary. Hence it is hidden and projected inside the surface of appearances. Gravito-electric force signals, expressing the commands and wishes of the psyche, propagate from the past sensor-effecter boundary into physical reality, here shown as a classic physical world. This changes the physical world that then radiates its own signals of changes back to the future sensor-effecter boundary and are then displayed as sensory experiences.

We defined the inside of matter as that unknowable internal entity hidden behind the 1st-person's theoretical projection of material objects. Hence the 1st-person is experiencing the outside of matter and projects what he or she believes is inside into this experience. But the opposite is also true. Figures 1.4-2 and 1.4-3 show the flow of influences is through the internal and external world of matter respectively. Each picture emphasizes a different aspect of the influence flow and only shows one stage in the propagation of influences. The propagation of influence does not stop at the boundaries of the figures. Figure 1.4-4 shows how the two external gravito-electric forces and the two conscious forces propagate in time through the external and internal stages of material.

The picture shows a time segment of influence traveling from the outside of matter, labeled objective, through the inside and back to the outside. Matter is shown as a hatched space cell representing charge and mass densities in a volume

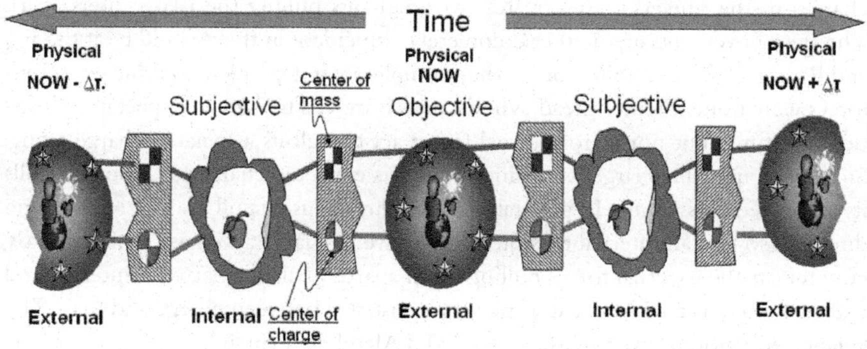

FIGURE 1.4-4 Force influence flow through outer and inner material

cell. The charge center is depicted by a round icon and the center of mass by a rectangular equivalent. The external real world is here represented by our old classic object model. Jagged external surfaces of the space cell are the sides of our sensors boundaries that transmit and receive gravito-electric signals. Between the straight-edged interior side of the cell, the crossed force lines of consciousness interface with the phenomenological world of sensations and feelings. An apple is shown in front of the nose in the 1st-person or mental view. The entity responsible for the apple's appearance is seen as a classic apple object icon in the 3rd-person objective view.

Physics has now been expanded to include a subjective, interior or mental phase. No longer is Reality simply material, which receives and radiates gravito-electric influences as shown in Figure 1.4-1. Instead, Reality is visualized as a continuous flow of influence in which inside subjective and outside objective phases follow each other, changing the pattern of mass and charge states as they go along. A single cycle consists of the physical and mental phases happening in a time interval "ΔT" associated with the local dynamic state "ζ(T)" of the cycle; a self-contained sequence of such cycles is in a global dynamic state "Z".

1.5 Physical implications of the mass-charge interaction

By introducing an explicit inside mental aspect of matter into physics while simultaneously keeping the external aspect of mass and charge already developed by classic theories, we have achieved an integration of mind and body in terms of influence fields that sequentially flow through both aspects in tandem. From the physical point of view, the masses and charges located in the rest of the material universe radiate their influence upon the mass and charge in any specific volume. Since the universe expects to be in equilibrium, these influence fields signal the mass to move toward a location expected by the rest of the universe of masses, and the charge to move to a generally different location expected by the rest of the charges in the universe. This creates two gradients pulling the two centers apart. The two movements are neither completely coincident as they would be if the F_{cm} and F_{mc} forces were infinite nor are they completely independent as if the conscious forces were nonexistent. Instead, when a mass is moved toward an expectation location, the finite but non-zero internal forces act to pull its associated charge along. Simultaneously, the charge is moving toward its expected charge location and pulls its associated mass along. In general, the two directions of pull are not in the same direction so that an internal tension exists between charge and mass, which exactly counteracts the external forces pulling them apart. A balance between internal and external forces is established at some vector distance between charge and mass. The balance equation is given by the extended d'Alembert Principle:

$$0 = F_{em} + F_{gi} + F_{mc} + F_{cm} + F'_{em} + F'_{gi} + F'_{mc} + F'_{cm} \qquad \text{Equation 1.5-1}$$

The primed forces represent backward traveling influences that can either be interpreted as reaction forces to radiation or actual backward traveling influences along the timeline (Baer, 2014c). The d'Alembert Principle is an extension of Newton's second law of motion. Newton, however, emphasized mechanical forces while the d'Alembert equation is the mathematical form of an equilibrium principle, which states that *in equilibrium matter only exists where and when all vector forces sum to zero.* A condition is not a causal statement (see Appendix A4.1). The same condition can also be formulated as the Least Action Principle, which defines the trajectory of particles as a locus of points along which all forces sum to zero. Such a trajectory is the trough of an energy surface, defined by all surrounding matter, along which the action of the motion is minimized (Goldstien, 1965b). What has been done to extend the d'Alembert Principle of classic physics in Equation 1.5-1 is to add the internal forces holding charge and mass together in order to achieve a global-force-equilibrium condition for the existence of material that includes subjective experiences.

The existence of internal forces implies that an internal energy pattern happens inside of material, which exactly counterbalances the energy pattern from the rest of the universe. This pattern is not necessarily an exact model of the external material configuration but should rather be interpreted as an *accommodation* made by both subjective and objective phases of our material structure to the influences from the rest of Reality. Since we normally believe what we see in front of our noses is at least a representation of the external world, the identification of a balanced internal mass/charge structure implies that we do not actually experience a reproduction of the outside, but each of us experiences our own personal interpretation of the influences to which we are subjected.

1.5.1 Space is a field of events

The mind-body sequence depicted in Figure 1.4-4 shows a series of a single volume containing centers of mass and charge. Single volumes were drawn for clarity and to more clearly support the discussion of internal and external forces involved. The expression "Vol" was defined previously in Section 1.4.1 and is a placeholder for the name of a single place of material happenings among many such places. Occasionally we want to deal with Reality as a single self-contained entity. In such cases we will let the letter "W" stand for the Whole. When all of Reality is intended then "W" is the name of the single place where all material happens. However, in most cases it is convenient to divide the Whole into smaller parts. For example, we will often divide the Whole into you (Y), I (I) and the rest of the universe (U) to analyze the interactions amongst ourselves. Further subdivisions are necessary to calculate the internal evolution of the major parts due to internal interactions. In the case of the universe this is usually done by parameterizing the volume with a coordinate system. For example, the letters x, y, z are traditionally used to give numerical names that replace "Vol" in a Cartesian coordinate frame. Figure 1.5-1 explicitly shows a subdivision of the large cross section, or volume, into a field of parallel cell strings. Each individual spatial cell string is a place in which charge and mass happens in a specific configuration designated by the state of the sub-volume $\zeta[x,y,z,T]$. Influences extend mainly along the time direction in such a field but also from neighbor to neighbor in the spatial direction. The cross section of such a field is identified as the spatial plane of a Now instance "T".

Linear and cyclic configurations of state sequences "$\zeta(T)$" are shown in Figure 1.5-1. Both show time sequences of material configurations in which subjective (S) and objective (O) aspects occur between inner and outer occurrences of material (M). A spatial cross section containing energy patterns are the Physical Correlates of Consciousness (PCC) pattern of observable experiences. There is no distinction between human bodies and any other material system. All material,

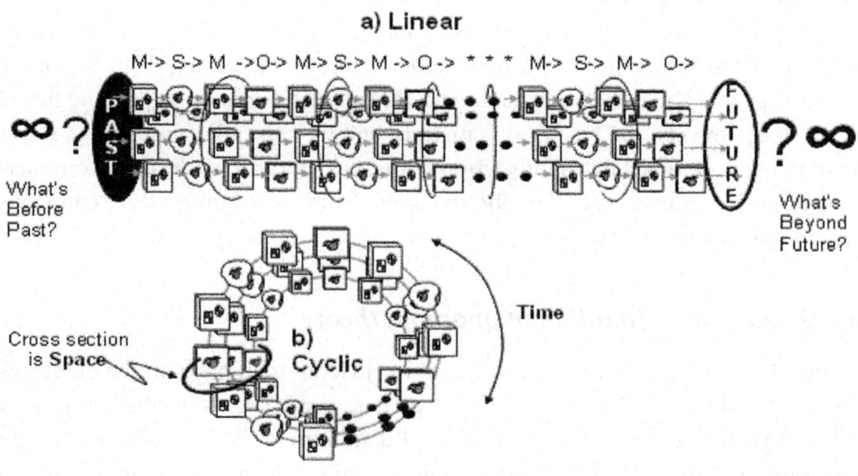

FIGURE 1.5-1 Linear and cyclic sequences of subjective and objective activities: space of parallel loops

whether the human brain or an inanimate rock, is composed of body-mind activity sequences. This shows how the pan-psychic nature of a primitive awareness is built into material itself and is not an ad hoc or emergent property. The difference between humans and rocks is the detailed organization of the material and the resulting intertwined action flows and not a qualitatively different substance or capacity.

The straight-line model sequence is useful in many practical problems in which a distinct beginning and end is required. Such impositions, though practical because it limits one's problem to a finite domain, leaves one with the question of what happens before or after the beginning and end, respectively. Within the evolution of the universe activity never stops but may transform itself into different patterns. On the cosmological level, the Big Bang theory suggests that the beginning of the universe happened when all action paths emerged from a single point. Though consistent with the Doppler interpretations of astronomic red-shift observations, it is difficult to imagine the spontaneous creation of something from nothing. A more prudent approach would be simply to acknowledge that all theories have limits of applicability. Such limits are called singularities, and the closer one gets, the less likely the theories in which they appear are applicable. The steady-state theories lead one to the logical conclusion that eventually the configuration of material must repeat, leading one to favor a cyclic form for activity as the architecture of the Whole. Such theories leave us with an equally puzzling question of how a Whole sprang into existence in the first place. Mechanisms for answering both these questions are given in Chapter 4, although the ultimate question of why an existence of any kind happens will be left for philosophers to argue.

In either case, the theory put forward in this book is that change propagates through the inside and outside of matter from which a conscious observer is constructed. This activity can then be correlated with consciousness when experienced as the flow of changes directly through the 1st-person's self-containing loop. However, the 1st-person is not alone. Parts of his or her material also interfaces with the rest of the matter in the universe either as influence leaking from boundary processing cycles or as specialized interface threads that terminate at past and future boundaries between the 1st-person's material and the rest of Reality. Thus, a linear action flow is modified by an interaction with a feed-forward cycle and a combination of both segment types describe the architecture of a human-level conscious system (see Chapter 6).

1.5.2 Event interpretation of quantum theory

Figures 1.4-4 and 1.5-1 use classic physical world icons to implement the observer's model of reality. This was done in the hope that visualizations of objective reality are familiar to the reader and their use will demonstrate the connection between sensations and the model explaining those sensations. As has been emphasized in Section 1.1, it is the architecture of this connecting activity, not the details of the models installed in such activities that combines the objective and subjective aspects of Reality. By replacing the classic physical world icon with a quantum model, a closer identification between the activity flowing through our event architecture and the nomenclature of conventional physics can be made.

Let us consider only the dark direct experience cycle from Figure 1.3-1 reproduced without the object recognition loop (Figure 1.5-2). It consists of a single loop that simply stores and regenerates a 1st-person optical sensation. This sensation is shown at the top as a spatial cross section of many parallel actions. This is the subjective phase of activity happening between two material cross section states shown in the left and right. The material consists of an array of cells whose upper halves are the inside aspect of matter, which are each influenced by the conscious charge/mass forces from the other side. On the external lower side of the matter arrays, the charges and masses would, according to our theory, be connected by electromagnetic and gravito-inertial forces. In this lower half, the 3rd-person view of an objective world would be located if we were using a classic "objective reality" model in a multi-cycle loop. However, this physical reality cannot be seen directly.

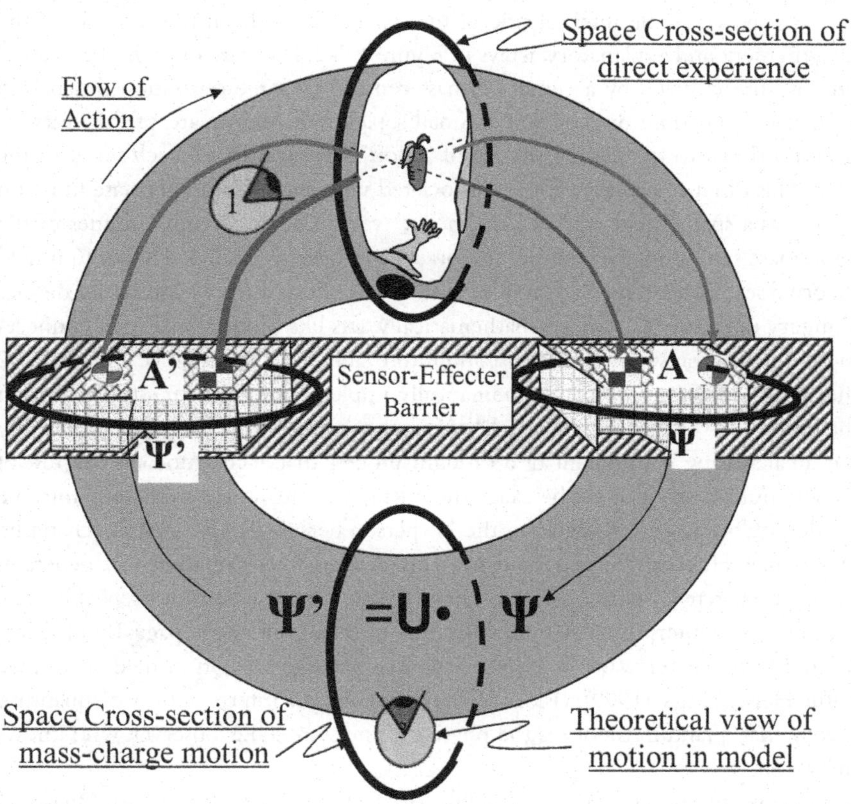

FIGURE 1.5-2 Optical sensation refresh cycle using Schrödinger's forward time propagation equation in the quantum model: 1st-person projects scene into Plato's cave

In other words, we can look down upon the event loop and see all phases because we have a *transcendental view* of our model. However, when *we are* the model, we would be inside, aware only of the observable patterns in the 1st-person view phase. This is the output of the interior-past side of the measurement array on the left.

The original developers of quantum mechanics were strongly influenced by the Positivist school of philosophy (Carnap, 2000), which insisted that it makes no sense to speculate about what physical reality actually is, since it can never be seen, even in principle. As discussed in Section 1.3, what can be seen is a fusion of a 1st-person qualia and a 3rd-person visualization of our reality model. Neither are physical reality but observable experiences. Although visualizations are useful heuristics tools, Niels Bohr, the father of quantum theory, strongly warned us not to fall into the visualizations trap since such images reflect the capabilities of our display systems rather than physical reality itself. Instead, he argued that only relationships between directly observable measurements should be used to build a physical theory. In CAT, the Physical Correlates of Consciousness are the directly observable action-flow patterns happening between the past and future sides of matter's interior. These actions implement the change between the charge-mass patterns shown as the internal side of the space-cell fields on the top side of the measurement and explanatory arrays in Figure 1.5-2. The state of each of these cell sides is characterized by a center-of-mass center-of-charge separation distance in both space and time directions. For small separations, the square of this distance is proportional to the energy, or rate of action flowing through each point of the array. This distance can therefore be associated with the Schrödinger state function treated as a spatial field $\psi[\underline{\mathbf{x}}]$, where the "$\underline{\mathbf{x}}$" vector labels the sub-volumes of the coordinate system into which the sensor-effecter barrier is divided. Quantum field theory does not pretend to deal with a model of physical reality but rather defines a unitary operator "**U**", which mathematically acts like physical reality in connecting the separation states on the past and future side of a time instance. Figure 1.5-2 shows the operator formula mathematically implementing this transformation on the bottom of the loop. The symbol "=**U**•" is not a representation of physical reality but a calculating component of a thought process that accommodates the rest of Reality outside the loop. To be exact, the operator in this single-cycle loop must be an identity, because it simply holds the 1st-person perspective as a static unchanging experience. However, in general it is a complicated transformation that generates the next expected sensations. In this general case the cycle does not repeat exactly and should be interpreted as a spiral heading into and out of the page. By identifying the Schrödinger wave function as the mass/charge separation field vector, we fulfill Heisenberg's (1999) vision of the Copenhagen interpretation of quantum theory, that quantum theory is the physics of the system, i.e. observer, who knows the world.

We now comment on the central linearity feature of quantum theory. Quantum mechanics is the physics of the system that knows the world when the displacements between charge and mass are small enough so that their motion can be described by harmonic oscillations around an equilibrium mass/charge configuration. When mass/charge separation becomes large, the force between mass and charge can no longer be approximated by linear reversible restoring forces, and contemporary quantum theory no longer accurately describes the situation. In such cases we encounter macro-size quantum phenomena including the creation and destruction of the underlying material arrays, i.e. our personal Hilbert Space in which objects appear. In physics experiments, this level of description would require the theory to include the setup and breakdown of the instrumentation required to explore atomic and nuclear phenomena, which are currently handled in the classic physics domain inside the von Neumann Cut. Further discussion of the relation between quantum physics and this simplified interior-material modeling approach is given in several references (Baer, 2014a, 2014b, 2014c) and will be elaborated in Part II in Chapter 5. Here we limit our discussion to the implications of the proposition, which identified the interior of matter as the holder of mind and its content, and thus provided a physical pan-psychic explanation of how we are conscious.

1.6 Event universe examples

The fundamental building blocks of the event-oriented reality include both open-linear segments and closed-loop segments of activity. Whether open or closed, the segments represent changing physical and mental state trajectories. This section presents alternative combinations of such trajectories in order to demonstrate important characteristics of the action model of reality.

For example, consider "Reality" as a single Whole. By definition the Whole must include all activity progressing in one universal dynamic state "Z". This means the material propagates through a single deterministic sequence of many correlated changes "ζ". This experience is analogous to a total Reality dreaming itself in a state of equilibrium forever. Since there is no "external" forcing the Whole out of its sequence, the charge-mass density configurations will eventually repeat and form a single closed loop. Such a single loop has been frequently drawn to represent the simplest and most fundamental "Form" of all activity. In order to understand how You and I fit into the Whole we must separate this Whole activity into constituent parts.

1.6.1 Division of the whole

To be compatible with conventional thinking, let's assume for a moment that the Universe is all there is. A model of the Universe as a Whole is useful when considering cosmological problems but does not correspond to the feeling of separateness and the necessity of dealing with smaller subsets of the universe that most of us encounter in our everyday lives. We can regroup the activities in many equivalent configurations so long as we remember that *the whole is equal to the sum of its parts plus all their interactions*. The simplest case divides the universe into the 1st-person "I" and the rest of the Universe "U".

We already encountered this division in Figure 1.2-4, where two single interacting cycles were shown. It is, however, instructive to consider how this two-part division would look when loop bundles consisting of many sequential and parallel cycles are involved. Figure 1.6-1 shows two bundles of loops drawn so that two closed sequences are explicitly represented. Two-sided dashed arrows show the interactions happening between them at different time points along their respective timelines. It is important to recognize that events include time, and all the interactions that either have or will happen in the lifetime of the event are here recorded. This view allows us to show the totality of both U and I as a combined record of a complete event. The separated lifetime loops connected by dashed arrows identify all interaction events contained in the Whole.

In the old object-oriented world view, the division between the I and the universe is made between the subject and the object. The English language incorporates this division when insisting that a proper sentence must have the subject-verb-predicate structure. The sentence, "I see the universe", expresses the belief that the universe is that separate thing in front of our nose, and influences flow from it through our sensors and into our brain where it is turned into observable experiences. Psychologists believe the separation between self and the rest of the world

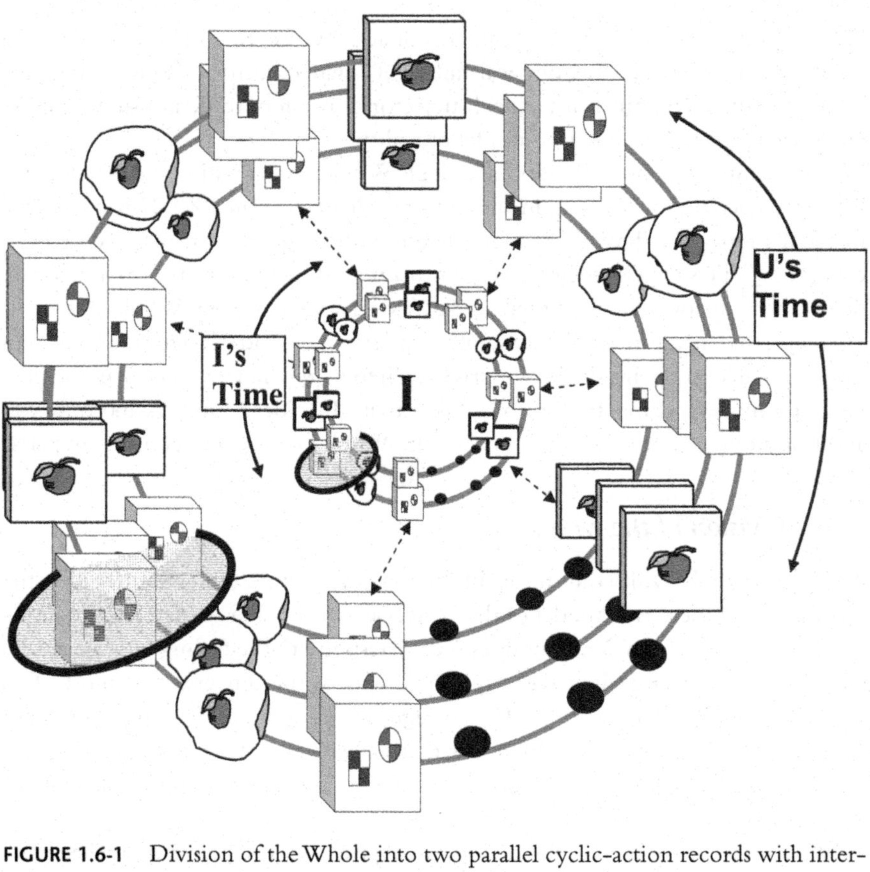

FIGURE 1.6-1 Division of the Whole into two parallel cyclic-action records with interactions happening along their lifetimes

is a necessary development in a child in order to allow it to properly deal with the objective universe. This same objective orientation is still retained in quantum theory because the von Neumann Cut is made between the observer and the external quantum object by a measuring instrument.

In contrast, the event-oriented world view approximates the Self as a closed action loop so that the flows of influences propagate primarily along its own timeline. The world in front of one's nose is an internal display of action flowing around one's own loop. Interactions with other loops initiate adjustments in both loops involved in the interactions. The symptoms of these adjustments are experiences described in the vocabulary of the display-generating mechanism constructed within each loop. In humans that vocabulary is composed of *the things* we sense. In different action loops the adjustments may require completely different display vocabulary. Whether or not we are capable of imagining the sensations of beings, such as an insect with compound eyes, is debatable. It is likely we are capable of imagining the sensations of more primitive beings occurring along the road of our evolutionary development, but it is extremely unlikely we have the capacity to imagine how more advanced beings interpret their interactions. What is clear is that the world we believe to live in is a visualization of an internal accommodation phenomenon and that world will change substantially if the display mechanism built into our loop evolves to achieve additional capabilities.

1.6.2 The three-person division

The multi-cycle bundles of parallel loops introduced previously are instructive for showing sequential parallel optic fields in memory records of past and future events expected to happen in our human lifetimes. They become overly complicated when attempting to show other important features of the event model. To simplify the figures when multiple interacting parts are involved requires the aggregation of parallel loops into more compact action lines and limiting the cross section display to single points of interaction. This can be achieved by showing only one set of parallel cycles occurring in *one Now time* slice while separating the parallel loops of all identifiable parts in separate places on a page. An example of three interacting loops representing three conscious beings is shown using such a compact format in Figure 1.6-2. Each arc between material icons represents an activity that is completed in the Now time interval "Δ" when the activity is in time-state "T".

Three inner cycles labeled "You", "I" and the Universe "U" are the essence of the beings depicted. Each of these cycles guides the interaction between the inner and outer loops to and from their respective models of physical reality. These models are hosted in the physical phases of the inner cycles. Observable sensations are attached to the cross sections of inner and outer loop interaction points. Sensations and thought bubbles indicate that a being, during normal everyday operation, pays attention to the interaction events while undisturbed space cells are ignored. What "I" see at the interaction points is the appearance of "You" holding a book, while "You" see the 1st-person perspective of yourself holding a book. You are

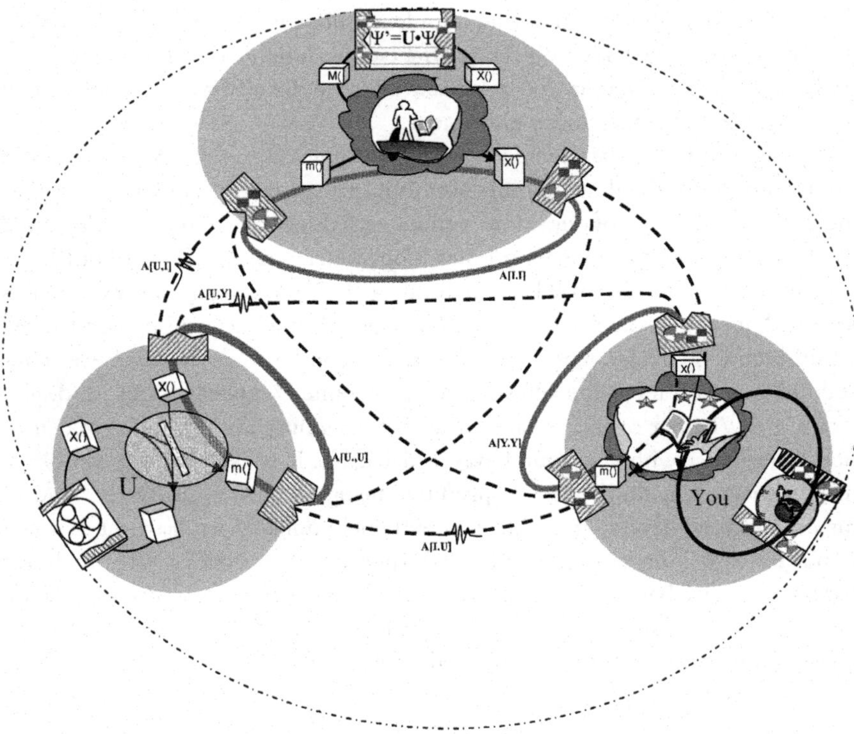

FIGURE 1.6-2 A three-person interacting event universe showing three different Reality Models and Model Leak interaction cycles as broken black line records. Each person is using different Reality Models and dot-dash Model Leak interactions are suggested. See Figure 4.4-3 for arc label definitions.

outfitted with a classic-reality model in memory, which looks like an objective three-dimensional world – no offense intended. This memory model interfaces through simulated sensor arrays, shown as single sides of mass/charge density structures, with the mental display of your cycle. I, on the other hand, am outfitted with a quantum physical reality model, which dispenses with any classic world visualization and instead uses a unitary transform operator "=U•" to directly transform the ψ displacements in my Hilbert space cells of simulated sensor arrays into the next expected array configuration. The Universe "U" is outfitted with a more abstract Conscious Action Theory model, consisting of a scale model of action cycles representing the larger event in which it is imbedded.

The drawing shows one instant of our existence. The static action cycles could be used as an empty space-time approximation in which observable content results from disturbances moving within the permanent repeating background. In this case mass/charge oscillations would flow in the external speckled-line interface arcs and some fraction of this activity is channeled through the solid-line internal cycles. The action lines are composed of space cells that repeat in the one cycle time period shown. If no disturbances happen, this single picture would describe an empty-space Now that repeats for all three parts exactly forever. *Such empty-space action-flow networks are the equilibrium ground state of our existence.* Disturbances will cause the equilibrium event cycles not to close. In this case a record of the event would require multiple different copies to be drawn on successive pages. When these are viewed like sequential movie frames, they would show empty space faithfully repeated and disturbance action structures moving through the space. The subjective experience in each part would experience a conventional movie of objects moving in a three-dimensional space. The CAT model adds the flow of action behind the scenes, which creates the 1st-person multimedia display we experience in real life.

Large broad speckled-line cycles labeled A[U,U], A[I,I] and A[Y,Y] represent the action loops of material controlled by each being, which also controls one's body. Built into the body loop are the actions producing the retina in a human optic system and also all other detector arrays such as in the auditory, touch or inner-body housekeeping modalities. Separately designated by the solid-line arcs are memory loops. Oscillations traveling through these arcs explain our sensory interactions, which are sensitive to electromagnetic stimulation in the optic, auditory and touch modalities but also to gravito-inertial forces through the semicircular canals of the ear. Small disturbances in a permanent space structure can be handled with quantum theory. However, this restricts the action flow to the existing space loop networks. A permanent space-time background is exactly the assumption underlying both quantum and classic physics. Larger action transfers of controlled material between beings modify the repeating spatial structure by transferring whole action cycles controlled by one being to another. This magnitude of change requires a CAT model.

In addition, we note that memory is typically protected from electromagnetic interaction. However, since no effective shielding isolates these components from gravito-inertial forces, the possibility of memory leakage interactions exists. Though gravity is quite a weak force, inertia is comparable in effect to electric forces. CAT allows possible memory-to-memory leakage interactions. These bypass the normal sensors and therefore provide a mechanism for extrasensory communication. They are indicated by the thin dot-dash lines in Figure 1.6-2. Since our traditional objective reasoning does not process direct memory-to-memory interactions, these signals show up as mysterious and illogical observables that are usually considered an artifact of our imagination. The ability of the event-oriented model to include extrasensory communication may lead to more rational handling of these phenomena and will be discussed in Part III of this book.

1.6.3 Cosmologic limits and the isolated systems approximation

In the last section we have assumed the undisturbed action loops can be used as a permanent repeating space background, which define the period of a Now.

Whether an activity can be approximated as an exactly repeating Whole depends upon the precision with which the activity must be repeated. To explore this relationship, remember that time is measured in cycles and a single cycle in CAT consists of a subjective and objective phase. The amount of activity happening in an elementary cycle is identified with the smallest measurable electromagnetic change requiring an amount of action given by Planck's constant "h" (6.02×10^{-34} Watt-second). A loop of period ΔT will have $\Delta T/dt$ primitive cycles in its circumference. If we designate the spatial volume of a primitive cycle by an infinitesimal cube as dx^3, the number of cycles in the cross section of the loop is "Vol/dx^3". Then the total amount of action required to close a loop is the amount of action in an elementary cycle times the number of such cycles in the circumference of the loop times the spatial volume as shown in the following equation:

$$A = h \cdot \Delta T \cdot Vol/dt \cdot dx^3 \qquad \text{Equation 1.6-1}$$

This is the amount of action in any isolated system's evolution. An elementary event has a period and volume equal to "$dt \cdot dx^3$" and an action of Planck's constant. This condition does not fix the shape of the elementary event, which when isolated may be a torus (see Section 4.3.3.3). If the cycles are exact in both their spatial cross section and temporal direction, then they can be lined up to repeat exactly at the end of ΔT seconds. However, if there is some small uncertainty in their time interval or spatial dimensions, then the repetition of the event is only approximate, and the ΔT seconds repetition time is a nearest integer approximation of the actual period. In this case, the true repetition time would be the number of approximate time periods "$\Delta T1 + \Delta T2 + \ldots \Delta TN$" in order to allow the deviations "δT" to make the repeating cycle complex line up at complete action "h" boundaries. An exact repeating equilibrium activity must have an exact number of action sizes "$N \cdot h = A$" in order for the activity not to have any residual action.

Equation 1.6-1 therefore is only exact for absolutely isolated systems and that can only be the entire Reality. For all other systems, the parameters should be given subscripts to define them as approximations. If the entire Reality is our Universe, then its existence would be completely defined by a single loop of size ΔT_U repeating exactly forever. However, any measurement by a subjective entity not accounted for in the Universe would imply the cycle will not close in time T_U. The repetition time of a loop and the action required to execute it will depend upon the precision with which one defines closure. By adopting Heisenberg's limit of uncertainty "h" as a fundamental principle we fudge the closure by calling the deviations "δT" intrinsic uncertainties of nature. This eliminates any inquiry of additional and possibly causal interactions with our Universe as nonsense and thereby dismisses rational subjective experiences from science.

Typically, one identifies some subset of cycles that does close precisely as the isolated empty space, which represents the first-order approximation of the system seen from the outside. If we are inside the material of such a system, then disturbances are displayed as content, which are the subjective experiences we see as objects. The inside of any system's material, when electromagnetically isolated, will be invisible and approximated by the equations of an empty universe or an invisible atom. For readers acquainted with quantum theory, this description should sound familiar.

From the outside, a hydrogen atom that is in a static eigenstate fits an exact number of matter-wave cycles around its orbit. In this state it is electromagnetically isolated and does not radiate or absorb light and is therefore invisible and modeled by Bohr as a small universe. However, Bohr assumed the inertial forces pulling the electron away from the proton was constant, when according to Mach's Principle it varies due to the motion of the surrounding masses. Ignoring this nearly random element makes quantum theory statistical. CAT eliminates this oversight returning physics to strict determinism at the cost of giving subjective forces inside matter a causal role that can modify strict physical materialism (Baer, 2015a).

1.6.4 The multiverse model

The division of Reality into three parts is useful for many applications. However, the process of division can in principle continue until all the parts have been broken down to their elementary event size. The number of elementary events encountered in human activities is so large that divisions will involve massive aggregations. Useful divisions are made by collecting groups of activities where internal interactions far outnumber external interactions. A conventional object is usually enclosed in a skin that is defined by a relatively small number of light interactions while massive internal interactions happen inside the boundary. For a typical one-gram object, the rate of action flow is given by Einstein's ($E = m{\star}c^2 = 9 \times 10^{13}$ Watt-seconds) equation while sunlight falling on its one-centimeter surface at sea level is .012 Watt-seconds. Thus, ten-thousand-trillion times more action is happening inside the object than the electromagnetic interaction with which we see the object.

In the visualization of the process model, the spatial boundary of a loop is defined by the interface loops containing sensor arrays, which interact with those of other loops. The action flowing through these interface arcs for most useful divisions will therefore be small compared with the action flowing in the internal loops. The division shown in Figure 1.6-2 will only represent well-individuated You, I and the rest of the Universe "U", if most of the action is flowing in our internal loops. In the extreme case, no external interactions take place, and we can imagine completely isolated stand-alone loops as shown in Figure 1.6-3. Here You, I and the rest of the Universe are shown as three wide internal loops suggesting massive internal activities and small normal sensory interactions. In addition, other loops representing people, places or things have been pulled out of the Whole to exemplify divisions applicable to more complex situations than simply You, I and U interacting in a general multiverse background. Although the normal sensory interaction channels with the loops outside our trio are no longer shown, some of the extrasensory connections may still be present. This is because normal sensory stimuli are easy to eliminate by closing one's eyes, falling asleep or even dying. The long-range gravito-inertial forces penetrate everything and may still influence us. The symptoms of internal accommodations in our loop may generate appearances in our dreams. These are occasionally remembered and available for recall when we wake up, but more often than not, they are dismissed as nonsensical or meaningless imaginations.

Figure 1.6-3 can be interpreted as a typical model of an event-oriented reality. It uses lines and loops along with process boxes to depict events and event interactions. The physical memory phase of each loop may contain different models of physical reality, which in extremely simple cases may transport influences rather than performing more complex processing.

Figure 1.1-3 introduced the object-to-event-oriented paradigm shift required to implement the next logical step in the development of science. There, a single event loop is used to represent the entire Reality. Here in Figure 1.6-3, the complex of interacting loops and process arcs show how such a single Whole can be expanded to depict details required to make an event reality model useful. We no longer think of objects moving around in a big three-dimensional box. Nor do we imagine probability packets moving around in that same box. Instead, an interconnected network of loops, arcs and segments of activities forms the visualization of a CAT reality, within which space-time and objects are incorporated. In this network, You, the reader, can find a record of yourself as a lifetime-loop in which the appearance of this book happens in front of your nose. When such a record is

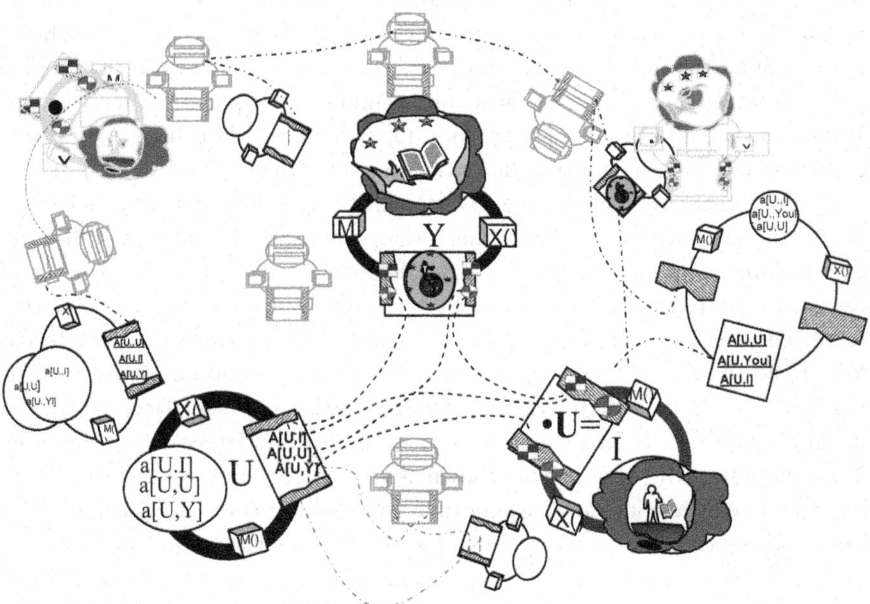

FIGURE 1.6-3 Three independent lifetime event cycles showing external force interaction flow records between I, You and U when I sees "you" holding a "book" imbedded in a multiverse

implemented so that the action flows through the structure of processing channels, the flow reaching you will produce a next external sensation in your mental space. Simultaneously, your internal action flow will produce an expected equivalent sensation. If the model is accurate and registered against your external stimulation display, the two will largely match. If small differences exist, they will send commands to the outside and absorb model updates back inside Yourself. Thus You, being an interacting action loop, will experience a lifetime of sensation that is being modified by mutual accommodations to other loops.

A multiverse of conscious beings completes our introduction to the event-oriented world view. The following chapters will elaborate our Conscious Action Theory to provide further details of how this model fits into and then expands contemporary science. The chapters in Part III will then provide examples of applications heretofore considered beyond the capacity of contemporary rational minds because with a valid theory the definition of rational will have been expanded.

1.7 Conclusion and summary

The main goal of this book is to integrate the observer's subjective experiences, feelings, pleasures and pains into a rigorous theory of reality that expands rather than negates technical advances of current science. To achieve this goal the introductory chapter claims:

1 *What-is* is not equal to *what-is-perceived.*
2 Reality is a process that connects what-is with what-is-perceived in a cyclic event.
3 Such *events* rather than *particles* are the building blocks of all there is including the universe as well as ourselves.
4 Therefore You and I are large processes that produces sensations of our bodies and the objective world We believe to live in.
5 The process of seeing objects requires two complementary cycles,

    a **M**odel-of-**R**eality (**MoR**) produces an expected sensation that is compared with a measured sensation to generate an error signal that corrects the **MoR** so it produces a more accurate next sensation.
    b The executing operations of the **MoR** is implemented through a second cycle which projects theoretical explanatory "**s**ensations" of what the **MoR** is into the measured "**s**ensation".

6 The fused measured and explanatory sensations are the experience of our everyday reality.

By understanding *what we do* to experience our everyday reality we have integrated mind and body in an abstract cyclic mechanism, which can incorporate any system of beliefs. A **MoR** is our memory structure, which operationally produces sensations and semantically produces visualizations of what the **MoR** is believed to model. We therefore experience direct sensation fused with sensations of meaning that express the Reality we believe we are living in. The beliefs coded into the **MoR** phase of our processing cycles determine the reality we experience.

This brings us to the question, "Does the **MoR** currently producing our objective reality experience represent the optimum truth or can it evolve toward something better?" This introductory chapter claims an event-oriented world view along with the Conscious Action Theory's reformulation of physics will integrate our subjective and objective experience into a new and better Model of Reality than we now have. The rational for this claim is summarized as follows:

1 Current science is based upon objective reductionism, i.e. the inside of material can be found by breaking objects into smaller and smaller objects until elementary objects are discovered from which all is composed.
2 Reductionism fails when objects are too small to be seen even in principle. At infinitesimal scales objective observation gives way to theoretical belief-dependent projection into the inside of material.
3 Quantum theorists project probability wave packets into material as quantum objects and fail to acknowledge the mental nature of their projections.
4 Replacing probabilities with interacting event cycles when one such cycle is the observer and the other is the entity of interest corrects these failures.
5 A new action cycle physics based on classic world concepts provides a physical implementation for subjective experience *if we assume* forces between charge and mass hold the inside of material together.
6 The new physics proposes object-subject time extensions execute cycles of activity in sequential and parallel action structures that form the space in which objects happen, and You are such a space.
7 Our old concept of objective Reality is replaced by an event Reality of interacting cycles. You are an event that always happens. You accommodate interactions by changing Your cycle of execution. The observable symptom of your internal changes is the appearance of objects in the subjective phase of your cycle.

Having summarized the logical arguments leading to a Reality concept of interacting events, the following chapter extends this introduction for the reader by giving a more detailed experience with action flow. Please pretend to be one of the prisoners in Plato's cave, who is locked inside your own skull. Rather than follow Plato into the blinding light of the external *ideal*, seek understanding and control of your cave by building models of material in the cave, which explain your situation and provide the control to improves the sensations you experience.

2

CONSCIOUS OPERATIONS IN THE 1ST-PERSON PERSPECTIVE

What is it like to know that we are living in a world of our own making? How can we look out past our noses and realize that the objects around us are like the icons on the desktop of a computer screen, somehow connected to reality in memory but *not* identical to that reality in position, form or material? How does it feel to be enclosed inside a simulation that is in principle unknowable from the outside, to be inside the control room of a great machine with no way of verifying the true nature of its existence? How can we live with the knowledge that every step we take, every move we make is based on an illusion that could suddenly disintegrate into nothingness? The answer is that we cannot operate in this state of absolute uncertainty and must believe in some Reality. The question is what to believe and how to incorporate those beliefs in one's bigger Self?

The Event-Oriented World View introduced in the previous chapter suggests that, no matter what we feel like, we are actually a processing loop that connects mental sensations with physical causes. If correct, the world that you see, the sound that you hear, the touch that you feel and everything you experience, including the experience of your body, happens in the display phase of an activity that is larger than anything you can imagine. We have introduced a graphic model of that larger activity as a conscious action cycle repeated here in Figure 2-1. It shows a cartoon of the experience of a person holding an apple, who believes he or she is holding an apple while standing on the earth surrounded by stars. This belief is shown as the icon of the 1st-person's (I's) physical reality model that is being updated to explain I's experience and measured to reproduce that experience. The closed action loop is a model of an isolated conscious being.

Yet immediately we run into the uncertainty described in the first paragraph of this chapter. This model cannot be understood objectively because the physical body phase is explicitly shown outside the observable mental phase and therefore can never be seen for what it actually is. Because we *are* such action loops there is

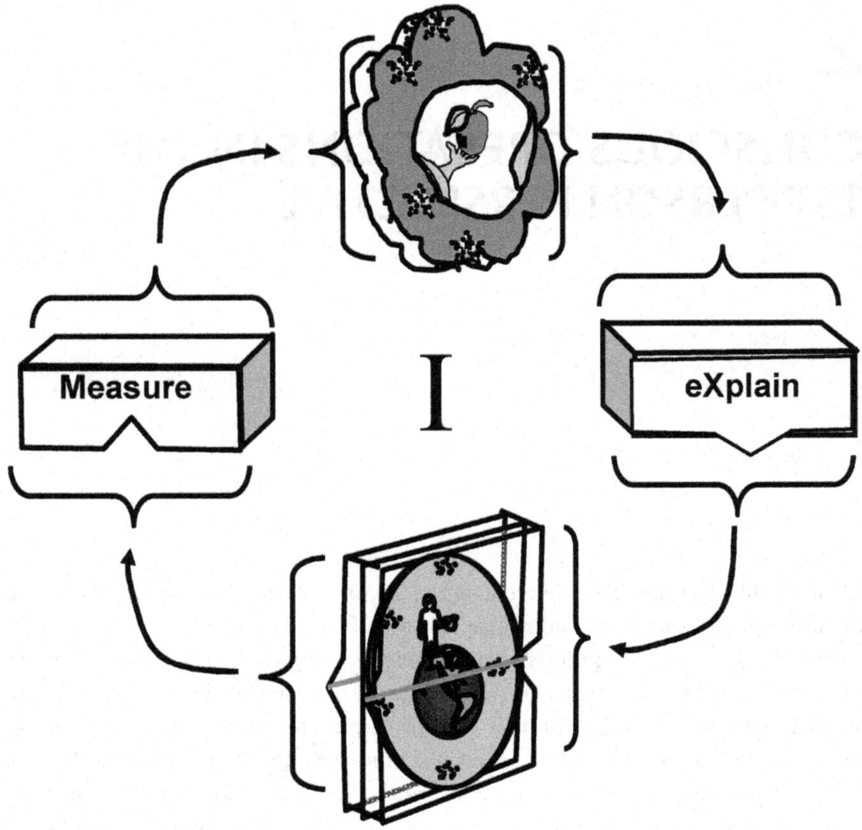

FIGURE 2-1 Functional description of the basic Conscious Cycle

no separate "we" outside ourselves to see us in the same way the reader can look down upon the loop drawn in the figure. All we can experience is mapped into the mind phase of our drawing. We can never experience the true cause of our sensations unless we conceive of an operation that transcends the loop we believe ourselves to be. However, even if we could, most of us do not wish to leave the comfort and safety of what we feel we are. Religious traditions claim to provide a mechanism of transcendence and control through meditation or prayer. Our scientific approach seeks to achieve whatever understanding is possible while remaining firmly anchored within our everyday 1st-person experience. This requires the use of symbolic models.

To ground our model, which emphasizes what we *do-to-see* not what we *see*, it is important to examine the processes we actually execute during our normal wakeful state. It is quite obvious that knowing what we *do* to have experiences, is quite different from knowing what we *do with* those experiences. The difference is similar to knowing how our automobiles work compared with knowing how and where to drive. We conduct our lives from a driver's seat that is centered just behind our eyes and treat the world of objects in front of our noses as though they were real. What is it about this position that makes it useful? How do we conclude our experiences are real? How can we trust the larger world we feel to be living in when our sensory range is limited to a small, almost infinitesimal fraction of what there is? Can we have confidence in our actions when our knowledge of the world beyond our sensors is at best a theoretical inference? This chapter answers these questions by examining the operations we execute to establish an actionable truth that is connected to the unknowable when our observations are limited to those that can be performed in the 1st-person perspective.

Our first task is to recognize that contemporary scientific theory is based upon an objective theoretical 3rd-person perspective but the experiences we use to build this perspective are gathered from our subjective immediate 1st-person experiences. If we are to ground our beliefs without looking through the prejudice of historically adopted 3rd-person theories, we must return to the undeniable truths of our immediate experiences.

Since we only experience mental sensations directly, not their causes, apparent manipulation of those sensations may influence but not directly control their causes. We will show how we overcome this limitation by making externalized symbols of what we believe caused our sensations and projecting their meaning back into our sensations as actionable reality. By carefully documenting the activities performed by a 1st-person creating and using such symbols, we will rediscover the architecture of a conscious loop as the activity we have been doing all along as conscious beings. Such loops connect observable sensations with explanatory models of physical reality. This architecture has already been offered as a framework of reality that is more fundamental than any specific physical theory we may choose to incorporate in it. It is the framework of activities – not any specific model of reality incorporated in those activities – that is fundamental. In later chapters we will show how the physics of interacting processing loops provides the theoretical framework we are calling Conscious Action Theory (CAT). This framework defines a universe whose parts act like conscious beings responding to each other's influences. By providing a context for both classic and quantum theory, action loops replace the dead material universe as the a priori starting point of scientific thinking.

2.1 The 1st-Person Laboratory

The first figure shown in Chapter 1 depicts the optical perspective of Ernest Mach looking out through his left eye into a room. In Figure 2.1-1 we reduce the graphic details of that picture and use cartoon icons to depict the 1st-person view of a typical scientist in order to examine what experiments actually look like in the only perspective we can experience directly. Here the 1st-person's view of Mach's body is reduced to a nose, an arm and one hand. At the same time, we have added a minimum set of objects that are required to conduct experiments in any laboratory. These include a coordinate frame attached to the corners of the laboratory room, a coordinate clock on the wall and an apple, which represents a typical system under study.

Figure 2.1-1 is an instantaneous snapshot automatically interpreted as a classic objective environment seen by a classic objective body from his or her own point of view. It is a record of a personal observation made from an everyday 1st-person perspective of our laboratory, where all these appearances are taken to be real objects. How they behave has been coded into the laws of classic physics. Classic physics describes the relation between appearances by proposing symbols of reality, such as charge and mass, which behave exactly in the theory as the appearances behave in the laboratory.

For example, classic physics assumes the simple experiment of throwing an apple shown in Figure 2.1-1 is explained by assuming an electric force, applied by the charges of one's hand, imparted an upward velocity to the apple's mass that is now in free flight controlled by its internal inertia and the force of gravity. The appearance attached to the mass is therefore accelerating toward the floor. By noting the position of the clock pointers simultaneously with the position of the apple, Newton's second law of motion can be verified to great accuracy, and the result of such experiments applied to predict the actual behavior of all similar appearances within the 1st-Person Laboratory (1st-PL).

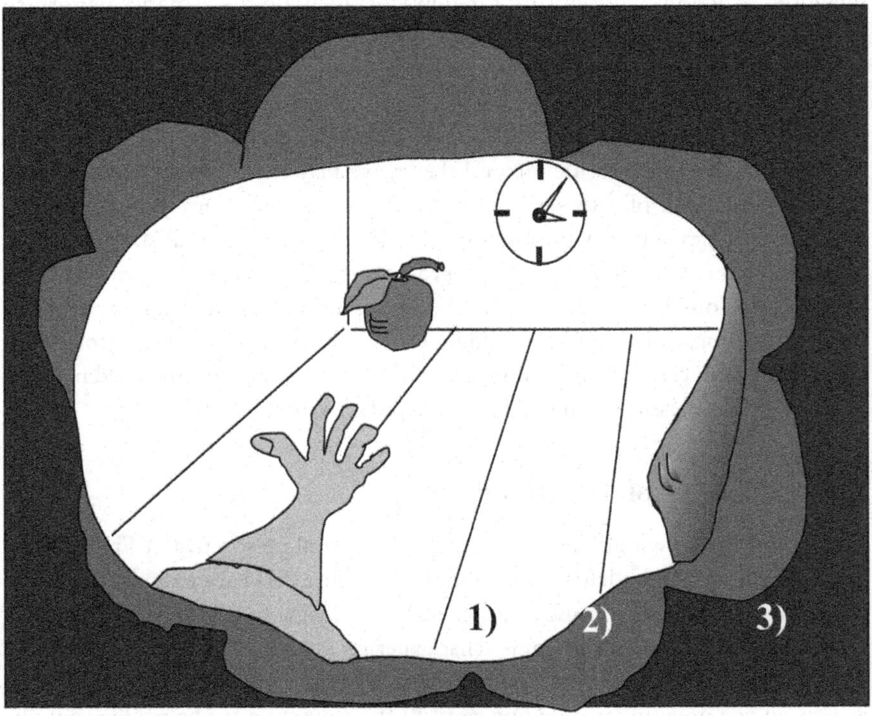

FIGURE 2.1-1 1st-Person Laboratory Plato's scientific cave: Object and space experience are registered layers of 1) Sensory interpretations, 2) Touch expectations, and 3) Belief visualizations

The utility of the laws of physics to predict and control our 1st-person sensations is undeniable. Their success does not explain how we see those appearances nor does it force us to adopt "objective reality" and believe the experience of objects in front of our noses *is* the independent reality we exist in. All we really know is the comfort, security and success provided by our historic utilization of the sensory display with which we are endowed. The reason for the comfort is the utility of expected touch sensations displayed in the dark space surrounding ourselves when we close our eyes. This perceptive space – we will call it the expected touch space when only the tactile sense is displayed – is represented by the thought bubble icon underlying the optic sensation of our 1st-Person Laboratory. Only by recognizing this world in front of our noses – this 1st-person real feeling experience – as a multi-modality registered display of optical, auditory and expected touch sensations, can we properly set the stage for more fundamental questions. What exactly is this experience we are conscious of? What causes it? How will it evolve? How can we further its evolution?

2.1.1 The feeling of reality

The drawing of the 1st-Person Laboratory is produced by mapping the world of appearances in front of our noses to a subset of those appearances located on the page in front of us (Baer, 2011). Faithful reproductions are designed to create the illusion that we are looking at an original. Our drawing is composed of icons that merely suggest a 1st-person experience. To the extent that it works for the reader, the illusion is broken only because he or she can look beyond the page and note the difference between the picture and the original. In one case we are looking at a flat optical image built of colored ink or a computer display. In the other case we are also looking at a similar optical image but endowed with the feeling of material solidity associated with our real-world environment. The sensory nature of this solid feeling can be examined by closing one's eyes and becoming aware of the black space around oneself. This space is filled with what some describe as white ghostly sensations that outline the objects we believe to surround us (Webster, 1835). These sensations define the location of touch sensations we expect to encounter if we move our body so as to have contact with the objects. Figure 2.1-2 depicts these sensations within a thought bubble. What is expected to be touched if we probe the space in front of our nose are the objects, including the walls, surrounding our location. The fact that this feeling of reality can extend centrally outward from our immediate environment and eventually to the earth, sun and stars is not explicitly shown on the picture. But such an extended mapping displays the solid material sensation one would expect to encounter if one were to move one's tactile sensors out to test the moon, stars and beyond.

For the sake of illustration in this book, the 1st-Person Laboratory walls also represent the limits of the 1st-person scientist's direct perception. We assume the scientist cannot get out and must use auxiliary sensors to probe the external world. In that sense, the walls are identified with a kind of externalized skull while the

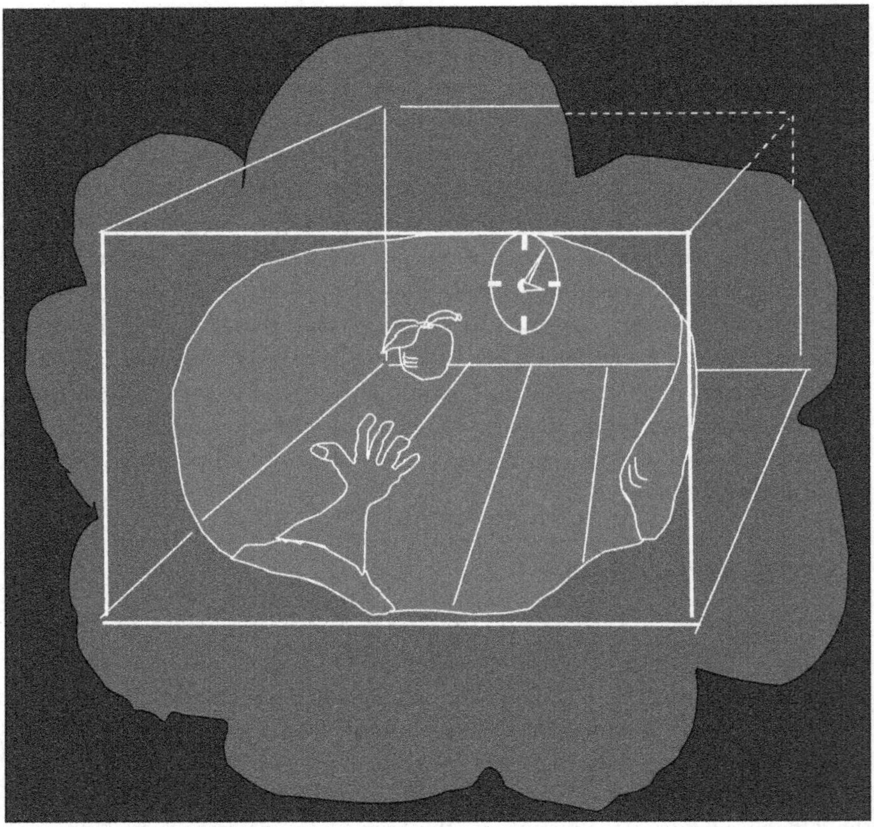

FIGURE 2.1-2 Expected touch sensation in the 1st-person perspective

scientist him- or herself is the little-man-inside who occupies the seat of his or her consciousness (Lehar, 2003).

The survival importance of a display that presents the location of potential collisions cannot be overestimated and hence this display is often taken for reality itself. The fact that it is an internal display of actionable information can best be illustrated by rapidly spinning around in a swivel chair to produce a dizzy effect. After a few rotations, inertial signals from the semicircular canals will rotate the expected touch sensations. If one rapidly stops the spin and opens one's eyes, the world will seem to spin. The expected location of surrounding objects will continue to twirl around while the optic display is stationary. The two conflicting sensation displays will generate discomfort until the motion of fluid in the semicircular canals settles down and the two sensation channels re-register. A similar false expectation effect can be observed when exiting a freeway after traveling at a constant high speed for a long time. The feeling that one is moving very slowly or even backwards is due to the latency between the expected locations of objects calculated for high-speed motion, which no longer predict their position when the automobile stops.

These simple observations show that expected touch sensations (ETS) are internally generated. They only display one's explanation of sensations rather than their actual reality. The dark space, within which optical as well as auditory sensations are registered, is often identified with the term mind. However, the term mind should be reserved for a more comprehensive display of all experiences – one which includes the display of space itself, our thoughts and hallucinations, not simply the expected location of objects. We will call the more restricted use of mental experience one's expected touch space (also abbreviated ETS since empty space is a sensation), and we will use a thought bubble to indicate its presence as a background sensation to the optical 1st-person view outlined in subsequent drawings.

An optical sensation registered with an expected touch sensation is usually considered to be real and is treated as an object. The veracity of the display can be verified by actually moving one's finger to the expected touch location and feeling an actual and usually much stronger sensation associated with touch or in extreme cases the pain of collision. The projection of explanatory thoughts into the sensation is a fundamental property of our thought process. Such projections are designed to establish the illusion of reality. Operating under such a reality illusion is a general characteristic of Western thought. The illusion is called Maya in some Eastern philosophic traditions. Without a display that is believed to be one's stake-your-life-on-it reality, it is impossible to act with conviction. It is fundamental to classic physics, chemistry and biology. The 1st-Person Laboratory is the place in this book that captures our reality illusion itself, and it is in such a display that the operations of our event-oriented CAT model must be demonstrated if understanding and utility is to be achieved.

2.1.2 The search for the feeling of reality

Once the internal nature of the ETS display is recognized, the feeling of reality previously associated with it in our laboratory is compromised. The challenge is answered by admitting the representational function of one's sensory display but at the same time generating a new sensation that marks a new "Ding an Sich" believed to have been the actual reality all along. This third layer of a more fundamental reality is represented in Figure 2.1-2 as an underlying black rectangle. In it a classical physicist might, for example, mark the reality of an object by projecting a center of mass symbol into the optical sensation and say, "I may be experiencing the qualia defining an apple but its appearance is evidence of a real object with real mass is moving through the real space in front of me". However, the objective world of classic physics is not the only reality one can stake one's life on.

After learning about quantum physics and Niels Bohr's contention that real objects are brought into existence through the measurement process, a new reality is found in the form of de Broglie's probability waves. In quantum theory an object is recognized to be the interpretation of observable reports from measuring instruments while probability waves take their place in the underlying black background. The visualization of these waves is registered and projected into the observables reported by a quantum physicist's biological measuring instruments. The physicist might then say, "I may be experiencing the observable light defining an apple but its appearance is evidence that real de Broglie waves have been collapsed into photon hits by my detectors measuring the light reflecting from its surface".

While it lasts, the quantum physicist might feel comfortable with the newly found feeling of reality but upon further investigation the physicist too will find his or her belief is insufficient. The sensation associated with the expected touch, like the sensation associated with a classic mass, like the sensation associated with the visualization of probability waves are first and foremost a sensation caused by something the physicist can never experience directly. The feeling of comfort in our current reality, destroyed by a realization that it is built on a sensation, followed by the search for a new reality, which is projected into the old sensations, is something we do over and over. The logic of our thought process needs to believe in something real. We will search for the feeling of reality and will always be disappointed in a futile and endless quest until we step back from what we are doing and realize that we must seek the answer to our fundamental question of what is really going on in a different way.

2.2 Symbolic transcendence

If we could get outside ourselves and watch the processes behind our observable layers of display, then the answer to our fundamental questions would be a recording of that external experience. Cataloging and compacting that recording into laws would then lead to a new integrated mind-body version of physics. Unfortunately, we cannot get out of our real Selves. The transcendental operations that promise to achieve a god's-eye view of ourselves and our environment are either straight out deceptions or at best extremely difficult to attain. Rather than argue about the possibility of 1st-person transcendence we will modify our search methodology to one that realizes we either cannot or do not want to get out. Therefore, in order to seek understanding, while holding solidly to the comfort of everyday 1st-person experience, we must evoke the use of symbols. We may not be able to get outside of our real "Selves" but we can easily mimic a god's-eye view with a symbol system designed to represent the "Reality" we seek to understand. The basic attributes of symbol systems, which allow a user to transcend the limitation of being one's real "Self" and obtain a useful tool that implements beneficial control over one's observable experiences, are symbols discussed in this section.

Observable symbols are seen as objects in the 1st-PL. What makes them symbols is the additional characteristic of meaning given to them by the 1st-person. That characteristic can be indicated by placing the object within an object that is generally recognized to contain symbols as shown in Figure 2.2-1. Here we have added an open book and a pen under the control of the 1st-person's fingers to the 1st-PL. The outline of the book divides the optical display into two distinct channels. The regions outside the pages contain everyday objects while the region inside the pages also contains objects that are automatically given symbolic characteristics

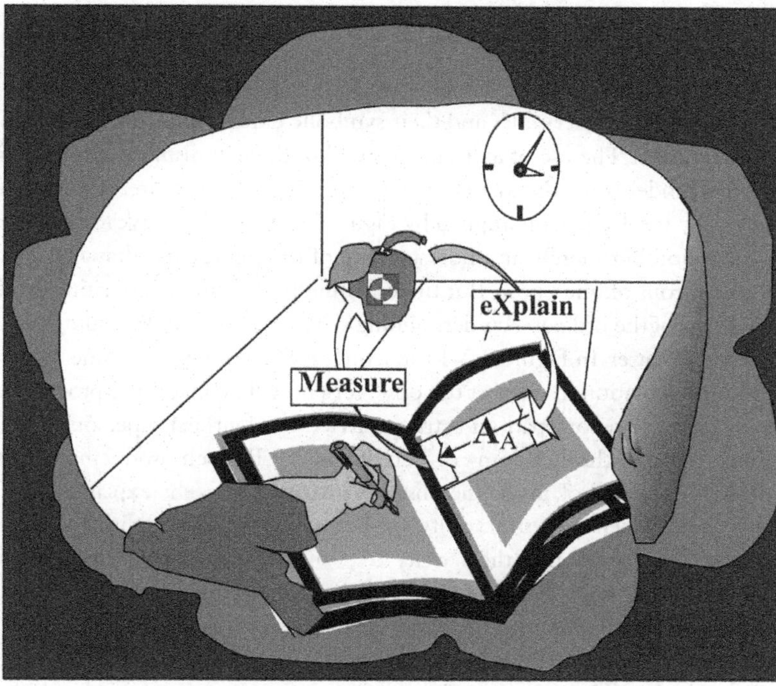

FIGURE 2.2-1 Symbolic transcendence view of connection between real sensations and externalized MoR symbols in the 1st-Person Laboratory. Here objects are assumed to be real although we know they are theory visualization experiences happening between the reader's physical sensor arrays; see Figure 6.5-1

within the context of the book in which they appear. The outline of the book represents the boundary between the two regions.

An abstract symbolic Model of Reality (MoR), which represents the physical explanation for what causes sensations to appear, is shown on the right-hand page. It is an idealist's 3rd-person view of matter with left and right functional interface icons connecting symbolic explanations to subjective sensations. It contains a bold first letter symbol of type "$\mathbf{A}_A$" intended to describe the physical change that causes the 1st-person's expected optical and touch experience. The "$\mathbf{A}_A$" is given an operational meaning because it is placed within the context of operations that generate observables. The subscript "A", described in the next section, is an abbreviation for the real "Apple" in which the change "$\mathbf{A}_A$" is believed to happen. The MoR is connected to the observable sensation it is designed to explain by two connecting function arrows which altogether makes a conscious action cycle. The cycle consists of an observable (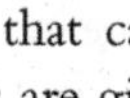), a MoR containing the symbolic change "$\mathbf{A}_A$" – "das-Ereigniss-an-Sich" – that causes that observable, and two connecting process arrows. These processes are given functional names eXplain "X()" and

Measure "M()" without any further details describing how they are implemented in the 1st-PL.

By placing symbols within symbols we have a mechanism for exploring the interaction between observables and their symbolic explanatory models within the 1st-person context. The use of icons in-line within the text distinguishes sensations outside the model from the symbols of the model. Furthermore, the operations carried out by the 1st-person implied by Figure 2.2-1 no longer ask for a transcendental operation but merely an understanding of the figures and drawings located in a book in front of one's nose. But there is a hitch. Reading and writing symbols is nothing out of the ordinary. Understanding what one does while reading or writing is another matter. In Figure 2.2-1 the icon "" without an outline, stands for the red round sensation in front of the observer's nose. The incoming process arrow stands for the explanatory path of activity carried out by the 1st-person who processes this sensation through him- or herself and out the pen producing an action record "$\mathbf{A}_A$". This symbol, inside the observer's MoR, names the explanation of the apple sensation. When a physical reality symbol is expressed in English terminology a more descriptive version of the activity "$\mathbf{A}_A$" might be the words "light emitting from the reflecting surface from a real apple". The outgoing arrow stands for the path of activity that generates the sensory stimulation expected in the optic and also the expected touch-sensation channel. In Figure 2.1-2, the expected touch is the white ghostly apple outline, in Figure 2.2-1 this outline is shown as a black line so it is visible against the white optic background. Under normal "objective reality" open-eye operation, one does not notice these separate sensations but simply recognizes the combined "" as something real.

Figure 2.2-1 connects an actual experienced object with its symbolic explanation. This is an absolutely vital connection that must exist in order to ground any explanatory symbol system within the context of the 1st-person experiences they are designed to explain. It is, however, common practice to implement this connection through intermediary symbols that define the observable sensations, so they can also be included in the book. We will use lowercase first letter symbols of type "a" to represent such intermediary symbols which then allows a completely symbolic conscious action cycle to be drawn in a book and relegates the vital grounding connection to a meaning assignment operation taught in language-specific reading and writing classes.

2.2.1 The meaning assignment operations

Under normal circumstances one is not aware of one's meaning assignment mechanism. For referential symbols, it happens automatically when two observables happen simultaneously and interactions – often represented by an equal sign – are created that connect their mutual appearances. The most common use of meaning assignments are translations between symbol systems. Examples of these are found in dictionaries, unit conversions, language translators and many scientific texts. However, unless one can produce the observable sensation of the terms in at least

FIGURE 2.2-2 From abstract to actual meaning along a symbol-reality axis

one system, such transformations will not provide a methodology for learning the definition of symbols from scratch. For this to happen, the chain of equal signs must eventually lead to something one considers to be "the real thing".

Figure 2.2-2 shows a graphic example of such a chain. As one moves from the more to the less abstract implementation of the symbol, a direction of change is defined. In Figure 2.2-2 that direction leads from an abstract mathematical symbol "a", to a word, to an icon, to a drawing in a book, to a painting in this actual book to a more accurate picture of a cluster of apples in a three-dimensional context, to an actual example off the page and, with the reader's cooperation, to the actual apple intended.

For objective reality model users, "the real thing" off the page equals what can, in principle, be seen. For quantum and CAT model users, the situation is substantially more complicated because such users are aware of the fact that symbols of inferences behind observables refer to meanings that can never be seen directly. In CAT symbol types, "a" indicates an observable event and the reality axis directs the reader to execute events that approach the referenced reality. Thus, with the use of a symbol-reality axis, we are able to direct the reader along a direction of change that can point to the actual meaning of a symbol even though that meaning cannot be represented in the symbol systems available to us within our media of communication. Nested book meaning chains are especially important to overcome this limitation.

2.2.2 Nested book meaning references

The process of nesting books within books provides a method for defining the relationship between symbols at different levels of reality. A book within a book can hold symbols that point to symbols that can be taken as their meanings. However, these meanings are in fact also symbols which can in turn point to meanings outside the enclosing book. In this way, a set of nested books can provide an enclosure for symbols at nested levels of reality. An example of such nested symbol structure is provided by the meaning arrows in Figure 2.2-3.

In this example, one meaning arrow runs along the symbol-reality axis from the small apple named "a", drawn in the observable phase of an action cycle inside the

FIGURE 2.2-3 Meaning assignment between two books at different reality levels

flipped open book upward to the drawing of a more real apple in a 1st-person's view. The reader is asked to extend the meaning arrow along the symbol-reality axis to produce a memory or an example of an apple in the environment outside the book being read. The critical point made by this example is that when the reader finds what he or she believes to be a real apple, it is only another "apple" appearance at a different reality level and therefore maps into the mental display phase of her or his action cycle. The real "Apple" actually names a Kantian unknowable that even in principle cannot be observed.

In comparison, consider the meaning arrow from the "**A**pple" symbol of the physical reality phase of the action cycle drawn on the notepad. For naïve realists this arrow points past the reader's nose into the brain behind the eyes where he or she believes the apple's memory is located. In CAT, that feeling of the brain is also an observable sensation. If the arrow were meant to point to an observable, the arrow from "**A**pple" in the notepad would first point to its visualization "**a**pple" in the observable phase of the cycle drawn on the notepad, and from there a second arrow would point to a 1st-person feeling of the brain behind the nose.

As drawn, the path of the meaning arrow indicates a path through the reader's bigger Self, which is symbolized by the action cycle on the notepad. The arrow points completely out of the 1st-person observable phase and travels around the observer's internal timeline through his or her explanatory activity "Ac(X(a))" and lands on an "**A**pple" shown as a model icon in the explanatory phase of the cycle in

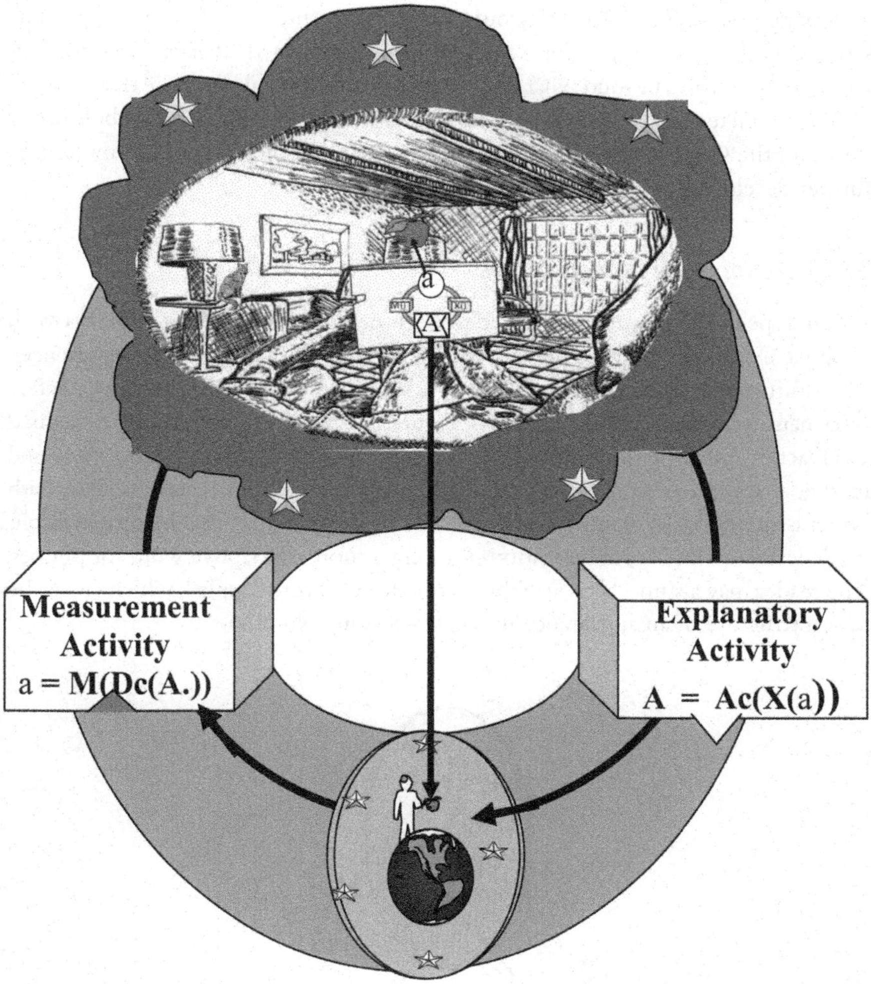

FIGURE 2.2-4 Mapping the conscious cycle between two reality levels

Figure 2.2-4. This represents the next level of reality for the symbolic action cycle drawn on the notepad. We are using an objective world model icon to emphasize the 3rd-person theoretical view we traditionally have of our imagined reality. The arrow therefore lands on a symbolic visualization of the memory that stores the external cause of the "apple" experience at the next level of reality.

Of course, this entire drawing is simply another symbol in this book. From there the reader is asked to trace the meaning arrow to the next level along the symbol-reality axis completely outside of this book. Since this does not refer to the observable sensation of the brain behind his or her eyes, the reader should look up and try to imagine a physical mechanism beyond the everyday observable feeling of the earth, sky and stars in which the reader believes to exist. He or she will then experience something completely outside the classic three-dimensional world sensation, and then understand this exercise has not yet defined "Reality" but provides a pointer to a world beyond what contemporary science assumes to be the universe.

To complete this discussion, we will summarize the definition of symbols introduced in the CAT action-flow architecture which will then be used in the text as further development of the theory unfolds.

2.2.3 Action type nomenclature

Action type nomenclature is intended to document the critical distinction between what we experience and the physical reality we believe is having those experiences. The distinction is enforced in the text by a set of alphanumeric symbol characteristics naming actions in CAT graphics. Figure 2.2-5 shows a simple self-contained CAT action model consisting only of the fundamental sensation action cycle and its theoretical projection cycle introduced in Section 1.3. These are labeled with symbols intended to demonstrate their role in the CAT model. In this example, single letters are used as abbreviations for longer more descriptive words or phrases. The reader may assume "a" is an abbreviation for the word "apple", which labels the action structure of an appearance in the 1st-person field of view.

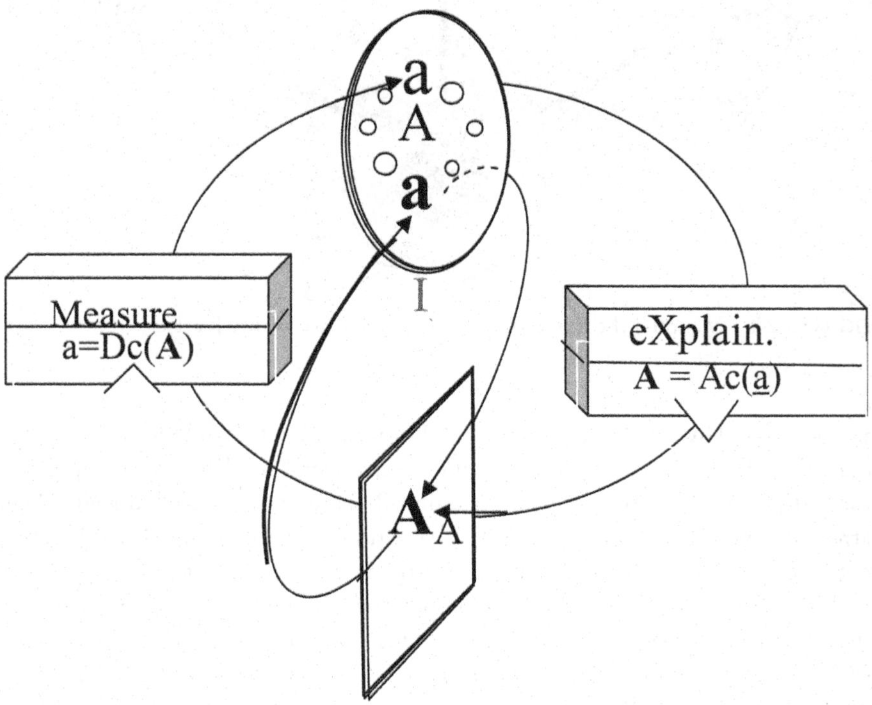

FIGURE 2.2-5 Sensation refresh and theory projection cycles (see Figure 1.3-1) labeled with abstract CAT nomenclature

Table 2.2-1 provides a list of symbolic action types along with the graphic they label introduced so far in CAT models.

The conventions introduced in Table 2.2-1 apply only to the parenthetical first letter of a name used in this book when referring to a CAT model. When the use is obvious the parentheses may be omitted. For example, "I" the observer experiencing an "apple", could be written as, I see an apple, without confusion. However, I see my body, would require using more accurate CAT conventions since the big "I" is a mechanism within which a little "i" references the experience one identifies with one's body in the objective world view. Implications of the fact that CAT identifies "I" as an independent event-onto-itself that may or may not interact with other events such as "You" or the "Universe" are discussed in Chapter 8.

Assuming the single letter types are substituted for longer descriptions, then "apple" refers to the sensation "I" experiences, "Apple" refers to the event itself, while "**A**pple" refers to the memory component that holds I's knowledge of the "Apple", and "**a**pple" refers to the reality feeling projected into the "apple" and is also the observable visualization of the operational symbol **A**pple. It is the automatic projection of type "**a**pple" sensations into type "apple" sensations that implements the illusion one's mental display shows, real objects. This illusion is indicated

TABLE 2.2-1 CAT model symbol types

Symbol	*ASCII graphic*	*Description*
"a"	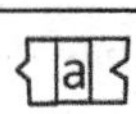	Lowercase first letter words mark the appearance of directly observable sensations, name action-flow icons with subjective straight outside lines.
"**a**"		Bold lowercase first letter words name the appearance of internally observable theoretical visualizations in the imagination, name action flow icons with subjective straight outside lines.
"**A**"		Bold uppercase first letter words name model processes, active memories that store/propagate states, name action-flow icons with classic objective past/receive and future/send direction flow angles on outside lines.
"A"		Uppercase first letter words name self-contained action loop complexes, Kant's "events-onto-themselves".
"Ac()"		Actuator phase of interface cells model actions that process subjective inside actions to objective outside actions.
"Dc()"		Detector phase of interface cells model actions that processes objective outside actions to subjective inside actions.
"X()"	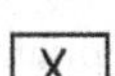	eXplanatory processing activity transforming subjective observable appearance actions of type "a" to actions driving actuator cells.
"M()"	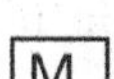	Measurement processing activity transforming from detector cells output to subjective appearance actions "a".

in Figure 2.2-5 by the thought bubble connections shown in the mental phase of the "I" cycle complex.

As a further example, if the symbol in Figure 2.2-5 were systematically replaced, so that "a" becomes the word "reality", which then would refer to all sensations experienced by an action cycle complex called "Reality". Its model storage element is **R**eality, while **r**eality refers to the objective sensation registered with sensations Reality experiences. The word Reality in CAT refers to the unknowable totality philosophers and cosmologists often attempt to model. For naïve realists there is no distinction between **r**eality and Reality because they believe their sensation of objective characteristics behind their vision – feeling when they close their eyes–captures what is actually there.

2.2.4 Operational and referential symbols

Symbols of type "apple" or "**a**pple" have referential meanings. One can in principle attach pointers to them that lead to observable experiences that a 1st-person observer can have. These symbols appear in the subjective phase of an action cycle and are created by a write and understood by a read operation. Observable experiences are not limited to the display of external sensations but include the display of internal pains, pleasures, dreams and one's imagination. Specifically, we have identified an "**a**pple" type symbol as referring to the visualization of the meanings of theoretical symbols like "Apple" or "**A**pple". Such visualizations are heuristic aids that support an illusion of understanding that often traps us as discussed in Section 1.3, and to avoid such confusion an explicit symbol type for such observables has been defined.

The referential meaning of symbols like "**R**eality" or "Reality" cannot be mapped into an immediate "Now" experience and therefore remains beyond the 1st-person's ability to grasp observationally. Words like "reality", "cause", or "das Ding an Sich" often used throughout English literature when referring to actual "**R**eality" or "Reality", do not make referential sense. When used in this manner, they have no referential meaning and do not point to anything we can experience directly. The meaning, if any, of symbols referring to entities outside of our direct experience must be operational because we cannot "see" what is beyond observable appearances or they would *be* observable experiences.

An operational symbol is just another object, a pattern of ink on a page. Searle's (1980) Chinese Room and machines trying to pass the Turing Test (2011) shows us examples of mechanisms that generate objects that look like symbols without any connection to experienced meaning. Symbols, used to build models of physical reality, cannot be directly translated into sensory meaning. They are operators that interact with each other in logic chains that produce referential symbols-of-observables at the detector interface "Dc()". Their significance is therefore to be found in their operational function within a symbol system, not in any sensory meaning they point to.

2.3 The basic symbolic operations

We have been careful to describe a cycle of activity summarizing the relationship between observable symbols and the operational symbols of a CAT model that explains the activity in functional terms. We will now expand the action-flow diagram in Figure 2.2-1 by adding observational symbols to our CAT model and the theoretical projection cycle to its Model of Reality (MoR). The resulting flow diagram will identify a set of operations that process action through the subjective and objective phases of a conscious being within the 1st-person perspective. These operations will define the transport and transformation functions required to process action through a CAT architecture. How such processes are implemented in physical terms will be discussed in Part II.

Five operations – "W(), R(), MoR, L_W(), P_R()" – implement the fundamental sensation processing cycle and four operations – M(), P_M(), X(), L_X() – expand the MoR to show its theoretical projection cycle. The functional purpose of symbols will be defined in the following list of processing steps:

1 : An apple is seen at time "t" measured from the wall-clock observables.
2 W(): Writes the sensation of the apple, and the rest of the universe is described as expressions of type "a" in the book.

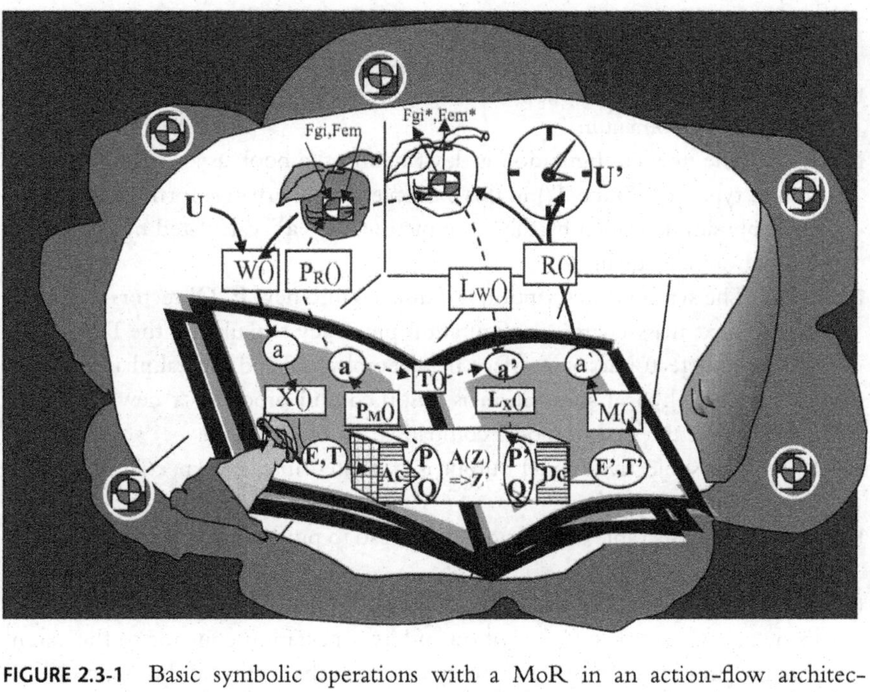

FIGURE 2.3-1 Basic symbolic operations with a MoR in an action-flow architecture. Dashed lines project classic physics MoR operations onto actual sensations

3 X(): eXplains the "a" description into the sensor configuration "Z(E,T)" where E and T are the energy and time parameters describing the action flowing *through* the observer's subjective phase.
4 Ac(): In CAT this is the "von Neumann Cut" interface between subjective and objective phases located at the modeled sensor boundary that translates the "E,T" subjective phase action flowing into the sensor mass-charge material that must-have-been the sensor response to physical stimulation into the Model of Reality generalized state length "**Q**" and momentum "**P**" vectors of the whole event.
5 $\mathbf{P_M}$(): The mass-charge model state is measured to produce an observable description "**a**" of what caused the sensation "a".
6 **T**(): The theoretical time transform operator changes the symbols of actual material to new symbols "**a'**". The action-flow architecture is independent of the reality theory, the MoR or its observable projection used. We have used a classic physical implementation to replace the abstract MoR() in Figure 2.2-3.
7 $\mathbf{P_R}$(): Reads the description "**a**" and projects as a theory-based mass-charge visualization symbol into the apple sensation.
8 : We now imagine the mass-charge position of what we believe is the real material of the apple located where its sensations appear.
9 Fgi,Fem: In classic physics, the mass and charge configuration of the apple is subject to the influences of all the mass and charges through force fields Fem and Fgi to produce a new configuration. The "**T**()" operator contains time derivatives of the Hamiltonian (see Process 0 in Figure 1.2-2).
10 ': We now imagine a new and expected mass-charge configuration at a new position and momentum.
11 $\mathbf{L_W}$(): The new configuration is described in the book as a symbolic expression of type "**a'**". Since **T**() in this example is an alternative formulation of the same physics described by the force picture, the "**a'**" calculated by both paths must always be equal.
12 $\mathbf{L_X}$(): The symbolic description is translated into new **P'**,**Q'** vectors that specify the next mass-charge configuration physically stimulating the Dc's in the simulated detector array interface between physical and mental phases.
13 Dc(): The physical stimulation is absorbed and produces a new subjective experience expressed in model compatible terms Z'(E',T').
14 M(): The subjective model output is translated into an expected observable description "a'".
15 R(): The observable description "a'" is read to produce an expected sensation '.
16 While all this processing happens, the apple sensation moves apparently under its own power so that the sensation and its expectation coincide to the extent that the processing model accurately describes the reality of the apple ' at the next observable clock time instance.
17 We now go back to 1 and repeat the processing cycle for the next time.

The architecture involves two parallel action cycles between observable sensations and the model of their physical causes. The first solid-line cycle "W()→X()→MoR()→M()→R()" moves the experience through a process that generates the next expected optic observable. In mathematical notation, this entire conscious cycle could be written using nested process functions as shown in Equations 2.3-1 and 2.3-2,

` = R(M(MoR(X(W())))) Equation 2.3-1

while the truncated objective reality version is

` = MoR() Equation 2.3-2

The objective reality version eliminates the distinction between sensations and real entities and reduces the X(W()) and R(M()) sequences to identity operations that do nothing. Therefore in classic physics, the state increment time operator T() directly increments the state of appearances because appearances are believed to be real objects in themselves. Such an approach clearly ignores the role of the subjective phase and fails to explain our conscious experiences. The observable phase of the solid-lined cycle is the sensation of the action flowing through the observer. Such actions are the Physical Correlates of Consciousness CAT proposes.

The second broken line cycle defined by "$P_M()\rightarrow P_R()\rightarrow$ Forces$\rightarrow L_W()\rightarrow L_X()$" deals with the implementation of modeled operations in the MoR and represents the functional implementation of the visualization cycle in Figure 2.2-5. This cycle sees the MoR from a 3rd-person theoretical perspective similar to the side look experienced by the reader looking down on the picture. In general, the operations in the MoR are mathematically summarized by "A(Z) → Z'". The "A(Z)" operation describes the activity that processes the subjective action state flowing into the MOR into a state flowing out.

How the MoR does this depends upon the 1st-person's choice of beliefs as expressed in the nomenclature of the chosen model. To make this example more concrete we adopt the nomenclature of classic physics and assume subjective action is described in the Energy-Time perspective. The interface actuator cells labeled "Ac" transform the subjective descriptions into a state function "ζ(**P**,**Q**)" composed of instantaneous position and momentum coordinates if a single cycle of a larger event is intended. The function "Z(**P**,**Q**)" refers to the state of a complete cycle. These vectors describe action flowing past us, because in the MoR we are looking down on that movement from a theoretical perspective.

A measurement made on this input state produces the theoretical action symbols of observables "**a**" that is connected through the time transform function "T()" to output "**a'**". In classic physics, "T()" contains time derivatives of the Hamiltonian (see Process 0 in Figure 1.2-2) that calculates the interaction between the apple and all other mass-charges in the universe. These operations are visualized by the 1st-person as changes in a mass-charge sensation "", which are moved by gravito-electric force influences from and to all the material in the rest of the universe. In later chapters, we will discuss how a general CAT-MoR model is reduced to quantum and classic functions that increment the instantaneous states of objects in contemporary theories.

Though we emphasized the processing of the apple sensation in the previous examples, we could equally well apply the same processing paths to project mass-charge configurations into all sensations experienced by the 1st-person. In this case, all sensations are used as input and the double process cycle shown in Equation 2.3-3

"` $=R(M(Dc(Lx(L_w(FemFgi(P_R(P_M(Ac(X(W($  $)))))))))))$",

Equation 2.3-3

where: FemFgi() = the classic gravito-electric propagator, which predicts the complete next sensation using classic physics.

It should be noted that the existence of the theoretical, dashed-line projection cycle is the reason consciousness is often called an epiphenomenon. If we fully believe our physical theory projections are the complete Reality, then in our model the symbols of type "a'" always equal "**a'**" and subjective phenomena are simply a kind of coating directly attached to the "real" mass-charge configurations. Thus, conscious experience rides along theoretical expectations, and it is not even necessary for a 2nd-person to have internal awareness of anything to explain his or her behavior. The current mainstream scientists hope to explain all behavior using a 3rd-person physical theory.

In contrast, CAT assumes conscious experience is directly attached to a subjective physical phase. In this example, sensations and theoretical projections are two phases of a complete processing path. Both these phases are action flowing through the "Now" plane. However, theoretical projections provide the reader with a feeling of reality that is characteristic of human thought but is not essential to primitive awareness. Under normal circumstances, the typical reader will not be aware of these separate operations; he or she simply does them and co-locates the two results as one. When they do coincide, thinking beings will also feel the comfort of believing they have grasped the apparent objective world around them, and their actions make sense.

To the extent these operations are done in real time and this model is accurate, the expected and actual next sensations should coincide. When they do, no corrective action need be taken. When they do not, the MoR must be updated. Action flows implementing corrections are discussed further in Chapter 6.

2.3.1 The self-contained Model of Reality

Figure 2.3-1 showed the processing activity occurring within one time instance that is punctuated by reality checks whenever an expected object position is compared with an actual one. The assumption of objects moving in a 1st-Person

Laboratory is that they are moved by forces that may be mimicked by action-flow calculations in one's model but not caused by them. However, if we are modeling the Whole of Reality, or self-contained approximations, there are no external interactions, since by definition the Whole includes all there is. In this special case, a completely symbolic self-contained action-flow structure as shown in Figure 2.3-2 can be constructed.

The output of the observable action-flow "a`", previously produced from separate apple, I and the rest of the universe sensations, here flows through the subjective phase to produce the input to the next cycle. Only a single cycle of a complete self-contained event is depicted. The actuator and detector sides of I's material is here enclosing the processing steps that implement its estimated next subjective experience. The "a`" expected sensation expressions generated inside the subjective phase are no longer compared to the external Reality of the model but are simply equated to the actual next "a" type expressions. There are no external interfaces "W()" and "R()". As long as the MoR addresses the Whole of Reality in which I exists as a sub-component, the model only stimulates itself through its deterministic lifetime.

Of course, such a self-contained model is detached from reality checks and would run accurately on its own only for a limited number of cycles. An ideal model of the Whole would be perfectly accurate, and its internally generated sensation would always match Reality whenever a check is made. We will find such self-contained models are useful as first-order approximations. The length of the time interval over which such approximations are accurate will necessarily be less, usually very much less, that of the lifetime of the Whole. But during such accuracy

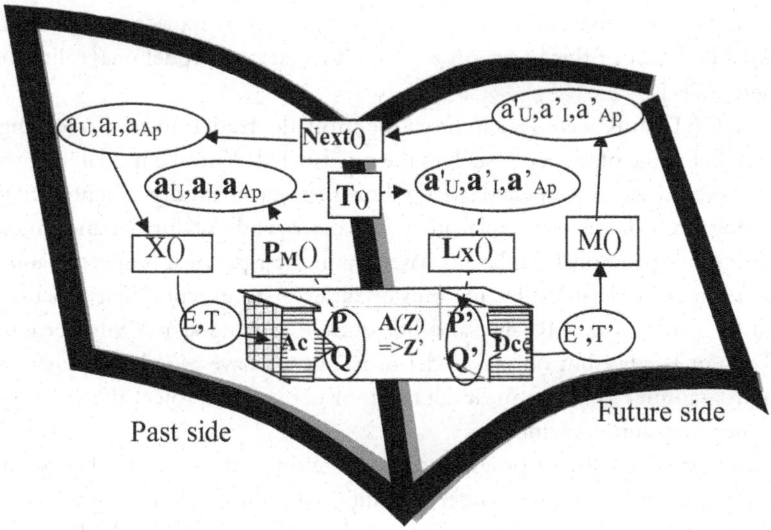

FIGURE 2.3-2 Self-contained CAT model of Reality: no user or accuracy verification interfaces shown

periods an approximate model can be used to furnish a steady space-time background within which content moves and reality-check interactions are added as small perturbations.

When interactions are added, the perturbed activity can no longer be easily drawn on a single page. In Part II we will show how multiple time cycles are drawn on successive pages of a book that include both external interactions, and the subjective processing here encapsulated in classic mass-charge state propagators. In Part II we will further develop the CAT event-oriented Model of Reality to show how its small perturbations approximation is compatible with current physical theories and thereby retains their calculation effectiveness while expanding its domain of applicability into the subjective realm. To do so will require a physical interpretation of the symbols being processed and those doing the processing.

2.4 The action-flow model of reality

In Figure 2.3-1 we enclosed a MoR inside the subjective flow of action in order to emphasize its role as a processing element inside the larger context of the thought process that included interactions with what appears to be a real objective world inside a 1st-PL. In Figure 2.3-2, we eliminated the off-page interactions by introducing a Next() function that duplicated the propagation of 1st-person observed behavior symbolically between symbols of type "a" and "a`" in order to completely contain subjective and objective aspects of reality in a single symbol structure. This forces us to acknowledge the 1st-PL has always been a convenient heuristic objective reality illusion that allows us to demonstrate the observable phase of action flow in terms compatible with the traditional readers' experience. We now invert the action flow of Figure 2.3-2 in order to construct a MoR in which interactions between external aspects of material (see Section 1.4.3) replace the classic force picture. The result of this inversion is a simplified action Model of Reality shown in Figure 2.4-1.

If the CAT-MoR were Reality itself then You, the reader, and I also reading this text would be one of the icons such as the one labeled "I" in the model. This model element would contain operational symbols that automatically execute functions producing both direct and explanatory sensations without further meaning. The processing of operational symbols is based upon their physical properties and does not need to be understood by any outside observer to execute their function. We would be a part in that Reality and not outside looking at it. Only because the MoR is not Reality but only a model of it, can we have a god's-eye view and – like a programmer assigning meaning to his or her code – project the sensations of those meanings into its symbols.

By analogy a computer program could be written that continually executes a physical activity to serve as a model of reality without ever knowing what its calculations or any output may mean. This would make the CAT-MoR, here defined as a set of cyclic processes in Figure 2.4-1, an incorporation of an abstract instrumentalist theory such as quantum theory, which requires symbolic interpretation

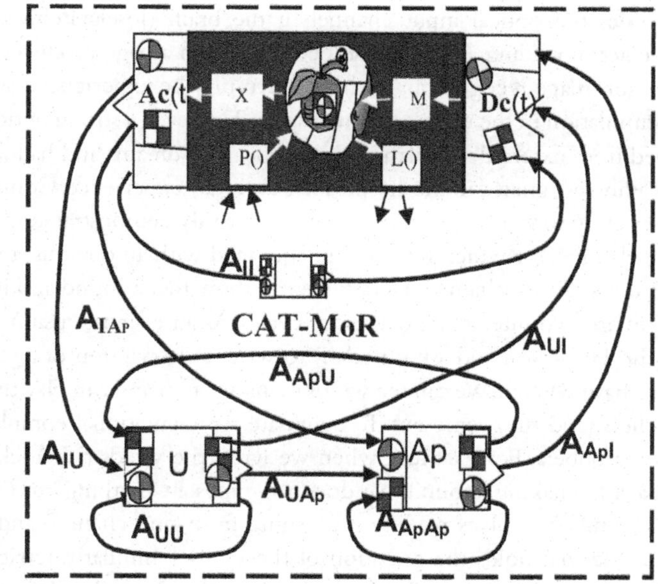

FIGURE 2.4-1 Inverted MoR modeling external action flow between I, U and Apple and showing I's observables on the inside aspect of its own material

to be understood. However, the CAT model has already introduced changes in a charge-mass density patterns to give visualizable interpretations to the action flowing through our abstract MoR. We readers are therefore urged to project iconic symbols of charge and mass centers into the action symbols presented in this book in order to ground their meanings in traditionally comprehendible forms. This does not imply we are reverting to a classic object model. We are not utilizing the graphic of an independent external world filled with mass-charge material that interacts with classic forces.

The CAT model includes interaction arrows between all the parts through external and internal material phases. *The universe as a Whole is a self-explanatory measurement loop consisting of objective and subjective phases that does not need to further understand itself. It just does what it does.* As will be developed in Part II, CAT proposes that action flow between four mass-charge degrees of freedom is equivalent to a force picture when internal conscious forces are added and thereby allows a superset of quantum theory to be formulated that is applicable to macroscopic phenomena and incorporates the subjective phase of human experience.

2.5 Examples of simple conscious action cycles

The use of optical observables and optical symbols introduces difficulties. Optical sensations are hard to describe verbally, and optical sensations are only generated by the 1st-person in hallucinations, dreams or works of art. Evidence exists that feedback primes the optical input channel in the brain (Joselevitch, 2008) and therefore the act of reading a description of an apple on a page produces a neural filter pattern for image recognition. Such a pattern may be experienced as delicate imaginary stimulation in the expected touch space. However, a strong optical sensation detached from external stimulation only appears in dreams and hallucinations and is not readily recognized in the 1st-person's everyday experience. Consequently, the conscious cycle through optical channels is not easily demonstrated in humans. The sensory channel, for which humans are equipped with an obvious stimulation generator, is the auditory channel. Hence, we can show that a sound and its optical representation are two interacting conscious cycles. As an exercise, assume we take the role of the 1st-person and ask ourselves to write a description of a sound and read what we have written. We can see words being written and can play them back by making the sound they represent. To eliminate representational complexity, we can use onomatopoeia. For example, when we write the words tick-tock, we can read them back by making a sound that does not represent anything but the sound.

Making a symbol involves reading a meaning from one channel and writing into another one that holds the sensation of the symbol. Similarly, retrieving the meaning of a symbol involves reading from the symbolic channel and writing back into the 1st-person-sensation channel from which the original sensation came. The pathway from an observable sound to the symbol and back to observable sound implements two sequential conscious cycles and each execution produces two conscious sensations as shown in Figure 2.5-1. The words "I am conscious of seeing an apple" implies the execution of a double-cycle loop that transforms an optical image into the symbol apple and back into an optical sensation. The words "I am

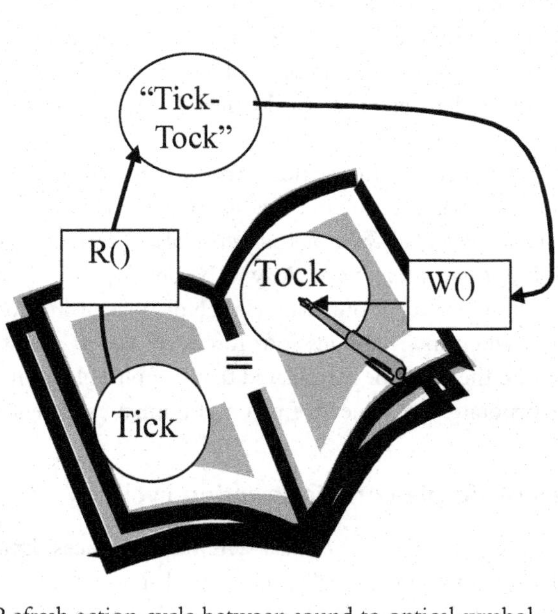

FIGURE 2.5-1 Refresh action cycle between sound to optical symbol

conscious of hearing tick-tock" describes a similar loop that transforms the sound "tick-tock" into a symbol and back again.

We do not need to experience both observable phases to be conscious of a "tick-tock" sound. Asking the 1st-person to write a symbol and read it back was introduced for the same reason the dashed-line loops are shown in Figure 2.3-1, i.e. in order to visualize a normally hidden part of the complete cycle. In doing so, the 1st-person becomes conscious of both the sensation of the words and the sensation of what they stand for. If we short-circuit the path through our hands and ask the 1st-person to repeat what he or she hears, a shorter cycle is performed. We hear the sound over and over, and as long as we do, we are conscious of "tick-tock". To produce this conscious effect, we carry out the single loop. We use the physical action, causing us to hear a sound, to stimulate the motion of our vocal cords that in turn produced the sound. Repeating a mantra or, for example, a telephone number over and over, is a common way to hold a pattern of information in immediate memory. Without the second meaning loop, we simply become aware of the sound for what it is and experience the "thing itself", which in CAT is the observational phase of the "event itself". By externalizing this activity, we can see that it consists of a loop between an observable and what is normally an unobservable stimulation of a physical sensation generator.

If all we were was a self-measuring audio generator feedback loop, the conscious cycle would close at the "a = a`" type descriptive level entities of the thought process, and we would be an isolated and self-contained being experiencing the "tick-tock" sound forever. In this case there would be no need for the symbols of a MoR or its X(), M() translation operators, because there would be no need to model an un-conceived external reality. But we are not that simple. We have learned to capture such action in sophisticated MoR structures precisely to understand what we believe controls our sensations so we can improve our dynamic state.

2.6 Example of an objective model in the 1st-Person Laboratory

Building models is a standard procedure utilized for both understanding what we believe is real and conveying that understanding to others. Externalized models of our thought process are visualized throughout this book, which utilize the little-man-inside the control room as the conscious element. How the little-man-inside the machine can be automated by systematic replacement of his or her calculation by electronic or biological circuitry is presented in Chapter 7. Here we emphasize the action flow that must be carried out in the little-man's 1st-person perspective when such a conscious element wishes to understand oneself and one's situation.

In Figure 2.6-1, we treat the walls of the 1st-Person Laboratory as the impenetrable barrier between what is our objective observable reality inside and what we believe to be the actual realty outside. Assume the scientist has built a measuring instrument, shown as a special camera that the scientist hopes is able to "sense" through a window, which we observers cannot see through directly. Remember the

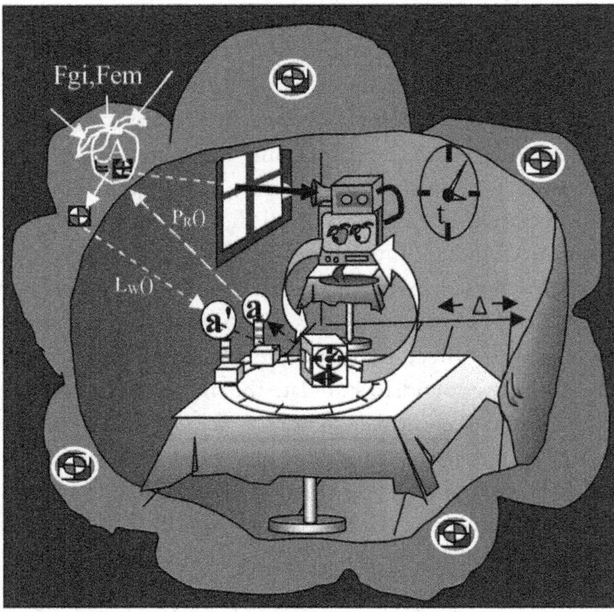

FIGURE 2.6-1 Flow of action using a Model of Reality built of apparent objects to describe what is outside the 1st-PL's sensor boundary

walls represent an externalized skull of the 1st-person, the window is an entrance of Plato's cave, the screen image takes the role of the consciously observed shadows in Plato's cave that in CAT are the appearance of objects in our everyday frame of mind. Unable to get out to see the causes of the screen images directly, the scientist builds a model of what we believe is his or her situation.

The components of the model are placed on the near table. The cube, showing a small window on the left side, represents an external view of the lab. The arrows between the screen display and its model equivalent represent the write-in "W()" and read-out "R()" functions, executed by the 1st-person, which connects the monitor screen with their model equivalents inside the cube (see Figure 2.3-1). From there and still inside the cube, the eXplanatory function "X()" transforms the simulated screen image to an actuator array "Ac", which produces the state description "**P**,**Q**" of the physical stimulation that is projected into a model object type "**a**" at some location outside the model cube. Here a "T()" function calculates the next "**a`**", which is here implemented by the forces of a pole moving the "**a**" objects along a deterministic track on the table. The meaning of these model objects and the model forces moving them is visualized by the arrow "$P_R()$", which projects the mass-charge icon outside the 1st-person's laboratory skull. They are moved by the gravito-electric forces due to interactions with the rest of the universe also imagined by the 1st-person to be outside his or her skull. The moved mass-charge icon gives meaning to the "**a'**" model objects through the write-in projection "$P_W()$"

and from there through the "Dc" and interface arrays inside our modeled skull cube. From there the Measurement process M() produces the model display, which is finally written back onto the monitor display as the expected next "" location.

If the actual forces of nature controlling the object the scientist believes is outside are accurately represented by the gravito-electric forces "Fgi,Fem", the next instrument display will move the actual measurement display "", and the scientist will believe he or she has built a good model of what cannot be directly observed and feel comfortable about the symbolic knowledge of material forces that have been validated through the 1st-person observable instrument and the measurements it makes. When the scientist or any observer can get outside to look at the objects directly, the example in Figure 2.3-1 describes a control-room situation. When the scientist or observer cannot, the situation is applicable to a quantum physicist, a cosmologist, the little-man or little-woman inside, who are intrinsically stuck inside a wall – penetrated by sensors – within which he or she must establish the reality outside through model building.

2.7 Controlling one's experience

Figure 2.6-1 defines the 1st-person observer as a passive entity whose only role is correcting and observing the model and thereby gaining symbolic knowledge of what the observer can only "see" through instruments. Perhaps knowledge is desirable in its own right, but it does not provide a mechanism for imposing the personal will and desire we need to control our subjective experience. However, once we believe to know our real situation in terms of a model, we have an actionable truth mechanism to express that desire by moving model icons from where they are to where we want them to be. Figure 2.7-1 shows the 1st-person's hand expressing desire by moving a model object.

Knowing what one wants is only a first step in getting what one wants. Symbolic expressions of intention would resemble voodoo magic unless the symbolic manipulation of a model element is actually connected to the real objects one wishes to influence. What turns magic into effective control in CAT is the interaction between the model and the actual experiences the model is intended to explain. Moving a model icon from the trajectory predicted by the well-established gravito-electric forces of physics would generate a will-based discrepancy between what is predicted and what is actually seen. If gravito-electric forces were all that actually controls reality, such discrepancy would simply be interpreted as errors in the model. The interaction arrow between the monitor screen and the model in Figure 2.7-1 would carry this error as an update signal used to correct the physical parameters controlling the model. *Knowledge is not enough*. In order to change the external world, the discrepancy must also be sent outside as a command, or more politely, a suggestion for the world to accept the desired change.

The mechanism for such a command-interaction flow is heuristically shown in Figure 2.7-1 where we have continued the action flow from the measurement display monitor through a semi-transparent mixing mirror. Signals from the outside

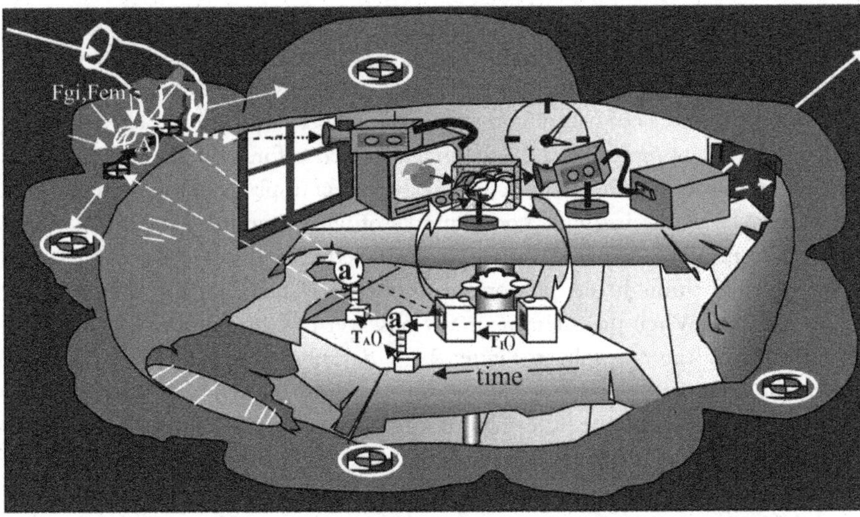

FIGURE 2.7-1 The 1st-person tapping the flow of action through the 1st-PL to update one's Model of Reality, which is then modified to express one's desires

are mixed with expectation signals from the internal model to produce two difference signals. The main flow is reflected from the back side of the mixer into a second camera, which captures the command signal and radiates it out the black window on the right side. The estimated reflected fraction mixed with transmitted measured signal is transported to the past side of the 1st-PL model, projected into the past "**a**" symbol type location, and time-transformed into its calculated new estimated state "**a'**". From there the expected state signals are processed through the model measurement apparatus and projected onto the comparator mixer screen. The 1st-person's desire is thereby transmitted through the semi-transparent comparator interface out into the world.

Whether the commands sent out will actually produce the desired result depends upon the accuracy of the calculations implemented in the model. Detailed calculation methods are addressed in Part II. What we have demonstrated is how a classic objective model constructed in a 1st-person's everyday experience is integrated into a CAT-action-flow architecture. Several liberties have been taken to illustrate the gist of the flow involved. First, the white window on the left acts like the entrance of Plato's cave that the 1st-person prisoner cannot see through directly. Action flowing through this opening is captured by measurement apparatus and displayed on the monitor. The monitor therefore is the source of light, which like the appearance of the sun illuminates our subjective experience. In actuality, the action would radiate from the monitor in all directions, bounce off objects and create flow rate variations across one's retina, which are normally explained as energy intensities. These variations allow us to differentiate optical sensation and process them into objects. The action would be absorbed by all objects including the scientist's body and turned into heat that is radiated into the blackness of outer space. For clarity we have concentrated most of this flow into a single main stream from left to right on the table and collapsed our night sky sensation into the black right-hand camera lens. The lens is black since we cannot see what flows out until that flow is processed by the external world around its action cycle and reemerges on the bright side as the next measurement instance.

White arrows indicate the flow of action out through the black window and out into the reality outside. The black background representing that reality is shown as a flat third layer background rectangle to simplify the drawing. In Chapters 3 and 4, we will make the case that the actual geometry of this background is toroidal so that the left and right edges connect. The white influence arrow comes around to the other side where the desire is implemented by moving the reality of the Apple, which is theorized as a mass-charge structure by this 1st-person scientist. Action flows through the laboratory from the hot, white left side through processing elements that include an interaction with the internal model and out the cold, black right-side window. The view for the 1st-person is a distorted version of one's daily appearance of sun and black sky with the time flow mapped into left-to-right line. The model, in contrast, moves the 1st-PL lab box along a model timeline drawn on the side of the table. This is theory preference. Even though the 1st-person feels him- or herself to be stationary, the 1st-person may choose a theory which depicts this individual as moving forward in time along with the apple.

In this picture, both the action flow through the laboratory equipment and the model are seen from a side view. The combined flow merges the expression of the 1st-person's desire into a passing activity stream. We thereby have a process model of his or her real Brain operations in the equipment in front of us. The model could run mechanically on its own as long as the 1st-person keeps his or her hands off the mechanism. But then, the 1st-person's will and desire would not be evident, and we would have modeled a zombie. The traditional metaphor used to add will into inanimate material is to assume the scientist is a little-man-inside the model boxes who is looking at the modeled monitors. The scientist's ability to think and be conscious is drawn as a thought bubble path shown in the figure between the past and future model boxes. Unfortunately, this little-man-inside analogy is as miraculous as assuming the hand in front of the first person's nose is moved by "will", which then moves the model objects to express what the scientist wants to happen in the external world. How that 1st-person generates desire involves the recognition of the actual loop in which he or she is imbedded. This expression of "will" in the 1st-PL makes a zombie into a conscious being and deserves some further comments.

2.7.1 Will and desire

Appearances in the 1st-PL are treated as classic objects in order to ground CAT in our everyday experience. Most of the objects are subject to gravito-electric forces and behave independent of our "will". However, some of these objects, such as the nose, arm and hand appear to respond to our wishes. These are identified as our classic body, through which our "will" is extended by physically controlling other objects and moving them as we want. As long as we remain in the 1st-PL view, the intent of one's desire simply happens. There is no explanation of why our body parts move the way we want since the controlling extension emanates from the mystery of conscious activity which we cannot objectively follow.

The recognition that the 1st-person in Figure 2.7-1 is taking a god's-eye view in which the action flowing in the 1st-person's own cycle is moving directly out of the page and around his or her own conscious cycle as shown in Figure 2.2-4 gives insight into the conscious mechanism. The 1st-person taps off a small fraction of the main action stream flowing past. This fraction is captured by the equally black windows of his or her eyes. It is then processed around the action loop and projected into the arm to produce desired hand and finger motions. The 1st-person's will and desire is built into properties of the action loop itself (see Section 4.2.2.1). It is the fundamental desire of all activity loops to increase the amount of an action it experiences in an equilibrium form that minimizes unbalanced forces.

To understand this un-seeable processing loop we have externally depicted the transfer of information between the measurement monitor and the model by the interaction arrows. When automated, the model equipment has a will of its own, and when its material is the material from which the 1st-person is built, then one would interpret Figure 2.7-1 as an out-of-body experience in which the scientist's body appears in the laboratory (see Section 8.3.3). To explain the origin of desire, the externalized model shown in Figure 2.7-1 is the best analogy we were able to construct in the everyday 1st-PL view. It demonstrates the flow of action along timelines symbolically mapped into the spatial 3D actionable truth display with which we are endowed. Conscious intervention happens between objective material states symbolically represented by the time transport function T() in the model. This example suggests what tangible equipment may look like when mimicking a conscious being.

In the following chapters we will delve deeper into the construction of symbolic models in order to incorporate subjective experiences in a comprehensive action architecture. The flow of activities between the unknowable external world and the model expressing our belief describing this unknowable nature has the basic structure of two interacting action cycles. One involving the two cameras shown on the back table in Figure 2.7-1 and the other implemented between observable monitor display objects and one's explanatory model. The use of a scale model built of moving objects is one of many alternatives that can be incorporated into this structure. We often imbed an object model in the larger action-flow architecture in the figures of this book because we assume the reader is familiar with such models in his or her own 1st-person experience. However, to go beyond objects, a more generalized version of a reality model is required. An adequate generalization will be introduced as a book powered by an operator in Part II Chapter 3. Whatever belief system is coded into a book can then be installed as our reality model in the processing flow. An operator is added to supply intrinsic properties of material that executes changes prescribed in the book. In actual implementations of such models intrinsic properties of model objects power its activities, but only when we readers can witness the physical changes as objects in motion from the outside will our Model of Reality be useful as a heuristic tool.

Thus, we propose a mathematician calculating formulas, a physicist processing equations or an artist manipulating diagrams will execute an activity that represents a kind of scale model of Reality conceived as an event. Even a silicon-based computer might perform the operator function as long as we realize that the model of reality is the physical event, which happens when its programs execute. It is not any symbolic answer it could output to the question, "What is reality?" In Part II of this book, we will explicitly develop an event-oriented book model that directs an operator to produce a physical flow of ink. This will model the flow of action between a physical aspect of an event and what it feels like to be that physical aspect. This flow of action will integrate the objective and subjective into a single action-flow framework. In Chapter 4 we will connect the flow of action in such book models with classic Hamilton-Jacobi action theory (see Goldstein, 1965, 273 and Chapter 7). In doing so, we will exploit one major improvement this theory portends. We will model completely isolated systems as the operator who is so engrossed in a book that he or she never looks up. Such a model runs at its own time and contains within itself the events of an operator's own isolated universe. Interactions between such self-contained models will then be used to explain the mysteries of quantum theory and provide a multiverse conceptualization of interactive conscious beings. One of whom is the I reading these words now.

PART II

Modeling reality

3

HOW TO BUILD A CONSCIOUS ACTION MODEL

This chapter deals with the problems and methods for building an observable event that implements an action Model of Reality (**MoR**) in the 1st-person perspective. Since "Reality" in Conscious Action Theory (CAT) is a structure of activity, it is the activity in the brain of a human mathematician or in the electronics of a modern computer, not the answers resulting from those activities that model Reality. In order to make such activity visible we need to externalize the operations happening in executing systems so they can be seen as moving objects in the 1st-Person Laboratory.

We will use the motion of ink carried out by a model operator on the pages of a book as our externalized model. The *flow of ink* is both a symbolic representation of the *flow of action* in Reality but also an activity of objects that must be controlled by auxiliary forces to fulfill its symbolic role. It is the evolution of ink patterns that constitutes the CAT-**MoR**. The operator and the pages are support structures that make ink flow as though it were action when it is not. Just like a model of the Earth is represented by a globe while the pins holding the globe at its north and south poles are ignored. So, the reader should imagine a river of ink as it evolves all by itself as our action model, while ignoring the operator or pages needed to hold the ink in place. A visualization of such a CAT-**MoR** event that can be constructed using such auxiliary support is described as follows.

The CAT model starts with an empty book and a pen filled with ink. The ink is transferred by writing a pattern onto the front cover of the book. The ink on the front cover is sucked back into the pen and placed as a new pattern onto the inside of the front cover. This activity, moving ink from one side to the next, is continued until all the sides of all the pages have been traversed and all the ink is drawn back from the back cover into the pen. This completes one lifetime of an activity loop.

The model is back to the state described in the first sentence of this paragraph and, if nothing changes, could repeat the event forever.

The movement of ink executed from the first to the last side is an activity that can be witnessed by the 1st-person observer from the outside. This is a 3rd-person theoretical view of an event being modeled. Ink bits flowing through the pages of a book are intended to model the pattern of action of the real event being modeled. To experience what it feels like to be the event, the observer takes the role of the operator. In doing so the observer experiences the feeling of moving of small objects. The symbolic significance of this experience is what it feels like to be a pattern of action executed.

We must distinguish this experience from the normal reading activity. It is not in the *meaning* of ink patterns appearing on the pages but the movement of the patterns that models action flow. When reading a traditional book, ink patterns that look like alphanumeric characters, words or figures are translated into sounds and visualizations of their meaning. This is not how the ink patterns in a CAT model should be interpreted. It is the action of physically making and destroying a word or picture that symbolizes what is being modeled.

How such an event can be used to simulate physically realizable happenings and the physical laws governing interacting activities will be the subject of Chapters 4 and 5. Here we restrict our discussion to the construction and operation of a book model itself. This allows exploration of scenarios limited only by what can be done with a model built by moving ink on paper. This freedom of imagination is important because CAT expands the laws of physics to include a subjective phase of matter.

3.1 Characteristics and requirements of reality model building

CAT reality book models consist of symbols, instructions and auxiliary support components constructed from ink on the pages of a book. A stack of pages into which ink can be written and erased provides objective characteristics that can be used to model an event-oriented reality. This section defines the essential characteristics of a book, which are exploited to produce the experience that models our event concept of Reality.

3.1.1 Book coordinates and symbolic material

Books and their content are classic objects that can be manipulated and observed by the reader in his or her 1st-person perspective. In this section, we will discuss how such objects can act as the objective instantiations of symbols representing the properties of Reality. Operations that can be carried out on these symbols will then be identified with actions in the Real World. In CAT, Reality is a form of action happening. Here is how action is represented in a book.

3.1.1.1 Book space as absolute nothingness

A book provides a convenient support media to hold symbols for a four-dimensional space. The points provided by such a media can be identified in the usual print nomenclature of column (c), row (r), depth (d) and page (p). In English, the word "page" refers both to a paper leaf and its two sides. When the intended meaning is not clear in the context of its use we will use "side" instead of "page". Depth is projected into each side by the user so its inclusion as a book-space parameter may be questioned. In a computer graphics display, depth is defined by the painter's algorithm – "print the farther distance first" – and implemented by a z-buffer distance. We assume the reader can project a depth direction into an open page. Hence the four variables c,r,d,p specify the location of a volume cell experienced by an operator that can be used by a printer or graphics display to build and manipulate its content. The size of the cell is conventionally specified by the font size given in print points. However, in anticipation of our use of figures and drawings, we will designate a media point by a non-zero-size cell of extension of the unit vectors $\underline{\Delta c}, \underline{\Delta r}, \underline{\Delta d}, \underline{\Delta p}$. The cell of a two-dimensional display is called a pixel and that of a three-dimensional display a voxel. Logically, the cell of a four-dimensional display should be a toxel and a multidimensional display a moxel. Figure 3.1-1 shows an example of a book parameterized by a c,r,d,p coordinate frame.

The Cartesian book coordinates and their frame are used to name and position ink relative to media points. They are support components purely introduced to organize and operate a symbolic model and do not imply any significance beyond this support function. The three coordinate axis icons and the page counter "p" are not part of the CAT model, and the book as shown in Figure 3.1-1 is to be treated as an absolute-empty-nothingness. To say that a symbol "a" is located at position c,r,d,p while a symbol "b" is located at c',r',d',p' does not imply any meaningful geographic relation or distance between "a" and "b". Even symbols located at the same media point are not physically at the same place until the meaning of media co-location is defined.

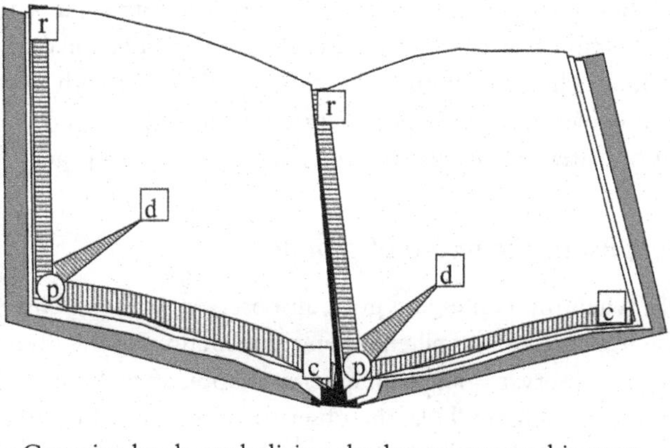

FIGURE 3.1-1 Cartesian book symbolizing absolute empty nothingness

The simplest method for specifying the distance between book media points is a distance vector "$\underline{\Delta b} = (b_c{\cdot}\underline{\Delta c}, b_r{\cdot}\underline{\Delta r}, b_d{\cdot}\underline{\Delta d}, b_p{\cdot}\underline{\Delta p})$". The vector array shows the number of book coordinate cells one must cross to get from one point to another. We will assume all book coordinate cell sizes ($\underline{\Delta}$) are constant throughout the entire book and are not functions of their location. Absolute nothingness is thereby assumed to be flat. Shortest distance vectors *in book coordinates* all appear to be straight lines.

The reader may ask, "How can empty pages represent nothing?" Here we must refer the reader to the symbolic relationship between a medium and its absence that must be applied by the reader to his or her 1st-person perception of empty space. The reader is asked to concentrate on an empty region in front of his or her nose. Allow that perception to be represented by a featureless layer of ink within a book. Then erase the ink. The meaning of this symbolic operation is taking the empty space in front of one's nose away. What is left is nothing. The absence of material defining empty space can also be experienced when one closes one eye and attempts to find the blind spot in the open-eye scene. *Without material underpinning, not even empty space is there.*

3.1.1.2 Using ink as the material of change

In order to introduce any content into the nothingness of empty pages, explicit symbols must be drawn with a material compatible with the media. Though electronic media may utilize a variety of technologies to implement symbols, the traditional material used to make symbols in books is ink and, in deference to the traditional hard copy, we will call the material from which symbolic structures are built by the name "ink", whether or not such material is actually used. Hard copies can usually be printed from actual media in which this book is delivered, so ink is the common material from which all content is built.

In the visualization of an event at the beginning of this chapter we assumed the ink can be written and collected back from a location "$\underline{b}$" on a page without loss. The two activities represent an amount of action that happened at that location. The amount of action that flowed through a point is proportional to the amount of ink at that point. The total amount of action that flows through all the points on any one page is equal to the amount of action contained in the pen reservoir. This is the amount of material available to write and erase on each page.

3.1.1.3 Using ink as the record of change

Unfortunately, when ink comes and goes, an observer whose attention is moving along with the flow may very well experience the lifetime of the event he or she is modeling, but the observer is left with an empty book after the modeling event is over. To grasp the event as a whole, the observer of the model may have made his or her own memory of the modeling event, but it is more convenient to use the book itself to hold such a memory. If instead of erasing the ink after it is written, new ink required for the next page comes from an additional reservoir, then the pages can hold a memory of the ink motion. The permanent ink patterns existing in traditional books are the records of a creation process executed by a printer that put each bit of ink from a reservoir onto a page. Of course, when reading a traditional book, the ink pattern is copied into an electromagnetic wave form that is then processed into the reader's observable display space. But we cannot follow the processing path through a traditional brain of a reader and therefore cannot observe the modeling activities. In the CAT model, we must completely externalize the modeling activity. Once ink is placed on the pages of a book, we have a record of an event. This means the ink placed on a page during a creation process must be interpreted as both the arrival and departure of action. To experience the event recorded, each bit of ink must be copied, and the copy put on top of the corresponding bit of ink on the next page. Only the amount of ink required to move copies through each Now experience of an open page during a playback event represents the action model.

The change of ink patterns between successive sides still represents the activity of the system evolution being modeled. Action, like ink, is the material in which changes are manifest. Therefore, if a permanent ink pattern is used to fill a book with a memory record, it will be the difference between the ink records on successive sides that represents the change happening in the interval between the pages. Such changes are actions modeled by the movement of copies.

The amount of ink deposited on all pages of a book representing an isolated event is a constant all-there-is, only the distribution pattern of the ink changes. To the extent that we can use the physical characteristics of ink to represent action, this is a fundamental characteristic of isolated events.

The amount of action in an isolated event remains constant.

It is critical to understand that identical repeating ink patterns on successive pages are simply a creation and annihilation action at every recorded dot. We will see that unchanging patterns represent the action of empty physical space that continually refreshes itself. Because we usually deal with records, unless otherwise stated, we will assume a permanent record version of CAT book models are implied throughout this book. However, explicit movement of ink from one page to the next models a reality described in the last section and may be appropriate for individuals who believe Now is all there is. The two models are not mutually exclusive. One deals with experience as it happens, the other with a record of that experience.

3.1.2 Operations in book coordinates

The introduction of permanent ink as the record of change and book coordinates as the location of endpoints in the emptiness of the book defines support components that allow the model creator and user to build and manipulate the model. It must be externalized if it is to be communicated.

Even though we know the appearances in the 1st-Person Laboratory (1st-PL) must be sensations, we invented this laboratory as a fiction precisely to define real "Objects". We are assuming the appearance of a book in the 1st-PL is evidence of an external real entity referenced with symbol type "Book", in which the motion of "Ink" is used to represent a **MoR**. We may not know how real "Objects" we see are connected to objects other beings see, but we accept that real "Ink" has an objective property and externalization in the 1st-PL captures this property.

However, the fundamental limit as to what can be externalized with a book is determined by the operations that can be performed with an object made of paper and ink. The pertinent operations limiting the reality that can be modeled are discussed in the following sub-sections.

3.1.2.1 Placement and removal of ink

At the most primitive level, the placement and removal of material ink in the right places on the paper are the only operations necessary to create a book. The operations needed are "write(c,b)" and "erase(c,b)" functions parameterized by the book coordinate vector "b", which specifies the media point to move to and put or take the content "c" of that point. Mechanically these operations might be visualized as a pen moving to "b" followed by a bit of ink "c" transported in or out of its reservoir. When the permanent record method is used to create an initial model, these operations are used as update functions in which ink records are moved from one place to another. Such update functions are implemented by an erase(c,b1) followed by a write(c,b2) pair. When one of the location parameters references the ink reservoir outside the pages, such pairs can be used as annihilation and creation operators.

The existence of ink at some media point is the record of an action. Some change happened to remove the ink from some previous location and place it at its current location. Hence every record of ink implies the happening of some erase(c,b1) • write(c,b2) change operation along a path between two points. As we shall see, 1st-person conscious awareness is associated with the change implemented by this erase-write activity.

An open book represents a time instance, which is bounded by the left(past) and future(right) page sides. Subjective experiences are associated with the difference between left and right page-action patterns. The change implementing such differences can be experienced by moving copies of ink bits between the past to the future side of an instance. In one instance, these movements are reversible and are not tagged by time differences. When pages are turned between an erase and write activity, a change involves the concept of time.

3.1.2.2 The turn-page operation[1]

An open book as shown in Figure 3.1-1 presents a single Now display instance during which the user is aware of facing the sides of two pages and the sides of

1 E-book readers will implement the turn-page operation as a button click. This obscures their path through the book or the form of action records stored in a book-model because it is practically impossible to follow the flow of changes through the electronic circuitry involved. To overcome this

two ink marks. Moving from the left to the right page does not require a physical change to the book pages themselves. Only the pen needs to be moved; the user sees both sides at once, and changes are reversible within a Now instance. Actions between different Now instances will require a physical turn_page(p',p) operation that changes the configuration of the book.

During normal reading, the pages on the left side have been read and are in the past, while those on the right are in the future. By turning the next page, the user operating the model moves forward in time by moving the ink on one side of a page to another, and thereby the action it represents flows from the future to the past. The erase→move→write operation, functionally implemented by "write(b2)•turn_page(p+1,p) •erase (b1)" simulates a flow of actions for which the operator does not have simultaneous awareness of both endpoints. This operation corresponds to the changes involving the physical phase of an action cycle and represents the theoretical flow of change from the subjective future side, through the imagined Now experience of the operator, and onto the past side of the next instance. When the ink moves from a passing "b1" side of a leaf to its next side location "b2" of the same leaf, the action simulates the physical response of the material underlying the subjective phases of an evolving event.

3.1.2.3 Representing physical space and format operations

To fill the absolute-empty-nothingness of a blank book, ink records are distributed into complex patterns. An ink record represents its own creation and destruction activity, which in turn represents the action of events being modeled. Static patterns that repeat on each page can be used to represent the material underlying the feeling of empty space perceived by the 1st-person and at the same time to represent the static material portion of any system one wishes to model.

A measurable physical space can be represented by drawing a three-dimensional coordinate frame into the pages of a book as shown in Figure 3.1-2. Only a hint of the total ink pattern is indicated since only the exterior outline of each space cell is shown, and many of the cells are implied rather than explicitly drawn. This is done to indicate the Cartesian structure of the entire volume and avoids a messy density of ink that would be required to show the action content of each 3D cell on a 2D page. In actuality each cell is a repeating system of its own, and the outlines should be understood to contain a large amount of action as a record of changes that create and modify space in the nothingness.

---

limitation, we urge the e-book reader to construct at least one page of a real CAT book model, such as Figure 3.2-6 or Figure 3.4-4, and experience the activities happening within him or herself while reading, projecting meaning and turning the pages. Once the feeling of one's involvement in this activity is firmly established, then stop and look at the record of the flow from a transcendental external point of view. The dynamic feeling of action is now projected into an object held in one's hand and from there can be transferred to all objects that one used to believe were just things out there.

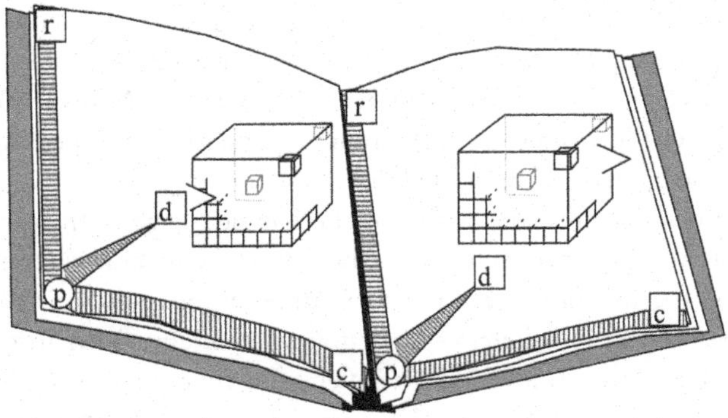

FIGURE 3.1-2 Cartesian space arrays imagined as records of repeating equilibrium activity between each page in Cartesian book coordinates

Cartesian space cells are usually given a name "$\underline{\mathbf{x}}$" and placed in a location defined by a book coordinate vector $\underline{b}$ = (c,r,d,p). Each cell can then be given a real location address relative to the other cells using four coordinate names (x,y,z,t). The real location vector name $\underline{\mathbf{x}}$ = (x,y,z,t) is a systematic shortcut notation. The placement operation of each cell can be defined by media formatting functions {$\underline{\mathbf{x}} = \underline{\mathbf{x}}(\underline{b},\underline{\Delta b})$ and its inverse $\underline{b} = \underline{b}(\underline{\mathbf{x}},\underline{\Delta \mathbf{x}})$} that provide the rules for connecting the space-cell names with their book coordinates. The simplest formatting functions occur when the book coordinate points and the space cell are both perpendicular three-dimensional arrays and lined up so that "c" lines up with "x", "r" with "y", "d" with "z", and "p" with "t". In vector notation, the formatting function locates the "xth" cell at

$$\underline{b}(x, \Delta x) = \underline{b}(0,0) + \underline{x} \bullet (\underline{\Delta b/\Delta x}) \bullet \underline{\Delta x} \qquad \text{Equation 3.1-1}$$

Here $(\underline{\Delta b}/\underline{\mathbf{\Delta x}})$ provides a constant scale change to the unit $\underline{\mathbf{\Delta x}}$ known as the metric tensor and (0.0) is the vector from the origin of the book coordinates to the origin of the real space representation in the book.

A constant metric tensor is characteristic of flat space. Since we defined the nothingness of an empty book to be absolutely flat, a constant metric tensor would format the representation of real space cells into a flat display support space. This makes the space icons drawn in Figure 3.1-2 look like Cartesian cubes. When these scale relationships vary from place to place, the real coordinate cubes become distorted and are called curvilinear. Curvilinear coordinates were introduced by Einstein in General Relativity to represent gravitational effects. Visualizing curvilinear space implies not only that the cubes on a single page appear distorted, but also that the cell labeled with the same real-time parameter values will show up on different pages. In other words, an operator of the model will experience many different real-time space cells on a single perceptive Now page.

It is convenient, but by no means necessary, to identify all the space cells appearing on one page with the simultaneous experience associated with the feeling of Now. Such an association would restrict the formatting functions by identifying the fourth dimension "t" with the book page coordinate "p". Because manipulating the book model becomes much simpler when a page is identified as a single time plane, we will adopt this association as a working approximation unless cosmological scales or General Relativity are being discussed. The blocks of cells drawn on each side of Figure 3.1-2 therefore represent two sides of an instantaneous real Now space that does not change. When combined they provide a snapshot of a cosmologically local flat space all happening at the same time. The in-pointing and out-pointing arrow features indicate that each cell array is a past "Dc" and future "Ac" interface, which between them contains the subjective experience of empty space.

Figure 3.1-2 only shows two pages of an open book. The whole book must be graphically formatted by drawing a similar pattern of space cells onto all pages. When the operator reads through the whole book, after the nothingness is formatted, copies of each page would be identical to the others, and the flow of ink experienced would repeat each time a page is turned. In this case the operator would interpret the formatted book as a physical vacuum also called a plenum. Such a vacuum is not empty and differs completely from absolute-empty-nothingness because a potentially large amount of action is required to define the space cells. By analogy, viewing a plenum structure is like viewing an empty computer screen. It is composed of an array of physical pixels that present a sensation of emptiness but is far from actual nothingness.

3.1.2.4 Representing the content of physical space

Space cells are modeled with ink, which represents a background system of events. Like an empty computer screen, such events are generally ignored. The material used to represent the content of the space is also ink. As an example, some of the space cells shown in Figure 3.1-3 also contain "1" and some of them are empty. The amount of ink per space cell defines the ink density in a region. CAT assumes reality is a form of action. By making the amount of ink proportional to the amount of action, patterns of action can be visualized as content of empty space.

The amount action contained in each cell can be defined by a density function "$\rho_a(\underline{\mathbf{x}})$" of the real space-time coordinates "$\underline{\mathbf{x}}$" describing Reality in CAT. The amount of ink contained in a region of cells is defined by the ink-density function "$\rho_{ink}(\underline{b})$" in book coordinates. By substituting real coordinates and applying a scale "$s_{ink,act}$" we can relate the visualizable ink pattern in the book to action in real space, using the formula

$$\rho_a(\underline{\mathbf{x}}) = s_{ink,act} \bullet \rho_{ink}(b(\underline{\mathbf{x}}, \underline{\Delta \mathbf{x}})). \qquad \text{Equation 3.1-2}$$

Where "$s_{ink,act}$" is a scale parameter converting ink material into action units. We now have a means to visualize objects in real space by scanning through the book

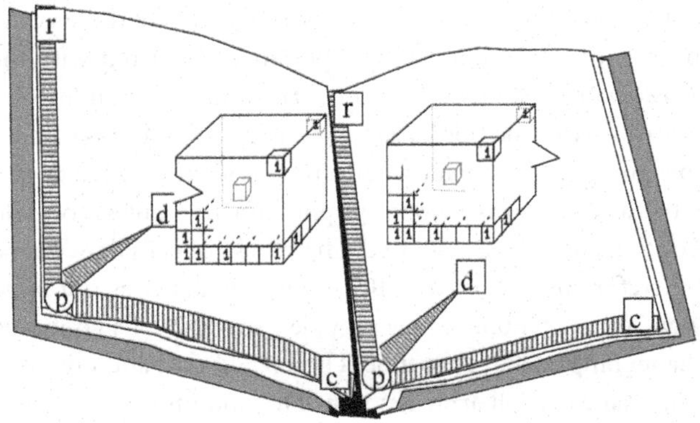

FIGURE 3.1-3 Space arrays represent action content as additional ink in each cell of the system being modeled

and interpreting the ink-density variations as a record of activity happening in a constant action space and time background. In classic physics only the material phase of Reality is considered and therefore the recorded action pattern as a function of space and time describes all there is. The amount of action per space-time cell "A(x,y,z,t)" is written in conventional units and is given by multiplying the action density function by the 4-volume of a cell as shown in the formula

$$A(x, y, z, t) = \rho_{act}(x, y, z, t) \cdot \underline{\Delta x} \cdot \underline{\Delta y} \cdot \underline{\Delta z} \cdot \underline{\Delta t} \qquad \text{Equation 3.1-3}$$

This classic action function represented by ink pattern difference between the two sides of every paper leaf constitutes a complete description of the classic objective universe. Thus, the book we have described so far can contain a graphic model of all there is in the classic paradigm. However, by including an ink pattern that can differ between open pages as well as successive pages on opposite sides of each leaf, we have added the subjective phase to that classic paradigm. This CAT extension includes the operator, observer or user and his or her experiences. Such an extension was also implied by quantum theory. Only CAT applies it to the totality of human experience and is not limited to atomic and nuclear phenomena.

3.2 Experiencing the model of an isolated system

We have discussed the properties and characteristics of an externalized model of reality consisting of a book in which a real space and its content is represented as patterns of ink. Patterns of ink on a page do not represent actions in themselves but rather are the records of an activity between changing ink patterns. It is the reconstruction of the activity producing the record, not the record itself, which provides the dynamic experience that models Reality. In this section we examine how a model user, interacting with the book, feels the sensations symbolizing the experiences of the real "System" being modeled.

3.2.1 Conscious experience in the playback of a prerecorded record

Let's assume an author has filled a book with a pattern of ink that upon playback is intended to simulate the experience of an isolated conscious system. This means a book has been created that records the physical evolution and accompanying feelings of a system and a reader is asked to experience a part of its lifetime.

At the most primitive level, a typical open page of such a book will look like Figure 3.2-1. We are still showing a Cartesian array from previous figures to emphasize the reality of material space and its content. The reader, when looking at the page, should imagine the cells without content appearing as empty space, and cells containing bits of ink appearing as surfaces of objects that can radiate light. The reader should be seeing a light pattern in the Cartesian array as a small picture of an everyday experience.

If a reader concentrates on the left page and flips the pages rapidly, then the reader would experience something like a frame sequence seen in a movie theater. The important difference, however, is that in a movie theater the scenes are snapshots of an objective, even if fictitious, world. The operations executed and feelings generated in the viewer when watching the movie are not explicitly recorded in the frames of the film. A CAT model book models the viewer, not the world seen in the movie. This includes how the viewer sees the film and includes feelings as well as the un-experienced flow of stimulation passing through his or her thought-processing mechanism. Therefore, each time instance is represented by two sides of time, and Figure 3.2-1 shows an observable action structure labeled "$a(x,y,z,t_p)$" on the left, or past page, and a second action structure labeled "$a(x,y,z,t_f)$" on the right, or future side. To see how these observations record a system's feelings, let's consider what happens when the reader operates a CAT model book.

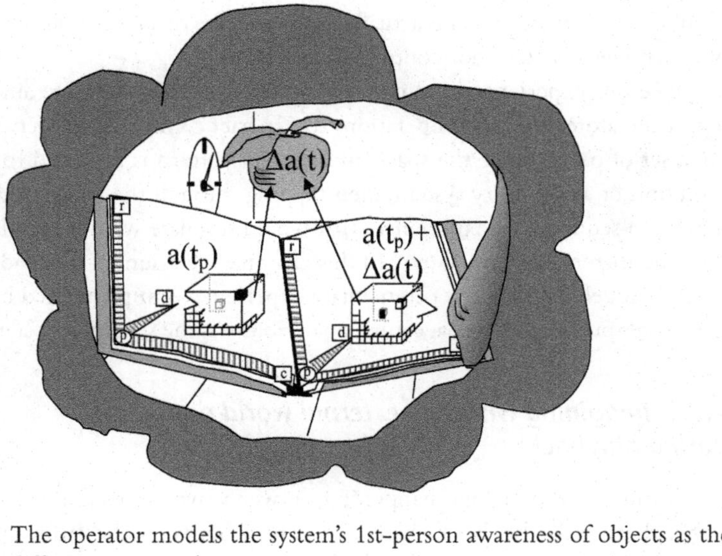

FIGURE 3.2-1 The operator models the system's 1st-person awareness of objects as the difference activity between two states

The reader shines light on the left and right pages in order to make a copy of the visual pattern onto the reader's retina. The copies are conventionally defined as electromagnetic intensity patterns but for our purposes, the only significance is that they are no longer action records permanently bound to the paper, but action bundles, called photons, free to flow through the reader. In the retina, these photons are converted to neuron pulses that carry the action through the reader's mental process. These processes consume, change and display the action patterns as they stream through the reader's mental Now space. The job of the operator is to note the pattern of ink, copied onto two channels of the operator's optical processing system, and two become aware of the difference as his or her Now experience. Thus, the reader becomes conscious of the change between the left and right frames. If the reader looks carefully at Figure 3.2-1, a bit of ink has been moved from the upper near corner of the space to a middle cell. This change experienced by the 1st-person is designated by the name "$\Delta a(t_p,t_f)$" or simply "$\Delta a(t)$" when sequential pages are assumed. A practical implementation is discussed in Section 7.5.

The mental calculation executed by the reader to experience this action flow as an apple will be thoroughly discussed in Chapter 6 where the fundamental algorithm of the CAT reality model is developed. It involves a recall of memories requiring the operator to travel back through the memory of the past pages seeking the cause of the current experience in order to define the change in the future that would modify its consequences. As each page is recalled, acceptable actions are immediately transferred to the future pages in his or her memory while causes of deeper significance are pursued further back in time. The ultimate cause is encountered at the front cover where the origin action is converted to the destiny on the back cover. The operator continues the journey through the memory record traveling backward from the future, interpreting action patterns as future plans until the operator reaches the immediate right side where the future of the Now time instance is recorded. In playback mode, the operator's projection onto the right side should be identical to what is actually there since he or she is duplicating the feeling of the modeled system not controlling its destiny.

Once this experience is complete, the operator turns the page and proceeds to repeat the aforementioned operations to experience the change between the next open set of pages. Since the space and content pattern is intended to simulate the evolution of an arbitrary system, then flipping through the pages of the book will result in a sequence of experiences that would simulate what it feels like to be the evolving material of that system. In this example we assumed the reader plays back a CAT model and his or her immediate experience – implemented by a sequence of changes punctuated by page-turn operations – is the sensation of a moving apple.

3.2.2 Imagining what the external world does during playback

In addition to the change happening between two subjective sides of an open book, there will also be a change of action between the front and back side

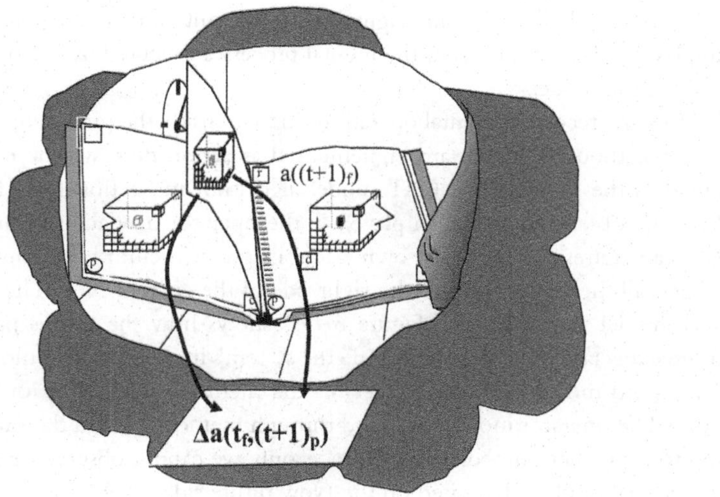

FIGURE 3.2-2 The operator experiences a visualization of the difference action between two states caused by objective forces between page sides

of the leaf being turned. The difference between the action patterns between the next time instance past page and the previous time instance future page, $a((t+1)_p) - a(t_f)$, is not directly experienced by the reader. The reader does not see them laid out within his or her Now time instance. Any conscious experience extracted from this difference would involve indirect mental processing. The difference is calculated between two different time instances as "$\mathbf{\Delta a(t_f,(t+1)_p)}$" as indicated in Figure 3.2-2.

This change can be imagined as a theoretical inference of the change mechanisms hidden inside the thickness of the page as it is being turned. Such theoretical inferences represent the actions in the material of the system being modeled. They are not equal to the external world. The "$\mathbf{\Delta a(t_f,(t+1)_p)}$" represents a theoretical 3rd-person view of the system's internal reality model components represented by type "**A**" symbols whose action is wedged between sequential directly observable experiences. In other words, "**A**" represents the cause of its experience and "**Δa**" represents how that cause is experienced.

3.2.3 Encoding the operator's subjective role into book symbols

Rather than constantly drawing external out-of-book operations as part of our model, we could explicitly document the operator's feelings by adding icons in the book that describe the operator's experiences as he or she reconstructs the action flow of the evolving system being modeled. The result of adding the operator's subjective mental operations within the boundaries of the book is shown in

Figure 3.2-3. Here the left and right space with content icons are connected by the simplest CAT descriptions of the mental processes executed by the operator when running the model.

How the record of mental operations hidden inside the processing pipes underlying the thought bubble are implemented as action flow will be explicitly presented as the fundamental CAT model algorithm in Section 6.4. Here we only show the observable result. In playback, the operator may actually turn the pages backward, refreshing his or her own electromagnetic memory copy until the operator gets all the way around to the right side of the current Now. The fundamental CAT model algorithm (see Figure 6.4-1) shows how the past is processed into future expectations, which determine the system's immediate next moves. In a pure non-record model the operator retains the memory copy of his or her past and future. The operator moves backward through memory to find the cause and reaction to his or her immediate experience, only we cannot observe these operations until a final result is deposited on the Now future side.

To make these unconscious operations visible the content of the book has now been expanded to include the subjective interpretation of the action flow. This means the book is no longer just a data storage device. Instead, the meaning of the subjective action-flow phase is now explicitly recorded in the book with icons and symbols that are answers to the question, "What does your material feel Now?"

The diagram in Figure 3.2-3 only shows one subjective phase of the past and future action patterns between two pages. The front and back side of these pages are connected by the page-turn() operation that moves the open book from one time interval to another. Figure 3.2-4 shows a book in the process of being turned. During this operation, the operator also intervenes to calculate motion of action and

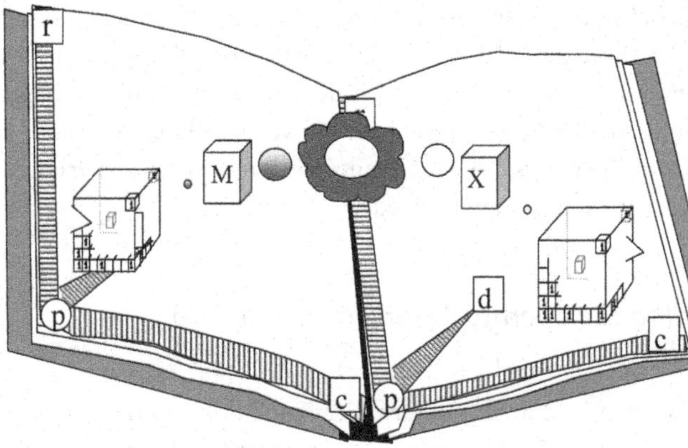

FIGURE 3.2-3 Recording a description of mental experience between successive subjective page sides in a CAT book model

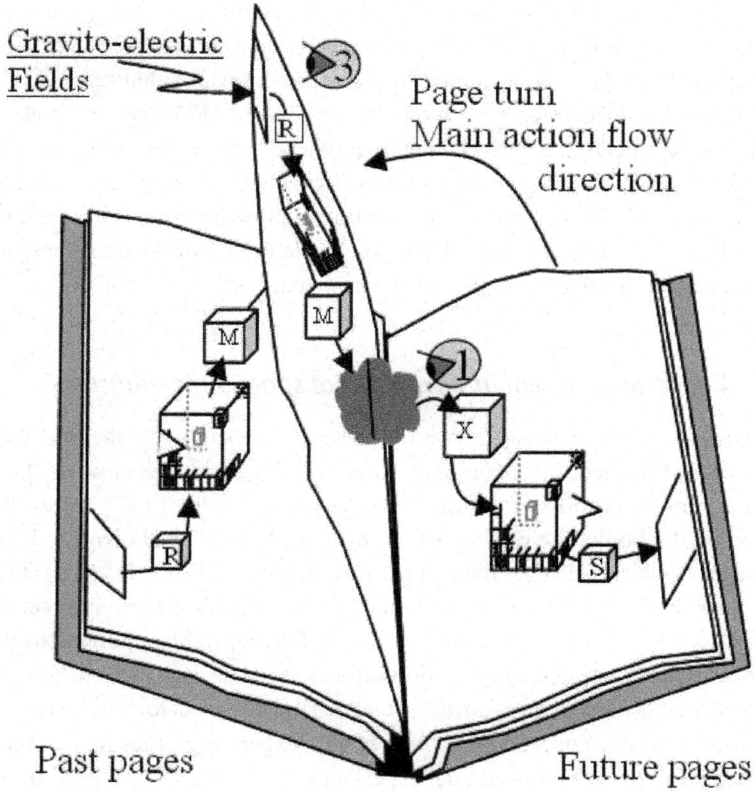

FIGURE 3.2-4 Adding a record of mental visualizations of the objective gravito-electric fields between two material states

move ink. However, rather than calculating the subjective experiences of the system being simulated, the operator calculates the proclivities of the physical material to evolve into the next time interval under its own inertia and possible influence of external material. As will be discussed in Chapter 4, we visualize the action pattern flowing through this phase from a theoretical 3rd-person perspective, showing the experience of the **MoR** implemented in the cycle. In CAT, the send and receive space and content icon have properties of material built of charge and mass, thus the classic gravito-electric forces (Fgi,Fem) dominate this calculation and classic physics applies. To indicate the connection from the front side to the back side of the page, a **MoR** location rectangle has been folded over the edge of each page. This rectangle is filled only with a field of gravito-electric forces connecting the past and future sides of the mass-charge arrays; it represents the bare bones, field only, physical phase of an action cycle.

These descriptions of objective and subjective experiences allow us to present a Model of Reality packaged into a book without explicitly showing the essential external operator. Such change has its dangers because the implicit inclusion of a ubiquitous operator will undoubtedly be forgotten by some users of CAT. So, let's make it clear. A book, like the memory of a powered-down computer, cannot be an adequate model of the event we believe "Reality" to be. When the symbols in the CAT book have been implanted by material whose intrinsic properties execute its symbolic functions, then the book symbols run themselves, no operator is necessary. Unfortunately, we are then back to postulating a ghost-in-the-machine who cannot be objectively observed. To build an observable model an operator must always be included to enforce the motions of the flow required.

3.2.4 A conscious system in a traditional space-time diagram

The physical calculation between two action arrays happens while the page is being turned. Hence the action happening during this calculation occurs while the page and all the ink on it moves from the future to the past side of the page stack represented by the book. The flow of action, named "$\Delta a(t_p,t_f)$", is shown on the open faces of the book and changes the past pages to the future. Similarly "$\mathbf{\Delta a(t_f,(t+1)_p)}$" changes the past into the future but while this is happening, the entire activity is moved into the past by the page-turn operation. This apparently contradictory flow of activity shows the interesting relationship between the main action-flow direction associated with the page-turn() operation and the feed-forward activity that implements the subjective 1st-person observable experiences and the theoretically calculated external real-world model experiences.

Drawn on a standard space-time diagram used to display the geometry of special relativity, the flow of action through a book model incremented by a page-turn() operation can be shown as in Figure 3.2-5. The coordinate time arrow points from the past to the future. This is the direction the operator moves his or her Now instant when we model observers are stationary with the book. The Now instance moves with the velocity "v_c" into the future pages. Thus, the action records make their way toward the past in Figure 3.2-5. The book is open to a time interval called Now. The feed-forward action directed by the CAT model to be applied at Now is shown as the instruction to feed-forward desirable changes carried out by the model operator. Instructions showing a thought bubble along an arc indicate the motion of activities by the operator in the direction opposite to the flow implemented by each page turn. This produces effects in the physical future and allows consequences of actions "caused" by the operator to show up later in the data stream.

Calculation of the physical response of the empty-space-cube and its content Icon continues in the forward direction by the operator. However, this happens during the turn_page() that moves events from future to past and is not modeled as a direct experience, but a theoretical inference. The overall effect is the illusion of forward events carried by the efforts of the operator against a backward stream implemented by the turn_page().

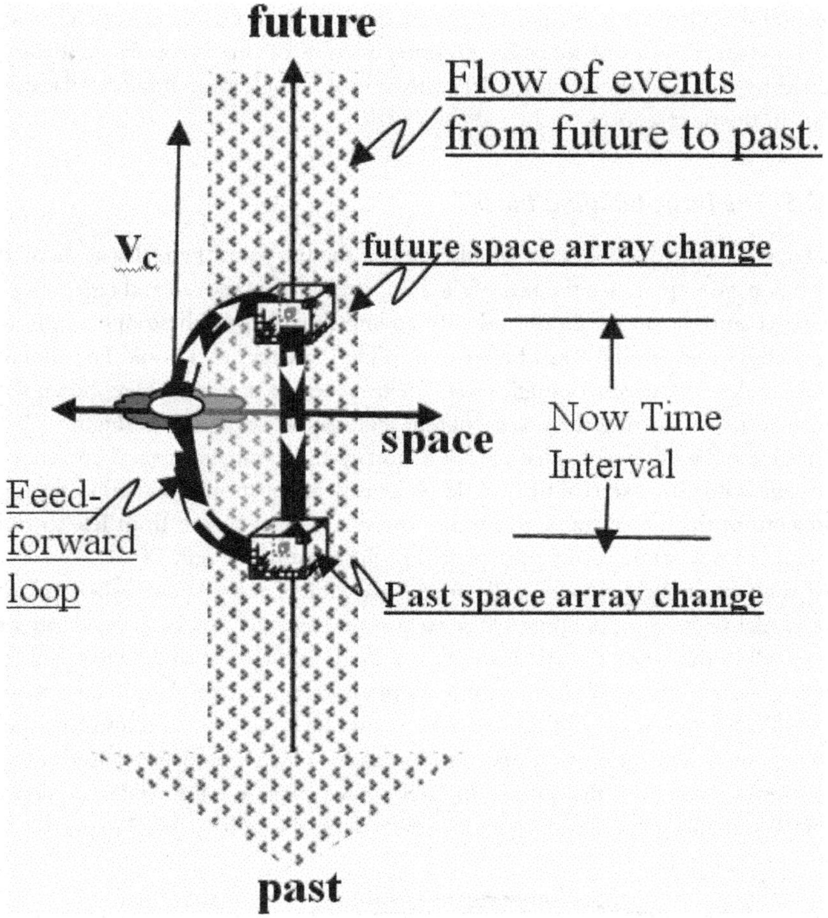

FIGURE 3.2-5 CAT feed-forward loop on a space-time diagram rotates between mass-charge densities as action flows through it

This diagram shows the significance of adding a subjective phase to our understanding of physics. If no subjective phase exists, the size of the Now time interval collapses to zero and a purely material body would have no subjective extension. In this case the material would be modeled by the purely exterior classic view of matter (Figure 1.4-1). In this view, matter receives gravito-electric influences from the past while sending out similar influences into the future at every point in time. Then it jumps to the next time point to repeat the absorption and transmission.

The introduction of the subjective phase shows up as a cycle of activity in time located between absorption and transmission. If the model observer moves with the Now, this cycle will appear to be stationary. The subjective action flow moves forward in time while the physical action flow passes from the future to the past.

Chapter 4 will show how such an action cycle in time exists between mass and charge characteristics of material. A clearer picture of this cyclic event stream is gained by reducing the book model to its simplest single page implementation as done in the next section.

3.2.5 The basic building block

So far, we assumed an operator would remove the ink from the real space icon on the past page, experience the feel of the ink pattern being moved and redeposit the changed amount on the future side. By adding instructions, these operations and the feelings they produce can be written inside the pages of a book. The simplest book model is reduced to a single page. The front and back side of it are shown with instructions connecting the space-content icons shown explicitly in Figure 3.2-6a and b. Here the observable phase of the action cycle is wrapped around one edge of the page while the external force-field phase is wrapped around the opposite edge. Instructions for the operator to modify the ink patterns move from left to right along each side while turning the page flips the right to the left.

Even a single cycle as shown will refresh a space full of many parallel cells. To reduce the model to its basic building block we would have to draw only one material-space cell in the arrays shown. In this case, a minimum cycle could be reduced to a single quantum of action. In contemporary physics terms we are describing activities at the Planck unit scale, and this example would be a continuous transmission and subsequent re-absorption of a photon (boson) by a system conceived as an object (fermion) as seen from the outside. In CAT, such a cyclic event includes an interior subjective mental experience, which closes the loop through its own happening.

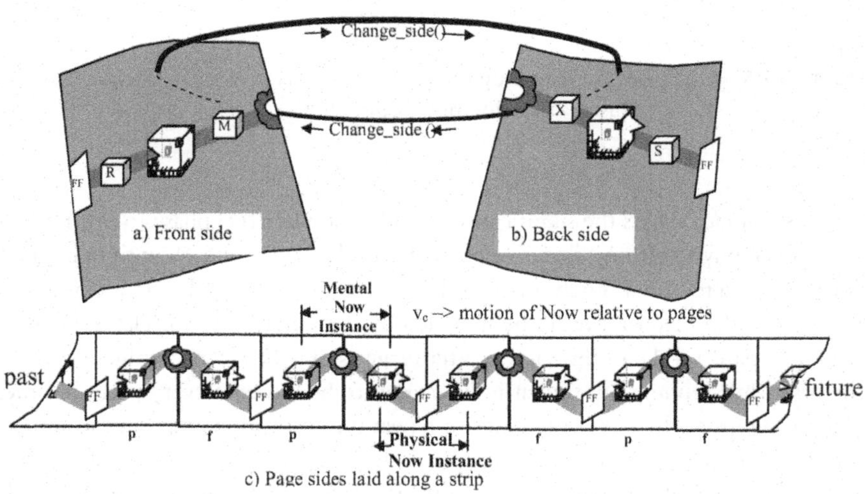

FIGURE 3.2-6 Front and backside view of a single page book model represents the mental and physical phases of a single isolated cycle (see Figure 1.1-2 or 2-1)

If the loop is closed by a double turn, the space-content action functions take on at most two configurations. On the front side, the measurement operations M() moves action from the past aspect of the space-content "Dc" arrays to an observable experience. This straddles the two-page sides. On the back side, the explanatory operator X() process activity to the future aspect of the "Ac" space arrays. The space content now sends S(), gravito-electric force-field influences FF, that are received, R(), by the icon on the front side.[2] A closed double turn simply refreshes the experience stored in the physical side of the cycle and in that sense simply maintains a single subjective feeling forever or until an outside influence disturbs the equilibrium.

A single-cycle loop, consisting of changing sides twice, is appropriate for showing the minimum components of the CAT model. However, even a completely isolated system will have both, many parallel space cells and many sequential cycles that all interact within the activities enclosed in an isolated stable action form. If we split a page made of paper into two leaves so each split page can be laid side by side, then we can get a visualization of our book model as shown in Figure 3.2-6c. Here successive front and back pages, separated by change_side() operations, are laid out on a line. Not shown on the sequential page sides are the processing operations (M,X,S,R) that transport action through the subjective and objective phases. The activity carried out by the operator runs from past-left toward the future-right. The change_side() operation moves the page sides from the future-right to the past-left.

If the observable Now instance of a reader of the book, or the operator of the model, is held stationary in the center of the drawing, then the pages of the book along with all the action recorded on it will flow from the future-left to the past-right. Against this stream, and coordinated with its flow by successive page turns, are the efforts of the operator, which produce observable sensations and the evolution of material. The space and content icon located along the horizontal center line divides the flow of action into an upper half cycle that contains direct 1st-person observables and a lower half that contains awareness of inferences of how the physical aspect of the cycle should behave. A full cycle in a CAT book model is composed of a subjective and objective instance that follow each other for the lifetime of the system simulated.

When looking at a flow of action, the nursery rhyme "Row, Row, Row Your Boat" describing our situation comes to mind. Only in CAT, the operator rows by turning pages and thereby drives the stream of time while modifying its passage with a feed-forward loop that contains the operator's feelings and desires. For a completely isolated system the feeling of his or her activities would most accurately be described as a dream. However, we are not always dreaming, and even if we are, there is often a separation between ourselves and our dream environment. Therefore, it is necessary to include interactions between systems to model our situation.

2 In Chapter 2 S() is composed of PM() and PR() functions while FF is the visualization of T().

3.3 Modeling interacting systems

The book model described in the previous section shows us how the records stored in a book can be read and manipulated by an operator to reproduce the activities described by those records. If the records store the activities of an isolated system, then to some level of fidelity the activities will repeat after a sufficiently long time sequence, and therefore the Reality of such a system could be modeled by the data and instructions contained in a book with sufficiently large number of pages. A completely isolated system only applies to the Whole of Reality. For, if every event is included, the Whole is completely self-contained and isolated, by definition of the Whole.

In order to model interacting systems one can either separate the Whole into parts or bring two previously separated parts together. From a book model point of view, the biggest issue involves the handling of time. We identified time with page numbers. If the Whole is modeled in a single book, then the pages would be coordinated with a global time. Breaking off pieces would disrupt this coordination. If we start with two initially isolated systems, each one modeled with its own book and its own operator, then neither the page rate or the actions bundled onto a page representing Now will necessarily line up in time. This means a message one part sends may solicit a response at any time and appear completely irrational and random. To make sense of this situation, interactions that are initially treated as perturbations can, as they become more and more frequent, be used to agree on a common time and meld the parts into a coordinated Whole.

Instead, it will be convenient to define the parts of a Whole first that become individually isolated but still within the context of a Whole. This allows the parts to be represented as approximate isolated systems in a single book model while interactions are treated as small perturbations, i.e. quantum approximation, in each empty space.

In either case modeling Reality will involve a set of interacting books each run by its own operator at its own rate. Such a configuration undoubtedly corresponds to the more general version of CAT and is its ultimate goal. However, treating Reality as subsets of a time coherent Universe that is already, at least in principle, modeled by the large Book run by a single operator will allow us to connect two contemporary theories with the more limited version of CAT and will therefore be presented first.

3.3.1 Modeling interactions between parts of a whole

Let's assume a large system such as the universe has been modeled and we divide it into two systems. Figure 3.3-1 shows the observable Now phase of the separated parts within one book. Each part is primarily identified by its non-interacting components and therefore two parallel action flows are shown. Here we have eliminated the subjective and objective transport operations shown in Figure 3.2-4 for clarity and only kept the space-content interface icons, the internal observables and external force fields.

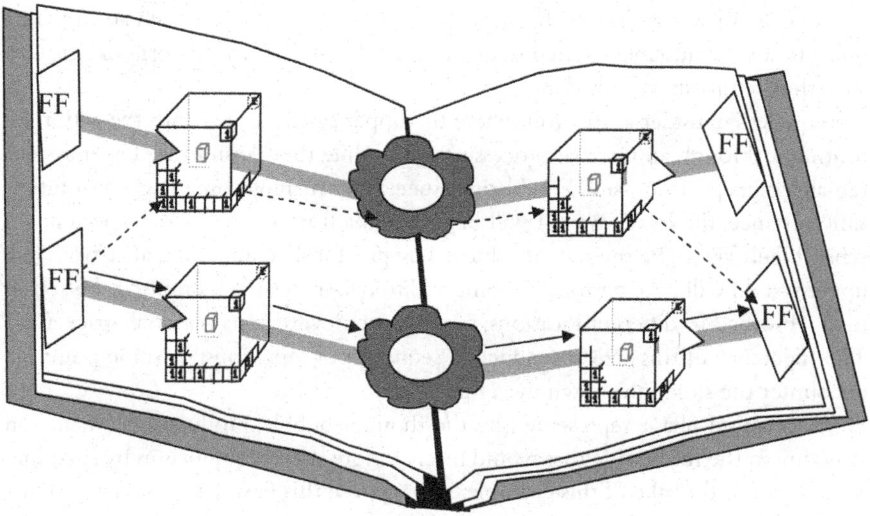

FIGURE 3.3-1 Lower system reflects photons off an upper system which experiences a reflex action

To first approximation, the two systems run in parallel from page to page without affecting each other. We further assume that the action densities have been selected so that the individual systems progress by the same time interval during each page-turn cycle. Of course, most likely two systems would not run at identical frequencies, and one might require many page turns to repeat the configuration, but we are considering an artificially simple case to demonstrate interactions.

As described, the book would be filled with two parallel systems that repeat in the lifetime of the Book and calculate their own experience page after page. The two systems may even have evolved a classic type physics to explain their experiences. As the operator turns the pages to the instant shown in Figure 3.3-1, he or she finds an interaction appears. As indicated by the dashed arrow, the external gravito-electric force fields FF of the lower system may have extended their influence to the upper space cells, modifying some of their content. Whatever the mechanism, some kind of collision is happening between the parts. From the operator's point of view this is a move of some action that would normally have remained on the lower but is now moved into the upper path. The solid arrow shows the changed flow propagating in the lower system. In both systems, the change alters the action structure in each physical-space icon and therefore an observable experience appears.

What happens next will depend upon how well each of the systems can accommodate the change. Shown in Figure 3.3-1 is a dashed arrow returning the change to the lower system so that both force fields are returned to the unperturbed equilibrium state. In this case the total effect is that for one instant both systems will have experienced something different than their isolated equilibrium sensations, but otherwise nothing has changed. The situation just described could be equated to a two-atom system in which one atom sends a photon to a second atom that is put into a very unstable excited state and quickly falls back to its original ground state thus returning the photon.

Now let's consider a situation where the upper system can absorb the action by routing it through an internal processing path while the transmitting lower system remains in its post-emission equilibrium state. After turning some pages to a future time instance, the lower system will happily remain in its new state, experiencing what it feels like to be the state it achieved by previously eliminating an action. The upper system will have performed some additional processing by routing the action it has absorbed to different locations, possibly memories, in its material-space array. The trajectory of this action produces a sequence of sensations. At some point we encounter the situation shown in Figure 3.3-2.

Here the mind phase, represented by the thought bubble, produced a new action structure in the future side that would reach a more stable equilibrium by shedding an action. For the sake of this example, let's suppose this new action structure contains a different excited atom at the end of its processing chain than the one absorbing the action in the previous figure. Then it may send a different action quantum, perhaps of a different frequency, down to the lower system. The absorption of this action is shown as a dot-dash arrow in Figure 3.3-2.

If we turn the page one more time, we would see the upper system happily running along its new isolated equilibrium path, and a lower system is stimulated by the new change, processing this action quantity through its structure. To conclude this

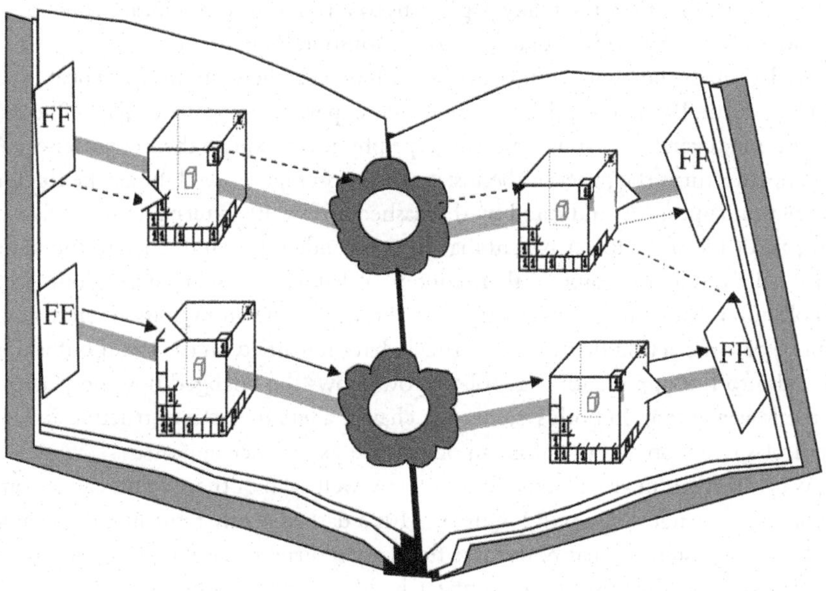

FIGURE 3.3-2 The upper system absorbs, performs internal processing and emission: has a primitive conscious experience

example, let's assume the lower system has the capacity to process its just-received action into an excited atom that remains stable for the remainder of the book and comes around through the beginning and remains in this quasi-excited state until it comes to the book instance page turn before the Now shown in Figure 3.3-1. It therefore was the excited atom state which radiated the photon at the next instance. If this is all that happened in the entire book, we would have modeled two nearly isolated systems with two interactions during their lifetimes. Further page turns would simply repeat this event. Except for these two interactions, both systems would evolve in their isolated-state-equilibrium configuration, but the combined system is modeled by nearly isolated parts coordinated by common time (Everett, 1957; Mensky, 2006).

As long as the activity is coordinated by the page turns defining the global time of a single book, the internal activities are not completely independent. As the number of interactions increase, the approximation of two isolated systems would be blurred. Given a sufficient number of interactions, no reasonable division can be identified and the total activity in the CAT book loop would become a single evolving system that feels like an isolated Whole . . . until . . . a new unexplained sensation pops up.

3.3.2 Modeling interactions between independent parts

In order to model interactions between initially independent parts, it will be convenient to go back to the examples of book models under the conscious control of an operator. Figure 3.3-3b shows an operator erasing ink from his past page,

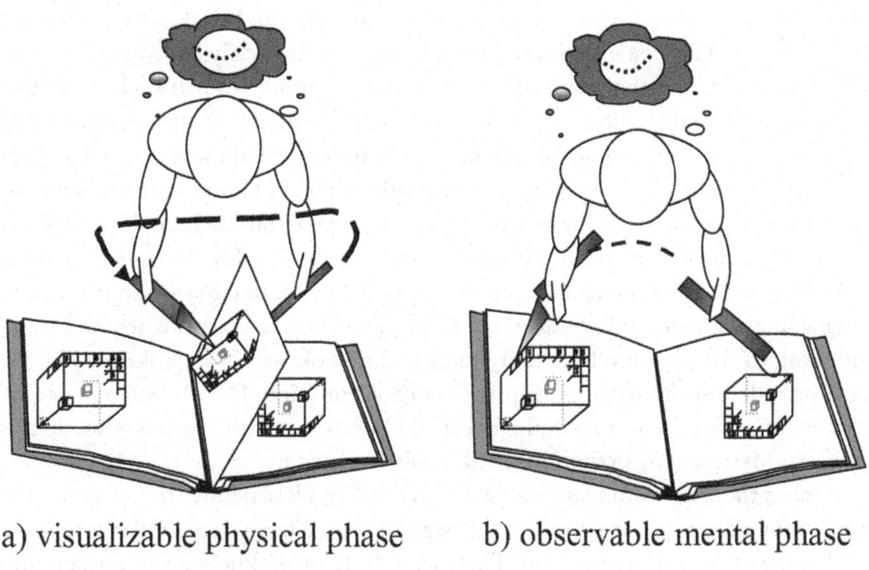

FIGURE 3.3-3 Action flow under operator control changes the CAT book beyond deterministic playback (see Figure 2.7-1)

applying his knowledge of the system being modeled, and writing the system's internal desires on his future side. This is the observational phase the modeled system "B" is conscious of. In contrast, the Figure 3.3-3a shows system "A" in a turn_leaf() operation, moving ink from his current future side to the past side of the next time instant. The movement of this ink represents actions due to the gravito-electric forces that connect charge with charge and mass with mass through their corresponding force fields. While this is happening, the page is turned and when completed, all the updated backside ink pattern is visible on "A's" new left-past page. The two models are independently run at different time rates and at different locations in the nothingness of this book you are reading.

The question now is, how would independent systems "A" and "B", modeled by our CAT model contraptions interact with each other? In the last section we assume the classic gravito-electric forces can spread their influences beyond the confines of their own space-content icons because they were parts of a bigger system and therefore their interacting force fields were always present but only neglected to first approximation. Here we are assuming some interactions exist between independent systems that are not parts of a local whole and capable of being modeled in a single book but rather truly independent for the lifetime of the model. The required model-to-model interactions are easy to draw when we jump from the reality of the book within the book to the next level in which figures are surrounded by the words being read.

Figure 3.3-4 shows external action flows between two CAT models entering and leaving through the actions of the operator. Hence arrows indicate some action would flow from the lower model to the upper one, and though not necessarily at the same instance, a similar action flow from the upper to the lower system is postulated. One would recognize such interactions as collisions between two universes.

In Section 3.2.3, we introduced the method for symbolically encoding the operator's experience of the action flow into the book model. When such subjective feelings are included, the book becomes a complete model of the subjective and objective phases of material. From within such an integrated model an action path leading out of the book would represent a path that would lead to the unknowable in contrast to the flow that travels from page to page within each model. Diagrams and an analysis of interactions between models are thoroughly discussed in Chapter 6. Figure 6.2-1, for example, shows the model of a conscious being named "I" interacting with the unknowable. Understanding such interactions requires transitioning to the next level of reality outside the book within a book. Section 3.4 will provide visualizations to help with such a transition. If each system's actions stay within their own models, the effect of interactions with the unknowable is a mystery. Mysteries, by definition, are difficult to explain.

Unless there is coordination between the two models, neither the location, the page number nor the rate at which the pages are being turned are similar at the two endpoints of the action transport. This means little or no knowledge of the transmitting system is available to the receiver except the fact that a change has been received. How each book model accommodates such change will depend upon its

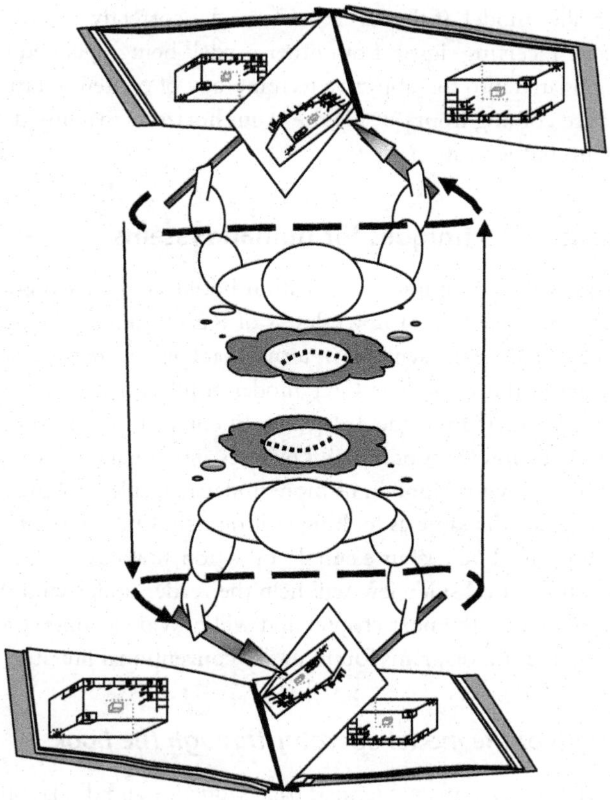

FIGURE 3.3-4 Interaction between two book models in their physical phase (see Figure 6.1-2)

ability to process the change into its remaining action structure. Presumably each of the book models will contain its own additional sub-model of what might be outside itself and the received change can be processed into a sub-model that will thereby exhibit a new look in subsequent observational phases. In this case, an explanation of the interaction has been found and the experience of each operator will include the "feeling" of an external presence within the observable objects he or she can create.

However, there is no guarantee that such speculations have any relation to the external book model that sent us a message unless the two are somehow coordinated by a supervisory operator who has built a larger model within which those shown in Figure 3.3-4 are parts working together. Such a coordination is provided by the reader and author of this book since we are the operators reading and writing at the next reality level. If we take a step to the reality off the pages of this book, we will be looking at our 1st-person three-dimensional scene of moving objects that should by now be recognized as the registered output measurement phase of our physical reality model. If the CAT book model correctly describes our situation then we are receiving signals from other models being operated beyond what we can see. Translated into the objective terminology of contemporary physics, this means signals are coming from outside the event horizon currently defined by the Cosmic Background Radiation.

3.4 Visualization techniques for human systems[3]

The CAT models Reality using books within books along a symbol-reality axis. As these books are moved up or down levels of Reality, one gets closer or further away from understanding the symbols in terms that apply to real-world experience outside the pages of this book. The CAT model of ink moving from page to page is observed by us readers from the 3rd-person theoretical perspective. Though we have added cross-section icons of thought bubbles and visual fields of view to make the effect of action flowing through us more understandable, looking at something flowing past us is not the same as looking at it directly. Only the immediate experience of reading this book is an example of action flowing through us directly. Nevertheless, a theoretical side view will help the reader understand the theory of action flow presented in the next chapter and will provide a context for interpreting the many theoretical diagrams found in the conventional literature.

3.4.1 The path of the model operator through the book

The book model consists of a predefined page sequence and display space. The ink patterns on each page record a sequence of events. When an operator erases and rewrites the ink pattern, he or she is reproducing an externalized version of the activities that created the explanation of his or her experiences. That explanation models the operator's physical reality which in turn produces the experiences. It is externalized so it can be communicated and gives the reader a god's-eye view of the modeled event at one instant. The event actually experienced depends on what is written in the book and the path taken by the user through it.

The standard user path suggested by the physical binding of a book starts at the right-side outer cover, followed by views of left and right pages, and ending at the left-back cover. When used as a CAT model there is no reason to treat these covers as anything other than more substantial versions of pages. Figure 3.4-1 treats the

3 Creating a book in the e-book reader's imagination and further imagining the flow of changes through this creation is not the same as performing these operations with real Paper and Ink. One misses the fact that observed paper and ink is actually attached to the real Paper and Ink by real Actions. It is the physics of this connection we are developing and demonstrating with the action flow diagrams throughout this book. When one imagines an explanation of one's observable with another observable, one connects a lowercase "a" type experience with a lowercase bold "**a**" type experience and it is easy to neglect its model cause "**A**" and mistake the "**a**" type reality one creates with the real "A" beyond one's Self. E-book readers are especially cautioned to avoid this visualization trap (see Section 1.3.1).

FIGURE 3.4-1 Closing an action cycle between the front and back cover of a CAT model feels like death and rebirth

back and front cover of a book as the past and future page of another instance. Such treatment logically implements a cyclic path for the user in which the last and first pages are connected. This configuration is equivalent to imposing cyclic boundary condition on the model and assumes the standard user path is a repeating cycle through all the pages.

If we close the book and view it from an oblique angle so that the upper edge of the pages are visible, the view defines a display space-time coordinate frame. The front cover shows a physical coordinate frame that is repeated on each page as suggested by the dashed-line re-renderings in the imagined volume inside the book. This visualization suggests a physical space-time that runs sequentially through the pages in the same direction as the user's standard path. A user reading through this model would traverse a physical instance of space repeated on each page along with the processes connecting each space with its next instantiation through the 1st-person observable sensation phase. The clock state in such a space sequence would increment along with the pages and although its rate might vary, it would fundamentally move forward along a parallel direction to the book-time axis defined by the page sequence (see Figure 3.4-2).

The rate at which the user reads through the book provides a velocity in pages per second. This rate requires the measurement of an external clock to define the second as a unit of time and hence as seen from the outside the user may start, stop, read fast or slow and follow an arbitrary path through the book.

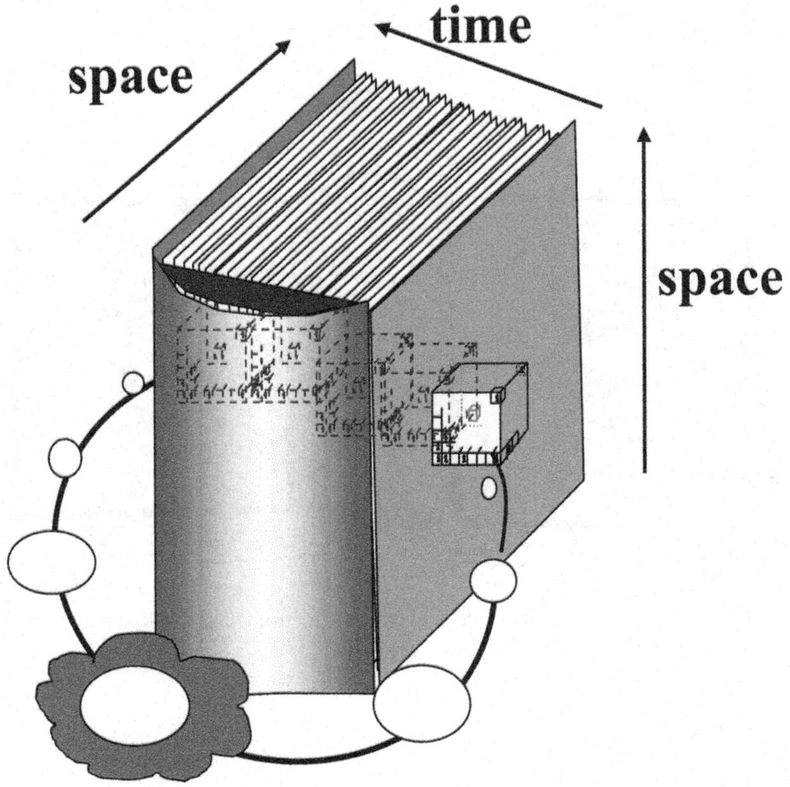

FIGURE 3.4-2 Standard action cycle around a book

If a clock is drawn into the space-content icon so that pointers from clock dials are available, then these time units can be read from the pages and the rate at which the user reads through the pages no longer depends upon arbitrary external whims and clocks but rather can be self-contained inside the book. Assuming a coordinate frame is drawn in the book to represent one built from standard Cesium beam clocks, then the standard second **s-second** unit is defined as $1 \cdot \underline{\textbf{s - second}} = 9{,}192{,}631{,}770 \cdot \underline{\textbf{Cs - cycles}}$

And the rate at which the user works through the pages is given by some number $\underline{\textbf{v}} = \text{v}\ \underline{\textbf{pages}}/\underline{\textbf{s - second}}$ It should be clear that the velocity provided is measured internally and is fixed by the relationship of the cesium beam clock-pointer records written into the pages of the book and their relation to the rest of events drawn into the space-content icon, not by the whims of the user.

3.4.1.1 Visualization of action cycles in book space

A cyclic path that follows the natural book-time sequence is only one of many possible action forms that can be represented in the pages of a book. The characteristic that makes a cyclic path appear to follow a course that is approximately parallel to the natural book coordinate axis is the fact that it must enter the front cover and exit out the back circumscribing the spine of the book. From a purely modeling point of view there are many paths that can be drawn through the same pages. If the orbits of action are encountered by a user who follows a different path than the orbit written, then experiences can be obtained that differ wildly from the activities that caused the original recording. As an example, if we bring an action cycle completely within the pages of the book, the action cycle pattern can be visualized as shown in Figure 3.4-3. The dashed lines suggest the pattern of the cycle within the book space while the projection of the cycle onto the top edge of the pages represents the book space-time view of the internally located loops.

When experienced with a standard observer path, the pattern on the left would first be encountered as a single creation event of two entities emanating in opposite spatial directions. Both entities would appear to travel forward in time as defined by the observer path and recombine in the future. Following the action cycle, one path is action going forward in time while the other path is the same entity traveling backward in time. The backward traveling path is typically recognized as a separate particle. After completing the cycle, the user following the standard observer path would see two entities come together and disappear, creating what appears to be an annihilation event. This is Richard Feynman's visualization of events encountered in positron-electron pair creation.

The pattern on the right of Figure 3.4-3 shows a cycle that is also inside the book space but oriented so that the entire cycle fits on one page. Such a cycle would appear at some time along the standard observer path as a simultaneous

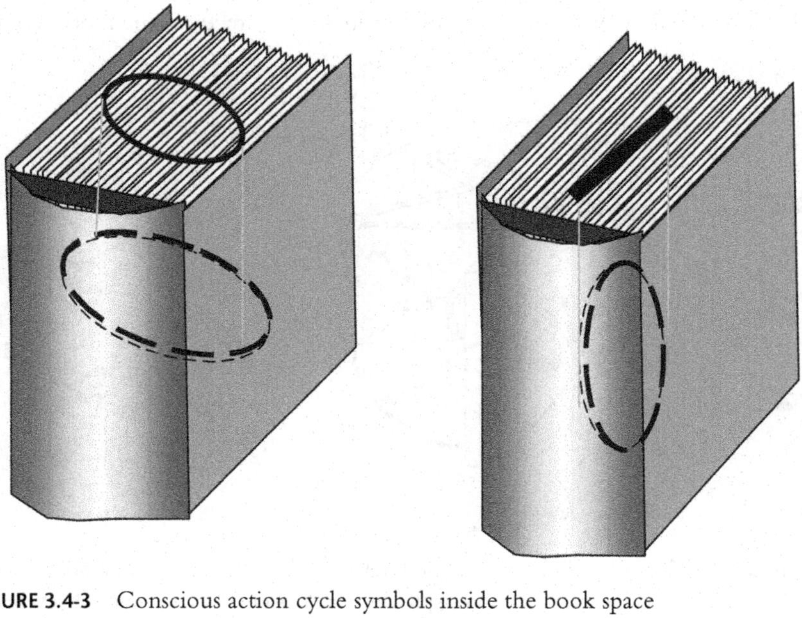

FIGURE 3.4-3 Conscious action cycle symbols inside the book space

occurrence of all the phases of a cycle collapsed into one time instance. Unless such a cycle is artificially created as an oval tube along the book-time direction for the purpose of maintaining a stable visual form, the single cycle appears for the duration assigned to a page-turn interval and then disappears.

The phases of such a cycle may be connected logically and recognized as measurement/explanation feedback loops. This is the form in which the conscious action cycle is often presented in this book along with the instruction to consider the line around the cycle as the event phase associated with time. However, in general phases of such cycles happening in parallel are often recognized as separate events without the logical connection made between them.

3.4.1.2 Visualizing action flow straight through book pages

In Section 3.2, action flow was drawn through connecting icons that crossed over sequential pages that represented the cross section of the 1st-person's experience on the bound inner side and the material theoretical response on the outer edge. In the previous section a visualization in which the flow travels straight through the pages is more suggestive of the actual experience. Figure 3.4-4a splits the physical pages of a book and spreads them apart into a star-like formation in which the material-space arrays are drawn so that the reader sees the subjective side directly in the front and the objective 3rd-person view seen over the top as the inside page expansion.

Figure 3.4-4b shows a top-down view in which a solid line indicates the flow of action through the perceived 1st- and 3rd-person view wedged between the physical-space interface icons. These are physically the gravito-electric field on the physical objective side and the mental fields on the subjective outside. Though only a connecting line is shown, the entire cross section of space and fields participates in the flow. The flow of action moves in the clockwise direction. The motion of the

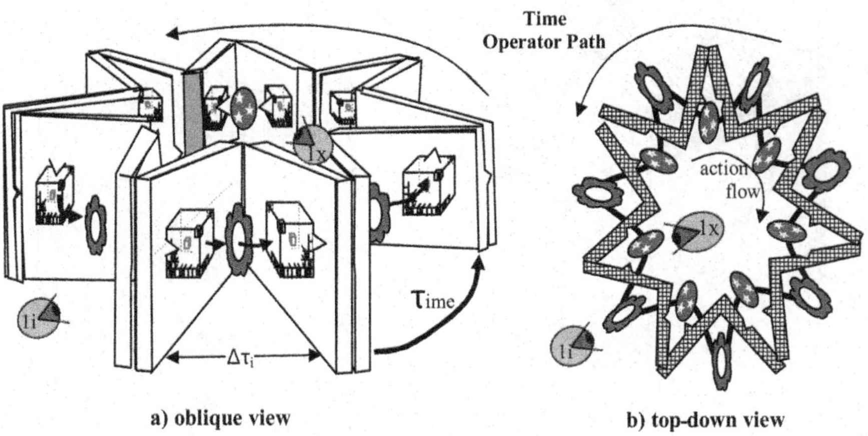

FIGURE 3.4-4 Flow of action through the interior and exterior pages of a book model provides sensation and explanatory experiences of a single sub-cycle

model operator moves in the opposite direction. We used an icon with three stars to represent the theoretical concepts of objects we believe are out there and a thought bubble to represent the 1st-person experience. To be more precise, the material-space arrays should be mounted on transparencies so the past and future can be seen from inner and outer sides depending on one's point of view. By doubling the pages, we explicitly integrate the subjective and objective aspect of material within a single physical framework composed of a network of action trajectories.

3.4.2 Eliminating the model support structure

The reader may consider the operations of the Book model described in this chapter as rather cumbersome. Erasing and drawing patterns of ink from one page to another by a normal individual in order to model cosmically large numbers of action transfers cannot be a practical way to imagine what Reality might be like. A major complexity however is attributed to support structures that are not part of the actual CAT model. The pages are required to hold the ink in place. If we move the symbols of the CAT model outside the book within a book and eliminate all the support components, then the essence of the CAT model for an isolated system is a cycle in time, shown in Figure 3.4-5. The cycle floats in "nothing". We see no pages nor an external operator who moves the symbols around to implement the flow of action. Instead action flows around the cycle due to intrinsic properties and forces inherent in the components we chose to build the model. Action flows around a

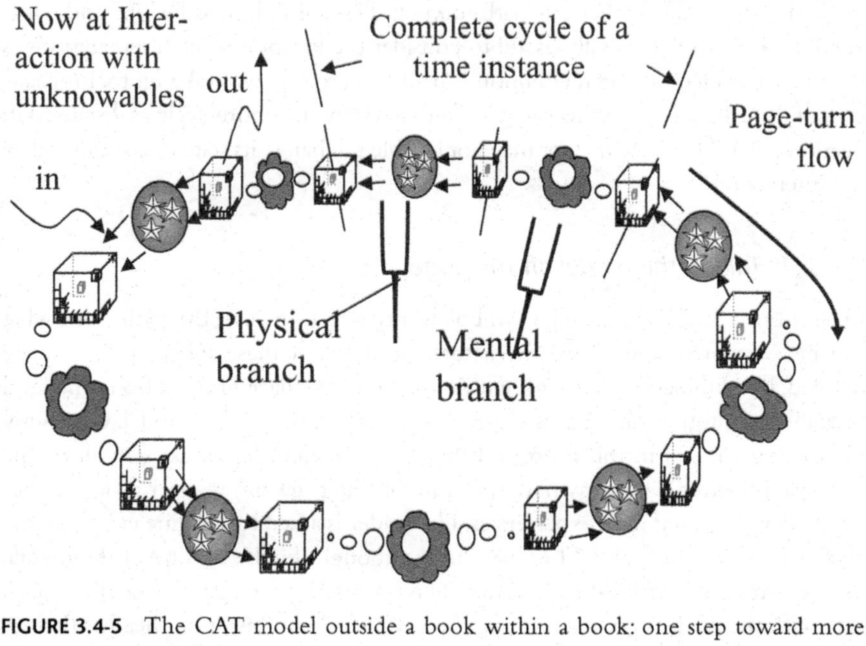

FIGURE 3.4-5 The CAT model outside a book within a book: one step toward more reality

cycle for the same reason that the earth continues to turn on its axis. It embodies homeostasis, which is the desire to move in the momentum of its material and there is only "nothing" to stop it.

The physical phases indicated by the double arrows is the theoretical side of utilizing gravito-electric forces to propagate change around the cycle. An icon of a classic universe is shown in the middle of each physical branch. This indicates the complexity of the material, which is represented by stars in outer space, being modeled to calculate the response to the influence of gravito-electric forces coming from and returning to the physical side of the physical-space icons.

These icons represent the detector cell interface between the subjective and objective phases of the action flow. The minimum complexity in this branch would occur if no material universe occurred between the transmission and reception of the forces. In this case no visualizable cause for the changes in the detector arrays are modeled and only rules connecting detector action records are used to explain our subjective experiences. In quantum theory these rules are probabilistic since we are dealing with interactions believed to be unknowables outside the cycle.

The mental phases show a trail of bubbles connecting the observable side of the detector array with the icon of a thought bubble containing a white oval. This oval represents the visual ego or third eye surrounded by the expected touch space. If the item labeled "mental branch" represents the observable Now instance, then the entire structure would rotate clockwise as indicated by the page-turn flow arrow. The observer would experience successive time instances as they flow through his or her Now, but in each instance, the observer would also affect the future due to past-based movement of actions into the future. The cycle represents a stand-alone isolated system but interactions with unknowables are indicated by "in" and "out" curved arrows. It is normally useful to consider the location of such interactions as the Now instance to which attention is paid and the one we wake up to. Propagation of disturbances from this point are processed by the entire cycle as discussed in Section 3.3.1. The cycle may or may not be able to change its state to accommodate the interaction.

3.4.2.1 Taking the model off the page

In Section 2.2 we introduced a symbol-reality axis by which the path from what can be written in a book to the actual meanings of these ink patterns can be defined. By eliminating the book within the book, we have jumped from one level of reality to another one that is closer to the reality we wish to model. Obviously Figure 3.4-5 is still in this book and therefore a symbol. The next step along the reality axis is to move this symbol structure off the page and register its icons with the reader's here and now experiences. The reader is asked to imagine enlarging the cycle so that the optical field of view in the thought bubble of one of the mental branches registers with his or her own. This means registering the nose in the picture with the reader's own and fitting the entire cycle on his or her head as though it were a kind of cap. The reader will then see his or her three-dimensional world while interpreting this experience with the CAT model. The rotating ink representing the flow of action must still be implemented by an operator. This job now belongs to the reader, who is asked to imagine action flowing through imaginary time instances. From this vantage point the reader may feel like time is passing right through his or her perceptive space.

Since the experience of that everyday world happens at one Now, only one thought bubble of the cycle maps into the reader's beyond-this-book experience. This experience is wedged between two sides of time represented by the observable side of the physical-space arrays. These arrays are not equal to the feelings of the eyeball and retina behind the reader's nose produced in his or her thought bubble. Instead they are mapped into a visualization of the space arrays out beyond and ahead of the three-dimensional world perceived as the direction of the flow of time. As we shall see, in Section 4.3.3, this direction is like an expansion coming out of or into the "small" at every point in the reader's scene. Probing further along this direction, the reader may encounter the appearance of deeper memories. These in turn become visualizations of mental experiences further into the past. So as one proceeds deeper and deeper around a cycle of experience, both memory recall and future planned expectation are being staged in the cycle to emerge as Now sensations at the next moment.

We will leave the next step down the reality axis as an exercise for the reader. The only guidance we can give for this step is to recognize that every sensation described in the last paragraph actually happens during the observer's Now experience. And therefore, a more comprehensive and deeper experience of detector cells, physical world images of past and future are evoked. This process down the reality axis is described in "The Search for the Feeling of Reality", Section 2.1.2, which must eventually end in the realization of a symbolic structure becomes the metaphor for what the reader believes Reality actually is like and in which the reader effectively lives.

4

THE ACTION MODEL

In CAT, we hypothesize that Reality is an activity that can be directly experienced in the 1st-person perspective and understood by experiencing a symbolic model of that activity from a 3rd-person perspective. The two experiences are fused to produce the world we believe to live in. Figure 4-1 shows an example of a model in which Reality is separated into two parallel, interacting action loops. Their physical components are shown as mass-charge density icons written on the future and past sides of each page, but here shown only on the inner and cover pages of a book. The model operator moving ink simulates activities being modeled. As the operator moves ink, action represented by ink flows from future to past. An open book represents a "Now" instance with two sides of time.

The upper and lower arcs show the flow of action producing subjective sensations mapped into the interior of matter. The arrows superimposed on the pages represent the interaction of gravito-electric force fields that connect the external send and receive aspects of matter. These are located on the inside of each single page, and the passing flow is perceived from a 3rd-person theoretical perspective (see Section 3.2). Each turn of a page moves the model operator to the next sensation instance, and moving through all the pages provides the lifetime experience of the modeled system.

Such process-flow diagrams provide visualizable records of what conscious systems are doing. They are not a mathematical theory and do not provide the detailed formalisms that can be used to build and control complex equipment. To overcome this deficiency, this chapter will first ground our graphic models in the terminology of classic physics and then expand those theories to include subjective experiences. The physics we introduce will emphasize a media in equilibrium through which changes propagate and the restoring forces each particle experiences when it deviates from its equilibrium position. Such forces will be connected to the action flow that generates actually observable experiences. We intend to replace the physics of objects and probabilities traditionally coded into contemporary theories with the physics of action flowing through interacting events.

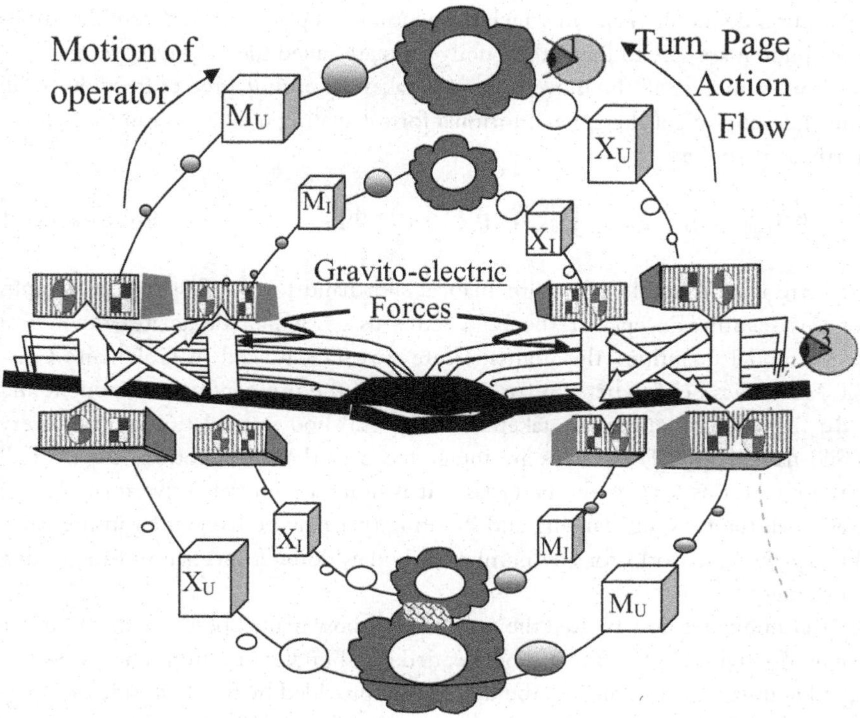

FIGURE 4-1 Lifecycle representation of a two system action model interacting through gravito-electric forces only

The terminology in this section will be familiar to readers who have a background in the physical sciences. However, the text is intended to convey concepts in English. The language of mathematics is used to define precise abbreviations for those concepts to avoid impossibly long repetitions of English text, which would be required to explain the behavior of complex systems encountered in everyday life. For readers without a hard science background, the formulas encountered should be treated as evidence that our CAT book model is a legitimate expansion of experimentally verified science that goes beyond philosophic conjecture. Our intent is to provide an introductory how-to guide for the development of engineering tools that apply to the objective and subjective aspects of our existence. Delving further into the meaning of equations, though useful, is not necessary to grasp the conceptual framework action physics provides.

4.1 The concept of action in classic physics

Action is a common term used to designate activity usually involving the motion of objects in the classic world view of things. At a child's birthday party, one may describe the scene of running and screaming children as an event. Material things are moving all over the place. *Action* measures the amount of activity, and the paths of motion define the *Form* in which the action takes place. The different directions the children are able to move their body parts are called their *degrees of freedom*.

If we sum over all the movement steps taken by each degree of freedom by all the children, we get the general formula for calculating total action in the "child's birthday party" as

$$\Delta A_{\text{Child's\_birthday\_party}} = \int_{\Delta q_{fN}} \Sigma_{fN} \mathbf{p}_{fN}\left(\mathbf{q}_{fN}\right) \bullet \mathbf{dq}_{fN}. \qquad \text{Equation 4.1-1}$$

Here is an example of a mathematical shorthand for the first two paragraphs of this section. Except for the bold letter usage, which designates theoretical CAT model quantities, the nomenclature was standardized in Goldman's Classic Mechanics book where "$\mathbf{p}_{fN}(\mathbf{q}_{fN})$" represents the momentum component and "$\mathbf{dq}_{fN}$" the length of the step taken by every "fth" body articulation joint of every child named "N". These steps are integrated over the total motion "Δq_{fN}" of all the joints for as long as the party lasts. It is quite a comprehensive formula that covers all the twisting, dancing and shouting that may be happening in the party. Furthermore, it works for any number of bodies doing a spectrum of interesting movements.

But no matter how twisted the moves are or how many bodies are involved, the *Form* of activities in that event can be coded into bundles of action trajectories in a graphic display that duplicates the description provided by the right side of Equation 4.1-1. This allows us to graphically describe Reality as an event by specifying the action densities along paths and in all degrees of freedom available to that event. In practice the complexity is overwhelming, and aggregations of events are used to combine the sums over some or all of the individual steps involved into approximate averages.

For a stand-alone "Whole" event, all the sums in Equation 4.1-1 can be summarized in terms of an average momentum "$\mathbf{P}_W$" in the entire event and the total path length "$\Delta\mathbf{Q}_W$" so the action "$\Delta\mathbf{A}_W$" required to implement the event is given by

$$\Delta\mathbf{A}_W = \mathbf{P}_W \bullet \Delta\mathbf{Q}_W. \qquad \text{Equation 4.1-2}$$

In CAT, the subscript capital letter is used to name any event. When "W" is used as a name, the event is the "Whole" or an approximation – such as the child's birthday party – the summary graphic form of its evolution becomes a simple closed cycle.

When the result of Equation 4.1-2 is equated with the result of Equation 4.1-1, a single condition is imposed on the many internal detailed combinations of momentum and path segments expressible in Equation 4.1-1. The trick is to aggregate these detailed changes into convenient parts that can be approximated by sufficiently stable averages. The two cycles shown in Figure 4-1 divide a Whole event recorded in the book into two forms of action representing interacting sub-systems. Interaction lines are shown as arrows happening inside the pages. The two parts are named cycles "I" and "U"; the Whole action combination is summarized by four terms as

$$\Delta \mathbf{A}_{W} = \mathbf{P}_{II} \bullet \Delta \mathbf{Q}_{II} + \mathbf{P}_{IU} \bullet \Delta \mathbf{Q}_{IU} + \mathbf{P}_{UI} \bullet \Delta \mathbf{Q}_{UI} + \mathbf{P}_{UU} \bullet \Delta \mathbf{Q}_{UU}. \quad \text{Equation 4.1-3}$$

The outer terms correspond to the straight arrows representing action flow within each part while the inner terms correspond to the interactions representing action flow between the "U" and "I" parts. Applied to the birthday party example, the party may split into groups of boys and girls who at certain ages interact very little. The Whole party may then be divided into "B" and "G" events within which average momentum and positions are combined in the form of Equation 4.1-3. By combining all three equations, we can show how alternative aggregations of parts and sub-parts are used to describe events between the extremes of a single whole and its infinitesimal details.

$$\Delta \mathbf{A}_{W} = \mathbf{P}_{w} \bullet \Delta \mathbf{Q}_{W} = \mathbf{P}_{II} \bullet \Delta \mathbf{Q}_{II} + \mathbf{P}_{IU} \bullet \Delta \mathbf{Q}_{IU} + \mathbf{P}_{UI} \bullet \Delta \mathbf{Q}_{UI} + \mathbf{P}_{UU} \bullet \Delta \mathbf{Q}_{UU} = \ldots = \int_{\Delta q_{fN}} \Sigma_{fN} p_{fN} \left(q_{fN} \right) \bullet dq_{fN}. \quad \text{Equation 4.1-4}$$

This introduction shows how action structures, whether presented in graphic or mathematical forms, can be used to describe events.

4.1.1 History of action in physics

Although Newton's first law – "for every action there is an equal and opposite reaction" – involves an important property of action, Newtonian physics focuses on forces as expressed by his second law ($F = m \cdot a$), not on action. Even the formulation of the Least Action Principle in the 19th century – "a physical system will chose a path of least action" – only provided a philosophical insight into the possible existence of an anthropomorphic pleasure-pain principle guiding the motion of particles. It was not until Max Planck discovered the fundamental action quantity "$h = 6.6 \times 10^{-34}$ Joule-Sec" that the importance of action as the smallest unit of electromagnetic change was recognized in physics. Though the quantization of action provided an initial explanation of spectroscopic experiments, the invention of matrix mechanics by Werner Heisenberg followed by wave mechanics by Erwin Schrödinger provided superior calculation tools for understanding the interior of matter in terms of energy-level structures. Since these calculation tools worked so well for developing valuable products, including the transistor and laser, it is hardly surprising that speculation regarding the deeper implications of Planck's discovery was largely relegated to philosophers. The most prominent of these was Alfred Whitehead (1978), who proposed that events, he called "actual occasions", should form the fundamental building blocks of the universe rather than fundamental particles.

4.1.1.1 The elimination of change in calculus

Though change is what actually happens, action has taken a back seat to the concept of an instantaneous state in the development of physical theories. This is both due to the way measurements are made and the language of mathematics we have invented to interpret those measurements. Physicists observe the state of a system by taking instantaneous snapshots that freeze the system in stationary measurement records, described by position and momentum vectors "$\underline{\mathbf{P}}$,$\underline{\mathbf{Q}}$". By adding the "Δ" or "d" prefix, the action equations introduced in Equations 4.1-1 to 4.1-4 above refer to happenings between states at average locations "$\underline{\mathbf{Q}}$" or the location of a sub-parts "$\underline{\mathbf{q}}$". Unfortunately, what happens between measurements has been coded in the language of calculus by mathematicians utilizing geometric analogies of points and lines. Calculus emphasize this state-point concept by defining the derivative as a limit process in which the interval between states is eliminated.

For example, the average velocity (v) of a particle is a change in position (Δx) divided by the time interval (Δt). Newton and/or Leibniz invented a mathematical limit procedure ($\lim_{\Delta t \to \to -0} \Delta x/\Delta t \to dx/dt = v$) in which time interval gets small enough to be considered a point instance. Classic physicists adopted the procedure by assuming snapshots of object positions can be made infinitesimally close to each other so that the interval between measurements becomes zero and can be neglected. They had also adopted the "objective reality" assumption that we see real objects that move through the neglected time interval in the form in which they appear. Thus, reality became a population of objects moving through a continuum of space-time as our Western legacy of beliefs. Even quantum theorists retain the continuum concept and talk about change as mysterious unobservable happenings in equally mysterious quantum jumps without recognizing that their own neglect of the interval resulted in the mysteries.

It is precisely the opposite emphasis on change, events and processes that characterizes action theory and the event-oriented world view. Though states are convenient ways of talking about recorded measurement results, it is precisely the changes happening between measurements that contain the dynamics and the time interval, which our mainstream physics has systematically eliminated. Action is the measure of the size of change. It is the abstract material from which events are built. Planck's quantum of action "h" is the minimum size of the change required to record electromagnetic state transitions. We must now reintroduce the neglected activities happening within those transitions. Because the elimination of the interval and the substitution of an infinite number of infinitesimally small points in calculus is such a deeply ingrained procedure, it is best to return to our actual experience of change and see what physical principles remain when the reality of the space-time continuum assumption is eliminated.

4.1.2 Examples of action in events

Like energy, momentum or electric fields, etc., action is not directly observable but inferred from what can be seen in the behavior of objects. Thus, action is a theoretical quantity whose existence is never detached from its manifestation in observable things. By examining a set of observable happenings, we can gain insight as to what action is, how it behaves and how it is calculated from what is actually experienced. In the following example, only one geometric degree of freedom is used, which is traditionally called "x". Here we use this shortcut instead of the generalized quantity label "q_{1I}" for a single degree of freedom along a line appearing in a 1st-person named "I".

4.1.2.1 Falling domino example

When we look at a line of dominoes, as shown in Figure 4.1-1, a limited activity happens involving three falling dominoes. The first one has some momentum, which builds up in the middle and declines when the last domino comes to rest on its neighbor. The area under the curve represents the action observed when looking along the horizontal x-axis. We can calculate the action if we let (p̲) be the average momentum in the pulse and multiply by the interval (Δx) over which the activity happens. The amount of action (ΔA) in the activity is then given by (ΔA = p̲·Δx). If instead our gaze remains at one spot, and we record what happens there along a vertical time axis, we see a single shaded domino. It picks up kinetic energy as it starts to fall, which builds up and then dissipates into heat after it comes to rest.

The energy flow is equal to the transfer of gravitational potential energy into kinetic energy as the standing domino gains speed, followed by the loss of kinetic energy as it comes to rest on its neighbor. Since the loss and gain are equal, the total

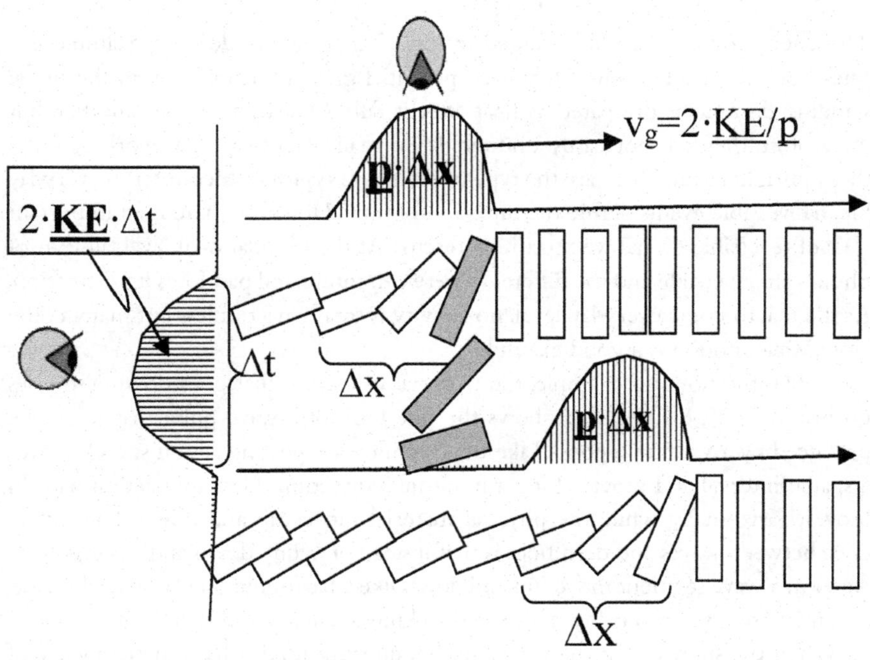

FIGURE 4.1-1 Action moving along horizontal space and vertical time dimensions

change is twice the average kinetic energy in the time interval (Δt) of the fall and gives the amount of action as ($\Delta A = 2 \cdot \underline{KE} \cdot \Delta t$).

In one case we see the activity spread out in space; the other we see it as spread out in time. Since we are looking at the same activity, the action should be the same no matter how we look at it. By equating the two we can extract the group velocity (v_g) with which the action moves along the x-axis as ($v_g = \Delta x/\Delta t = 2 \cdot \underline{KE}/\underline{p}$). The particle velocities inside the kinetic and momentum calculations are the falling velocities of the dominos. These are not equal to the velocity of the group moving forward along the x-axis. A domino mass falling all by itself would only move half its height along the x-axis. Because of neighboring interactions, this motion will be transported along the spatial axis with the group velocity. The change of a standing domino just being touched on the right side of the pattern is identical to the change that will happen to the domino a distance ($v_g \cdot \Delta t$) further right in a period of time Δt later. Therefore, *the change moves* with the group velocity. Moving change does not connect the same domino but the same state of change. The middle gray domino in Figure 4.1-1 is in the same state of change as the falling domino on the left of the top gray one. *What has moved here is the change.*

What we have introduced with this example is that a stable form of activity is the observer-independent event that can be viewed as momentum spread out and moving in the space direction ***or*** energy spread out and moving in the time direction.

4.1.2.2 Wave motion example

The energy difference implemented by the change in the domino example is a one-shot irreversible event. Organized potential gravitational energy in the initial standing domino is dissipated as heat after it falls. One thing causes another, but once done they are not easily undone. It normally takes external work to stand them upright again. These are the type of events we typically encounter in everyday life. Irreversible events define the direction of time. However, there is an important class of reversible events we must now discuss. At the foundational level, all laws of physics are reversible and the difference between future and past loses its distinction. At the macroscopic everyday level, no activity is totally frictionless but many come close. Wave motion is a good example.

Unlike the domino example, the material in a wave that goes down also goes up just as easily. Figure 4.1-2 shows the side look of a wave pulse that might be produced by a wave in a pond. Like the dominos, a repeating action stretches over a spatial interval and moves along a horizontal direction. The same action pattern moves horizontally while the physical material moves up and down. The difference between waves and dominoes is that instead of falling down and staying there, water in a wave segment moves up and down like a harmonic oscillator. In this case, potential energy is reversibly transferred to kinetic energy and then back.

When the surface is at the flat-water equilibrium level it has kinetic energy of motion. When the water is above the flat surface it is pulled down by gravity and

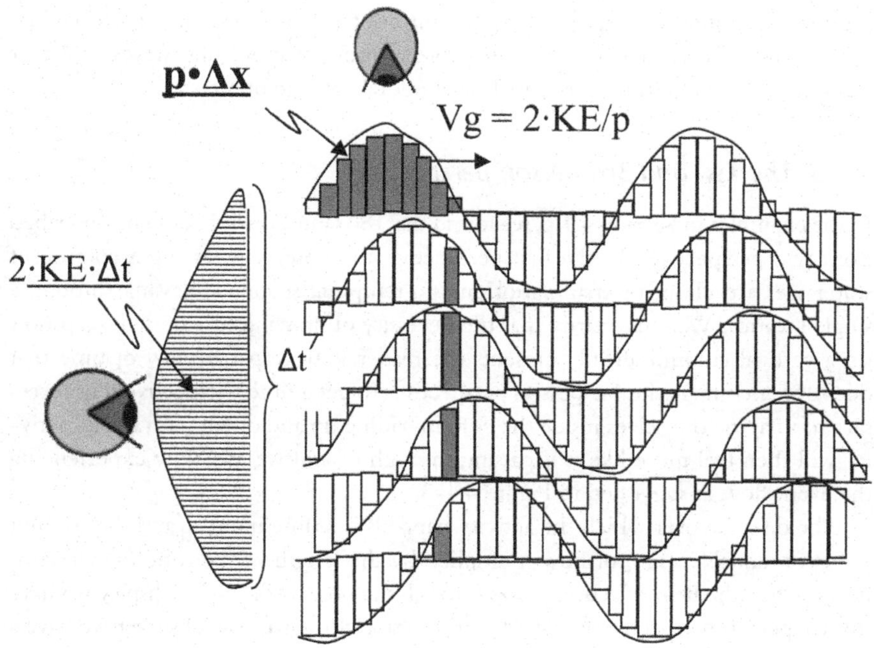

FIGURE 4.1-2 Wave motion example of a moving reversible action pattern

when below it is pushed up by buoyancy. Surface tension between water columns provides for lateral energy transfer. The states of the surface are again spread out along the spatial axis for a wavelength "Δx" and the action is related to the average momentum by the formula (ΔA = p·Δx). If we record the wave on a time axis by looking at one column, it would oscillate up and down as the form of the wave passes. A single up and down cycle happens in a time period "Δt" and requires an amount of action "ΔA", which is again related to the conserved average kinetic energy of the up and down motion by the formula (ΔA = 2·KE·Δt).

As in the domino example, something, which is not a thing, but rather an arrangement of change moves with a velocity ($\underline{v}_g = 2 \cdot KE/\underline{p}$). If a pattern of action happens here, and then again there, has the event moved? Certainly, when we look at wave motion it would be natural to conclude the form of action implementing the change has moved. Is it the same change? Could we say the action has moved? Certainly we say the people we meet every day are the same people even though they happen at a different place and time. But are they the same material or are they simply the same form of material? Is what we see actual material or an activity that creates its appearance in ourselves?

Event-oriented thinking requires us to consider events and hence action structures as possessing a kind of permanence that moves. As we develop an event-oriented action physics in this chapter, the form of a constant pattern of change experienced in our selves will become more and more fundamental. The theoretical projection of objective material particles into our experiences will be replaced by the equally theoretical projection of stable motions that act like waves. and that motion can be viewed from a spatial or temporal vantage point.

4.1.3 The 1st- and 3rd-person perspectives

In the examples in Section 4.1.2, we found that the same activity could be described from two perspectives. In the first perspective, the observer viewing a column of water sees a cycle of reversible motion as a temporal sequence passing through a single location. We must clarify that the necessity of drawing several state snapshots on a vertical column already presents the reader with a spatial view of time that does not encourage the 1st-person perspective. To get a time perspective it is necessary to imagine our selves inside the column riding up and down with it. The activity will then feel more like it is passing through us and we are Now experiencing the event flow, as suggested in Figure 4.1-3.

The distance over which the activity happens is a time interval, and the amount of action equals its rate of flow multiplied by the length of the time for which it flows. When the flow of action passes through the observer's "Now" display we have the 1st-person perspective while when the action flows past the observer we have a 3rd-person perspective. The direct 1st-person view looks at the output of a process. The observer is feeling the action flow passing directly through his or her "Now" space straight down the timeline. What the observer experiences is a pattern of

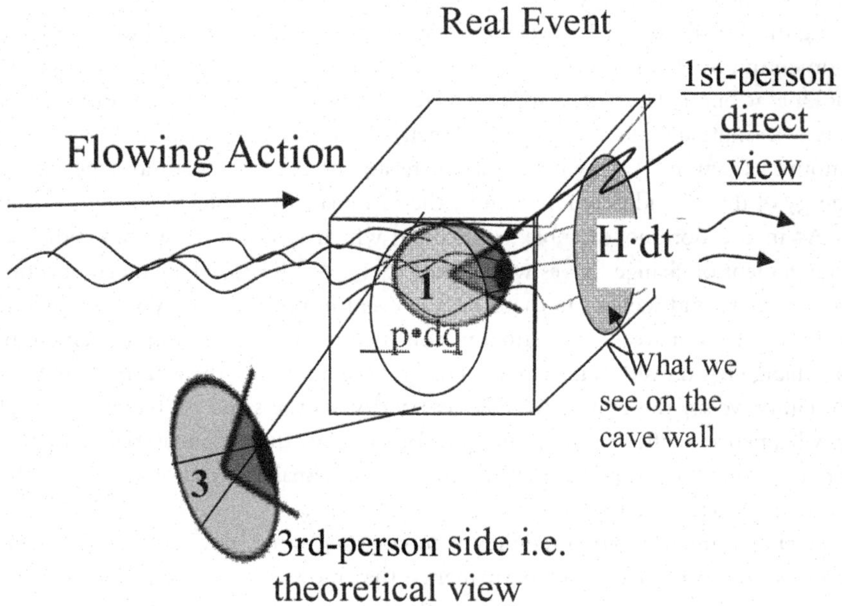

FIGURE 4.1-3 Time vs. space views of action flowing through an event

action-flow intensity per time interval, called energy. When adopting a clock in the Universe, the time measured is the coordinate time interval given the letter "dt". The total energy measured is traditionally coded into the letter "H", the Hamiltonian, to honor one of the founders of action theory. The amount of action "dA" flowing directly toward and through the observer is calculated from "dA = H·dt". This perspective is like watching cars role out the assembly line of an auto factory. We see what is produced but not the mechanisms that produce the output.

In the 3rd-person perspective, the observer steps back and genuinely sees the sequence laid out along a spatial line. Here the distance over which the activity is spread out is a spatial interval and the amount of action ($dA = \underline{p} \cdot \underline{dp}$) is the action density in each interval multiplied by the length over which the action is spread. When looked at from the side, it is like watching the operations acting on the raw material as they move through the assembly line, which gives one some idea of how the product is produced.

The realization that energy and momentum describe two observer dependent aspects of the same activity is central to the derivation of CAT from the concepts of classical physics.

4.2 Characteristics of action structures

The examples of action provided in the last section will now be examined to extract characteristics that are ubiquitous properties of all events. These properties will be generalized to build a physical theory in which the behavior of events rather than objects is paramount.

4.2.1 Characteristics of the medium

Each of our example events happened in a medium. The medium in our examples have general characteristics tabulated in the following paragraphs:

1 Material: the medium consists of classic physical material consisting of a line of wood and an expanse of water that, in our examples, changes its shape. In classic physics all material is composed of mass and charge, and the medium consists of mass-charge density aggregations.

2 Cells: the medium is divided into material cells systems consisting of dominoes in the first example and water columns in the second. Dominoes are clearly separate self-contained systems. Water columns are artificial divisions in a material density created by superimposing a coordinate grid giving each column an address and a size. The medium cells are approximated as self-contained systems.

3 Degrees of freedom: the cells have a specific but limited set of directions of motion. Dominoes move along an arc as they tumble onto their neighbors. Water columns move up and down along a vertical axis. In general, medium degrees of freedom are all the directions along which a cell can expand or contract.

4 Instantaneous states:

> Individual cell states are defined by the instantaneous location and momentum of all the cells' degrees of freedom. The domino is in an instantaneous position and motion along its falling arc.
> Medium states are the combined instantaneous states of all the cells producing a pattern or shape, i.e. the surface of the water.

5 Event-states: also called dynamic states, event-states combine all instantaneous states of a medium into a single interrelated pattern of motion.
6 Interactions: flow of action accompanied by forces between neighboring cells. The dominoes push horizontally and vertically on their neighbor as they fall, while the water columns pull their neighbors up and down with friction, and "van der Waal" forces are applied at the boundaries between them.
7 Neighbors: neighbors are defined by touching boundaries between material cells through which forces act without passing through intermediary cells. In the domino, neighbors are adjacent cells along a line while water columns have four neighbors among which forces change each other's up-down motion.

In summary, the generalized medium is a material extension organized into a set of cells characterized by individual degrees of freedom that interact directly with each other to change the shape of the medium extension. Each repeating evolution of shapes is an event-state.

4.2.2 Reversible and irreversible changes

The domino provides an example of an irreversible change in which the end result is *not* easily undone. Let's see why. The potential energy stored in the upright dominoes is converted to kinetic energy of motion as they tumble along an arc. The arc is the internal degree of freedom in a medium cell along which each domino is allowed to move. When they hit bottom, the kinetic energy is converted to heat and dissipates into the rest of the universe. Irreversibility is a property of interacting systems in which action is transferred out of the system involved.

Reversibility is a property of isolated systems in which action stays within the medium involved. An example of reversible change is provided by the water wave example. When the water column rises above the surface it is pulled down by gravity. When it is below the surface it is buoyed back up by water pressure induced by gravity pulling the rest of the surrounding surface down. Each water column therefore oscillates like a mass on a spring. The column would oscillate up and down in place containing a constant flow of action forever if it were completely isolated and action flow were not transferred in and out from neighboring columns.

The transfer of action to a neighboring column retains the amount of action flowing in the degrees of freedom defining the entire medium. If the shape of that medium repeats, such as standing waves of water contained in a bucket, the amount of action flowing per repetition event will remain constant. If, however, some of the interactions happen between media degrees of freedom and other degrees of freedom, the action per event is lost to the greater universe. In practice friction between water columns or containment walls drains action flow out of the vertical motion and reduces the wave amplitude and hence the amount of action in sequential repetition cycles until the media becomes flat and the medium reaches its ground state in which zero amount of action flows through its vertical degrees of freedom.

Action flow contained in an isolated medium does not change the dynamic event-state of that medium although action flow between internal degrees of freedom changes the instantaneous state of the entire system and the value of individual degrees of freedom in each cell.

4.2.2.1 Entropy and our fundamental desire

Since most change patterns we see in our experience are always coupled by friction to the rest of the universe they only approximate truly reversible changes and eventually run down. This tendency for systems to run down is expressed by the second law of thermodynamics, which states that the entropy of a system will spontaneously increase. Alternatively, one might say it is impossible to isolate a system and eliminate friction completely. However, at the fundamental level of gravito-electric forces, friction is simply a flow of action that expresses our lack of control over the action's migration.

In CAT the fundamental desire of any activity is:

1 To increase the amount of action experienced.
2 To experience that action in an event-state of equilibrium.

If a Whole is divided into two self-contained systems, I and U, each one will remain in a state of equilibrium as long as it is completely isolated from the other. In order to increase its action experience, each system must interact with the other in hopes of gaining a flow of action and absorb it by transitioning to a new equilibrium state – also called phase transitions in chemistry. Both systems have the same desire. A sloppy interaction may lose action flow and therefore must be carefully planned. The activity loop inside living systems does the planning (see Section 6.4). If successful, a living system will gain action flow and decrease its entropy at the expense of increasing entropy in its environment "U". Failure to control all the details of our interactions may have more to do with the fact that we are an activity loop in which our attention is focused on our most important interactions at our localized "Now", and as we grow, small leakages will occur without our notice.

Negative entropy measures an event's success in achieving its fundamental desire.

4.2.3 The action flows in classic physics models

We have discussed several examples of events visualized as the motion of material that could be observed in the 1st-Person Laboratory, where such material is assumed to be independently real. A classic physicist experiencing the motion of such material would naturally build a model to explain what he or she believes is going on. We will accordingly build such a model using traditional physical concepts of energy and momentum in this section and then convert to an action flow as a prelude to our expansion of physics that incorporates the subjective aspect of matter in Section 4.3.

4.2.3.1 The block universe model

The block universe is a classic model of the universe, or any isolated system, that can be envisioned as a static description in which future and past are depicted as a sequence of causally connected snapshots. The snapshots are perceived by the 1st-person like the images recorded on successive movie frames. Each frame shows a space-time instance and records the position of all the objects at that time. A stack of such frames viewed from the outside by the 3rd-person describes an event. The term "block universe" is due to the appearance of the space-time record as an unchanging four-dimensional "block" of pages.

Parameterization of a classic physical block is shown in Figure 4.2-1 with generalized position "q", momentum "p" vectors attached to mass-charge icons occupying a region of space shown as an oval on successive pages. Each rear page radiates influences to the next front page as the charges and masses are carried from past to future. Each page contains sufficient information to calculate the state on the next

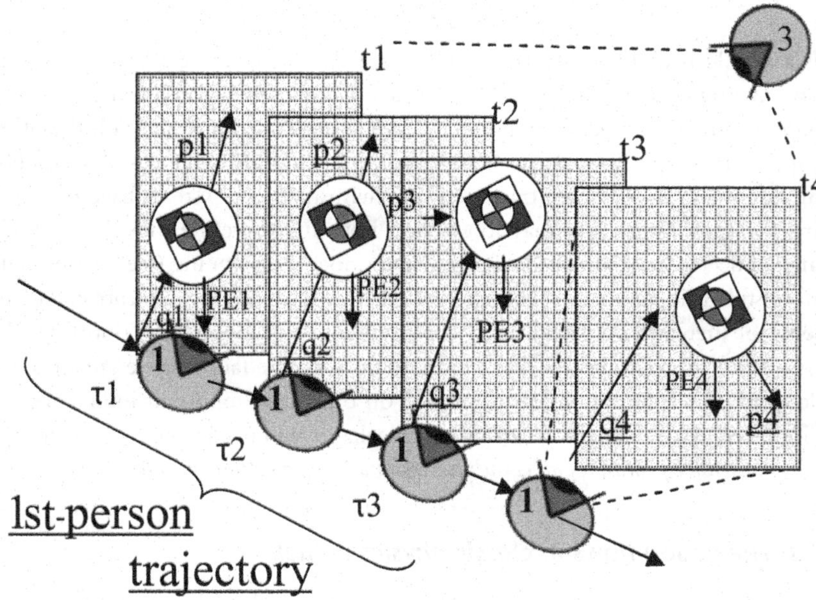

FIGURE 4.2-1 States in a classic block universe are viewed sequentially like the frames of a film

page. The classic momentum for material composed of rest charge and rest mass is given by

$$\underline{p} = m_0 \cdot \underline{v}_m + ch_0 \cdot \underline{\mathbf{A}}_e / c_p \qquad \text{Equation 4.2-1}$$

Where $\underline{v}_m$ is the instantaneous velocity of the mass, (c_p) is the phase velocity of light and "$\underline{\mathbf{A}}_e$" is the magnetic vector potential in Gaussian units.

Charge momentum expressed by "$\underline{\mathbf{A}}_e$" is a property of space due to motion of the rest of the charges in the universe. Mass momentum has traditionally been attributed to intrinsic properties of matter. However, calculations by Sciama (1953) utilizing Mach's Principle show momentum is also a property of space due to the motion of the rest of the masses in the universe (see A4.3). The momentum specifies the "KE" of the mass-charge complex and defines its expected location on the next page if no additional forces are present. The Coulomb and Gravitational force potential "PE" adds the influence of these additional forces. The expression for the total energy "H = PE+KE" is used to determine the position and momentum on the next page.

The expected position on the next page is an expression of the equilibrium condition imposed by the existence and motion of the whole charge-mass distribution in the universe on every material component within it. The combination of all gravito-electric forces can be interpreted to suggest that when the whole Universe is in equilibrium, all charges and masses are where they are expected to be at all times. This means the trajectories for the whole event are determined and the entire evolution of the material states from beginning to end can be permanently recorded on the pages of a block universe model. If one wanted to look up what happened thousands or even a million years ago one just goes to the right frame and reads what is there. We could also look up any future date and find what will happen.

4.2.4 Action-flow structures in a classic block universe model

The same trajectory of all the masses and charges in an isolated system can equally well be calculated by considering the action flow. This perspective is achieved by looking not at the state parameters "$\underline{p}$" and "$\underline{q}$" at each measurement snapshot but rather the action flow happening between snapshots. In Figure 4.2-2 we have flipped the transparency labeled "t3" and "t4" so that the action per time interval arrows indicating the energy at different horizontal space cells are now seen from the back side. The 1st-person riding along the data block's timeline now concentrates on the dynamics between the states. Here we kibitzing readers see the trajectories of action flow spread out before us in a 3rd-person perspective where the partial time interval "∂t" is mapped into a space interval "$c \cdot \partial t$", where "c" is the speed of the 1st-person. From this perspective we can follow the trajectories that move action from a space point (q_x,q_y,q_z,t2) to a second point (q'_x,q'_y,q'_z,t3) in our Figure 4.2-2 example.

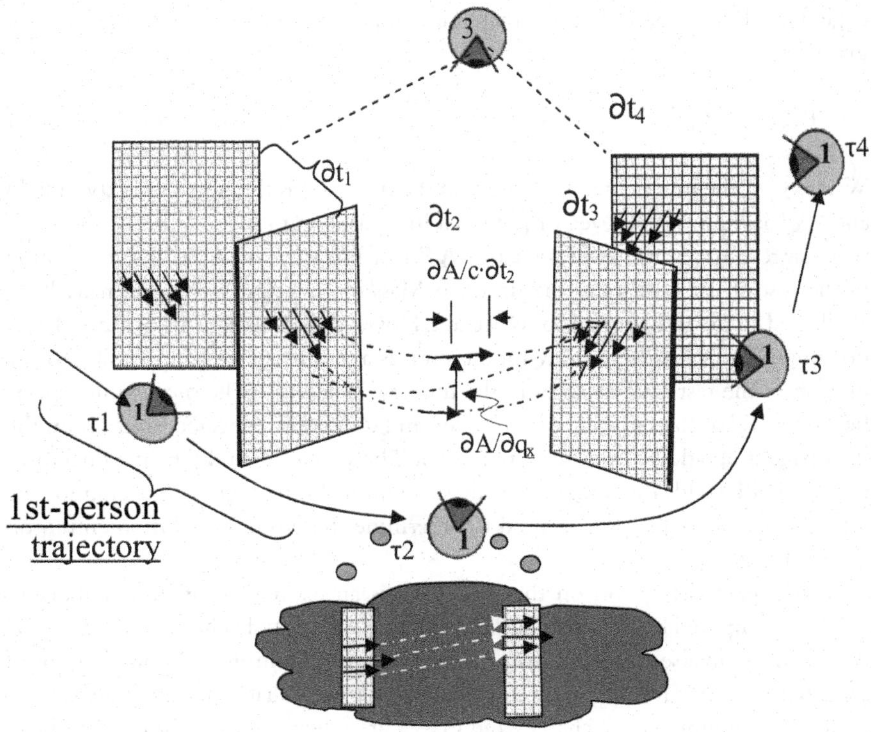

FIGURE 4.2-2 Propagating action structure in a classic block universe, mind phase ignored

For nonrelativistic situations most of the action will move along the time direction because particles move slowly. However, moving particles will require action from the trailing edge to be moved to the leading edge. This means some action is transferred along the direction of motion and that action must be subtracted from the amount that would have been transferred along the timeline if the particle were stationary. In Cartesian coordinates, the change in the amount of action moving from one space point to a neighboring one is shown in Figure 4.2-2 as "$\partial A/\partial \underline{q}_x$" while the loss of action out of the flow along the timeline is shown as "$\partial A/c \cdot \partial t_2$". These partial derivatives are the definition of momentum and energy divided by "c", respectively. When added together, the relationship between action flow in intervals between state snapshots and the state formulation of classic physics modeled in the last section is as follows.

$$dA = \partial A/\partial \underline{q} + (1/c) \cdot \partial A/\partial t = \underline{p} - E/c = 0 \qquad \text{Equation 4.2-2}$$

Besides demonstrating the equivalence of the state and interval formulation this equation is also a kind of continuity equation that expresses the fact that action is neither created or destroyed and flows like an incompressible fluid, i.e. ink, through our model of physical reality. For further information regarding action formulations of classic physics and the Least Action Principle from which Newtonian equations of motion can be derived, the reader is referred to standard texts (Goldstein, 1965, 273). Our task now will be to expand the action-flow model of classic physics into the CAT model developed in Chapter 3 in order to integrate the subjective aspect of conscious beings in a comprehensive physical framework.

4.3 The CAT block universe model

Action is an abstract concept. It can only be visualized as a property of *something happening*. That *something* has been reduced to a material medium that can be characterized by charge and mass. In classic physics, the *happening* is the movement of matter that is calculated using external electromagnetic forces between charges and gravito-inertial forces between masses. The primary deficiency of this scheme rests in the assumption that what happens between recordable states of matter is completely determined by these external gravito-electric forces, leaving no place for subjective experience. In Chapter 3, we introduced the CAT book model to overcome this deficiency. In the next section connects that model to classic physics by proposing an internal aspect of matter and forces between charge and mass as the physical correlates of subjective experiences.

4.3.1 Adding the subjective phase to classic action theory

The conversion of a classic block universe model to a CAT model is accomplished by adding a page between classic physical recordings and explicitly showing objective and subjective phases on the front and back side of the absolute nothingness provided by each page. Figure 4.3-1 shows an oblique view with the 1st-person traveling through the CAT model exactly as he or she would have traveled through a block universe. Figure 4.3-2, however, shows the same model from a 3rd-person god's-eye view in which the material aspects and the action flow through these aspects is more clearly seen.

The extensions we have added to the classic block universe graphic model are summarized as follows:

- Material space is formatted onto the "absolute-nothing" of support pages.
- Matter has future and past as well as subjective and objective sides.
- Matter is basically composed of charge and mass densities.
- Mass and charge centers equate to mass-charge particles in the calculus limit when densities are constant enough to be approximated by points.
- Internal subjective forces are introduced between mass and charge.
- External objective forces remain the gravito-electric classic categories.

Given these additions, the conscious 1st-person experience involves a fusion of the immediate sensations to an icon labeled "1i" and explanatory sensations "1x" of action flowing through the inside and outside of matter.

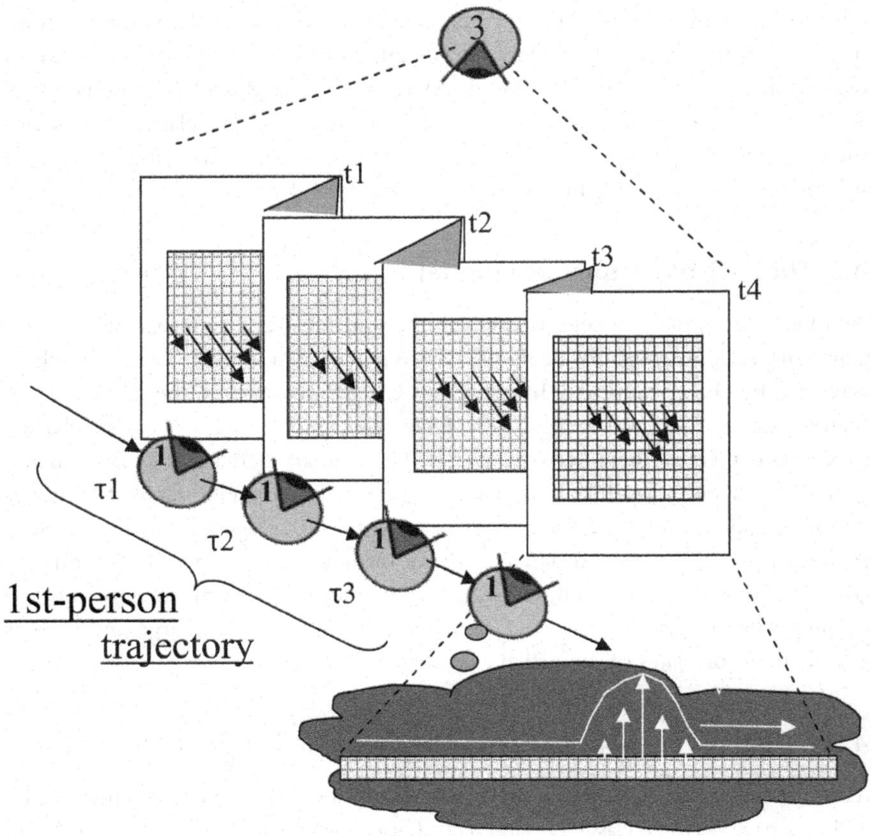

FIGURE 4.3-1 Oblique view of a CAT block universe model mind phase added as second hidden pages

4.3.1.1 Identifying the subjective phase as the inside of matter

Macroscopic objects are constructed by combining infinitesimal volumes of charge and mass into a coherent ensemble that looks similar to the drawing shown in Figure 4.3-3a. We are looking here at a sketch representing an object as seen in the everyday human perspective. We have projected macroscopic charge and mass centers to indicate our belief that material is composed of mass and charge. These absorb and radiate gravito-electric influences from and to the rest of the universe and would be composed of external material cells shown in Figure 4.3-3a.

The traditional method of finding what is inside material is called reductionism and consists of breaking things into smaller pieces. If we break such classic objects into two parts as shown in Figure 4.3-3b then besides the influences coming from and radiating to the rest of the universe there will be gravito-electric interactions between the charges and masses of the parts. These are the forces of classic physics. As we divide the material further into three or more parts, the parts get smaller and

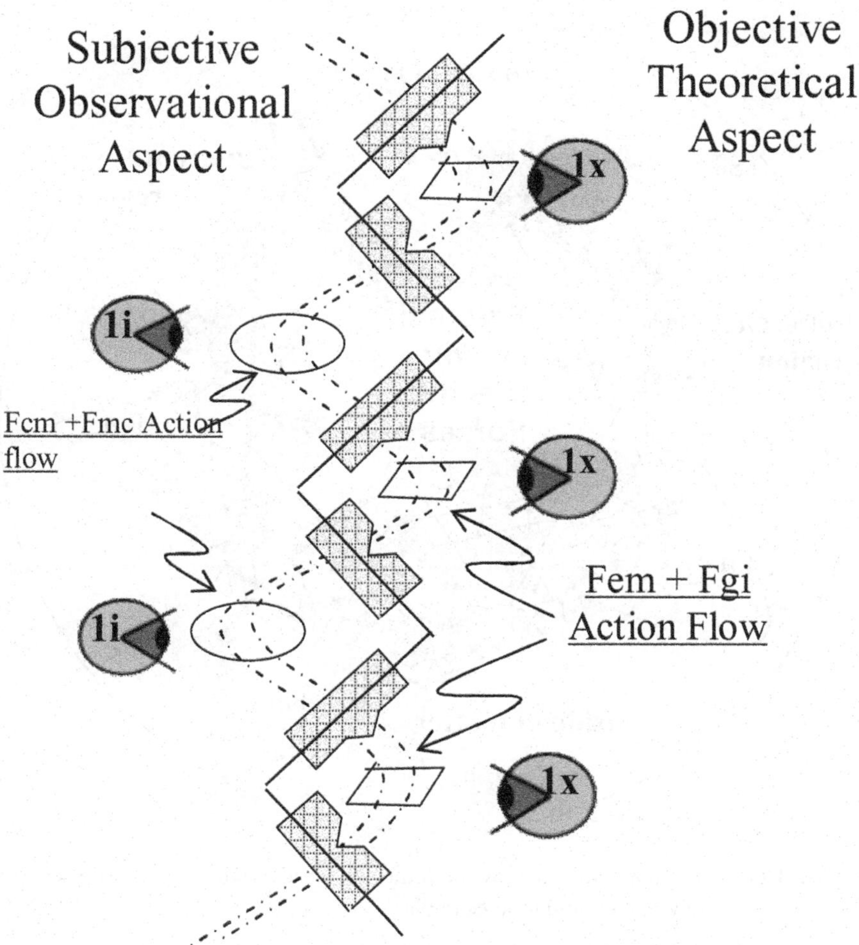

FIGURE 4.3-2 Top-down, god's-eye view of a CAT block universe model

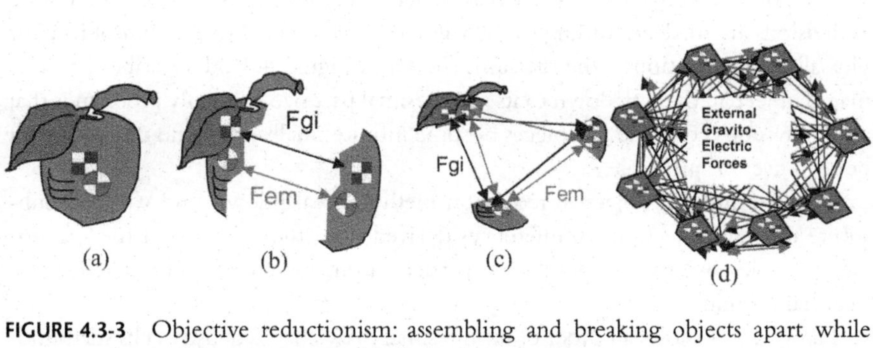

FIGURE 4.3-3 Objective reductionism: assembling and breaking objects apart while keeping gravito-electric forces between parts

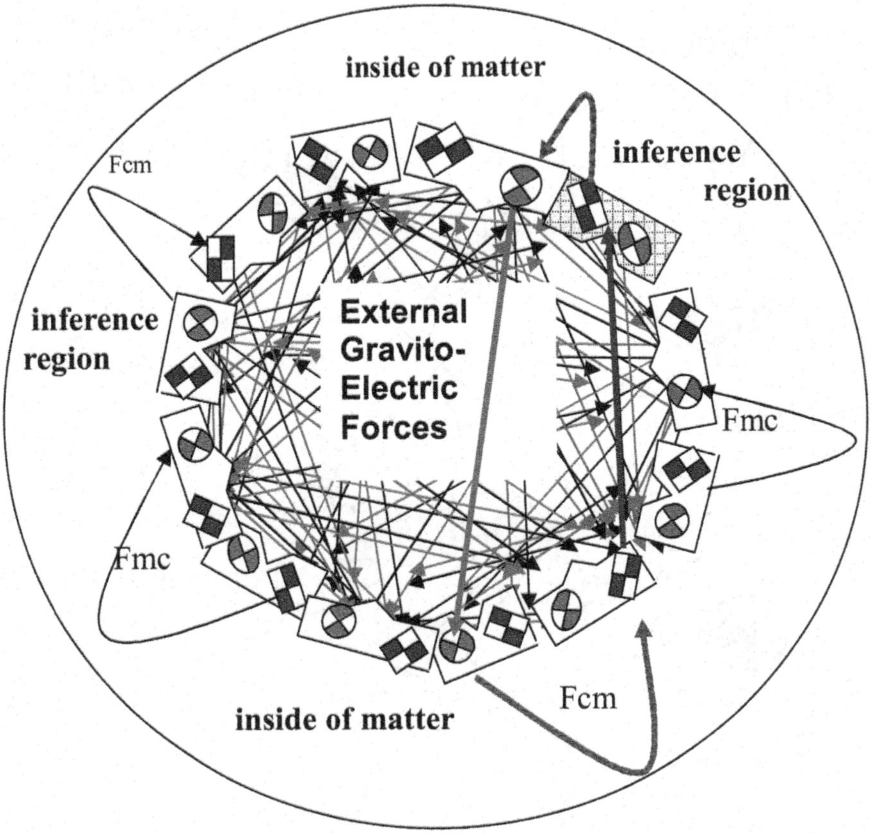

FIGURE 4.3-4 The subjective phase is the limit of objective reductionism: thick lines show one closure loop example

smaller but interactions between parts continue to be implemented with gravito-electric forces external to those parts as shown in Figure 4.3-3c and 4.3-3d. As long as divisions are made according to the rule "a whole is equal to the sum of its parts plus all the interactions", the divisions shown in Figure 4.3-3d describe the same macro object all the way down to its infinitesimal part size. The only problem is that as the divisions continue, the pieces become infinitesimally small and can no longer be seen even in principle.

At this point the objective reduction method breaks down, and we must substitute mental projections of inferences derived from the behavior of the gravito-electric fields in order to define the particles from which we hope macroscopic material is built.

Figure 4.3-4 shows a border of infinitesimal mass-charge density cells surrounding a region of gravito-electric fields. Outside this structure is a theoretical region where inferences and mental projections, no matter how well founded, are all we have to describe the inside of matter.

4.3.1.2 Force lines and fields stay in their domains

By identifying the external view of objects with our everyday experience we relegate the internal aspect of material to the portion inaccessible to our senses and therefore to the domain of quantum theory, which is one example of the broader domains of knowledge generally accessible only through symbolic representations. External gravito-electric forces have been extensively measured and are represented by the straight arrows between parts shown in Figure 4.3-4.

It is important to realize that the arrow tips start and end at the external side of material. That they continue to penetrate into smaller and smaller spaces and particles *is speculation* that requires the classic assumption of a space-time continuum and infinitesimal point particles. Both these assumptions have been challenged by quantum theory and the CAT concept of material-space cells of a finite action size. Thus, a ring of icons forms a boundary between objective and subjective regions where different force fields control the behavior of material.

In CAT, empty space is defined by adding material media to nothing and that material has an exterior and interior side. In the standard model of high-energy physics, all forces are carried by some particles. In the electric domain, the photon is emitted and absorbed at two sides of a force line. In the gravity domain, gravitons connect two sides of mass. It is only when the force carrier is absorbed that a force is exerted, and therefore the two ends of the trajectory of a force-carrying particle always begin and end on material. According to CAT, this interior is governed by new forces between charge and mass. This means gravitational forces, and Maxwell's electromagnetic force fields existing between external sides of material do not penetrate into the interior where conscious forces take over. When density regions of charge and mass are drawn with exterior and interior boundaries their force lines stop at those boundaries.

4.3.2 The nature of material

In our everyday experience, objects consists of solid material we can see and touch from the outside. Adding an inside aspect to a classic block universe allows us to recognize that the perception of solid material is actually the experience of action flowing through the subjective phase of our own cycle. The nature of matter itself has therefore been changed from a thing, moving through time as the solid object it appears to be, to an event happening in all the bigger "Selves". This change introduces modifications in several physical concepts. Specifically, the questions "What is material?", "How is material visualized?" and "How is material shaped?" will be addressed in the following sub-sections.

4.3.2.1 Grounding abstract action with mass-charge visualizations

In classic physics, objects are considered fundamental, and action is an abstract quantity derived from objects moving through space and time. In CAT, action is fundamental, and material is a form of an action. Action per se is a theoretical quantity that cannot be seen directly. It is visualized as the change happening between past and future states of mass-charge densities that are connected by internal subjective and external objective forces. When an activity is closed, the mass-charge densities and their connecting forces are depicted evolving around a cycle (see Figures 2-1 and 1.1-2). These are typically drawn so that the left density performs a measurement and sensation-projection function, and the right density performs a sensation-explanatory and memory-recording function. When the cycle is not closed, the spatial surfaces connect to the surfaces of previous and subsequent cycles forming chains of activity.

In Figure 4.3-5 we show the left and right densities, combined to form three theoretical visualizations, which are typically projected into directly experienced sensations in order to explain their "real" cause. Each projection represents what a piece of matter actually is to adherents of the three main belief categories discussed in this book.

a Materialists believe what they see is the external sides of matter. This is the classic physics theory view of external objects where the internal subjective side is hidden. Here the future-outside of the past instance receives gravito-electric illumination, and the past-outside of the next instance transmits it.

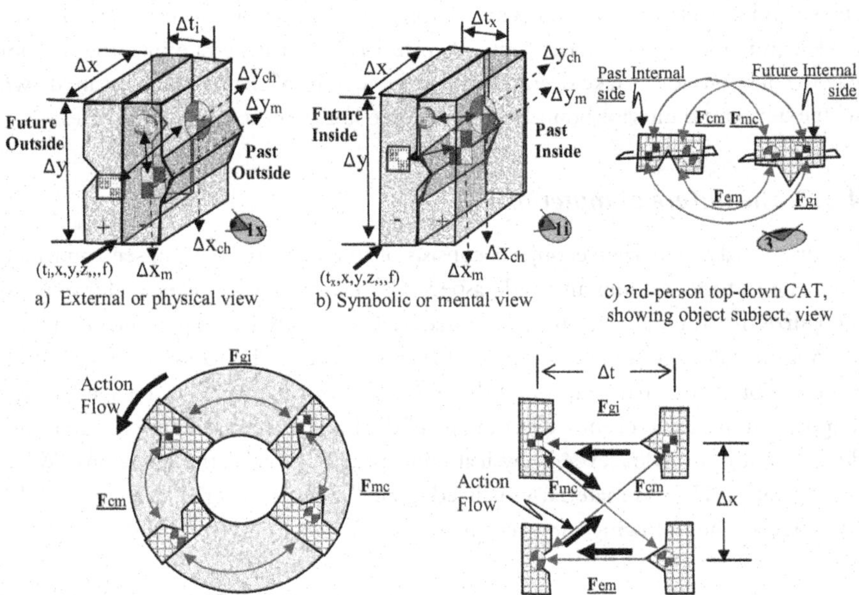

FIGURE 4.3-5 Alternative views of matter density icons with embedded charge and mass centers

Interior force arrows are the forward and backward forces between charge and mass. Exterior force arrows between charges and between masses are not shown for clarity but the action from these forces would flow through the 1st-person external icon labeled "1x".

b Idealists believe what they see is the interior mental side of matter, and the physical side is hidden. Inside, the external gravito-electric forces connect the past external mass and charge with their respective future mass and charge. A symbol is always incorporated in an object but is clothed in its meaning, here represented as the inside surfaces of matter.

c, d, e Three CAT views imaged from a god's eye, or the reader's point of view, where the complete event can be observed. The three views emphasize the object-subject division, the cyclic-action flow and the physical-forward mental-reverse configurations respectively. In these examples, the activity is closed for this small event. It should be noted that transmission and absorption of influences appear to propagate from past to future sides. However, the action in these events continues to flow from future to past due to the motion of the operator's "Now" when executing a "turn-page" in a model or when a "next" operation happens in Reality.

Figure 4.3-5 describes three alternative ways of explaining the same happening. The main direction of change is time, which is symbolically mapped into pages of a book space and here given the coordinate label "t". Views "c" and "d" show time as a cyclic coordinate appropriate for self-contained isolated systems. The quantum spinner double cycle in "c" is due to the inclusion of the subjective mass-charge phase missing in standard quantum theory. Unfolding the double cycle in "d" shows a clear picture of action flow in a self-contained isolated event. There would also be only the sensation of empty space in the observer. If the material part were truly isolated there would be no interfering neighbors. All we would have is the projected visualization of a non-interacting event. In this case, instead of the Cartesian cell shown in Figure 4.3-5a, b and e, the material density would curl up in all directions. The sides would all be directly connected to their opposites and take on the topological form of a multidimensional toroid (see Section 4.3.3.3) in which all the action flows around internal cycles, connecting its internal mass or charges in perpetual motion.

Views a, b and e show linear time and space geometries that are appropriate for representing cyclic activity cells in larger systems. The temporal neighbors are previous and subsequent events, and most action moves along this line. We use Cartesian coordinates "x,y,z" as part names of material cells into which an external object may be divided. In case the cell activity is imbedded in a much larger material event, then all its sides would be abutted against neighbors and thereby subject to action patterns propagating through its imbedding volume of events. The action flow is visualized as the motion patterns of mass and charge centers inside the boundaries of each cell length "Δt, Δx, Δy or Δz". Figure 4.3-5e is especially suited for displaying the isolated action cycle as a building block of larger systems.

Adding such complete cycles in the time and space directions produces the linear space-time plane of special relativity while when such a plane is extended to cosmological scales, the entire structure again closes to produce toroidal displays. Such self-contained cycles become toroidal surface cells representing an observer in his or her universe as shown in Figure 4.3-8.

4.3.2.2 The extension of matter

The visualization of an isolated event is produced in the display space of the visualizer. Such a space is equivalent to the support pages of a book (see Section 3.1). Take the pages away and the real isolated event happens in absolutely nothing. We then have the pure action flow happening in nothing. Unfortunately absolute-nothing has no space points or distances between them and therefore we cannot talk about action happening anywhere unless action itself provides the space by naming its own parts. Such a naming is called formatting and was discussed as a functional operation in Chapter 3. Here we take the next step and transition from function to implementation.

On an abstract material formatting can be imagined by assuming one is completely surrounded by a dense uniform fog whose gray-shade color is proportional to the amount of action happening. Formatting the fog implies inserting systematic color changes by etching black gridlines into the fog, which would signify boundaries of low action between cells. The boundaries of cells outlined by such lines are shown above and the "x,y,z" addresses name the cells. If there is no action, there are no cells and no space is happening.

A flow of action in the form of waves could identify nodes of minimum motion that actualizes such an operation. However to provide a closer tie to classic physical concepts we should remember action measures change and a change in "nothing" creates its opposite which we call something composed of mass and charge. If ch+ and ch- are not separated there would be zero charge. If m+ and m- are not separated there would be zero mass. *Without mass or charge separation into past and future there would be no time. If further charge were not separated from mass there would also be no space.* Thus in the CAT model space and time are properties of the activity which separates mass and charge along directions action may flow.

Action is the material of an event. Its value measures the heftiness or magnitude of change happening in an event. The greater its value the more change has happened in the event. A change that separates the properties of matter requires a commensurate amount of action. In CAT action is the fundamental ingredient added to the "nothing" from which all else is created and therefore action is conceived as a fundamental material of change. Action flowing in nothing separates charge and mass into forms and shapes characterized by the amount of action able to flow in the directions available. However material, whether wood, marble or the wires of a communication network always comes in a form or shape. The form of an event is the shape of its volume. Volume measures the geographic size of an event but does not specify the detailed shape. Shape is defined by the directions material can extend and these directions are its degrees of freedom. How force interactions between orthogonal degrees of freedom form the shape of an event is explicitly addressed in Section 4.4.2.2.

In summary, classic physics assumes matter exists and moves in empty space without changing or involving that space. CAT recognizes space as the fundamental extension property of matter not its container. Material defines space and space requires material to define it. Without material there is nothing.

4.3.2.3 Material degrees of freedom

Figure 4.3-5 shows a finite extension of charge-mass densities along with four center icons and forces between them. These centers are treated like four individual entities that have the ability to move *in the dimensions supplied by the mass-charge density extensions*. Though only three dimensions are easily shown in the human display space the number of extension directions that exist in Reality must be empirically determined by the number of measurable quantities attributed to a material complex. In our example each center has "f" degrees of freedom and can move in any one of them. If the densities were completely homogeneous then all four centers would be collocated at one point in the material medium and one would only speak of a single center of matter. If on the other hand the density gradient exists then the amount of material would be greater on one side rather than the other. Such a gradient can be indicated by a separation between equal and opposite charge or mass centers. For example if some charge moves from the past to the future along a timeline then there is an absence of charge in the past and an excess of charge in the future. Similarly if some charge moves in a spatial direction but the mass does not then the centers of charge and mass would be separated in space. The nonhomogeneous gradients in charge and mass densities can therefore be represented by the four positions of charge and mass centers and the forces inside the density distributions can be summarized by the forces between these four centers.

The identification of center displacements with gradients is convenient when the containment borders of the material region are fixed. This is usually the case for everyday material objects where charge and mass center displacements identify internal gradients along with stress and strain forces. Alternatively when the regions become *small enough so that the attached regions remain homogeneous* then the centers are rigidly attached to the material and their movement signals a displacement of the entire region. In this limit "Δ→→d" and calculus applies, the densities can be treated as infinitesimal mass-charge center points.

The single future absorbing charge center "ch-" of such a homogeneous density is subject to the "Fem" from transmitting "ch+" and the reaction force "<u>Fcm</u>" from the "m+". A center will be in equilibrium if the forces on it are equal and opposite. An entire region will be in equilibrium if all four mass and charge centers are simultaneously in equilibrium. This condition expressed in the following form when the forces pulling all the centers are all in a line and equal,

$$\ldots \rightarrow \underline{Fem} \leftarrow ch^{-} \rightarrow \underline{F^{*}cm} \leftrightarrow \underline{Fcm} \leftarrow m^{+} \rightarrow \underline{F^{*}gi} \leftrightarrow \underline{Fgi} \leftarrow m^{-} \rightarrow$$

$$\underline{F^{*}mc} \leftrightarrow \underline{Fmc} \leftarrow ch^{+} \rightarrow \underline{F^{*}em} \leftarrow \ldots, \qquad \text{Equation 4.3-1}$$

and has been named the extended d'Alembert Principle and is equivalent to the Least Action Principle, which governs all stable states of material. If the force cycle is closed the "F★em" pull force on the past "ch-" is equal and opposite to the opposite pull force "Fem" on future "ch+" and a stable configuration can be found. If the cycle is not closed so the left and right sides are connected to further past and future cycles on each side then the forces may not be equal and position adjustments that change the forces will take place as disturbances in the equilibrium. The construction of larger structures out of building blocks described in Figure 4.3-5e produces empty space when its material remains in equilibrium states. Thus material in equilibrium can form the background plenum through which disturbance action structures propagate. We normally experience these disturbances in the equilibrium space of our own material as objective content. Objects will propagate through the equilibrium mass-charge structure adjusting equilibrium positions until a new equilibrium configuration is reached.

4.3.3 Characteristics of empty material space

Space is perceived as the sensation of equilibrium happenings flowing through the "Now" phase of many parallel action cycles. The action-flow pattern through the "Now", the physical volume and shape of the space, the position and momentum of the charge-mass aspects and the forces between those aspects will all depend upon the equilibrium state of the entire event. In this section we will examine the interrelationship of these parameters and how they determine the activity of the system being modeled when only the material in equilibrium states that form the empty-space background of our experience is considered.

4.3.3.1 The volume of action in equilibrium states

Normally objects are seen contained in space, but space itself is contained in nothing so that its size and shape is determined by the extension of material from which space is composed. The volume "ΔVol" and shape of a finite space region is the sum of the infinitesimal volumes "dVol" of each of the points composing that space "$\Delta Vol = \int all\_points dVol$". These infinitesimal volumes are calculated from the mass-charge center icon separations along available degrees of freedom.

The shape of this volume is determined by the direction of material expansion which in turn is determined by the direction and strength of forces pulling the charge and mass apart. The direction of pull depends upon the number of dimensions available in the generalized coordinates of the media. The action required to extend a volume in any direction is given by

$$dA = \rho_t \cdot (\partial Vol/\partial q_t) \cdot \underline{d}q_t + \Sigma_{all-f} \rho_f \cdot (\partial Vol/\partial q_t) \cdot \underline{d}q_f$$
$$= p_t \cdot \underline{d}q_t + \Sigma_f p_f \cdot \underline{d}q_f$$

Equation 4.3-2

Where the volume gradient is the surface area perpendicular to the expansion direction. When this area is multiplied by a constant density "$\rho_f(q_f)$" at point interval "q_f" the product is the momentum along the spatial extension, which is the linear action density (see Equation 4.1-1). For example, when calculating the extension in the time direction, the spatial cross-section "$\partial Vol/\partial q_t$" is multiplied by a unit dependent constant density "ρ_t" to give the momentum "p_t" along the time extension. This momentum is called energy and when multiplied by the mapped time distance moved "dq_t" results in the action density in the time direction.

When generalizing the expansion in a single direction to a multidimensional space the individual extensions multiplied together are a volume,

$$dVol_f = dq_0 \cdot dq_1 \ldots dq_f = \Pi_f dq_f.$$

Equation 4.3-3

If all degrees of freedom comprising a self-contained Whole is included, this volume is directly related to the amount of action in that Whole by

$$\boxed{A_W = \mathcal{A}_w \cdot Vol_W}.$$

Equation 4.3-4

Where $\mathcal{A}_w$ is the constant average volume density. To the extent action can be visualized as an incompressible fluid, one might imagine the space defining a self-contained event in the form of a circular tube made of pliable material. As the tube circumference lengthens the walls get stretched and become thinner. The volume swept out by the tube material, our timeline, remains constant in proportion to the amount of material action contained in the cycle. We can increase or subtract the volume only by adding or subtracting more material, and with each amount the internal forces will balance when a stable shape is achieved. If this reminds the reader of black-hole properties it is because we self-contained action cycles are viewed from the outside as black holes because the internal subjective phase is ignored.

4.3.3.2 Volume of empty-space equilibrium states

In equilibrium the vector sum of all forces on all the components of a system are zero. A ridged body is an observable example of a system in equilibrium. A block universe or CAT book model of permanent records also describes an equilibrium event in which nothing moves. Figure 4.3-5 shows four forces between charge and mass aspects and Equation 4.3-1 shows the eight ends of these forces as they pull on a charge-mass configuration cycle. When the sum of these forces are zero,

$$0 = \underline{F}_{em} + \underline{F}_{gi} + \underline{F}_{mc} + \underline{F}_{cm} + \underline{F}^*_{em} + \underline{F}^*_{gi} + \underline{F}^*_{mc} + \underline{F}^*_{cm}, \quad \text{Equation 4.3-5}$$

the extended d'Alembert Principle is satisfied and the system is in equilibrium. Since the direction of these forces in an f-dimensional space is arbitrary, the condition is not easily achieved. A trivial condition that satisfies these equations is when all forces are zero. Because all the forces are attractive this can only happen when all the charge-mass centers are co-located at one point in a homogeneous medium. In this case there is no volume to the infinitesimal point, no action expanding the material and no physical volume of the space composed of such points. Such a system is a formless blob of zero volume, where all charges and masses have no location, but their visualization can still be spread out in the "absolute-nothing" of book space. This is the absolute ground state of material, one level of something above nothing. The Big Bang before the energy of action flow is added. This is modeled by an empty book with all the ink in a bottle, which may exist in this action-less state forever.

To examine the next simplest example let's consider isolated material whose only degree of freedom is the time direction in an equilibrium state shown in the god's eye perspective of Figure 4.3-6.

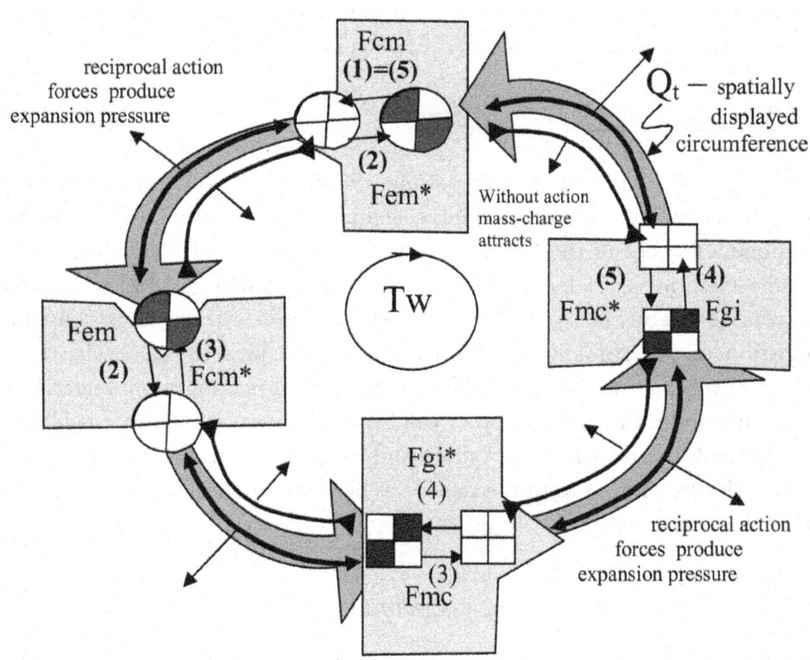

FIGURE 4.3-6 Oscillation waves in four degrees of freedom of a time cycle balanced by reciprocal expansion and mutual attractive forces

Here the cross-section volume "Vol_{w-1}", having one less degree of freedom than the Whole is small enough to be approximated as a line. The total volume of the event "$Vol_w = Q_t \cdot Vol_{w-1}$" can be considered a single line of extension "Q_t". In this approximation we can consider charges and masses to be point particles. Forces as well as action can only propagate along the material length of the timeline represented in book space as "Q_t". The un-filled icons represent the force-field equilibrium positions desired by the material of the Whole while the filled icons are the actual locations' charge-mass points. We now list the sequence of changes that can propagate through the material at the charge or mass positions indicated by the numbered list.

1 A force "Fmc" pushes the upper charge from its current equilibrium position (filled icon) forward along the timeline.
2 The move exerts a force "Fem" on the left charge pushing it forward while the upper charge feels a reaction force "Fem*" that retards it back toward its equilibrium position.
3 While the left charge is moved from equilibrium it exerts an internal "Fcm" force on the bottom mass while feeling a reaction force "Fcm*" back toward its equilibrium.
4 While the bottom mass is moved from equilibrium it exerts a force "Fgi" on the right mass while feeling a reaction force "Fgi*" back toward its equilibrium.
5 While the right mass is moved from equilibrium it exerts a force "Fmc" on the upper charge while feeling a reaction force "Fmc*" which returns it to equilibrium. We are now back to 1).

Because the system is isolated there is no dissipation into external degrees of freedom and the oscillation continues to move as a compression wave around the timeline circumference forever. The physical length of the circumference "ΔQ_t" is determined by the size of the oscillating motion. An analogous phenomena can be observed when a metal ring is hit tangentially. As the compression pulse from the collusion point propagates around the ring, friction heats the molecules expanding the ring. When the length of the circumference is increased, the volume "$Volw = (Qt+\Delta Qt) \cdot Vol_{w1}$" is also increased.

Our step-by-step description of activity in this cycle was appropriate for a pulse of action. From our god's-eye perspective an action density rotates infinitesimal bits of action through each of the charge-mass points thereby producing the infinitesimal vibrations around each equilibrium point. If the shaded arrows represent mass-charge densities their action content is incorporated as distributed oscillations expanding the circumference. Since the icons have always represented fictitious centers of *homogenous enough* densities, the material and the same vibrational activity is distributed around the entire circumference of the cycle thus maintaining the cycle at a given radius and a physical volume proportional to the action held in the loop's dynamic configuration.

4.3.3.3 The topology of an isolated system

Figure 4.3-6 showed how the force lines in the material medium accompany a flow of action around a time cycle. The cross section of the cycle was assumed small enough so we could ignore the action in the spatial degrees of freedom. The addition of parallel time cycles introduces a space-time topology. The nature of that topology is guided by the symmetry of our subjective experience. In CAT an isolated event having a permanent center is perfectly reasonable since we conscious beings usually feel as though we are at the center of our own Universe. However a theoretical model, constructed from a 3rd-person perspective, must deal with representations including all of us beings and must explain how each one can logically conclude – not intuitively feel – that he or she is at the center of their universe.

We have usually represented space cells as a cube of material that recreates itself by exactly repeating an activity cycle between each page. Such cubes represent small Cartesian spaces in which local experiences are displayed in front of one's nose. By treating the front and back covers of our CAT book models as the origin and destiny respectively, a closed time loop was assigned to such spatial cubes. The edges of these cubes could collide with neighboring loops (see Figure 4-1) so that interactions between the parts of an approximated Whole could be represented. If each of these space-cubes are at their own centers, the combination of all the space-cubes must form closed spatial loops in all directions.

If all the cells in the first single space direction are added together to make a circular "Q_1" axis and these are multiplied by all the cells that make the time loop "Q_t" axis, the result is a two-dimensional volume in book space. Temporal cross sections look like a circle on each page as shown in Figure 4.3-7a. The thin line is the only material volume in the nothingness of the pages. At this one page instance it consists of many space cells mapped around the circular "Q_1" axis and many time cells mapped around the book page axis. A blow-up of a segment on this line shows the time and 1st space direction but also an additional 2nd space direction. This second "Q_2" direction is the surface of the line which is actually a small tube

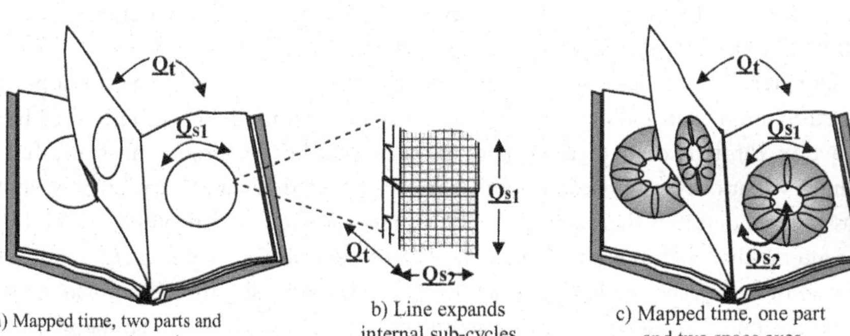

a) Mapped time, two parts and one space axis each

b) Line expands internal sub-cycles

c) Mapped time, one part and two space axes

FIGURE 4.3-7 Closed time and space dimension in a CAT book model: three orthogonal degrees-of-freedom space is a torus on each page

shown expanded as a torus in Figure 4.3-7c. Again the actual space cells are located on the surface of this now three-dimensional torus. Each such cell has six immediate neighbors, two in time, and two in each of the space direction. Adding more dimensions becomes difficult to visualize. Mathematically the operation of multiplying all cells in an axis with all the cells in another is called an "outer product" of the axis vectors indicated by an "x" in a circle. Multiplying many dimensions together gives a multidimensional f-volume shown in Equation 4.3-6.

$$\mathrm{Vol}_f = \underline{\mathbf{Q}}_t \otimes \underline{\mathbf{Q}}_1 \otimes \underline{\mathbf{Q}}_2 \ldots \otimes \underline{\mathbf{Q}}_f \,. \qquad \text{Equation 4.3-6}$$

Such volumes look like surfaces in a higher dimension, but such a surface is composed of individual cells that have f-dimensions and "2f" direct neighbors. Every individual who feels him- or herself located at any here-and-now cell array shown in Figure 4.3-7b will be in a completely symmetric relationship to his or her Universe space as long as the axes are closed.

Since the human display space is limited to three dimensions, we can only visualize a two-dimensional torus at one here and now instance. Figure 4.3-8 shows the human view of a torus with symbolic time and a single space axis mapped onto its surface. Time is mapped into the large circles. The small circle represents a cyclic space axis which when copied into the Now instance of an open CAT book would look like the circle on the left page. Pages can be imagined stacked around the circumference. A 1st-person eyeball is located at one space-cube in the space-time surface. The internal action-flow structure of this cube was shown in Figure 4.3-5e. As the human projects action-flow disturbances from the retina further out into space he or she also projects the sensation of their causes back in time. The dashed lines emanating from the eyeball represent the edges of a light cone.

As long as the observer projects a cause trace – here in a linear tangent plane to the toroid surface – but the actual light causing the observer's sensation rotates around the curved surface and the projection will end at his or her event horizon.

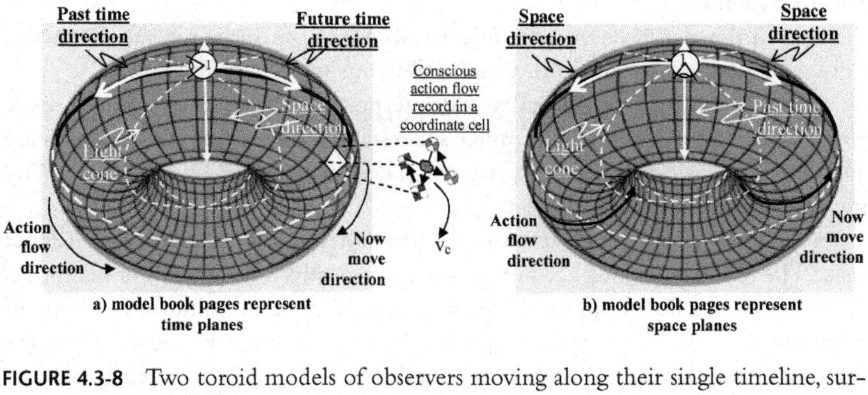

FIGURE 4.3-8 Two toroid models of observers moving along their single timeline, surrounded by neighboring timelines making a closed orthogonal space-time

A contemporary cosmologist would interpret the time rotation as a red shift and postulate space shrinks as we look deeper into space. A cosmologist would further postulate a big bang at the center of the donut hole. Such cosmologists have not incorporated the subjective phase into their calculation and therefore have not closed the loop through themselves when they project their theory out from their "Now" instrument measurement records.

The form of a perfect multidimensional torus is symmetric in all directions and at all space-time points. Its surface volume determines its size and the amount of action stored in its form. The extension of its degrees of freedom determine its form. When undisturbed, its complete symmetry implies symmetric gradients exist and all charge and mass density ratios are constant for all "dVol" points. Such forms are the empty-space ground states of all isolated action structures and disturbances in these structures become the content experienced by that empty space.

4.3.3.4 1st-person experience in an isolated universe

The readers 3rd-person visualization of empty space shown in Figure 4.3-8 is an external point of view in which we see action mapped into volumes that are visualized as surfaces in our display space. In this section we will connect this with our personal experience by entering the space in which the eyeball is located and see what things look like from his or her 1st-person location.

The single degrees of freedom along a line we modeled in Figure 4.3-6 is relatively trivial. To model nontrivial empty space, as encountered in everyday experience, we will imagine reentering a 1st-Person Laboratory and map the wall joint lines appearing in our field of view with the "dt,dx,dy,dz . . . qf" space axis lines of a multidimensional toroid. Now imagine yourself moving in time in a 1st-Person Laboratory (1st-PL) looking at the model of the 1st-PL, which is seen as a cube imbedded in a space-time surface. Only the "dt" and "dx" edges can be explicitly shown in Figure 4.3-8, but as you look at the tables inside the walls of your laboratory you can easily imagine yourself located on the surface of the Earth surrounded by a homogeneous spherically symmetric distant masses, as is the case in the classic observable universe where the material mass is symmetrically extended in all directions. Graphically your imagined situation is depicted by Figure 4.3-9a. Classic physics would interpret the situation as a distant outer ring of material surrounding an inner spherical ball of local material producing a downward gravitational force of attraction counterbalanced by a corresponding upward electric force of repulsion.

In CAT the forces are symptoms of action flowing through phases of material space. The reader is looking at a purely spatial perspective in which his or her model "self" is feeling a flow from the outer past ring into the center future "Now" point while the reader's motion in time is perpendicular to the page. Figure 4.3-9b shows the same event only turned sideways so that time is shown along the horizontal axis. The directions of forces from one material component to another is indicated by

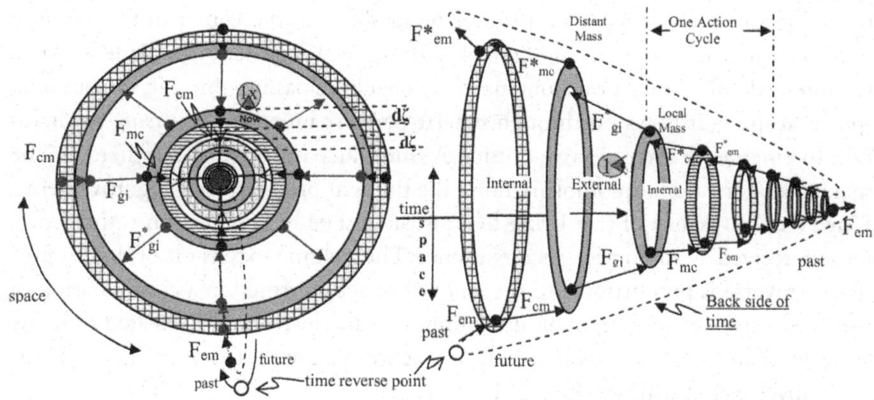

a) Seeing volume when looking down the time line at the past

b) oblique view of the space-time torus in discrete steps

FIGURE 4.3-9 Action flow of a symmetric matter distribution in equilibrium, forces balanced, 1st-person time flow mapped to radius along a large-small axis of one's universe

the arrow point. The pull of such forces is from the tip side back to the ball side of the arrow. The sequence of influence can be described as follows:

1 Gravitational forces “F_{gi}”, from the distant mass ring to the local mass will pull the local mass outward in all directions. A reverse force “F^*_{gi}” pulls the outer ring inward.
2 The local mass force “F_{mc}” pulls on the negative charge outward, separating the charge component of its material.
3 A electromagnetic force “F_{em}” is now created between the separated negative and positive charge pulling the positive charge outward while its oppositely directed “F^*_{em}” pulls the negative charge inward.
4 The positive charge density then pulls “F_{cm}”, the next mass ring, inward while the reverse force “F_{mc}” pulls the next mass outward. Force labels are no longer shown as the spatial extension of the cycles get smaller.
5 Next, the outer mass having been pulled and separated from the next inner mass, a gravitational force pair appears which except for scale repeats the situation encountered in step 1 between the distant and local mass densities.
6 The further inner mass pulls on deeper charge volumes, separating positives and negatives, which pull on each other and on to yet deeper masses.
7 The direction eventually disappears into the small spatial sizes where we can no longer draw the material but the progress is indicated by the dashed line which wraps around to the positive charge ring outside the original mass ring we started with in step 1.

The diagrams show how the force lines in the material medium accompany a flow of action around a cycle that travels from large to small and back to large in both directions. The 1st-person believes he or she is in the center of the universe but from our god's-eye view in Figure 4.3-7b we see his or her Now plane is a cross section to the flow of action along parallel radial lines passing through surrounding spherical space. It flows on through the 1st-person's inner self, reversing its direction to emerge on the objective outside. As introduced in Section 3.2 there will be many feed-forward loops implementing the thought processes of a cognitive being. However the essence of that being in an isolated state of equilibrium is the action loop perceived as an empty-space existence. The volume extension of this empty-space universe is proportional to the amount of action stored in a configuration of balanced forces extending in all directions. For an electronically isolated universe conventionally known as a black hole, the action volume relation has been extensively investigated (Brown et al., 2016).

We have cheated a bit. Figure 4.3-7 does not accurately represent our situation on the Earth because the action turn-around happens in material sub-surface layers long before the Earth's center of mass is reached. Electromagnetic forces hold the mass up and action flows back to outer space at lower (colder) frequencies. What we have actually shown is the 1st-person's model when he or she is in the center of a homogeneous universe. In other words we have replaced the gravito-electric interaction in the Earth with the idealized model in which all the Earth's material is concentrated as a black hole in the center to make *the point* shown in my thesis (see Figure 1). Parallel action appears to flow from the large through our Now into the small and back. From our god's-eye perspective in Figure 4.3-7b we see that our Now plane is a cross section to the flow of action along parallel radial lines passing through spherical space. It flows on through our inner-subjective self, reversing its direction to emerge on the objective outside.

In CAT we conscious beings experience the inside of our own black hole through which action flows from a subjective inside to an objective outside giving new meaning to the worm hole tunnel of science fiction fame.

4.3.4 Time, phase and distance

In CAT the words time, phase and distance are names for the extensions defining the *form* in which action exists. For models of isolated events, such as the universe, we can no longer treat time as an external independent parameter, because our own self is also represented in the model and must measure time from intrinsic model quantities. This section will explain how this can be done by considering the following analogies.

If we take a road trip with a car from some start point "0" along a path to some endpoint "L", our position will have changed. The path length of the change is a function of the two endpoints and the path taken between them. Assume we are restricted to measure such a length from within the car. The odometer measures the distance by the number of wheel turns. The fuel gage measures the distance by the amount of gasoline burned. We could take the same trip symbolically with a ball point pen on a map and measure the distance by the amount of ink used or the number of turns the ball makes. In CAT the meaning of the "ink used" or "gas burned" translates to the amount of action happening in the event. The path is the form of the action and movement along the path defines the change of state. Its endpoints are the states Q_0 and Q_L. The trip is the whole event being modeled.

Using CAT notation the amount of action per wheel rotation at a single point is

$$dA(Q) = (dA(Q)/\underline{dQ}) \cdot \underline{dQ}. \qquad \text{Equation 4.3-7}$$

Where: Q = the position label for small-enough points along the path Q
$\underline{dQ}$ = the distance for a wheel turn
$dA(Q)/\underline{dQ} = \underline{P(Q)}$ = the rate of gas burned per $\underline{dQ}$ at point Q
dA = a small-enough amount of gas burned

The rate of gas burned per wheel rotation is called the generalized momentum in classic physics. P(Q) normally varies as the car moves along the path because acceleration, hills and valleys require variable amounts of gas.

We can measure the distance traveled by making marks at every 2π wheel rotation or making marks every constant amount of gas burned and counting the number of marks shown in Figure 4.3-10.

The total gas burned on the trip "ΔA" is the sum of all the gas burned during each wheel rotation along the path.

$$\Delta A = \Sigma dA(Q) = \Sigma(dA(Q)/\underline{dQ}) \cdot \underline{dQ} = \Sigma \underline{P}(Q) \cdot \underline{dQ}$$
$$= \underline{P}_{\Delta Q} \cdot \underline{\Delta Q}. \qquad \text{Equation 4.3-8}$$

Where: Σ indicates the sum over all cycles (wheel rotations) between Q_0 to Q_L.
ΔQ = the sum of all wheel turns or the total path length of the trip
$P_{\Delta Q}$ = the average momentum (burn rate) along the total path

The analogy of the car trip or its symbolic pen trip will be used in the remainder of this section as a heuristic aid to explain the concepts of time, phase and distance

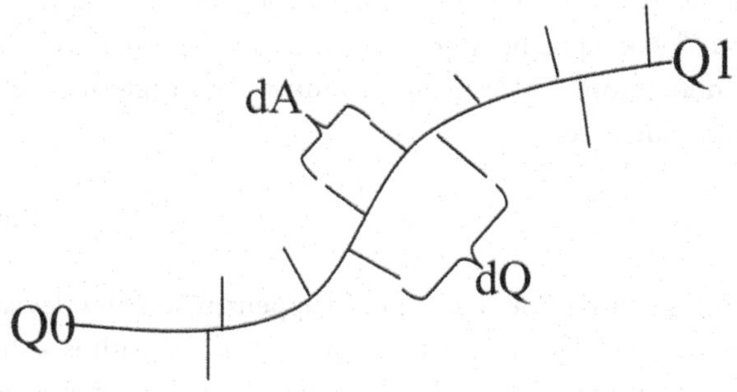

FIGURE 4.3-10 Constant action and state distance marks along a system timeline path

within the context of an event containing a 1st-person. The use of variables such as P and ΔQ are concepts of burn rate and path intervals along which a car travels. They are all simplifications used for summarizing the detailed internal changes (p_f, dq_f) happening in a complex system.

4.3.4.1 Path selection and the Least Action Principle

We have shown how to calculate the action for a trip by counting the gas burned and the length by counting wheel turns along the path. But what determines the path? The shortest distance is how the crow flies. But a car must travel on the ground. Passing over hills and dales or plowing through walls and fences burns a lot of gas. On the other hand selecting the most even terrain, even if paved, requires long circumnavigations that require many wheel turns and may burn more gas. A logical compromise, and the one that Nature takes, is to minimize the product of gas-burn-rate times wheel turns thus calculating the total amount of gas or ink and by analogy the action required for the trip. This means taking reasonable short cuts, driving around steep mountains and over small hills. In mathematical nomenclature this compromise is known as the Least Action Principle and can be calculated by the techniques of Variational Calculus (Morse and Feshbach, 1953). The idea is to consider each wheel-turn "dQ" and make a decision regarding the direction to turn the steering wheel. For each direction angle "θ" we calculate the gas-burn P(Q) required and choose the direction that minimizes the action for that step. In mathematical notation the procedure is denoted by the variational symbol δ, and the right direction is the one that requires the minimum action,

$$\delta dA(Q) = \delta \underline{P}(Q(\theta)) \bullet \underline{dQ}(\theta) = \text{minimum} \qquad \text{Equation 4.3-9}$$

Actually calculating the minimum rests on the realization that if one has the best path and knows the best angle "θ", and one deviates from it by dθ, one will be following a worse path because the burn rate would go up. The situation can be described graphically by plotting the angle relative to the burn rate as shown in Figure 4.3-11.

The minimum burn rate happens at the bottom of the valley when the slope is zero. *In CAT we also recognize this as the equilibrium point the rest of the universe wants any system to be at this instant.* The slope at the minimum point is calculated by taking the change in momentum "dP" required to move an infinitesimal distance "dθ" at the equilibrium point as zero,

$$\underline{dP}(Q(\theta))/\underline{d\theta} = 0. \qquad \text{Equation 4.3-10}$$

The minimum burn rate or action flow happens when any deviation from the lowest point in the valley is zero. This does not mean the path is a straight line but rather that it is determined by the shape of the momentum curve as it progresses through time. That curve models the bumps with features encountered along the

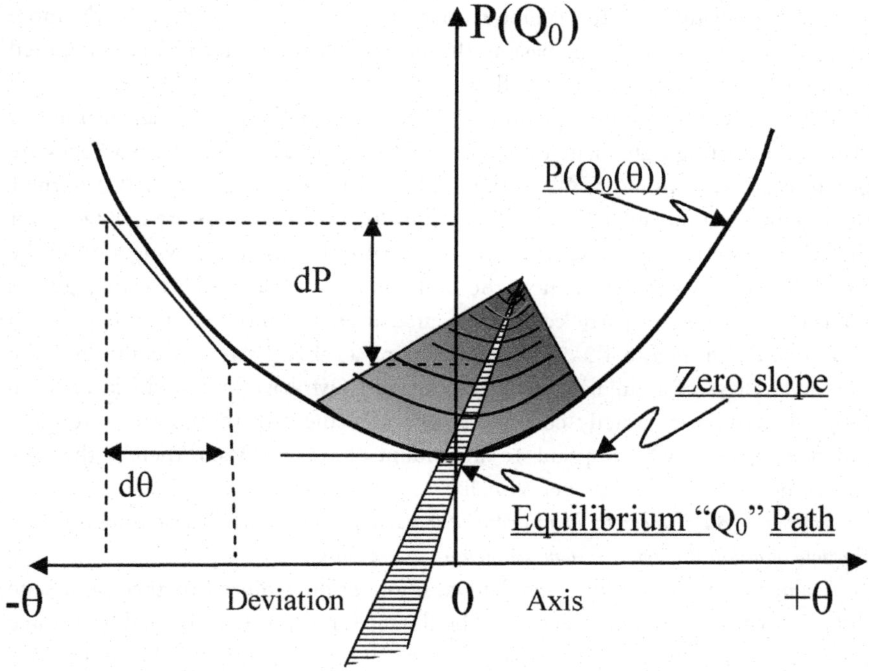

FIGURE 4.3-11 Minimum-action point defines the equilibrium path

way. It resembles the shape of a mountain valley through which a river flows. The water moves along the lowest path. If one were to ride a motorcycle down a smooth version of the valley the forces on the wheel would automatically guide it down the lowest path. However if the driver interferes and turns the handlebars so that the bike climbs up the sides a restoring force would push the bike back to its dynamic equilibrium path. This tendency for an undisturbed system to follow the minimum-action path and when disturbed to oscillate about such a path describes a universal behavior encountered in both physical material and many disciplines built from aggregations of such material.

The lesson here is that the natural measure of distance is measured in constant action units not meter units. In these units the path chosen by any system is a minimum distance and can also be identified as a straight line in an appropriately curved coordinate frame.

4.3.4.2 Definition of time

Time is what clocks measure. That "what" is associated with something felt flowing through the 1st-person's perceptive space. What is flowing through Now is action coming from the future and projected into our observable experience in the past as we move into the future. The 1st-person point of view is projected straight down the timeline and experiences the flow of action directly. The 3rd-person view is a theoretical explanation of the same flow viewed from the side using an internal visualization channel of the symbolic elements processing the flow. To do more than have a feeling of change passing through one, a clock mechanism is required to appear in the 1st-person action flow.

Clocks are physical systems. Equations 4.3-7 and 4.3-8 provide a generalized nomenclature for relating state changes to action flow in an arbitrary system. Clocks are not arbitrary systems. What makes them different is that the action dA(Q) burned, the distance dQ moved and the momentum P(Q) for each step, are constant over the whole path traveled. The trip is now the path of a pointer moving around the clock dial. The wheel turn is now the cycle of an oscillator. Each rotation pushes the car, now a pointer particle, around a circular energy-momentum valley shown as a clock dial in Figure 4.3-12. By constructing a car and carefully controlling the hills and valleys of a circular test track it traverses we have built a clock. The trip progress marks here exactly coincide so the movement of the pointer through a distance dQ exactly corresponds to an amount of action dA and thereby the flow of change we call time has been visualized.

Time in CAT is therefore identified as a measure of change, and change is measured by the flow of action through a system we identify as our clock.

Change is measured by a standard flow of action required to traverse a state distance of a clock at a constant rate. The distance in this case is defined by a single cycle, which in our car analogy was the distance of wheel rotation, but in practice our unit of time is defined as the duration of 9,192,631,770·dt, where dt is the cycle of radiation from a transition between two hyperfine energy levels of Cesium 133. At the fundamental level we define time by the action happening in a system constructed to report every time a constant amount of action has passed. The standard amount of action is given by Planck's constant h = 6.62607004 × 10^{-34} Joule-Seconds. This action is the minimum irreversible change required to record an

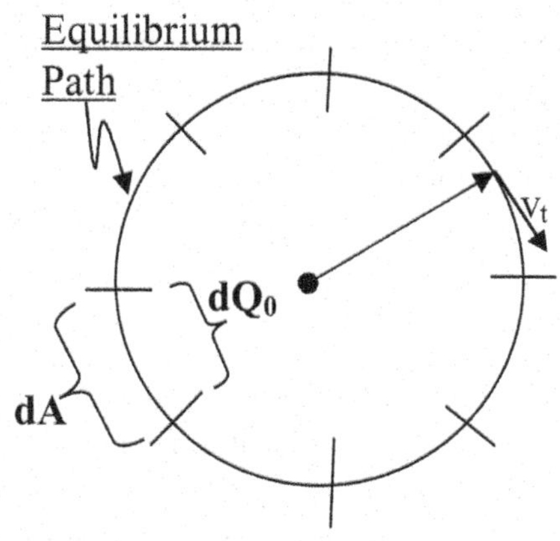

FIGURE 4.3-12 A clock-pointer motion changes position state proportional to action

interaction. Once this value is known we can measure time by counting the number of actions happening in a system through which action passes at a constant rate.

The constancy of the action flow rate is guaranteed by the hyperfine line width produced by the Cs 133 energy transition. This is an empirically measurable fact. It means we do not need to know the underlying details happening inside the action cycle as long as we can be sure the average action flow between completions marked by interactions remains constant. We do not know the exact mechanism which connects the activity producing the radiation from a Cesium clock to the state of the universe as seen in the motion of the stars and the macroscopic objects observed in daily life, nor is current physics much concerned with the cause of the infinitesimal variations in "dt". For practical purposes it is sufficient that nine billion variations occurring in such activities statistically cancel when the measurement of one second is carried out.

4.3.4.3 The phase of an action cycle

The phase of an event is directly associated with the stages or parts of an overall activity. Phases are marked by recognizable activity features. If we apply objective reductionism to look inside an automobile, we would observe the four phase combustion cycle which repeats every "2π" phase angle to move the rubber wheels' interfacing with the ground. If the car were isolated – jacked up – this "2π" phase sequence would still execute, only no movement along the road would be detected. In Appendix A4.2 we show how the internal activities of an isolated system with an arbitrary number of degrees of freedom can be reduced to a single degree-of-freedom system by calculating two global parameters,

$$E_w = E_w(pf,qf), \qquad T_w = T_w(pf,qf), \qquad \text{Equation 4.3-11}$$

where "E_W" is the total energy in and "T_W" is the name of the global state interval in which the action flow occurs. Often the event name "W" used as a subscript is omitted when a Whole or its approximation is obvious. How fast the global state proceeds through a "2π" cycle of phases cannot be specified until the car is put back on the road and its speed is measured by an external observer. Of course auto mechanics can look inside the car and make such external measurements on its moving parts in the repair shop, but when the National Bureau of Standards defines time by counting cycles of action they cannot directly see how the phases of the internal events produce the motion they can observe.

The cause of the observed radiation cycle, which we have associated with a small-enough measured time interval "dt", cannot be directly observed because it happens inside material (see Section 4.3.1.1). Quantum physicists have theories that explain why the state sequence "Tw" produces such extremely consistent wheel turns in our analogy, but practically speaking its constancy is an empirical fact. The Cs 133 energy-level transition is called hyperfine because the radiation frequency emerging from it produces extremely narrow spectral lines. Such lines are found experimentally and they are narrow because the radiation producing them are nearly monochromatic.

The quantum theorists acknowledge that some activity happens inside material and whatever it is can be mapped around a phase line parameterized by a phase angle "φ". This angle rotates from zero to "2π" whenever a complete execution returns to the initial state. In CAT we adopt the nomenclature of classic physics for describing whatever mechanism is inside material in order to be able to visualize the flow of action as moving things. A time period "ΔTw" required for such a system to repeat its state is therefore simply a name change for the "2π" activity. Whether the duration of such a state change is labeled by "ΔTw", "ΔQw" or "$\Delta\varphi$" and the corresponding *rate of action* flow is termed "Ew", "Pw" or angular momentum "Aw", is a preference of language. Such preferences are not as important as understanding the flow of action and interaction that actually happens inside material in any language. The various definitions of time encountered when an isolated system is divided into two parts will now be discussed.

4.3.4.4 Measuring time in an isolated system

Since Newton, time was specified by an external parameter that moved relentlessly from past to future, driving all activity along its steady course, unaffected by any efforts from us mortal beings. The practical use of time required the construction of systems called clocks. The traditional clock is the universe. The pointer is the earth's prime meridian, which rotates against the celestial sphere with constant angular momentum "P_φ" stored in its angular motion. The state of the earth clock is measured by the phase angle "φ" of the pointer. A complete rotation consists of $\Delta\varphi = 2\pi$ radians, which is called a sidereal day. The action due to spin in a sidereal day is

$$\Delta A = P_\varphi \cdot \Delta\varphi = P_\varphi \cdot 2\pi = E_{spin} \cdot \Delta t =\sim 4.46 \times 10^{34} \text{ Joule-Seconds}$$

Equation 4.3-12

Where: Δt = the sidereal day of 86164.0916 Seconds
P_φ = angular spin momentum of the earth ˜ $7.10\text{x}10^{33}$ Joule-Sec/Rad
URL: http://web.mit.edu/8.01t/www/materials/InClass/WE_Sol_W11D1-1.pdf
E_{spin} = Spin energy of the earth

The amount of action in the earth rotation event is the fundamental measure of change. The terms in Equation 4.3-12 shows it can be specified in time, phase or distance units but ultimately change is perceived as a flow of action.

When the rest of the universe is identified as our clock, and we are measuring it, the Whole is divided into two parts, us and the clock. We introduce Figure 4.3-13 to explore the use of the Universe as a clock in a CAT book record describing two systems. The center of this diagram shows a top-down view of the split page book model shown as a cycle in Figure 3.4-4 and linearly in Figure 4.3-2. This view allows us to map sequential interior and exterior aspects of matter around a loop of activity records. A pointer arrow moves around the pages indicating the progress of the model operator as he or she copies, processes and projects the meaning of the symbols in playback mode.

We've drawn two shaded rings outside the circle of pages in Figure 4.3-13. The radial thickness of these rings represents the instantaneous energy of the systems simulated in the book. The inner ring represents a system recording a constant amount of action on each pair of the split pages. An operator moving at a constant page rate would experience a constant amount of action per page. The total area of the inner ring represents the total action of the system "A_c" recorded at a constant action per page.

If the spinning earth in the universe has been adopted for our clock, the energy "Ec" and angular momentum "Pc" are constant since phase (2p) and time period (Tau) are simply different ways of labeling the distance around the ring. The total action for the system is expressed in these two coordinate frames by, "$P_c \cdot 2p = A_c = Ec \cdot Tau$". In our 1st-Person Laboratory view the motion of the spinning earth is tethered to the wall clock; therefore if the operator turns the pages at a constant wall-clock rate the operator would experience the action flowing through this simulated system at a constant rate and would be justified in calling the record of this inner rim system his or her clock. Once the wall clock is registered with the operator's page-turn rate, the operator would be justified in concluding that the rest of the recordings gives him or her an accurate experience of a scaled reality.

The reason for this accuracy is that the wall-clock mechanism was simulated by the action flow in the inner cycle. If the author of the CAT model had chosen to record the motions of the second system in constant actions per page, then as shown in the lower left of Figure 4.3-13 the time or phase intervals would no longer map into the constant time or energy of the inner rim system. Turning pages at constant action rate of the second system would not be constant when measured by wall-clock intervals. This does not mean choosing one or the other system necessarily leads to an incorrect description of reality, but *by choosing any part of a Whole as one's clock forces energy and time definitions onto the parts not chosen.* If instead of the wall clock the operator had chosen to register the page-turn rate with the second system, then an equally accurate experience of the scaled reality would be achieved. The only difference is that what is hanging on the wall is no longer one's clock.

The CAT model represents a single isolated system, such as a universe, with a formatted book. When such a universe is divided into parts then the rate and distance is calculated from the whole activity as shown in Appendix A4.2. In energy-time units the average energy is "E_w", while the distances are the time intervals of the whole ΔT_w, and both these quantities are functions of action rate and distance of all the constituent parts. For small-enough action intervals in our two system example, the incremental action of the Whole is given by

$$dAw = E_w\left(E_c(t), E_s(t), t\right) \cdot dT_w\left(E_c(t), E_s(t), t\right). \qquad \text{Equation 4.3-13}$$

Where the individual energies and moment are calculated using a measured clock system time "t". By choosing one system as a clock and assuming it runs at a

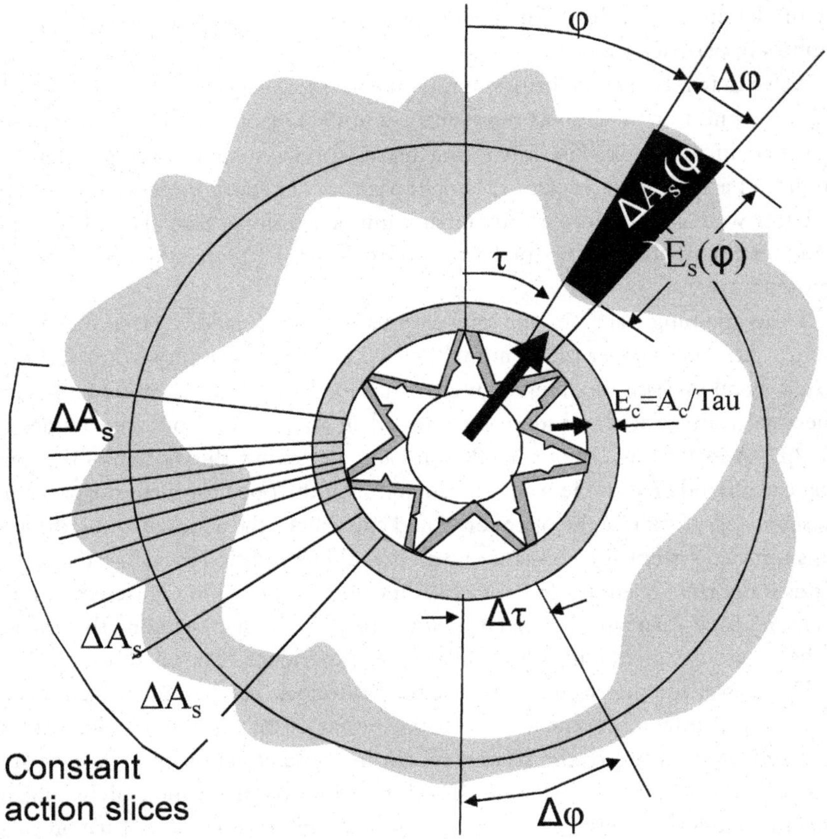

FIGURE 4.3-13 Two parts of a whole one defined as a clock creates variable personal time for the other: shows three times "T_w, t, τ" that are involved

constant action rate, the energy of the second system is no longer constant. The effect of this calculation for the total distance based upon the amount of action flow implies that both systems will not run at exactly constant energy or at a constant distance. No matter how big the clock, if the whole is divided into two parts the parts will interact and change each other.

The significance of this interaction is enormous. The definition of time is no longer the god-given external parameter introduced by Newton, which was carried forward into classical and quantum physics. Time as measured by a clock no longer proceeds at its steady pace irrespective of the action executed by separated parts. *To the extent our bodies are parts of the Universe they effect the clock rate.* In CAT measured time is directly related to the state of the specific system or action loop whose interactions are adopted as one's clock. The evolution of every identifiable system, or action loop when approximated as an isolated system, can however be assigned its personal time. Because the distance between the phases of one's own lifetime are of personal significance they might better be measured by one's personal time. Personal time is the abstract Newtonian parameter of classic physics calculated from the average motion of the entire event in question. When "You", the reader, models your observable body self as the second system in Figure 4.3-13 your own action flow rather than the rest of the Universe becomes your measure of time. Implications of such changes will be addressed in Chapter 8.

The realization that time is no longer an external parameter, but dependent upon the observer was first popularized by Einstein in his special and general relativity theory. In Einstein's theory the letter "τ" is called the proper time. Proper time is defined as the time measured by a clock moving in a coordinate frame whose activities are synchronized by coordinate clocks measured to produce coordinate time "t". In our previous discussion the coordinate time is associated with system "1" while proper time is identified with system "2". The critical difference is that Einstein's clocks are parts of his concept of an independent physical reality. In CAT that reality is a Whole, which is its own observer and we independent beings are approximated as Wholes in which we are the observer. That observer experiences space as his or her own subjective aspect buried in the interval between two phases of the observer's own material. Any clock appearing in the space of a Whole is an artifact, explaining an interaction, which is subject to the physics of that Whole. When isolated during periods between interactions an external Whole evolves independently of the time defined by any observable clock outside that Whole. The realization that we are all, to first approximation, isolated systems running at our own rate explains both the statistical nature of quantum mechanics and its incompatibility with Einstein's theories.

The only time satisfying Newton's criteria for absolute progress is the abstract personal time of the Whole given by the distance measured by the "Qw" or "Tw" scale. These are calculated from all the position and momentum states in all degrees of freedom (see Appendix A4.2) in an isolated Whole. In our universe time Tw is usually approximated with measured time given the letter "t" used in classical and quantum theory. This leaves us with three distinctly different time definitions depending upon how change is measured.

"Tw" or just "T" references the Newtonian abstract time derived from the global flow of action in a Whole system.
"t" references the time derived from the action flow in a clock system separated from the Whole and used in coordinate frames to locate other events.
"τ" references the time derived from the action flow in other separated parts of a Whole that are usually the systems being located by a clock in a coordinate frames.

In practice the difference between abstract Newtonian time and clock-measured time is often small, requiring only special relativistic corrections when an electromagnetic clock is built and used in similar gravitational environments.

4.3.4.5 The ultimate ambiguity of time

Recognizing time as the measure of change in a physical system impacts our ability to predict the future. We have shown that when any self-contained system "W" is arbitrarily divided into a clock "U" and the rest of the Whole "I", then the clock state can be used to predict the state of "I" because both are governed by the self-consistency of the Whole. However the state of the Whole cannot be logically predicted because the equations of motion are ambiguous. Mathematically the Equation 4.3-11 implies a circular definition because the state of the sub-parts making up the Whole are functions of time, energy and constants of motion "$\alpha_{f-1}, \beta_{f-1}$",

$$p_f = p_f(Tw, Ew, \ldots \alpha_{f-1}, \beta_{f-1} \ldots), \quad q_f = q_f(Tw, Ew, \ldots \alpha_{f-1}, \beta_{f-1} \ldots).$$

Equation 4.3-14

The energy is usually assumed to be constant as well. When such sub-part motions are substituted back into Equations 4.3-11,

$$Ew = E(p_f(Tw, Ew ..), q_f(Tw, Ew ..)),$$
$$Tw = T(p_f(Tw, Ew ..), q_f(Tw, Ew ..)),$$

Equation 4.3-15

the result are equations that represent *a condition of self-consistency* because we end up with 2f+1 constants and 2f+2 equations. In other words the Newtonian time "Tw" is dependent upon the choice of its value. Such a condition is expressed as an eigen-value equation. This means the equation is only true for certain values of time called its eigen-values of the state "Tw". Exactly which eigen-values satisfy the condition depends upon the structure of the function and the constants α_f, β_f and E. Knowing which values of time can be realized does not tell us when any one specific value is realized. This ambiguity is fundamental.

Even if one of the sub-systems is a clock and Equation 4.3-13 tells us the state of the rest of the Whole as a function "t", and even if we have a Least Action Principle that tells us the shape of the path taken between two endpoints, we still do not have an equation that tells us how those endpoints are selected. In the car trip analogy the endpoints are selected by the driver. In quantum theory the endpoints of an experiment are selected by the driver of the experiment. In CAT the endpoints are eliminated by the cyclic structure of isolated events. Then the whole loop is in some event-state, but which one is not determined. The internal self-observer of its own Whole knows what eigen-value of the time state it is experiencing because "Now" is its own observation. But *when the "Now" takes place* is no longer predictable from within its own self. Implications of the realization – that the true nature of an isolated being is a self-contained physical action – for the wider scientific community will be addressed in Part III. In the meantime we will concentrate on the action-flow control mechanisms internal to material that enable such choices to be made.

4.4 Translating the graphic action model to physics nomenclature

The graphic CAT model of an isolated system is useful for demonstrating the principles of an event-oriented physics when the subjective phase is taken into account. A single arc of a graph is a convenient representation of a form of action that summarizes the activity by four graphic features. These are the amount of ink, the density of ink drawn, the length of the line drawn and the endpoints of the line. Because a graph is laid out in space, an arc having a length ΔQ, and the momentum function $\mathbf{P}(Q)$ representing the linear action density along the length are the most appropriate set for parameterizing the flow of action ΔA in a graphic model. Alternative sets of canonical variable pairs are often used to parameterize this transportation of state change between endpoints in physics. The Newtonian time interval "$\Delta T = \Delta Q/\mathbf{V}_w$" and energy $E(T) = \mathbf{P}(Q(T)) \bullet \mathbf{V}_w$, where "$\mathbf{V}_w$" is the velocity of the activity along the arc length ΔQ of the whole, are two important alternatives. These parameters and amount of action are not independent because the condition

$$\underline{\mathbf{P}}(Q) \bullet \underline{\Delta Q} = \Delta A = E(T) \cdot \Delta T, \qquad \text{Equation 4.4-1}$$

implies only two parameters are necessary. The third is always determined by the action density definition expressed by Equation 4.4-1. Un-subscripted capital letters will be used without subscript names when self-contained whole events are obvious from the context.

4.4.1 Parameterization of the action model

An action-flow diagram is a record of activity and thereby represents the activity itself. The connections of arcs and endpoints of material states completely describes the dynamics of an event. Looking at an action graph in a CAT extension of a block universe model presents the dynamics of reality in a simultaneously experienceable format that is more easily grasped than mathematical notation. Unfortunately such simultaneous presentations are only readable when a small number of parts are involved. This is useful to introduce the concepts, but for larger systems usually encountered in practical applications a mathematical notation is required. This means introducing a nomenclature at least one step of abstraction above the action graph so its symbols can be used in verbal discussions and mathematical relationships. The following sub-section will show how graphic features are labeled to transform CAT graphics into a mathematical model.

4.4.1.1 The action model in classic physics parameters

We start with a god's-eye view of a block universe model at the summary level showing the total action of a whole event. Figure 4.4-1a shows a form of action as a graphic record of a classic isolated event divided into three interacting parts. The arcs are the record of all the action of three interacting systems. To include further details the arcs could be expanded into spatial cross sections and divided into smaller sequential records placed on successive pages of a block universe book. Here only the three icons of an external or physical aspect (see Figure 4.3-5a) of a "Now" instance are shown. This form emphasizes the external classic view. The location of the model operator's "Now" experience is located inside the past and future side of each part where the gravito-electric interaction points meet. The total amount of action in the Whole must equal the amount of action in each part plus all the interactions between parts. The reader could in principle scrape all the ink of the page and collect *half* the external representative action of the event into a bottle. The other half is located in the subjective interior of matter.

In Figure 4.4-1a, each part is labeled with "1, 2 and 3". The arcs connecting these parts are labeled with the amount of action happening between the parts. For example, the amount of ink in the arc connecting part "2" and part "1" is a record representing an amount "$A^2{}_1$" of action happening between part "2" and part "1" when the whole event executes. In general, the arc length between these parts is $\Delta Q^2{}_1$. The distribution of ink along this arc represents the action density or momentum $P^2{}_1(Q)$ as a function of distance along the arc. The average momentum between part "2" and part "1" when the whole event executes is given by $A^2{}_1/\Delta Q^2{}_1$. The entire graph of all explicitly labeled action quantities $A^{from}{}_{to}$ and implicitly presented intervals $Q^{from}{}_{to}$ is the record of a three-part event.

Because the graph shows the parts of a single Whole event of equal time display length ΔQ, the separated individual arc distances are all this same time length, thus "$\Delta Q^i{}_j = \Delta Q$" for all paths. This allows us to calculate the total action density flowing into the "j'th" part as

$$P_j = \Delta A^1{}_j/\Delta Q^1{}_j + \Delta A^2{}_j/\Delta Q^2{}_j + \Delta A^3{}_j/\Delta Q^3{}_j =$$
$$\Delta A^1{}_j/\Delta Q + \Delta A^2{}_j/\Delta Q + \Delta A^3{}_j/\Delta Q, \qquad \text{Equation 4.4-2}$$

and the total amount of action in the total Whole event as

$$\Delta A = \Sigma_j\, P_j \cdot \Delta Q^j = P_1 \cdot \Delta Q + P_2 \cdot \Delta Q + P_3 \cdot \Delta Q. \qquad \text{Equation 4.4-3}$$

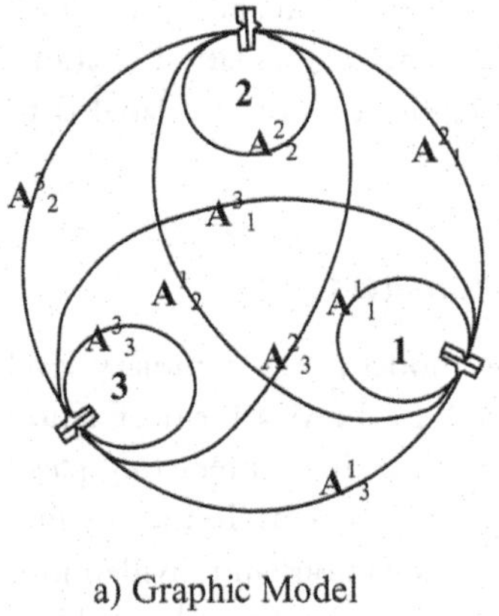

a) Graphic Model

$$\Delta A = \left[\frac{1}{\Delta Q}, \frac{1}{\Delta Q}, \frac{1}{\Delta Q}\right] \begin{pmatrix} \Delta A^1{}_1 & \Delta A^1{}_2 & \Delta A^1{}_3 \\ \Delta A^2{}_1 & \Delta A^2{}_2 & \Delta A^2{}_3 \\ \Delta A^3{}_1 & \Delta A^3{}_2 & \Delta A^3{}_3 \end{pmatrix} \begin{pmatrix} \Delta Q \\ \Delta Q \\ \Delta Q \end{pmatrix}$$

b) Interaction Matrix Notation

$$\Delta A = (1/\Delta Q)_i \bullet \Delta A^i{}_j \bullet \Delta Q^j = \mathbf{P \bullet \Delta Q}$$

c) Matrix Index Notation

$$\Delta A = A(P_1, P_2, P_3, \Delta Q^1, \Delta Q^2, \Delta Q^3)$$

d) Analog Notation

FIGURE 4.4-1 A Whole form of a classic three-part action record in graphic and mathematical notation with equal change-state arc lengths

This calculation is duplicated by the matrix multiplication of the left array (covariant) vector components of the distances on the left by the first column of the interaction matrix in Figure 4.4-1b. Here, the covariant left side row vector components have the value "$1/\Delta Q$". Use of the lower index of the covariant vector is to indicate that the reciprocal of the value of the arc length is to be used. The right side contravariant column vectors have the arc length values "ΔQ".

The constancy of action in an isolated system approximation also provides a condition on the possible inner behavior of a quantum system. If, rather than using vectors to sum all the action, we use Form matrices $(1/\Delta Q)^k{}_i$ and $\Delta Q^j{}_1$, the interaction matrix can be transformed to a new event-state as follows:

$$\Delta A^k{}_1 = (1/\Delta Q)^k{}_i \bullet \Delta A^i{}_j \bullet \Delta Q^j{}_1 \qquad \text{Equation 4.4-4}$$

Remember, we are using Einstein notation in which the multiplication product of all doubly appearing indexed quantities are summed. The new interaction matrix will have the same total action as the old, and inner physical state changes can be interpreted as a rotation of a multidimensional hyper-sphere of radius ΔA.

The action matrix in Figure 4.4-1b describes the physics of the event because the volume extensions are all coordinated by a Newtonian-like time making all the arc lengths equal. The task of connecting CAT graphics to classic physical nomenclature is only possible when we realize that this nomenclature is based upon the assumption that physical reality happens in a single Universe, in which all activities are coordinated by equal time intervals. Such an event is completely characterized by an *amount* of action "ΔA" happening in each element presented in the *form* of an interaction matrix. The different amounts of action happening between different endpoint states in equal time intervals describes events in classic physics and therefore only this special case of equal arc length CAT diagrams can be equated to the matrix notation of contemporary quantum physics.

In order for the action matrix to depict an exactly repeating cycle of states, the individual action elements must be symmetric. If the changes expressed in index notation by the interaction matrix during one cycle in each part satisfies the relationship $A^i{}_j = A^j{}_i$, then for a complete event period the total flow of action into and out of each part will be equal. In the matrix model this means outflow from a part is represented by horizontal rows while inflow is represented by vertical columns as shown in Figure 4.4-2. The condition only applies to the Whole. Within individual segments of a whole time loop imbalances may occur but they must cancel when summed to the Whole.

4.4.1.2 The action model in CAT parameters

In Figure 4.4-1 the subjective aspects of matter inside the three classic material icons located where the intra and inter action arc meet. The expansion of this interval to show explicit graphic and matrix representations of subjective action flow and of time-state interactions are shown in Figure 4.4-3a. Both the 1st and

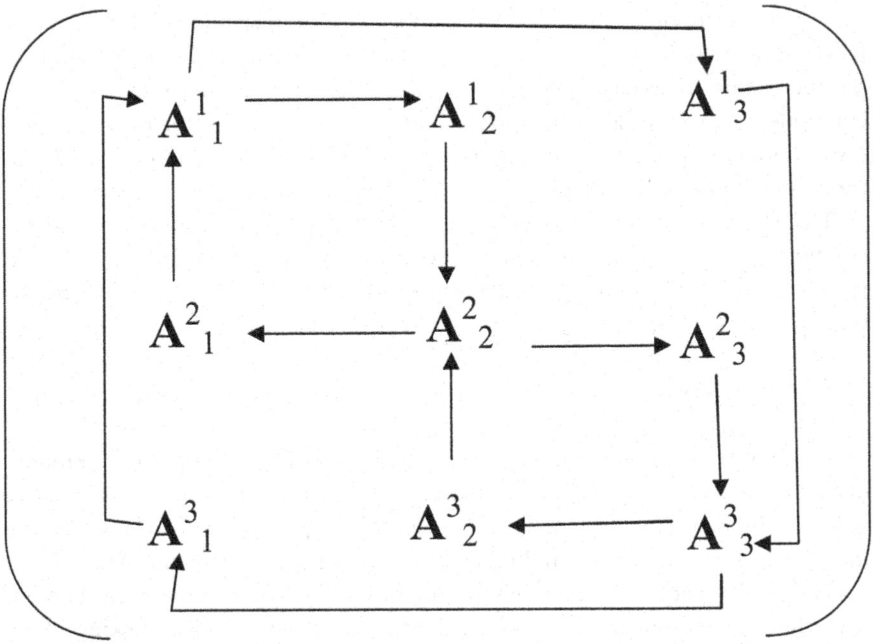

FIGURE 4.4-2 Action flow of one cycle in an interaction matrix

2nd-person show explicit feed-forward cycles required for modeling their reality and experiencing conscious self-awareness.

This thought-processing mechanism may not be necessary when the 3rd-person is most of Reality. However its physics would still contain a subjective gap shown only as a thought bubble indicating a ubiquitous awareness and reflex reactions for all material. Labeling and developing interaction matrixes become very intricate when time instances, material types and inside phases are added to the simple $^{to}_{from}$ notation adequate for describing interactions between classic material parts. For example, time ticks dividing the action arcs into smaller cycle instance records would be synchronously rotated to provide three moving subjective experiences where the actions meet.

Figure 4.4-3b shows the endpoints of a self-contained one-time event named (N), the material type (m or c), the internal or external edge (i or x), and the side of time from which a change emanates (1 or 2). Even for an isolated single degree-of-freedom model the four arcs connecting four endpoints are involved. So Equation 4.4-1 expanded by explicitly identifying each endpoint for the momentum and distance as,

$$\Delta A_N = \Delta A^{Nc1i}{}_{Nm2i} + \Delta A^{Nm1i}{}_{Nc2i} + \Delta A^{Nc2x}{}_{Nc1x} + \Delta A^{Nc2x}{}_{Nc1x}$$
$$= \underline{\mathbf{P}} \bullet \Delta \underline{\mathbf{Q}} = P^{Nc1i}{}_{Nm2i} \cdot \Delta Q^{Nc1i}{}_{Nm2i} + P^{Nm1i}{}_{Nc2i} \cdot \Delta Q^{Nm1i}{}_{Nc2i} +$$
$$P^{Nc2x}{}_{Nc1x} \cdot \Delta Q^{Nc2x}{}_{Nc1x} + P^{Nc2x}{}_{Nc1x} \cdot \Delta Q^{Nc2x}{}_{Nc1x} .$$

Equation 4.4-5

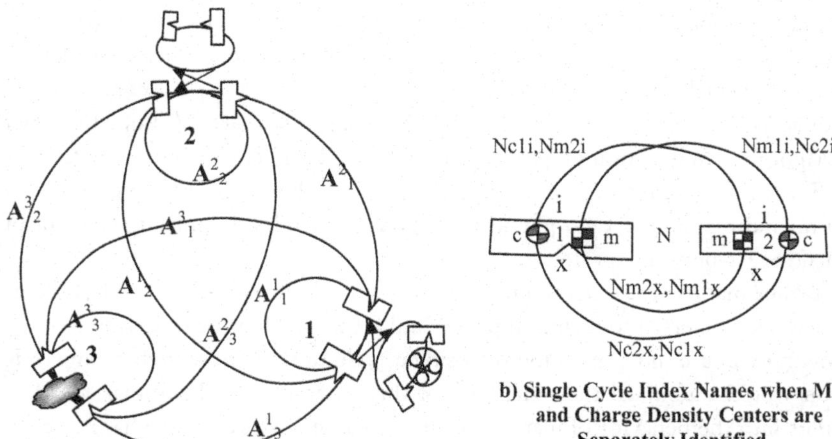

a) Action Flow Diagram

b) Single Cycle Index Names when Mass and Charge Density Centers are Separately Identified

FIGURE 4.4-3 Adding the subjective phase inside classic material

The first line sums the action in each arc, the second line uses the momentum and length. When all the actions are collected together the isolated event is characterized by single degree-of-freedom vectors $\underline{\mathbf{P}}_N$ and $\Delta\underline{\mathbf{Q}}_N$ when a single subscript is adequate to name it. A single degree-of-freedom summary is useful in a cosmological context to describe the Universe as a whole, or when approximating systems as completely isolated systems. The more usual applications require some modeling of the internal structure of isolated events so interactions can be treated as perturbations. Lowercase momentum and distance are often used when building up the single degree-of-freedom action structures from internal degrees of freedom. Then the change-state and momentum vectors look like $\mathbf{P}(\ldots p_{fc}, q_{fc}, p_{fm}, q_{fm} \ldots) \bullet \Delta\mathbf{Q}(\ldots p_{fc}, q_{fc}, p_{fm}, q_{fm} \ldots)$.

4.4.2 Insights provided by mathematical notation

By labeling arcs and endpoints we have transformed a graphic representation of dynamic reality to a matrix of symbols. The rows and columns of such a matrix defines the "from" and "to" endpoints of arcs carrying action between them. The arcs in CAT graphs use ink, length and density to represent action flows A^{From}_{To} required to implement changes in structure of distances Q^{From}_{To} with action density P^{From}_{To} defined by the ratio $A^{From}_{To}/Q^{From}_{To}$. These graphs or their matrix or index notation equivalents describe Reality.

A^{From}_{To} is the symbol that answers the ontological "what is?" question.

We can expand a graph from a single arc to many arc structures just like we can expand a single action into many values in a matrix in order to describe details of interest. By labeling the edges and nodes in a graph with physical parameters we have converted our graphic CAT book model to more traditional mathematical terminology. *To provide a visualizable physical theory that includes the subjective and objective aspect of Reality we doubled the degrees of freedom in classic physics formulations, introduced internal forces between charge and mass, and added an internal aspect to material as endpoints that define an arbitrarily complex form of action flow.* We hope this brief description of how action graphs are parameterized will convince the reader that the flow diagrams presented in the main text of this book are based upon a solid footing and represent a valid physical theory that includes the missing element of subjective 1st-person experience.

Further mathematical development is only suitable for advanced CAT students and has been deferred to technical papers and future work listed in Chapter 9. The following will use index notation on a single cycle to show how such parameterization would unfold. In the remainder of this section we will summarize a few insights into the behavior of material at the fundamental level which has not been available outside of CAT.

4.4.2.1 The fundamental desire behind event interaction

CAT assumes reality is action in a form. In classic physics the shape of that form is governed by the Least Action Principle, which states that stable systems only exist in forms which minimize its action. If we label the action record of two interacting systems with classic physics parameters we get Figure 4.4-4, then the Least Action Principle for System "1" within one time step is given by the formula,

$$\delta dA = \delta\left\{\Sigma_f p_f \bullet dq_f - H\left(p_f, q_f\right) \cdot dt\right\} = \text{minimum} \qquad \text{Equation 4.4-6}$$

Because classic physics did not distinguish between measured and Newtonian time, here "dt" is equivalent to "dTw". The symbol δ indicates a possible variation in the direction of the steps "dq_f" followed by a system. In other words a System 1 appears to act as though it has a choice but will choose the step which minimizes the difference between the two action terms in its lower physical activity phase and its upper mental activity.

This makes sense in the CAT architecture of Figure 4.4-4 because we can see that the difference between the action flowing through the observer producing the 1st-person experience ($A^1_1 + A^2_1$) and the action flowing through his physical phase (A^1_1) is in fact the incoming interaction (A^2_1). Due to the definition of signs in classic physics this difference is negative. Minimizing a negative means the System "1" acts as though it wants more of the desirable quantity A^2_1, i.e. the action it receives through interaction.

The same Least Action Principle applied to System "2" shows it also wants more of the desirable quantity A^1_2, i.e. the action it receives. Since action is defined as energy multiplied by time, the CAT action-flow diagram shown in Figure 4.4-4 demonstrates a fundamental motivational principle that governs the behavior of all parts of a Whole, which can be stated as follows:

"All parts of a whole will interact to maximize the action they experience".

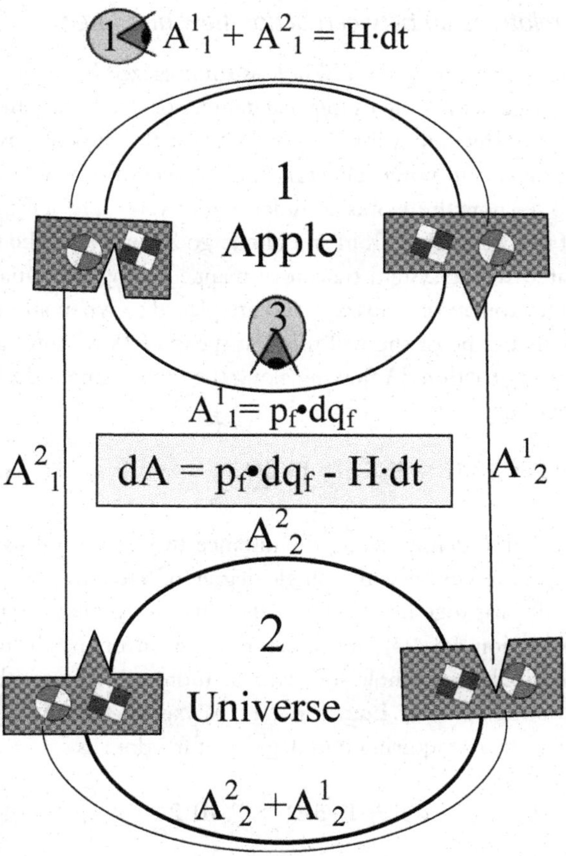

FIGURE 4.4-4 Interaction between two cycles shows the action of classic physics "dA" is only interaction "A^2_1", not the internal existence action

If Systems 1 and 2 were an Apple and the Universe, this principle states that an interaction will happen when both parties make choices to the internal parameters they control to maximize their action experience. Since the rest of the universe in this example includes You and I we would see the apple object move along a path that maximizes its negatively defined apparent action. This means the Minimum Action Principle of classic physics is no longer simply a sophisticated description of observations but rather logically explained by an innate desire of all parts in a Whole to gain action flowing through themselves. Furthermore because both systems only experience the flow of action through their mental phase this desire motivates continuous interactions that appear to satisfy the desire of both participants. This may be an illusion since the total action in the Whole remains constant, but because we only face in one direction in the flow of change, i.e. time, a continuous experience of apparent self gain drives a dynamic activity even when the Whole is in equilibrium.

4.4.2.2 The relationship between action flow and forces

System dynamics when treated as a Whole is summarized by single system trajectory through a space defined by its internal degrees of freedom. When action flows between degrees of freedom a force exists between the dimensions which causes a curvature in the system point trajectory and an accompanying acceleration and deceleration. To see how this works consider Figure 4.4-5. The left panel shows the CAT model of the action flow from an oblique god's-eye view. The thick circle on top is the isolated whole system trajectory mapped along its spatial extension of length "ΔQ". Newtonian time marks "Tw" are placed so when an operator replays the recorded activities he or she will move at speed of "**V**w" through the stack of pages. The amount of action dA flowing along the time segment dT is given by the differential equation

$$dA = E \cdot dT + T \cdot dE = E \cdot dT = \underline{\mathbf{P}} \bullet \underline{\mathbf{dQ}}. \qquad \text{Equation 4.4-7}$$

Where **P** is the action density along the distance **d**Q at interval named Q. When representing an isolated event with a single degree of freedom the total energy and momentum in all parts together can be made constant by adjusting the time interval length (see Section 4.3.4.4) and therefore terms involving dE or **dP** are zero. However if we divide any Whole into two or more sub-systems their individual energies need not be constant. Equation 4.4-7 is expanded, in the E,T representation, as two sub-systems requiring two degrees of freedom as

$$dA = E1 \cdot dT + E2 \cdot dT + T \cdot dE1 + T \cdot dE2. \qquad \text{Equation 4.4-8}$$

The condition Equation 4.4-8 on the whole is satisfied as long as E1+E2 = Ew and the change in the energies is zero, i.e. 0 = dE1+dE2. Figure 4.4-5b shows what happens when action flows from one degree of freedom to another. In this example the thick line of the system point moves in a straight line until it reaches T1w. From T1w to T2w an amount of action $\Delta A^1{}_2$ flows from the **Q1** to the **Q2**

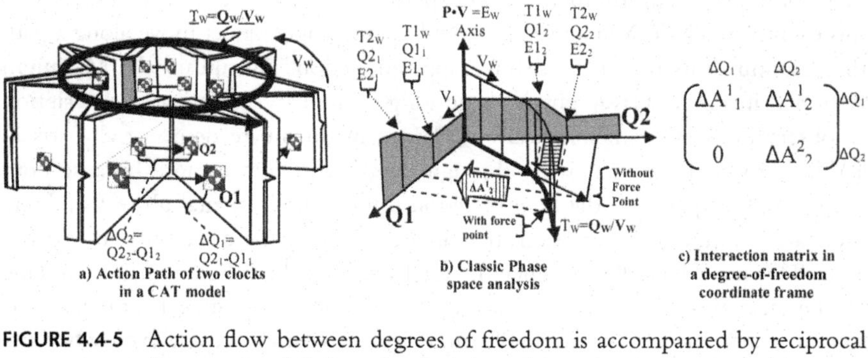

FIGURE 4.4-5 Action flow between degrees of freedom is accompanied by reciprocal forces and and defines the direction of time

degree of freedom. These are the two axes in 4.4-7b. If action flows out of axis 1 the action density P1 along the $\Delta Q_2 = Q2_2\text{-}Q1_2$ segment is reduced. This is shown by a reduction of the shaded area above the **Q2** axis. The shaded area is simply $\mathbf{P}_2(Q_2)\bullet\mathbf{d}Q_2$ which equals the action dA_2 in an infinitesimal distance and therefore one can see the shaded area is decreasing as we move in the Q2 direction. The change in momentum is $\Delta P_2 = P2_2\text{-}P1_2$, which when divided by the time interval $\Delta T_W = T2_W\text{-}T1_W$ gives the equation for the force in the first quantity in Equation 4.4-9,

$$\mathbf{F}^2_{\ 1} = \Delta P_2/\Delta T_W = \Delta\mathbf{dAw}/(\Delta T_W \cdot \Delta Q_2) = d^2A/dtdq_2\,. \qquad \text{Equation 4.4-9}$$

However, we also know that momentum is the action density so the third term shows the force is explicitly a change in the change of action divided by the time and space interval. We have taken some liberties by mixing "Δ" and "d" intervals but this example uses linear straight-line changes in momentum to avoid integration. The last term in Equation 4.4-9 shows the mixed intervals in more conventional notation as a second derivative. The "t" here refers to Newtonian time, not measured clock time and "q_2" here is the degree of freedom of a clock pointer of an otherwise stationary clock.

A similar calculation applies to the action received by the Q2 axis, only here the momentum density increases and therefore the sign of the momentum change is negative.

$$\mathbf{F}^1_{\ 2} = -\Delta P_1/\Delta T_W = -\Delta\mathbf{dAw}/(\Delta T_W \cdot \Delta Q_1) = -d^2A/dtdq_1\,.$$

Equation 4.4-10

By adding Equations 4.4-9 and 4.4-10 we see the forces are equal and opposite. This reflects the fact that forces balance in isolated systems and any action flow inside the parts of such a system retains this balance. From a transcendental perspective this is an obvious result of the isolation condition. If internal forces were not balanced by internal forces then some latent force is left over. This must in turn be balanced by an external force accompanying an interaction with an external system. The system cannot be isolated if all its forces were not balanced.

Further implications are deferred to the technical papers on CAT but a few more comments should be made. In Figure 4.4-5b the straight line of the system trajectory would end up at the point expected without forces. The degree-of-freedom Q2 falls short of this point, indicating the force decelerates the projected motion along this axis while at the same time the motion in the degree-of-freedom Q1 jumps ahead indicating acceleration has taken place. If we were so inclined we could identify the momentum in an axis as an intrinsic property of that degree of freedom and completely dovetail with Newton's force view of physics without recognizing the action flow involved.

It is also of interest to note that the action actually lost is half of the interaction since $\Delta A\text{lost} = ½ \cdot \Delta P_2 \cdot \Delta Q_2$ as can be seen by noting the triangle of area produced by the changing momentum in both axes. This means the total action remains a constant of internal interactions but the total change is doubled. For example when an atom emits a photon, the rate of action flow is transferred to a receiving atom. Half the change happens in one atom, half in the other. The two endpoints are classified as Fermions with spin 1/2. The action carrier is assigned the total change and is classified as a boson with spin 1.

Lastly a circular pulse of action on top of a steady flow between four degrees of freedom drawn in four quadrants would produce forces and oscillations around an equilibrium extension determined by the action in the steady flow. When these four degrees of freedom are the inside and outside aspects of mass and charge as shown in the basic action cycle of Figure 4.3-6, the magnitude of action in the steady flow would determine the volume of empty space while the oscillation in the flow would determine the material content in that space. Please refer to Section 4.3.3.2 to see how action stored in the separation of charge and mass is proportional to the volume extension of an interacting mass-charge structure.

4.5 Examples of action model analysis

In this section we will analyze several simple physical situations to show how action flowing through material composed of separable mass and charge centers can be applied. These examples will demonstrate how the flow of action in the electromagnetic and gravito-electric force domains can be projected onto objective experiences encountered in daily life. This will provide examples for how to relate the abstract quantities encountered in CAT physics to observable phenomena and lay the ground work for quantitative analysis of complex systems that include mental phenomena.

The first example includes the calculation of a stationary object in a gravitational field held in place by an electrostatic counter force. This will show a flow of action through the external support structures, the internal material components and the masses producing the gravitational effects. The second example will analyze a standard spring driven harmonic oscillator to show how action flows from an extended spring through an attached mass and into the gravito-inertial field determined by the rest of the masses in the universe. This example will demonstrate how the classic physical approximation, which assumes an infinite force holds charge and mass together, eliminates any activity in the internal mind aspect of matter and has prevented a physical explanation of consciousness. Relaxing this assumption then provides a physical explanation for activity associated with cognition and consciousness. Lastly we will include the effect of the spring on the support structure to which it is attached. This will allow us to identify a closed action-flow loop that will serve as the prototype for the event structures with which an event-oriented world view organizes reality.

4.5.1 Stationary particle example in CAT

Some time ago I was fixing some cracked stones on the chimney of our house with my son. Whenever I needed a new brick he would lob one up to my height. At the top of its trajectory the upward motion of the brick would stop. At that instance I could reach out and grab the stone. It had no weight. As it started to fall I could feel the tug of gravity increasing as it swung down on the end of my arm until it stopped at the height of the roof. I now felt its full weight.

To examine this phenomena let's look at Figure 4.5-1. On the left side a free-falling apple is shown at the top of its trajectory. At that instance its position is "q(t) = z" in height and its momentum is zero p(t) = 0. If at exactly this instance we move a table under the object, as shown on the left, there would be no force between the table and the apple's surface. As the apple settles in, however, the apple would be pulled down against the table top until an equilibrium was reached. The apple center of mass would be slightly below its apogee height "z-Δz" with momentum zero, only now the force of gravity "Fg" pulling the apple down would be counterbalanced by the electric force "Fe" of the table holding it up.

In classic point particle physics there would be no difference in the state between these two configurations. In both cases the point charge and mass centers would be at the same height with zero momentum. If we accept that objects are not points we would build a finite element model of the internal apple and calculate a stress and strain of the electric force pushing up against the force of gravity pulling down, distributed throughout the bulk of the apple's material.

These stress and strain forces hold potential energy that is ultimately attributed to forces between atoms and molecules. These would be treated as distortions of electron and proton location probabilities that would be visualized as infinitesimal distortions in their probability clouds distributed throughout the material. In CAT we retain the simplicity of the point particle approximation but allow mass and charge centers to separate. We would calculate the potential energy in the material by noting the center of mass is pulled down by gravity while the center of charge is

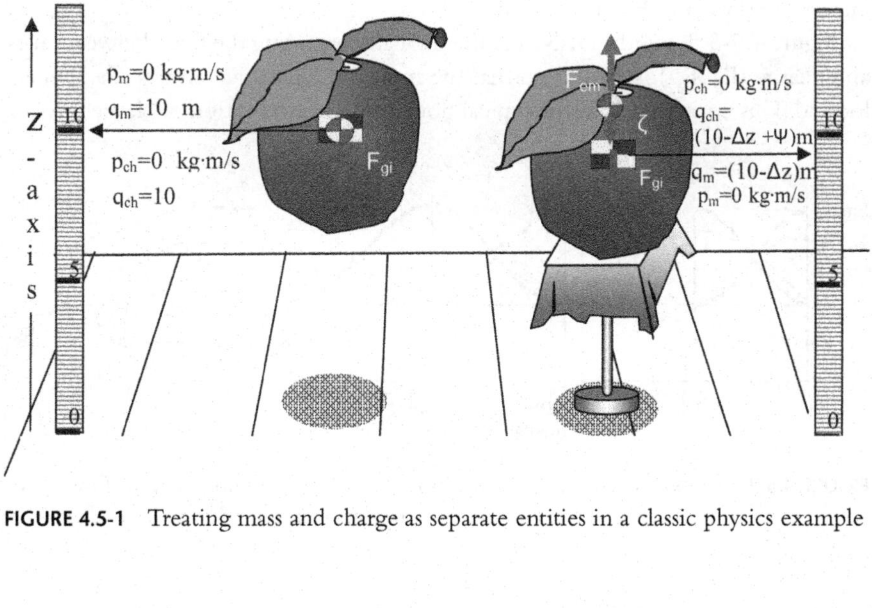

FIGURE 4.5-1 Treating mass and charge as separate entities in a classic physics example

pushed up by Coulomb repulsion. This separates the center of mass from the center of charge and introduces the internal attractive forces, Fcm and Fmc. These hold the apple material together and balance the opposing Fgi and Fem forces impingent on the apple from the outside. What we notice is that the action flow rate described by the potential energy ($m \cdot g \cdot \Delta z$) of the apple as it settles into the table surface is transferred into the action flow rate described by the potential energy ($k_{mc} \cdot \psi$) stored in the separation of the charge and mass during the settling time. Where k_{mc} is the spring constant associated with the separation from collocated equilibrium.

Of course the use of charge and mass centers is a vast simplification describing the actual details of changes propagating the through-the-apple material between the time it first touched the table surface and the time it settled in. No matter how the electromagnetic girders and beams of the apple's atomic material are compressed, they are also attached to the mass distribution in the same material. The distribution of mass-charge forces in the bulk of material is conveniently summarized by introducing the abstract centers. Adding charge with its own degrees of freedom is a natural extension to classic physics and provides insight into the happenings inside material. Stable and repeating motions of charge and mass forms the background of material empty space cells. When space equilibrium is disturbed oscillatory motion is treated as a perturbation that describes the content of space in quantum theory. How oscillators are constructed to incorporate subjective forces will be discussed in the next section.

4.5.2 Harmonic oscillator example

Assume a mass of material is attached to a spring laid horizontally on a frictionless surface. The mass, initially in its equilibrium position is pulled slowly stretching the spring to an extension x_max and let go. The mass executes harmonic oscillations. Graphs of the position (x), momentum (p_x) and its kinetic (KE_g) and potential (PE_e) energy are shown in Figure 4.5-2.

Figure 4.5-3 shows the analysis of the oscillator assuming the force between mass and charge (F_{cm}, F_{mc}) is infinite so that the mass and charge are always exactly collocated. This corresponds to the typical point particle assumption of classic physics.

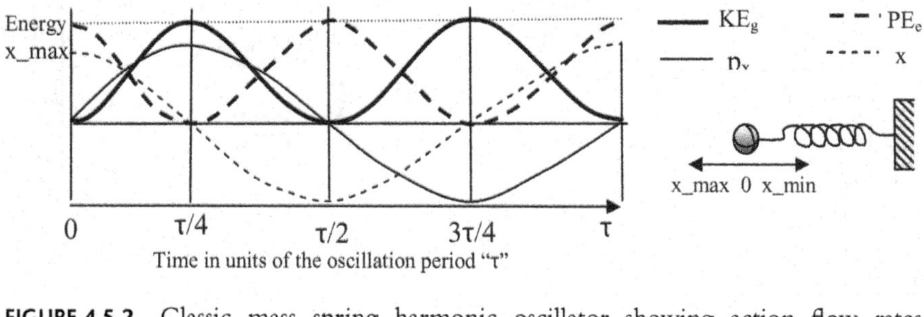

FIGURE 4.5-2 Classic mass spring harmonic oscillator showing action flow rates (energy) between electric and gravitational force domains

According to Newton's Laws only the electric force is present but it is balanced by the inertial force calculated as mass times acceleration expressed by $F_{em} = m \cdot a$. In CAT we say the spring wants the charge to be at its equilibrium (x = 0) charge field icon location and the masses in the rest of the Universe want the oscillator mass to be where its velocity would put it, as indicated by the mass field rectangle in Figure 4.5-3.

When the charge and mass is not where these desires want them to be, then action flows, forces arise and motion adjustments occur in interacting degrees of freedom as explained in Section 4.4.2.2. How these desires move a classic harmonic oscillator is explained next. The explanation of activities can be quantified by 1) balancing the electric force with the observed acceleration using Newton's Second Law, by 2) assuming particles have an intrinsic property to move at constant velocity unless acted on by a force using Newton's First Law and 3) assuming charge and mass are always co-located properties of particles. However further insight can be achieved by utilizing the CAT assumption that charge and mass are independent entities that are attracted to each other by a finite force which at small separations is approximated by $F_{cm} = -F_{mc} = k_c \cdot \zeta$, where ζ is the separation distance and k_c is the small-enough separation spring constant. The activities producing harmonic oscillations can then be further explained as shown in Figure 4.5-4.

The balance of four force types in the extended d'Alembert Principle (see Equation 1.5-1) can be explicitly seen in the intervals between equilibrium and maximum extensions. The electric field icons are positioned by the Coulomb forces in the spring at the spring's equilibrium point. The mass field icons are positioned by an application of Mach's Principle which suggests the inertial tendency

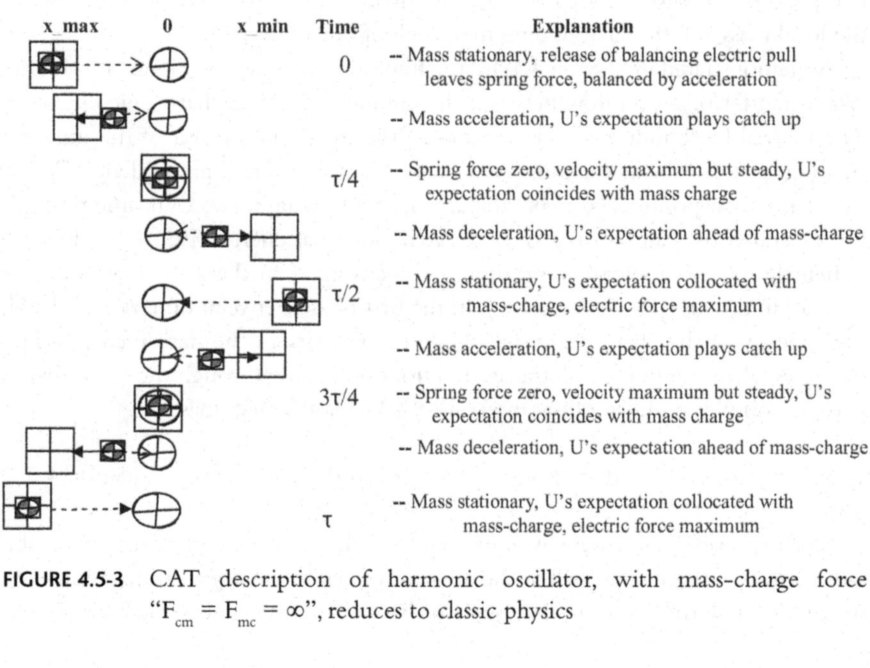

FIGURE 4.5-3 CAT description of harmonic oscillator, with mass-charge force "$F_{cm} = F_{mc} = \infty$", reduces to classic physics

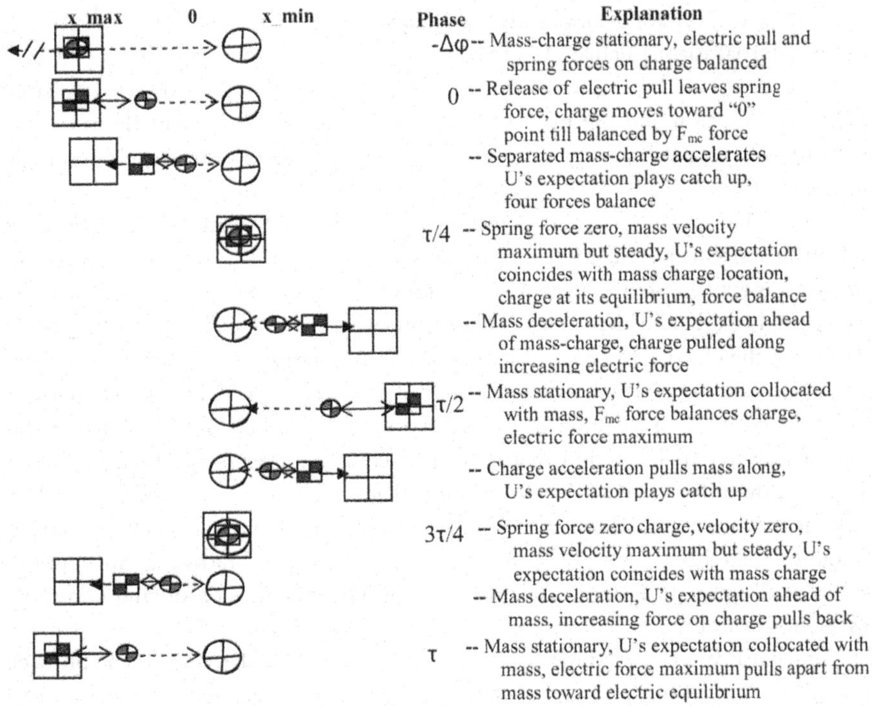

FIGURE 4.5-4 CAT description of a linear harmonic oscillator, mass-charge force $F_{cm} = -F_{mc} = k_c \cdot \zeta$, reduces to quantum theory

expressed by Newton's First Law actually involves an inertial interaction between the local mass and the surrounding mass shell of our Universe.

As demonstrated in Section 4.4.4.2 the force arrows shown in Figure 4.5-4 indicate a transfer of action flow between the components of the harmonic oscillator. The inertial force indicates a flow between the mass and the rest of the universe (U). Figure 4.5-2 shows the four phases typical of the external physical view. When the charge is at position (x_max), the action rate flowing forward in time through the extended oscillator spring is the electric potential energy ($PE_e = ½ \cdot k_s \cdot x^2$). When the mass is moving at maximum velocity (x = 0) the action rate flowing forward in time is ($KE_g = ½ \cdot m \cdot v^2$). In the first phase, between time zero and τ/4, the position of the charge decreases while the velocity of the mass increases. The incremental amount of action transferred from the spring through the mass-charge particle complex to U at a time interval "dt" during the first phase is

$$dA_{OU} = ½ \cdot k_s \cdot x(t)^2 \cdot dt = ½ \cdot m \cdot v(t)^2 \cdot dt, \text{ while } dA_{UO} = 0. \quad \text{Equation 4.5-1}$$

Since the time increment is equal when both sender and receiver are in the same universe, the rate as well as the amount of action are equal in magnitude. At time t = τ/4 all the action in the oscillator has been transferred to the inertial field of the universe and flow of action reverses. The explicit time, position and velocity expressions remain the same but the role of dA_{OU} and dA_{UO} reverses so that in the second phase, between time $\tau/4$ and $\tau/2$, the action flows back into the oscillator spring. The action transfer process repeats in the third and fourth phase. Although observable motion of the particle differs in each phase, the energy and action flows back and forth twice because position and velocity appear as squared quantities and the sign difference is eliminated.

Figure 4.5-3 shows the case in which the mass and charge are collocated by an infinite force. Equation 4.5-1 reflects the classic physics approximation when it was not even known that the interior of matter existed. Knowledge of electricity in the 19th century increased our understanding, and quantum theory opened the door for exploring this interior. The CAT shortcut introduced mass-charge separation as a heuristic tool to demonstrate the equivalence of mind with the interior of matter and Figure 4.5-4 shows how action flows through the mass-charge separation gap on its way between the oscillator and the rest of the universe. We therefore have the buildup and decay of a new potential energy ($PE_\zeta = ½ \cdot kc \cdot \zeta^2$) where ζ is the mass-charge separation distance. The rate of action flowing from the spring to the separation is now ($PE_e + PE_\zeta = ½ \cdot k_s \cdot x_e(t)^2 + ½ \cdot k_c \cdot \zeta(t)^2$) where the position of the charge $x_e(t)$ at time "t" is different from the charge-mass complex used in Equation 4.5-1.

Similarly the velocity of the mass is no longer equal to the classic velocity but is also dependent upon the rate of expansion and contraction of the separation distance. The kinetic energy of the separation distance interval is $KE_\zeta = ½ \cdot m \cdot v_\zeta(t)^2$ where v_ζ is the separation distance velocity. So that the rate of action flowing to the U's inertial field from the separation interval is $KE_g + KE_\zeta = ½ \cdot m \cdot v_m(t)^2 + ½ \cdot m_\zeta \cdot v_\zeta(t)^2$). The incremental amount of action transferred from the oscillator to the inertial field through the particle complex in the first phase, then,

$$A_{OU} = ½ \cdot k_s \cdot x_e(t)^2 \cdot dt + ½ \cdot k_c \cdot \zeta(t)^2 \cdot dt = ½ \cdot m \cdot v_m(t)^2 \cdot dt + ½ \cdot m_\zeta \cdot v_\zeta(t)^2 \cdot dt, \quad \text{Equation 4.5-2}$$

while the reverse action-flow A_{UO} is zero. As in the classic point particle mass the action flow reverses in the second and again in the third and fourth phase. Furthermore since the transition points $\tau/4$ and $3\tau/4$ the mass-charge separation distance is zero so the action flow over half the cycle is equal and opposite; however the motion, as described by the individual charge and mass, follows four paths which equal those shown in Figure 4.5-5, only at points $\tau/4$ and $3\tau/4$. In the next sub-section we add the interaction of the spring with the wall to show how local activities are part of a closed action loop.

4.5.3 Oscillator loop closed through the universe

The oscillator example in the previous section assumed that one end of the spring was attached to a ridged wall that provided a permanent anchor with no other

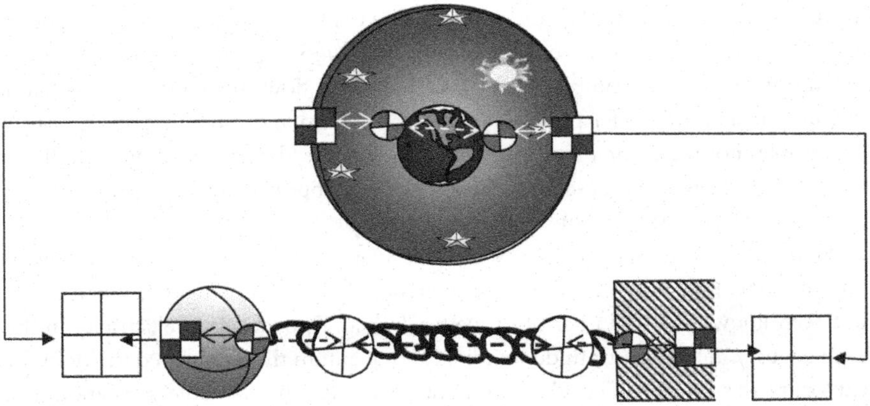

FIGURE 4.5-5 Oscillator universe action loop: the mass of the wall is always attached to the masses in the Universe: see Figure 7.6-3

physical implication. Such an anchor does not exist and by including the interaction of this end of the spring with the mass of the wall and all that holds it in place we will provide an important example of the closed action loop. In Figure 4.5-5 we show only one instant of the oscillator cycle where the spring has expanded to its furthest point and is now contracting so that the charge in both the ball and wall ends are being pulled toward their respective electronic equilibrium points. As shown in Figure 4.3-9 this in turn pulls the internal masses along, accelerating them away from their inertial equilibrium points and producing the acceleration force of Newton's second law.

At this point the inertial field attached to the rest of the universe comes into play. The inertial equilibrium points must now play catch up to the accelerating masses and move an amount $\Delta v = a(t) \cdot \Delta t$. This change requires an adjustment from the masses in the rest of the universe represented by the icon placed directly above the oscillator spring. In CAT the universe is also represented by mass and charge centers. The movement of the inertial equilibrium pulls the universe masses centers apart which in turn pull the charge centers apart as indicated by the arrows. The upshot of this activity is that as the oscillator spring contracts toward its electronic equilibrium point, the universe charges, which may also be treated as connected by a spring, are pulled apart.

The reader may now visualize how the rate of action flowing through the oscillator spring is transferred into the mass-charge configuration in the universe and back again. In the first phase between 0 and $\tau/4$ the oscillator spring contracts toward its equilibrium point losing action while in the second phase between $\tau/4$ and $\tau/2$ the oscillator spring compresses, requiring further energy and an increased action flow. The transfer of action flow are reversed in the third and fourth oscillator phases.

No matter how we anchor the mirrors, wires and detectors in our experimental laboratories when all the transmitted and recoil forces are taken into account, a flow of action closes a cycle between the universe and our apparatus. This maintains the Whole in a stable dynamic equilibrium. Failure to recognize all aspects, including ourselves, in such cycles introduces explanations in our theories that obscure and complicate our world views and the sciences that support them. CAT physics will be approximated in the next chapter to show how quantum theory can be derived. How we conscious beings fit into our physical world and how such understanding can improve our situation will be discussed in Part III.

5

THE QUANTUM AND CLASSIC APPROXIMATION

In this chapter we will show that the CAT model of interacting conscious beings is a superset of quantum theory. Quantum theory itself will be derived as a linear approximation applicable when disturbances in the material-producing experiences are small enough to be reversible oscillations around a dynamic equilibrium state. For a computer, such a restriction means reducing the power of internal signals to levels that do not to destroy the electronics doing the processing. For humans, it means such disturbances do not destroy the fabric underlying the perceptive space in which our experience appears. CAT includes vastly nonlinear activities such as the construction, repair and destruction of the hardware in which such appearances happen. By showing CAT is the comprehensive context in which quantum theory applies, we expand our knowledge beyond current limits, legitimize the physical basis of our 1st-person experience, and build consciousness into the foundations of scientific thinking.

5.1 Classic and quantum theory

Historically quantum theory grew out of classical physics as an attempt to explain how light interacts with matter to produce the colors that were observed spectroscopically. In doing so many fundamental tenets of classic physics were kept. This includes the notion that an independent space and time provided a common container for quantum objects such as atoms and elementary particles as well as our own bodies and the experimental apparatus involved in experiments. When such apparatus were able to make measurements without disturbing the objects being measured one could conclude that reality is what we see. The discovery of the action quanta by Planck introduced the notion that a measurement apparatus always disturbs the systems being measured and therefore the state of such systems could only be defined within the limits of the disturbance. This gave rise to

Heisenberg's Uncertainty principle and a probabilistic interpretation of quantum objects since the disturbances cannot in themselves be seen or controlled at the Planck scale. Furthermore, when de Broglie introduced a wave representation of particles, they were quickly interpreted as packets of probability amplitudes, leaving us with an unrealistic ontology.

In CAT, we eliminate the common and permanent container concept of space by recognizing that space, like objects in it, is perceived and generated by the material from which an observer is built. Therefore, objects are indeed oscillations, as de Broglie contended, but such oscillations occur in the material from which the observer and, by extension, all systems are built. This gives quantum waves an ontological interpretation of oscillations in real material. However, it also raises the possibility that the configuration of material, producing a constant and empty sensation of space, may itself be subject to construction and destruction. Quantum theory assumes the abstract Hilbert space of material in which such oscillations occur remains intact, and the oscillations do not get large enough to destroy the permanent configuration of material in which they occur. This means quantum theory is restricted to small oscillations in a permanent common space while CAT allows the modification and association of material space to describe the creation and destruction of systems including ourselves.

5.2 The CAT context for quantum theory

In this section we will show how the essential components of quantum theory already model an action cycle. Next, we will place this representation of quantum theory inside the brain of a quantum physicist to show how this person, having a quantum MoR in the brain, interfaces with an external world through a sensor/actuator interface. Lastly, we will divide the external world into the laboratory equipment enclosing the quantum physicist and separating him or her from the rest of the universe, which interacts with that equipment. This will show how the quantum physicist projects his or her quantum MoR into the interior region of that equipment where the physicist believes quantum laws prevail. All along we will point out that quantum theory tacitly assumes the brain and the externalized equipment will remain stable so that small-enough reversible disturbances will not destroy the equipment. This small-enough and reversible condition is then identified as the quantum approximation to Conscious Action Theory.

5.2.1 The action cycle in Conscious Action Theory

In Figure 5.2-1a we identify the operations of a self-contained action cycle consisting of a field of space cells using quantum theory nomenclature. The cells of the field are named by the space vector [**x**]. The action phase density due to objects in empty space in each cell is a[**x**,t](φ) where "φ" describes the phase angle that measures the progress of the cycle as it proceeds through the activities of its event. As the action flows around the phases, each complete cycle is in a dynamic time-state "t".

In the material interface of the von Neumann Cut, it is processed by the explanatory functions

$$\psi[x,t](\varphi) = e^{+i\cdot\int a[\underline{x},t](\varphi)\cdot d\varphi/h}, \text{ and } \psi^*[x,t](\varphi) = e^{-i\cdot\int a[\underline{x},t](\varphi)\cdot d\varphi/h}$$

Equation 5.2-1

into the motion of the material space $\psi[x,t](\varphi)$, which is responsible for the action required to enable the motion. Here "φ" is measured in radians, "h" is Planck's constant and "i" is the square root of minus one. By executing these functions, we have processed through the von Neumann Cut from symbols of perceived action hits to the symbols of the CAT extension to quantum theory. This operation adds a perturbing motion ψ to the model of empty space to define the combined motion $\zeta[\mathbf{x},t](\varphi)$. The phase-time operator ($= T[t',t](\varphi',\varphi)\bullet$) calculates the propagation from the phase angle interval taken up by the model in the main cycle. Note the CAT model is a cycle of motion consisting of a forward and backward propagation from the injection of the disturbing motion to its rejection. If the disturbance does not change the time state, the perceptive universe is simply refreshed. When the disturbance propagation through the main cycle is absorbed into the original "ζ" motion, a new time-state "t'" applies, and the appearance described by a[x,t'] will have moved.

The two transforms in the model reach the same phase from two sides and together form a closed cycle. This is the mathematical version of a CAT-MoR, which models the cycle in which it is imbedded. We can extract the action function in the main cycle by applying the action operator $\mathbf{A} = (-i\cdot h/2\cdot\pi)\cdot d/d\varphi$, and using an indefinite integral over the phase angle as follows:

$$\int\{\psi^*[\mathbf{x},t'](\varphi)\cdot\mathbf{A}\cdot\psi[\mathbf{x},t'](\varphi)\}d\varphi =$$
$$\int\{\psi^*[\mathbf{x},t'](\varphi)\cdot\psi[\mathbf{x},t'](\varphi)\cdot(-i\cdot h/2\cdot\pi)\cdot d\left(i\cdot a[\mathbf{x},t'](\varphi)/h\right)$$
$$/d\varphi\}d\varphi' = a[\mathbf{x},t'](\varphi').$$

Equation 5.2-2

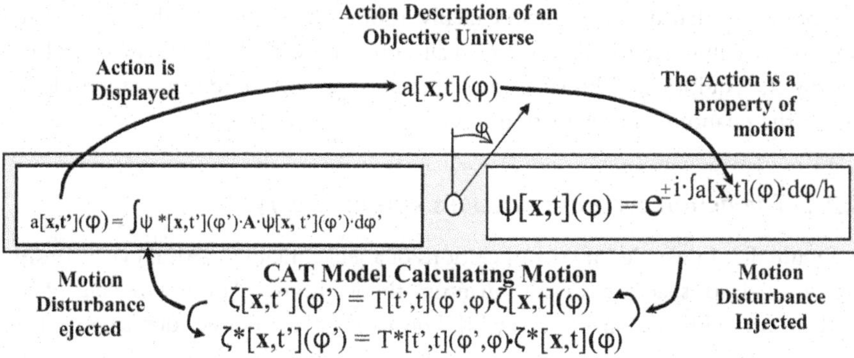

FIGURE 5.2-1A The action cycle using a Conscious Action Theory Model of reality that propagates a Dirac-like forward and backward disturbance forming a time loop model of itself

This integral can be carried out because the complex conjugate CAT wave function "ψ^*" differs from "ψ" by a negative sign in the exponent so multiplying these two terms gives "1" and the integral and derivative cancels.

The formalism here retains the phase angle as a parameter that summarizes the progress of the main action cycle event which in CAT is precisely the activity modeled. The physics of modeling a cycle with a cycle contained within itself describes the unknowable aspect of matter with a theory that can be approximated by quantum theory when the disturbances are small enough.

5.2.1.1 The quantum approximation

Rather than dealing with what happens inside an action cycle, standard quantum theory assumes the disturbances to the motions in the cell are so small that the action phase density "$a[\underline{\mathbf{x}},t](\varphi)$" is no longer a function of the phase angle and therefore can be replaced by its average. The integral of Equation 5.2-1 can therefore be evaluated over the entire cycle as shown in Equation 5.2-3.

$$\psi[\underline{\mathbf{x}}, t](2\pi) = e^{i\cdot a[\underline{x},\, t]\cdot\int^{2\pi} d\varphi/h} = e^{i\cdot a[\underline{\mathbf{x}},t]\cdot 2\pi/h} \qquad \text{Equation 5.2-3}$$

In the middle term, we are keeping the integral in the phase in order to remind the reader that the "ψ" function still describes a motion in a "2π" interval located at "$\underline{\mathbf{x}}$" that is in a state "t". "ψ" is not simply a complex scalar but shorthand for an event completing its full cycle of activity. Our interpretation, however, is more akin to the sloshing motion of a material density rather than a probability amplitude. Visualization of the action cycle in quantum terminology now looks like Figure 5.2-1b. Again, the conversion from observable action is converted at the von Neumann boundary to the Schrödinger wave function, which is assumed to represent a disturbance in a time-state "t". The now quantum unitary operator (=U[t',t]•) adds a state change to ψ calculated by the Schrödinger equation to the original displacement to get a new time-state "t'" of motion executing through the 2π-phases of the next event $\psi[\mathbf{x},t']$ in cell "**x**". Note the integrals over the phase angle are now trivial resulting in the 2π-radians of a complete cycle and thereby converting the phase action density into the action in a complete cycle.

The exact mathematical formula for Schrödinger's equation is derived from the more general "T" transform because the phase motion describing empty space is assumed constant and can be neglected. Any small-enough disturbance to the fixed repeating space motion will act like oscillations of a coupled harmonic oscillator and such oscillations are solutions to the Schrödinger equation. The derivation of this equation is qualitatively discussed in Section 5.3.2.1 and mathematically derived in Appendix A5.1. It shows that the fundamental formulation of quantum theory is applicable when oscillations around empty-space equilibrium states in CAT are "small enough" so that only reversible changes happen, which do not destroy the cycles of empty-space motion. When the fabric of empty space itself is changed, quantum theory is no longer adequate, and CAT is required. Therefore,

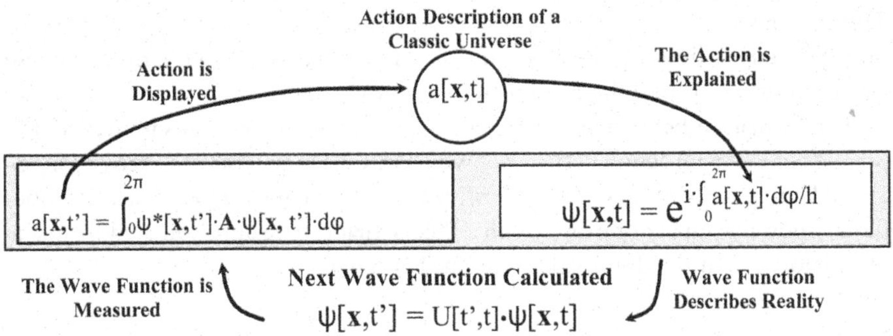

FIGURE 5.2-1B The action cycle with a quantum theory model using Schrödinger's forward time propagation equation that closes its time loop but does not model itself

quantum theory approximates CAT when the disturbances described by y are "small enough".

If the unitary operation does not change the time state of "ψ", then the observable action will remain constant and permanently appearing observable will refresh every execution of the cycle. To be constant requires all internal sub-parts of the system that is the space cell [**x**] to have completed all intra-actions and returned to their initial state. Thus, quantum explanation and measurement of an unchanging action structure can be considered the existence operations that replace the fundamental particles of quantum physics with their fundamental CAT event counterparts.

In summary, the quantum action cycle shown in Figure 5.2-1b is constructed from symbols found in standard texts on the subject. The only symbol that can be directly related to human experience is the action field a[**x**,t], used to describe the total amount of action flowing through the Now during each complete cycle. When this information is used to calculate the wave function ψ[**x**,t], standard quantum theory leaves us with an implicit 2π-motion of a completed cycle that masks the details of its role in reality. However, if we carefully look at the activity of a scientist executing the methods required to implement quantum experiments, we find the 2π-motion inside material can be naturally associated with the scientist's mental experience, thus placing quantum symbols into the context of a CAT action cycle phase. A comparative list of symbols in Table 5.2-1 shows how the phase measuring progress in a CAT cycle has been eliminated.

The next section shows how a CAT action cycle is incorporated into an observer, who provides the context within which quantum theory is actually implemented.

5.2.2 The CAT action cycle for a human observer

In addition to the action loop using a quantum model, we will now add the icons describing the subjective experiences within a real brain to demonstrate how a

TABLE 5.2-1 Summary of the quantum approximation

	Conscious Action Theory		*Quantum theory*
Next state operator	$=T[t',t](\varphi',\varphi)\,\bullet$	→	$=U[t',t]\bullet$
State function	$\zeta[x,t](\varphi)$	→	$\psi[x,t]$
Phase motion	$\int d\varphi$	→	2π
Subjective-objective	$e^{\,i\cdot\int a[xt](\varphi)\cdot d\varphi/h}$	→	$e^{\,i\cdot a[xt]\cdot 2\pi/h}$

1st-person interacts with what he or she believes is a quantum world beyond personal sensors.

In CAT, we assume personal sensations are located inside the observer's real brain material. Sensations are sandwiched between interface cells which transform neuron gravito-electric pulses to and from neuron processing channels, which carry action from the past and to the future actuator/detector arrays. These arrays constitute the von Neumann Cut. They are placed as icons that represent the future and past side of the real human retina and muscle actuators. In other words, the classic objective world a human observer sees in front of his or her eyes is the interpretation of what happens at these interface boundaries. The lines in the icons divide the multiple sensory channels and movement control paths (optic, auditory, memory, etc. See Section 6.3). Parallel processing pathways are bundles of action cycles labeled by cell address vectors "$\underline{\mathbf{x}}$". The wave function ψ, representing motion inside of the "Ac()" cell material, is calculated using the action flowing out of the observer's Now. The **a**[$\underline{\mathbf{x}}$,t] represents the average action phase density per channel per cycle, which in quantum theory is no longer dependent on the phase angle.

For heuristic purposes, in Figure 5.2-2 the motion inside-of-matter is interpreted using two alternative theories. The inner loop uses the symbols of the quantum reality model (=U[t',t]•) to calculate the next dynamic state of the motion cycle propagating forward in time. This calculation remains in the inside aspect of material and corresponds to the belief that the world beyond the von Neumann Cut is a quantum world.

In contrast, the reverse ψ*[$\underline{\mathbf{x}}$,t] output of the actuator arrays is channeled through the CAT model interpretation that the wave function is a disturbance in a mass and charge density field configuration. These disturbances are reverse processed through a simulated measurement function and then converted to gravito-electric influences, which must have stimulated our sensors in the real-world model of the unknowable. This identifies the physical cause of our perceptions in the model of reality (**MoR**) constructed in the observer's material.

The immediate unknowable past is here depicted as an objective universe **MoR** represented by the familiar icons of a man on the earth holding an object of interest. The interface icons send gravito-electric action to the objective side of the observer's detector/actuator array model, and the signals flowing through these arrays move the observer's body in the model. The model processes the observer's motions along with motions in the rest of the universe backward through its past

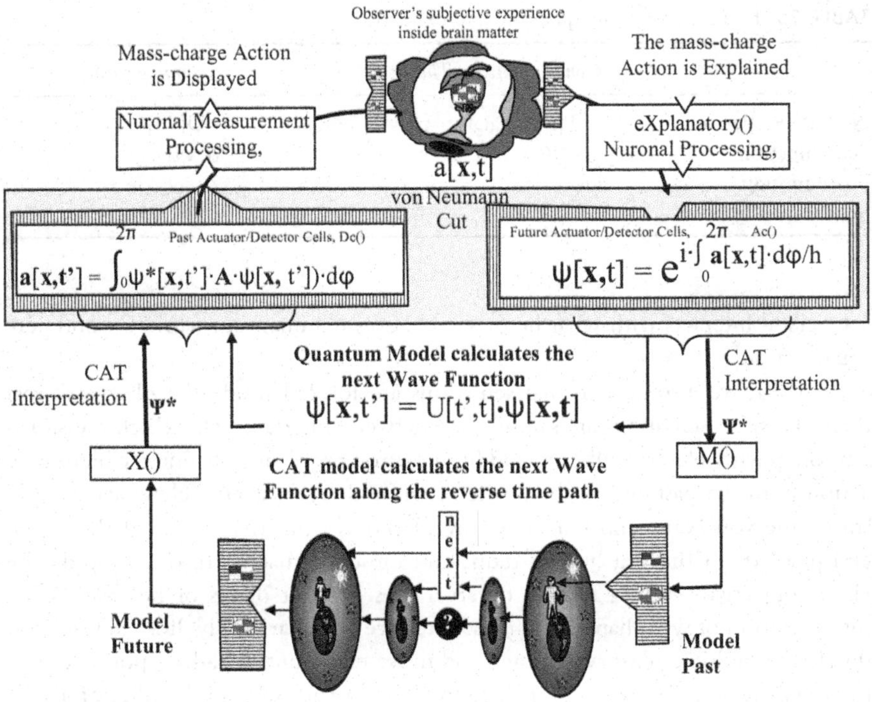

FIGURE 5.2-2 The quantum action cycle when the CAT framework uses an object model: shows quantum forward CAT backward time propagation

causes. The algorithm skips directly to the next future when a changeable goal is identified (see Figures 6.4-1 and 6.7-1). It produces the next stimulation to the observer's model of him- or herself. This stimulation is converted into inside-of-material disturbances that are processed and delivered to the past actuator/detector arrays as the next $\psi^\star[\underline{\mathbf{x}},t']$. The action density is here calculated using the action operator "$\mathbf{A} = (-i \cdot h/2 \cdot \pi) \cdot d/d\varphi$" which is integrated over 2π to get the total grav-ito-electric action in cell "$\underline{\mathbf{x}}$" state "t"". Neuron measurement processing drives neural pulses that produce the operator's next sensations.

By showing an icon of a classic universe and interpreting the probability amplitude into a visualizable mass-charge separation, the backward flow of the $\psi^\star[\mathbf{x},t]$ field through the model is thereby given an ontological reality in terms of the physical characteristics of material. In quantum theory, the role of the **MoR** is fulfilled by unitary time propagation function U[t',t] applied to the inside or mental aspect of matter. The Copenhagen interpretation makes no attempt to model a real world, or anything of that unknowable structure that might be the actual cause of our experiences. Guessing what such structures might be is considered too metaphysical by most quantum physicists.

At the bottom of the cycle in Figure 5.2-2, CAT normally substitutes whatever model of reality is installed in the observer's brain. We only used the icon of an objective universe to emphasize the point that what belongs there is a model of one's physical reality belief. We assume the reader comes to this book believing we live on an earth surrounded by stars. Most likely what is out there is not an object with particles and fields moving around in empty space. But the exact physical model placed into this slot is not as important as the fact that the activity of the cycle actually happens in a conscious being, and some **MoR** must be included to fulfill the role of the unknowable in it.

Thus, the CAT action cycle gives the quantum or any **MoR** a context in a larger event. CAT furthermore suggests that "Reality" cannot be completely described by a quantum theory that only connects inside-of-material sensor motions with each other. As Einstein argued, quantum theory is incomplete. The fact that all operations shown in Figure 5.2-2 are mapped as models that happen inside a human being's action loop corroborates Heisenberg's belief that quantum theory is the physics of the system that knows the world not the "World itself". The only interaction with the "World itself" occurs at the observer's subjective experience. This interaction will be modeled as external sensor/effecter processing channels in Chapter 6.

In the next section, our human sensory boundary is externalized so that the subjective experience of the von Neumann Cut becomes the quantum experimenter's view of his or her laboratory equipment. Though we know the 1st-PL is a subjective experience inside of our "Brain" material, we treat these experiences as real objects. This "objective reality" fiction allows us to employ the analogy between the growth and decay of conscious beings with the construction and destruction of experimental equipment that provides the Hilbert space in which the ψ-waves propagate.

5.2.3 Externalization of the von Neumann Cut

For the human, an array of six million cones and 120 million rods form the detector array in the retina of each eye. For the quantum scientist, the detector arrays are pieces of equipment that interact with what is believed to be the Reality beyond the detector cells and report the results of their interaction on their dials and printouts. These reports are then interpreted as symbols referring to what is beyond the equipment's detector cells. Figure 5.2-3 shows a representation of a sensor array as a tangible object in our 1st-PL. A quantum scientist, shown as a 2nd-person, would assume the equipment is stimulated by a quantum system that is described by a wave function field $\psi[\underline{\mathbf{x}},t]$. Neither the quantum system nor the wave function can be seen directly without looking through a screen of detectors.

In CAT, the icon of such a screen is visualized with a peaked reporting side of a measurement apparatus. The screen array is a classic object but the data it reports provides a symbolic tunnel to the inside of matter, which cannot be objectively seen (see Section 1.4.2). The 2nd-person interprets the appearance of the screen report in his or her mind by projecting the theoretical interpretation $\psi[\underline{\mathbf{x}},t]$ into the equipment that is believed to interact with quantum entities in the interior of matter.

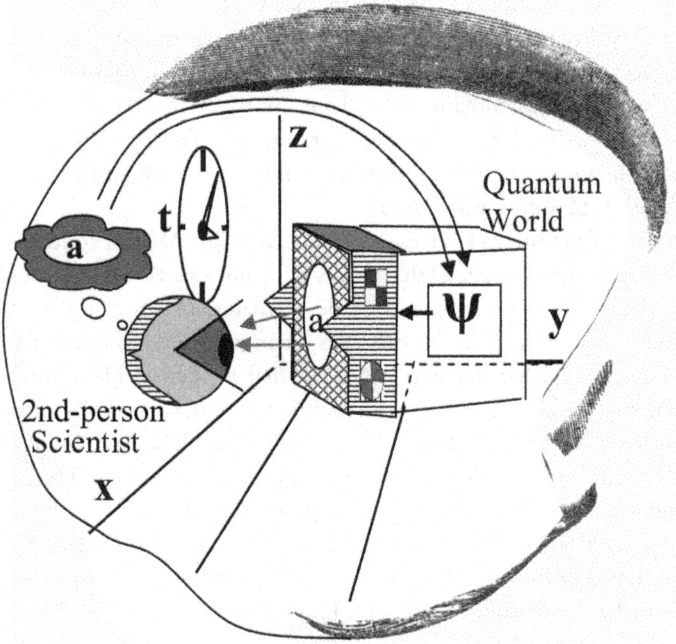

FIGURE 5.2-3 Detector array report in a 1st-Person Lab and a scientist projects a quantum interpretation into the equipment material

The 1st-PL perspective shows what the reader would see in his or her own mind since the 1st-PL is always looking through his or her own sensor array. Of course, the 1st-PL cannot experience the exact actions flowing through the 2nd-person but rather experiences duplicate members of an ensemble of actions that flow through him- or herself. If this reader happens to understand and believe quantum theory, the reader will also project a ψ-function into the equipment and agree with the experimenter that both are measuring a quantum entity. The reader may understand the experimenter is projecting the theory of a quantum world into the material of the equipment. But these mentally projected happenings inside material and the projection of their theoretical understanding of this equipment builds a consensus reality, which often feels very real to such individuals, perhaps more real than the sensations of their equipment they actually see and feel.

5.2.3.1 Action flow through an externalized von Neumann Cut

Figure 5.2-3 showed an experimenter as might be seen by the reader observing a quantum experiment. We now analyze this situation by extending the transcendental top-down view of an action cycle, developed in Section 5.2.2, with classic action-flow segments between the experimenter and the equipment. This means we are no longer dealing with subjective experiences explained by two alternative models implemented in the material of an observer. Instead in Figure 5.2-4 we show two parallel processing loops. The inner dot-dash line loop shows the quantum modeling process projected into the inside material of the experimental equipment by a quantum scientist. In this loop, the only experience being processed is that of the symbol a[**x**,t], which is believed to be a measurement result of the quantum system believed to be inside the laboratory equipment. The outer solid-line loop shows the modeling process of a scientist who treats the laboratory and its equipment as an objective world, in which action flows through object/subject sequences that explain phenomena using a CAT model.

The von Neumann Cut has been moved into the 1st-Person Laboratory apparatus while the human experimenter is treated as a 2nd-person little-man-inside the 1st-PL skull. Above the von Neumann Cut and throughout the lab, classic physics applies. The scientist sees the laboratory equipment as objects. This region may look like mirrors, wires and many boxes of interconnected equipment but none of these observables are the inside of material. However, some of those objects are dials and displays that also carry a symbolic significance because their objective states are connected to detector cells that respond to the un-seeable inside of matter where events are governed by quantum theory.

The motion disturbance inside the past detector cells of the equipment are recorded in observable dials and displays. The state of these dials is treated as real objects that transmit classic signals to the experimenter's retina. From there they are channeled to the experiment-result-processing operation that merges the actual and theoretically calculated result and that identifies the observable "a[**x**,t]" as symbolizing the happening of a quantum activity inside the equipment. These observable action hits are explained by projecting a stimulating activity "a[**x**,t]" into a von Neumann Cut where action patterns are converted to internal motion disturbances "ψ[**x**,t] and ψ*[**x**,t] " that carry action into the scientist's quantum model of the inside of material. At the detector cell interface, the experimenter believes classic action signals are transformed into quantum disturbances. As in Figure 5.2-2 the action is summed over a phase cycle so the wave function at time "t" represents a cycle of motion. These are processed in the quantum model by U[t',t] and U*[t',t], which produce the output disturbance through two opposite phase directions. The action response from the quantum cycle model is then recovered in the "next-time" detector cell that changes the output display. It is to the inside of matter that the symbols of quantum mechanics refer. This quantum world is accessed through mental projections into an equipment detector interface, and theorists agree this quantum world is not only reality but an observer-independent reality of probabilities between measurements.

In contrast, CAT models reality as a flow of change characterized by an amount of action in a form. This action flow is implemented by gravito-electric forces on the outside of matter and mental mass-charge forces on the inside. Probabilities occur because of a lack of knowledge in the observer. Figure 5.2-3 showed a scientist projecting the belief that an action a[x,t] must have happened inside of matter in

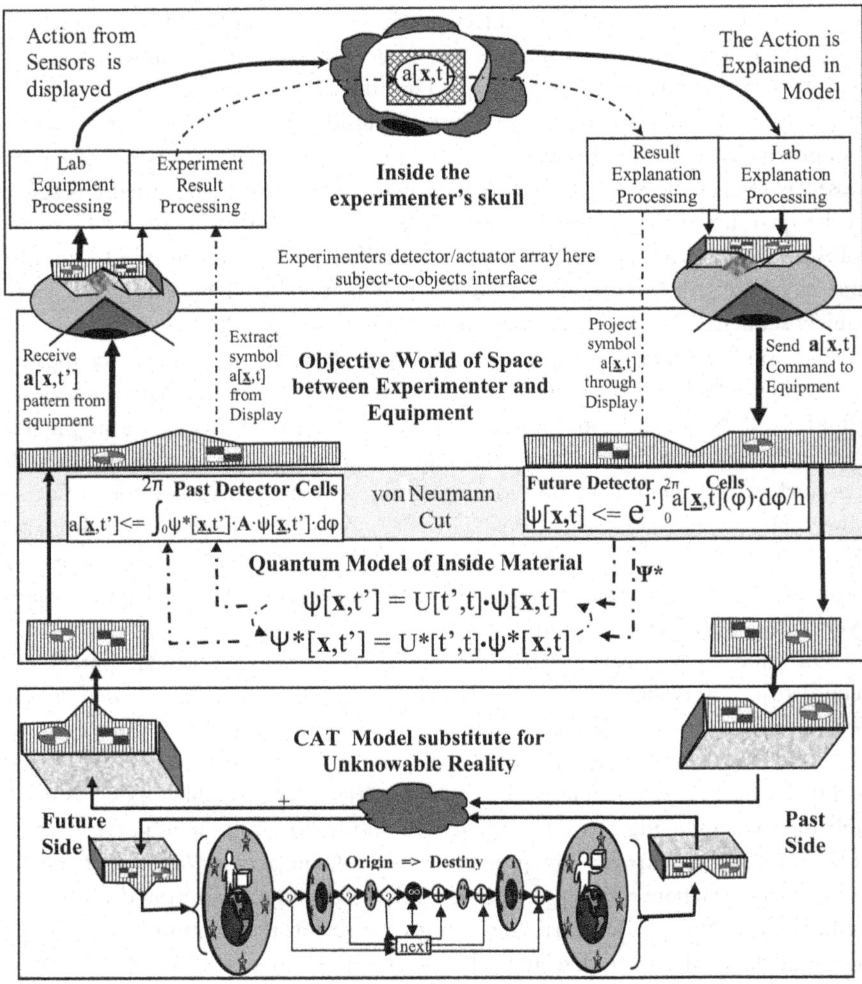

FIGURE 5.2-4 The action cycle with externalized quantum measurement equipment and a CAT model bypassing quantum calculations

the form of a motion disturbances, and therefore the scientist would expect to see a predictable action response of a[**x**,t']. However, expectations are not reality and this projected action and calculations have no effect on the inside of the equipment. Instead the real stimulation the calculation output describes must have come from the real equipment that executes real processes different from the quantum calculation. That action may be implemented by motion inside of matter is not in dispute. That the happening of such disturbances and their probabilistic interpretation are the complete description of "Reality" is being challenged. CAT proposes that the disturbing motions carry action through the von Neumann Cut and emerge as gravito-electric action forms that interface with the rest of Reality.

The lower half of Figure 5.2-4 shows a CAT model of the unknowable reality interacting with the laboratory apparatus. Here we have drawn the processing algorithm using objective universe visualizations that close a self-explanatory measurement loop. Again, we chose this visualization as a placeholder for the unknowable because it duplicates the action-flow algorithm of a real conscious being. This choice emphasizes how both a memory of the past and expectations of the future are computational elements that predict the next time instant and will be discussed in Chapter 6.

The actual **a**[$\underline{\mathbf{x}}$,t] – note the bold letter – stimulating the equipment is processed through the actual inside of its material. This process may very well have been correctly modeled by the quantum scientist but here is calculated using a CAT model based upon charge-mass interactions. The action from the scientist is relayed directly through the equipment and wall surfaces of the 1st-PL to interface with the unknowable Reality. Remember the 1st-PL is composed of observational experiences from which the 1st-person consciousness, like the prisoners in Plato's cave cannot get out of. This means the surfaces of equipment, like the surfaces of the walls, are boundaries to the unknowable Reality outside. This entire Reality receives action and responds with the next action patterns **a**[$\underline{\mathbf{x}}$,t'] that in the left side of Figure 5.2-4 stimulate the scientist's retina with sensations that include the experiment report of dial-state results.

The dial-state results started our description of the scientist's processing at the beginning of this section. We have replaced the quantum theory applied to small-scale material with a general action flow through the observer, or here, the 2nd-person scientist for whom all the walls that block direct sensory experience are the border between objective and subjective experience. The formal name for the sensor wall is called Hilbert space, and how the symbols of this space relate to the tangible visualizations of Reality provided by CAT will be discussed in the next section.

5.3 Hilbert space

Hilbert space is introduced in quantum theory texts as an abstract reference frame in which the Schrödinger's state function is defined. However, in practice such a space is implemented as the detector cells of real measuring instruments and is therefore not abstract at all. The cells of such measuring instruments are observable classic systems which form the von Neumann Cut, mentioned earlier as the barrier between the 1st-person objective view and the interior of matter. It is these cells that interact with the quantum world and report the passage of an amount of action through themselves. These reports are the database from which our models of that quantum world are created. We can therefore treat the Hilbert space formalism of quantum theory as simply a mathematical notation for keeping track of where, when and what amount of action pass through an array of coordinate frame cells.

The key to understanding a Hilbert space (H-space) is to recognize it as a general reference frame, composed of objective detector cells, through which one looks at the unknowable world beyond the impenetrable sensor boundary within which all quantum scientists operate. A number of such cells are usually organized into lines, areas or a three-dimensional volume but in general, such organizations are special cases of networks. Networks are no longer limited to the immediate six-neighbor interactions suitable for three-dimensional arrays but may be connected by communication channels that can in principle allow interactions between any cells in the network. This generalization allows us to use the term "space" for multidimensional organizations of detector cells and mathematically describe measurements of non-spatial sensation classes in new, non-geographic dimensions.

These H-cells, and the H-space they define, are not equal to the three-dimensional coordinate frames in which their appearance is located in the 1st-PL. In classic physics, the traditional labels for the Cartesian coordinate frame are "x,y,z", while time has been called the fourth dimension since Einstein's relativity and is designated by t. But in CAT, as well as quantum theory, detector cell names tag the detector cell reports that are encoded in the flow of action that produces a 1st-person display. In this section we will use generalized coordinate labels $q_1, q_2, q_3 \ldots q_f$ to name such cells and q_0 for the time tag when necessary. When looking through a coordinate frame of sensors these labels define the H-space in which the "ψ" function oscillates. To get a feeling of what this means, let's look more closely at an H-space in the perspective of the 1st-PL.

5.3.1 Analysis of a Hilbert space array

Figure 5.3-1 shows the basic "what", "where" and "when" tags of a measurement interaction. The entity participating in the interaction reported upon is shown in the inside of the equipment material where a quantum object symbolized by ψ is thought to be located.

The "what" reported by the H-space cells at the fundamental level is reduced to the amount of action $a[\mathbf{q}_f, q_0]$ passing through the H-cells at time "q_0". The rate of flow in the direction of a specific neighboring cells is called the momentum vector "$\mathbf{p}_f$" where "f" is the generalized axis along the "f'th" direction. In case the flow is in the direction of time, the momentum p_0 is given the special name "energy".

The "where" report is the name of the H-cell in which the interaction happened. One might think one could use the location x,y,z of the H-cell in the laboratory to locate ψ; however, as discussed in Chapter 2, this is the address of the visualization of the cell in the 1st-person display perspective, not the addresses of the H-cell in its Hilbert space network.

For example, to specify the location of a color interaction in one's retina, one needs to specify four types of values. These are left or right eye, x and y locations in each retina, and one of four color-response types. Thus, to answer the question, "Where did the action happen?" one answers, "It happened in the left, 1000, 3021, green H-cell". It is from this "where" information that the mental display of one's surroundings is generated, not the location of the retina cone or rod in the x,y,z location of the 1st-Person Laboratory. The generalized name of the H-cell is mathematically handled as a vector "$\mathbf{q}_f$", which specifies the internal pixel location of the detector relative to the other sensors in the Hilbert space network.

The "when" is often added as an additional dimension to the "where" thus leading to the concept of the relativistic 4th dimension. This works because recorded memories are often displayed in space-time diagrams, calendars or sequence numbers for movie frames that are in fact displayed in space. However, in CAT, time is associated with the state of the Hilbert space, which is represented but is not equal to our perception. Chapter 4 calculates time as an abstract quantity derived from the isolated state approximation of a clock in a system of interest. This abstract time is used in CAT, like Newton's god-given time "T". However, when the Hilbert space contains its own clock, "q_0" or the Greek letter "τ" defines the personal time state of the H-space, then these parameters label the "when" portion a measurement report. This reserves "t", the wall-clock time state measuring the state of the universe the quantum experimenter has adopted for his or her laboratory clock.

With these clarifications the measurement report received by the 2nd-person contains 1) what happened as an amount $a[q_f,\tau]$ flowing parallel to the direction of the H-space clock, 2) where it happened is the name of the f-axis cell vector "$\mathbf{q}_f$" and 3) when it happened as the state of the Hilbert space, while the duration and sizes of each measurement is labeled by $\Delta\tau$ and $\Delta\mathbf{q}_f$ respectively.

5.3.1.1 Interpretation of Hilbert space measurement reports

It is important to remember that the H-cell measurement is performed through an interaction with the unknowable outside-the-perceptive experience common to all of us communicating beings. As shown in Figure 5.3-1 the reporting arrows point to the 2nd-person icon, known as Wigner's friend, who is looking at the report and thereby believes he is seeing through the H-cells and measuring a quantum object.

We 1st-person observers can theorize that the flow of action carrying the report has been processed into the 2nd-person's quantum object symbol ψ, which is projected into the interior of the H-cells where we 1st-persons have also projected ψ. By using the same symbol to communicate between us regarding what we believe happens in the unknowable interior of matter we have established a consensus reality. We mutually reinforce each other's belief that ψ defines what actually happens inside the material beyond the H-cell boundary leading to the quantum world.

Furthermore, because we are looking straight into the 1st-Person Laboratory, it is typical for us to fall into the visualization trap and assume that our own theoretical projections are really out there. Given this belief, we may then utilize our laboratory reference frame to state that the quantum object happened at the location defined by the wall dimensions "x,y,z" at the wall-clock time interval "t". To understand why this is an error – perhaps the main reason quantum and relativity theory cannot be reconciled – remember that the marks on a ruler give names that format our retina detector cells recording a measurement. When using the x,y,z,t wall coordinate frame in the 1st-Person Laboratory to locate an object, the names of the points along the walls are used to format the retina detectors of us

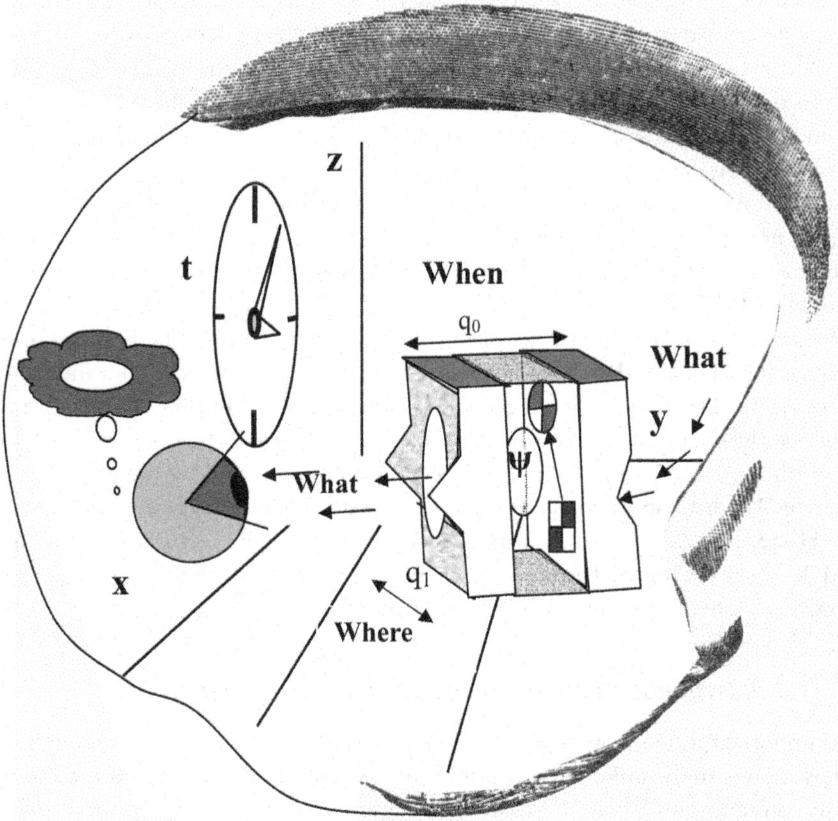

FIGURE 5.3-1 Detector cells report inside material equipment parameters not external to "what, space, time" locations in the 1st-Person Laboratory

1st-person observers. We use these axis labels to calibrate our retina when looking at the experimental equipment from the outside. When looking through the equipment the q_0,$\mathbf{q}_f$ labels of the material must be used to define the locations of events inside the material.

What we have described is the typical viewpoint of a quantum experimenter who believes that what surrounds him or her in the laboratory is an independent reality of objects including the quantum objects, which the experimenter believes exist as independent-of-him-/herself probability amplitudes. In CAT, however we acknowledge that interaction reports are explained by our own projections. These meanings of symbols describing these projections are our own mental constructs. The validity of these projections is their utility in manipulating our sensations. We are therefore free to suggest a better interpretation of ψ than the one suggested by the Copenhagen School. In CAT, we give ψ the physical meaning of mass-charge displacement oscillations, rather than probability amplitudes of conventional quantum theory. The inside of matter can then be visualized and quantified as will be done in the next section.

5.3.1.2 Small displacement oscillations

In this section we assume the interior matter beyond or internal to a Hilbert space-cell boundary is composed of mass and charge densities. The mass and charge densities move relative to each other in order to maintain their equilibrium positions. For small-enough volume cells, such motion can be approximated by the motion of centers of mass and charge. Figure 5.3-2 shows the icon for a typical cell volume taken out of a larger action structure forming a Hilbert space. For the time being we assume the specific structure and its action flow is self-contained and not interacting with other Hilbert spaces. Think a multidimensional "toroid" where the square edges of a CAT book model are connected to their opposite sides, and the time states are closed through the back and front cover, although we are only able to show a static snapshot of a small Cartesian array in Figure 5.3-2. The reader is reminded that action is here flowing past this "Now". This means the charge and mass positions change as the reader imagines the action flowing along the spatial timeline being watched.

To calculate these motions, remember that when matter in a non-interacting system is in a stable equilibrium, all forces sum to zero. There are three force types on the charge and three on the mass. The flow of change passing through the cell will in general dictate a motion in the vertical direction in response to the changing force-field variations. For an isolated loop segment, the forces flow along the timeline. But the gravito-electric forces, $F_{gi}\star$, F_{gi}, $F_{em}\star$ and F_{em}, on the outside side of each "Now" instant, do not always cancel each other as they propagate past. This

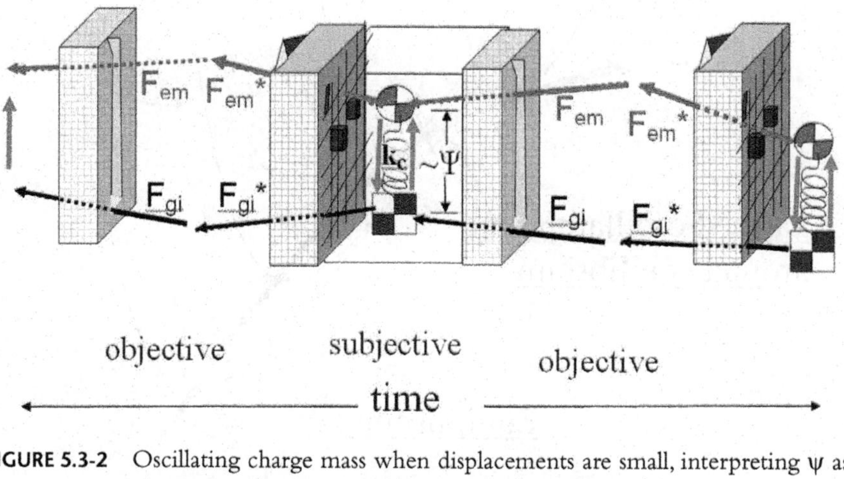

FIGURE 5.3-2 Oscillating charge mass when displacements are small, interpreting ψ as charge-mass separation state

means the internal Fmc, Fmc★, Fcm, Fcm★ forces must take on values so that the total vector sums to zero.

Consider an empty-space equilibrium action flow running through an action loop. The flow does not stop. It is just featureless. Since we are visualizing centers of mass and charge in time and space of a cell extension, the charge and mass centers would represent an average location for the motion defining an empty space cell. Furthermore, the activity in such a cell would repeat exactly by definition of the space cell, and hence be in a stationary position throughout the lifetime of the isolated event structure. However, content associated with particles in empty space could be visualized as changing the up, down, forward and backward positions as action flows along the timeline. Any deviation from equilibrium would be experienced as a disturbance separation of charge and mass. In CAT, these separation distances can become large. Implications of large deviations beyond physics are discussed in Chapters 7 and 8. However, when the CAT displacements are restricted to be "small-enough" distances, we reach the quantum approximation.

All classic systems subject to small-enough disturbances will experience a linear restoring force and follow motions similar to those of harmonic oscillators centered on the equilibrium motion. Since we are treating the mass-charge centers as classic objects responding to force fields, the theory of small oscillations applies. The motion of the charge relative to the mass would be an oscillation about the dynamic equilibrium state of empty space. Figure 5.3-3 shows a graphic representation of

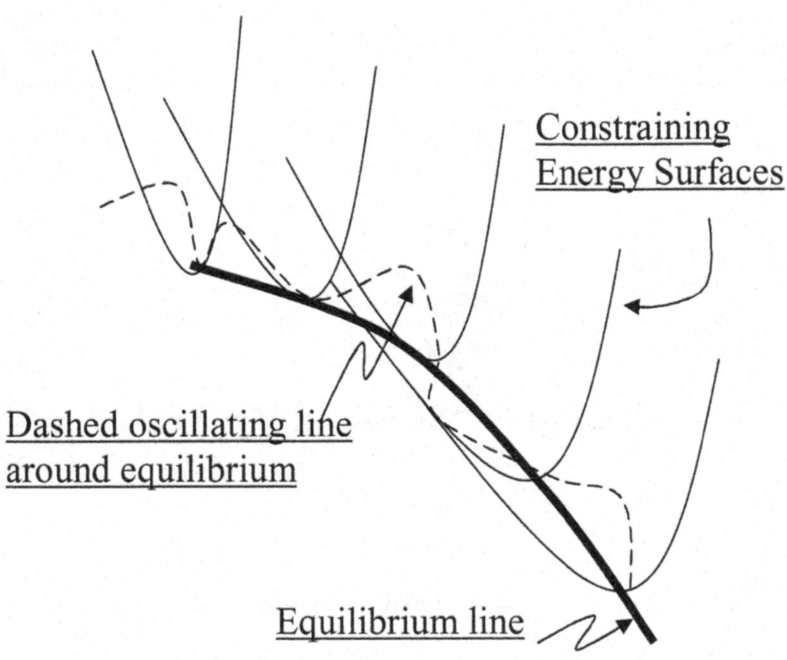

FIGURE 5.3-3 Oscillating path around energy valley

an equilibrium line forming the valley of a potential energy surface provided. The equilibrium line would correspond to a river flowing down the bottom of the valley. A ball rolling down such a valley would oscillate from side to side. Each time it tries to climb the wall, a resorting force would drive it back to the lowest point in the valley. The difference between such a valley and our situation is that the main direction of the equilibrium line is time, not a path down the mountain.

The mechanical model for such a situation is the motion of two balls connected by a spring. The two interior forces at each end of the spring shown in Figure 5.3-2 would couple the charge and mass together. The spring constant "k_c" determines the strength of the internal forces F_{cm}, F_{mc} holding the charge and mass together while the strength of the gravito-electric forces impingent on the future and past sides of the Hilbert space cell's "Now" determines the balancing forces. Classical and quantum point particles approximation is approached when this spring constant approaches infinity for then the charge and mass are always co-located.

The mathematical expression describing this oscillation is $e^{i\cdot 2\cdot\pi\cdot\varepsilon\cdot\pi/h}$. Here π is the personal energy and τ is the personal time for the cells in the structure. These intrinsic parameters are applicable for an isolated action loop. It should be noted that this converts to the expression for the instantaneous wave function shown in Figure 5.2-1, $\psi[\underline{x}](\varphi) = e^{i.\int a[\varphi]d\varphi/h}$, because the action is integrated over the $2\cdot\pi$ radians defining a space-time instance. We have thereby identified the quantum mechanical expression for the Schrödinger's wave function with a visualization of oscillating charge-mass separation distance inside material. This gives the quantum symbol ψ an ontological meaning and gives us a visualization of what is vibrating. The next section shows how these oscillations satisfy Schrödinger's wave equation. This will further demonstrate that quantum theory is an approximation of CAT when displacements are small enough.

5.3.2 Motion in coupled Hilbert space cells

In the previous section we examined a single isolated action loop. Such loops are only exact for Reality as a Whole or when used as approximations for systems whose interactions are small when compared with internal activities defining the bulk of the system happening. In all other cases action loops come in parallel configurations and interact with their neighbors along the whole timeline of their loops. Instead of a single address vector "$\underline{\mathbf{q}}_f$", this symbol will now be used as a variable addressing a field of parallel loops. This situation is more appropriate for describing arrays of sensors such as the human retina. To analyze this parallel loop interaction, Figure 5.3-4 has added neighboring Hilbert space-cell "Now" instances next to the one we analyzed in Figure 5.3-2. The coupling between neighbors is accomplished through leakage of the external forces, F_{em} and F_{gi}, from one loop to another. These past and future interaction forces are considered to be smaller when compared with the majority of influences flowing through the main timeline of the loop. We can therefore assume that to first approximation the charges and masses in each cell continue to move action along the loop's timeline as though no cross-loop

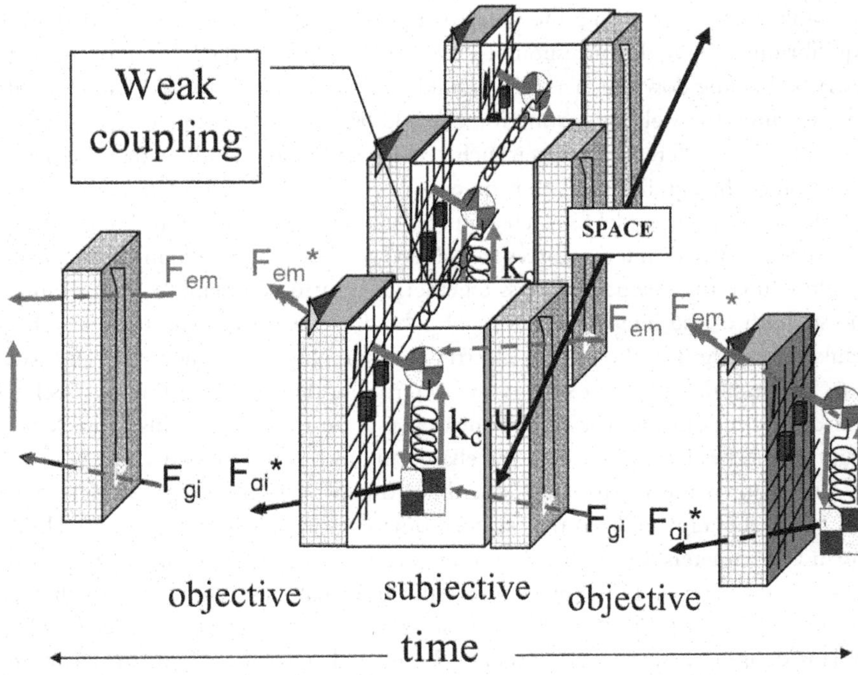

FIGURE 5.3-4 Coupled Hilbert space cells support Schrödinger oscillations

interaction occurs. However, in addition to this primary motion, the cell is also subject to a perturbing potential energy field from the charges and masses moving in all the neighboring loops in its environment.

We again utilize the spring analogy to visualize the connection between spatially separated time instances in terms of springs. Since the main influence is along the timeline, only relatively weak forces leak between neighbors. This weak coupling is represented by weak springs with small spring constants as compared with strong springs coupling the cells along the timeline. The interaction strengths are justified by remembering that centers of mass and charge are an approximation to the mass-charge densities filling the cross section of each cell. In such sheet-like configurations only the perimeter material interacts with the perimeter of its neighbors.

To visualize what an empty-space model of these parallel time loops connected by springs might look like, consider an old-fashioned box-spring mattress with all the springs connected to each other. When left alone, the springs in the mattress are all at rest, and though there is plenty of force in the springs tying up the material, nothing moves. At some point a pebble falls on the mattress causing a small disturbance. The disturbance spreads in wave-like patterns. If we assume ideal springs without friction, the disturbance spreads throughout the structure, reflecting from the sides and perhaps achieving patterns of standing waves. Of course, an actual demonstration would have friction. Moving springs push air molecules creating sound. Flexing and extending creates heat and so does movement of the joints. The disturbance in bed springs would quickly fade. However, activity at the elementary force-level friction does not exist and the vibration would go on forever.

5.3.2.1 Derivation of the wave function ψ from the CAT model

The patterns appearing in those vibrations are not random. A standard analysis in Goldstein's *Classical Mechanics* (1965, chapter 10) provides an analysis of small oscillations. The analysis is applicable to all systems independent of the material and nature of the forces involved. A tailored summary of the analysis is presented in Appendix A5.1. This shows that when the disturbance is small enough, any system of "j" particles connected by springs will produce a vibration pattern that is governed by a Schrödinger-like equation. A cube of Hilbert space cells, each labeled with generalized addresses, variables qj_1,qj_2,qj_3, etc. and personal time "τ", could support a pattern of oscillations that satisfies a Schrödinger equation. A normalized field of such oscillations, described in quantum theory as $\psi(qj_1,qj_2,qj_3,\tau)$, is visualized in CAT as small motions of a center of charge relative to a center of mass in the jth cell of small-enough side lengths dqj_1, dqj_2, and dqj_3. By demonstrating how quantum oscillations can arise in coupled classic particles, the CAT model provides a physical basis for the existence of wave patterns that appear as probability amplitudes in quantum mechanics but are actually the appearance of thought.

An example of coupled motion in a system of two particles, having equal masses and charges, and connected by linear forces between individual mass-charge degrees of freedom, shows that the motion corresponds, in quantum theory, to Hilbert space cells designed to measure the location of a quantum particle. The amplitude of oscillation will move from one cell to another. If the energy in the amplitude is taken as a measurement of the location of such a quantum particle, then it will show up in location 1 or location 2 defined by the two cells with probabilities given by $\psi^{\star}{}_1 \cdot \psi_1$ and $\psi^{\star}{}_2 \cdot \psi_2$ exactly as predicted by the Schrödinger equation and quantum theory. However, the example provides an ontological visualization of a reality causing these probabilities and identifies what we believe is a long-standing misinterpretation of quantum measurement results. Namely that *interactions causing motions in detector cells have been mistaken for particle locations themselves.*

5.3.2.2 What is a quantum particle?

A measurement consists of an interaction between the detector cells that are seen on the boundary of the Hilbert space from the outside as objects. In CAT, the reality of the interior of the material defining a Hilbert space is a system beyond its appearance in the 1st-person perspective. When a measurement takes place, an amount of action "h" is transferred from the Hilbert space out into the objective recording apparatus of the lab equipment. The H-cell that engages in this recording must have the action or it would not be able to pass it out to be recorded. *In quantum theory, the location of the cell from which action is extracted is the location assigned to the existence of a quantum particle.* When the cells are viewed from the outside, the cell positions are given laboratory coordinate vectors **x1** and **x2**. Since in our two-particle case, the action rate moving back and forth between H-cell at **x1** and **x2** is in each cell half the time. Measurements will find the "quantum particle" at either position half the time. This half-time result is naturally interpreted as a probability of finding a quantum particle at either position because the existence of quantum particles is the explanation of measurements projected by the founders of quantum theory into the location of their equipment in the laboratory.

Appendix A5.1 only derives the Schrödinger's equation for a single free particle moving in one dimension, as might be visualized as a disturbances traveling down a very long and narrow system of bed springs, but the lesson is obvious. If coupling energies exist along a path but reduce to zero at some path-width boundary, the oscillations will remain within the width of that path. In three dimensions, the width is the volume of a particle and the path is the particle's world line. In other words, because 1) *interaction locations are interpreted as particle locations* in quantum theory and 2) particles, when described as wave oscillations distributed in their volume, are likely to interact across the entire volume of the H-cells in which the oscillations occur, therefore 3) quantum particles can appear to be at two places at once. This usually assumed interpretation leads to the collapse of the wave function, wave-particle duality and other touted quantum mysteries of Nature. When the symbols and equations of basic quantum theory are given an ontological and visualizable interpretation within CAT, such strange properties disappear. The CAT interpretation provides a mathematical equivalence to quantum theory when Hilbert space cells are identified as the external objective view of material, and small-enough motions between charge and mass centers do not destroy the cells. In this case the oscillations can be interpreted as the wave function. In other words, quantum theory is the linear approximation to CAT when the observer is taken out of the formalism but the observer's mental projections are interpreted as probabilities of a quantum reality.

5.4 The quantum model of a conscious being

Figure 5.4-1 is a flow diagram of the "Now" instant of an interacting being using both quantum and classic physics symbols to model Reality. The being is experiencing a room with an apple in his visual ego. Both the expected and measured visual images are shown. A visualization of the explanation of his or her visual sensations are shown in the thought bubble. First the white touch outlines of objects are experienced in the thought bubble, and second theoretical visualization of mass-charge centers contained in the surrounding rectangle are fused with the thought bubble. Under normal operation, all three data flows are registered and co-located providing an everyday feeling of a solid objective world. The upper external visual observable is derived from the unknowable outside. It is compared with the expected visual observable, which generates commands back to the outside and updates into the model of reality used by the being. Most likely only reset and gain adjustment commands are sent to the past side of the retina; however, the interface with the unknowable is intended to represent all modalities of sensations available including muscle actuators.

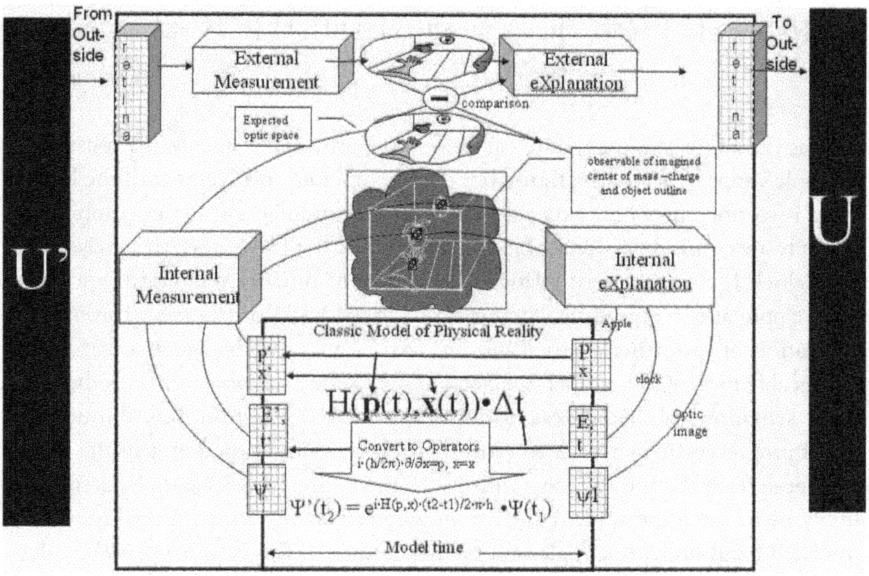

FIGURE 5.4-1 Process diagram of "I" outfitted with a quantum model interfacing optically with the external universe

The two lower observable regions are connected to the models of physical reality by oval lines representing action flow inside the being. The graphic cycles transport update signals through the internal eXplanation function and are connected to two models of physical reality. These are only shown for comparison. Under normal operation, the being would only install one or the other. These models calculate the changes in the expected touch and physical theory visualizations, which are expected if the commands sent to the outside do what they are intended to do. The two models are shown within the context of the CAT flow diagram in order to exemplify how each of them performs their intended function. For heuristic purposes we restrict the example to the appearance of the apple. The classic model uses the position $\underline{\mathbf{x}}(t)$ and momentum $\underline{\mathbf{p}}(t)$ of the apple centers as they are experienced in the thought bubble when the clock experience stands at "t" o'clock as input. These parameters are used to build the Hamiltonian Energy $H(\underline{\mathbf{p}},\underline{\mathbf{x}})$, which is the sum of internal Kinetic Energy $KE(\underline{\mathbf{p}})$ plus the Potential Energy $PE(\underline{\mathbf{x}})$. This Hamiltonian is effectively the classic model of reality. By applying the Least Action Principle one can derive the canonical equations of motion for the apple as

$$dx_f/dt = \partial H/\partial p_f \text{ and } dp_f/dt = -\,\partial H/\partial x_f, \qquad \text{Equation 5.4-1}$$

Which can be solved, numerically if necessary, to generate the next expected position and momentum at o'clock time $t_2 = t_1 + \Delta t$ by adding the change happening since the current o'clock time t_1 as

$$\underline{\mathbf{x}}(t_2) = \underline{\mathbf{x}}(t_1) + \{\partial H/\partial \underline{\mathbf{p}}\} \cdot \Delta t \text{ and } \underline{\mathbf{p}}(t_2) = \underline{\mathbf{p}}(t_1) + \{-\partial H/\partial \underline{\mathbf{x}}\} \cdot \Delta t .$$

Equation 5.4-2

This classic physics procedure calculates, to reasonable accuracy, the location of the apple's appearance in the future but the unconscious involvement of the human being is so obvious when expectations meet measurements that the combination is simply recognized as a real object out there. In CAT, we note that t_1 is always the o'clock time in the past relative to the current instance. Finding the location of the apple at t_1 required the "being" to calculate backward in time, through the stimulation of his or her sensors, and on into the unknowable. Such a feat is only manageable in the CAT model (see Section 6.4). When the observer finds the cause of the sensation, the being's calculation implemented as action flow through this model progresses further back to cross the origin destiny time point in the model to emerge from the future along with his or her desire. In this example, desire may simply be to catch the apple. Thus, a configuration change in the model moves the simulated hand under the apple at some future time. If this is to happen, the calculating action still flowing in the same direction must instantiate a trajectory for his hand, which will emerge as a change between what the unknowable measurement result and the expected observable contains. The comparison function now contains the muscle-actuator command. That controls the body movements and updates the model of reality to expect the motion of his or her hand at the next instance.

The last paragraph was a summary description of the fundamental CAT algorithm, which will be thoroughly discussed in Chapter 6. It is here provided to show how classic physics fits into the larger action flow promulgated by the CAT. Its popularity and success mean the unknowable consists of centers of charge and mass described by coordinates and momentum that move under the influence of gravito-electric forces. All we can say is that the calculations seem to work well when we want to catch apples. For other challenges the quantum model has also been profitable.

The conversion from classic to quantum physics is shown in Figure 5.4-1 as the notation in the downward pointing arrow inside the model square. The momentum and coordinate vectors are converted to mathematical operators so that we now have a Hamiltonian operator acting on a wave function $\psi(t)$ rather than a temporal function of p(t), x(t) trajectories. This Hamiltonian operator is formally placed into the exponent of Euler's number "e". Exponents allow addition in the exponents to be equated to multiplication in the function so we can write the time difference (t2-t1) as two sequential operators,

$$\Psi(t_2) = e^{i \cdot H(\underline{\mathbf{p}},\underline{\mathbf{x}}) \cdot t_2/2 \cdot \pi \cdot h} \; e^{-i \cdot H(\underline{\mathbf{p}},\underline{\mathbf{x}}) \cdot t_1/2 \cdot \pi \cdot h} \; \Psi(t_1) = e^{i \cdot H(\underline{\mathbf{p}},\underline{\mathbf{x}}) \cdot t_2/2 \cdot \pi \cdot h} \cdot \Psi(0).$$

Equation 5.4-3

The right-hand operator in the middle term transforms the y-function to the origin of time as shown in the right term while the left-hand operator in the middle term transforms the ψ-function from the origin across the destiny line and on back from the future to time t_2. This quantum formalism exactly implements the fundamental CAT algorithm when the y-function is interpreted as real oscillations in Hilbert space, and Hilbert space is interpreted as the inside material behind the detector cells facing the unknowable. In CAT, we visualize an oscillating distance between charge and mass propagating through this inside material of the H-cells comprising our lab equipment. Lab equipment is seen as objects, but we assume these are some unknowable reality outside our 1st-person experience that we can only model. The quantum model provides one mathematical formalism which describes this unknowable.

Remember that a 1st-person is the action loop who feels the flow of change pass through his or her "Now". When the changes produced in the loop of parallel cells are exactly identical to those measured from outside without any differences, then the 1st-person observable "Now" instance would feel like empty space. This feeling arises when the observer's **MoR** exactly predicts the next observable and the being's loop state is in equilibrium with the unknowable. If the disturbance to the equilibrium state is small enough, appearances would arise in this space, but the perception of space would not be altered. One would see the appearance of everyday objects moving in a permanent space. This situation is described by the quantum approximation that allows the equilibrium to be reversibly altered. If, however, the disturbances become large enough, the equilibrium loop state itself is altered. This would show up to the 1st-person as a disruption of the space he or she perceives, not just a change to the objects in that space. Nonlinear displacements are often reversible and selected nonlinear extensions to quantum theory have been developed but more serious cases leading to permanent disruptions of space is outside the quantum theory's domain.

In summary, the quantum model of reality consists both of a small-enough disturbance in Hilbert space given the symbol ψ and a process U() that manipulates that disturbance. The definition of "small enough" is that the externalized detector cells can accommodate the disturbance without themselves being destroyed. In this case, the disturbance will propagate indefinitely in the permanent space of cells. If, however, the disturbance becomes more violent so that the detector-actuator cells are themselves modified, then we cross from the quantum into the CAT domain. In this domain the theory becomes much more comprehensive since it includes the activities that create and destroy the laboratory equipment and the experimenter him- or herself. In fact, if we consider just the experimenter under the quantum approximation so that the detector-actuator arrays remain unchanged by the disturbances processed through them, then the experimenter's experience would be described as a fixed space in which appearances move around like the objects we see. This describes a mature human being with a stable memory. Such an individual will be happy with classic or quantum theory. However, once we must deal with the growth and destruction of those memory cells, which surely happens, it will be necessary to adopt CAT and the event-oriented world view. The physical understanding of permanent disruptions in space and further applications of this expanded theory will be discussed in Part III of this book.

PART III

Implications and applications

6

MODEL OF A CONSCIOUS BEING

In the last chapter we presented an action-flow model to describe the fundamental reality happening in all isolated systems coordinated under one global state-time. This chapter introduces the specific architecture of that flow, which gives rise to conscious activity experienced by a human being. We will accept the basic action cycle as a continuous happening between mental experience and physical explanations of that experience as a solution to the "hard problem" of consciousness. We now know the physical basis of consciousness is the Now phase of an action loop. How an action loop structure can implement the detailed functions required to perceive as well as act in the manner of a human being is now to be discussed.

6.1 Interactions between two almost isolated beings

Figure 6.1-1 shows the use of two book models that display the essence of the reality a self-conscious being encounters. Each book has been formatted with a mass-charge medium that contains interactions between internal parts. These interactions happen inside the pages of each book during the changes executed by the page-turn operations. Each book individually describes the dynamics of a nearly completely isolated system. The framework of both models is the same, whether we are modeling the universe, a conscious being or an elementary particle event. Only the scale and the detailed action-flow patterns differ. That action-flow physics was applicable to such systems was demonstrated in Chapter 4. There we reintroduced the Newtonian concept of an immutable time of an isolated whole "T_w" and its spatial mapped length "Q_w", which coordinates all activity under its loop state "Z_W". A measured clock time "t", which approximates Newtonian time, becomes available when a dominant sub-part of that Whole is identified as a clock. This left us with a picture seen by a godlike Reader, who is coordinating interacting sub-parts in his or her own Whole, as a deterministic clock-like universe. A picture of two such sub-parts, the first containing your body "**You**" and the rest of your universe "$\mathbf{U_Y}$" and the second containing my body model "**I**" and the rest my universe "$\mathbf{U_I}$" as action cycle complexes shown in Figure 6.1-1.

The godlike Reader has now identified two approximately isolated models within a larger Whole that is believed to be Reality itself. That godlike Reality includes two models of beings whose Newtonian time T_I and T_Y and the measured clock time within each model, t_Y and t_I, correspond to the instantaneous state of nearly isolated beings named by "You" and the "I". These operational symbol types refer to what these models actually are intended to represent. Each of these events is governed by the physics of an isolated system outlined in Chapter 4. In that sense, each of these whole "You or I" events are their own self-contained universe (Chopra and Kafatos, 2017; Baer, 2017b).

Using the analogy of our book model we can imagine two readers sitting at two desks, each one reading at different rates or even skipping back and forward. Each one experiences a different story depending on the path through the book, and each one experiences a Now instant dependent on the pages one happens to have open. Occasionally one of the readers looks up and sends a message to the other. Since action is conserved there is no ink outside the pages, so messages must be composed of material extracted from the book. The receiver attempts to incorporate the message by modifying his or her own book and will presumably do so if the receiver's lifetime history is thereby improved. If absorbed, the message modifies the state of both events. The receiver may return another message, perhaps as an acknowledgment including some payment. However, these are not the deterministic state changes within each universe but involve mental evaluation and are akin to the jumps happening during the measurement process of quantum theory.

Exactly how, when or where each interaction message is perceived by the other system will depend on their individual configuration. What is clear is that the interactions between otherwise isolated events will result in accommodations to those

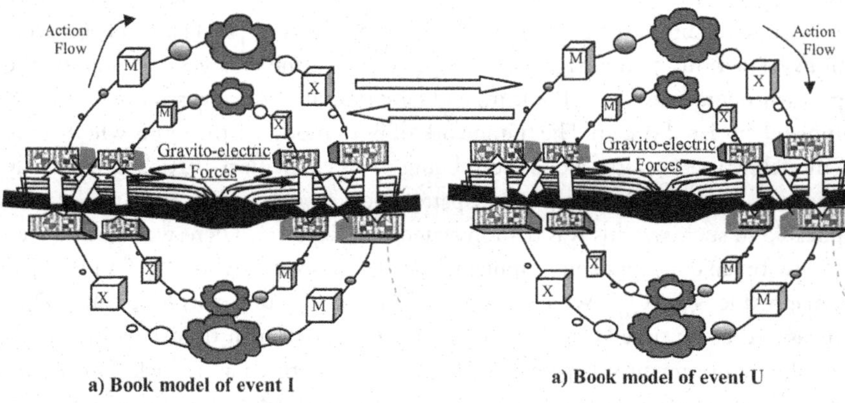

FIGURE 6.1-1 The graphic action model of two isolated events with two parts each

messages in each of the participating systems. This accommodation will consist of updates to a model in each participating universe that explains what caused the message and how interactions with it can be formed to achieve the desired improvement.

Figures 6.1-1 and 6.1-2 set the stage for the development of the detailed action-flow model that is constructed in each isolated system in order to acknowledge and manipulate whatever it believes exists outside itself. This development transforms a stand-alone system that may contain a solipsistic dream to an interactive action-flow structure. Such an interaction structure will become our model of the conscious being described in this chapter.

Toward this end we will modify the self-contained action loop by identifying specialized space cells that divert some of the action flowing through the internal model back into the external unknowable. A CAT flow model of an interacting conscious being is then analyzed by tracing the logic flow required to receive, become aware of and send action commands back to the outside. The fundamental CAT algorithm in this model explains sensations by tracing a cause-and-effect chain backward in time and then creating action plans that stretch back from the future to terminate with the immediate Now commands sent to the outside. The ultimate cause in the model will be identified as the symbolic origin of what the Being believes to be its Self, and the significance of this symbol to control the fundamental tenets by which the higher processing levels are controlled will be explained.

At this stage we will have documented a single optimum response based on a single set of knowledge coded into a being's memory of the external world. However, the typical human is aware of the limitations of his or her knowledge and hence the flow of action cannot be singularly deterministic. Instead a simultaneous calculation of possible alternatives, each appropriate for a different guess as to the actual state of the external world is required. The presentation of multiple

FIGURE 6.1-2 Two models of independent conscious beings with occasional message exchanges

parallel executions followed by an optimum command selection then completes the model of a cognitive being. In Chapter 5 we showed that when the action flow is restricted to "small-enough" reversible changes it can be represented with linear algebra. In that case, we will show in Chapter 7 that our theory reduces a cognitive being to an operating quantum computer.

6.2 Building an action-flow model of a conscious being

In Chapter 4 we developed an action model of physical reality as a stand-alone independent event. Such an event is a self-contained activity that transforms material into the sensations experienced by that material in an endless cycle of activity. As such, the hard problem of consciousness is solved by the pan-psychic assumption that conscious experiences are built into material at its most fundamental level. The experience of a conscious human being is not simply described by feelings inherent in a stand-alone action cycle. A conscious human being does not only experience a self-contained dream but also a specific set of sensations attributed to entities believed to exist outside the body, entities the human being believes he or she must manage in order to control the sensations the human is subject to. For this reason, the architecture of an action structure describing a human being consists of an interacting action loop. Such a loop generates within itself a model explaining external interactions, sensor-actuator interfaces and action-flow channels connecting all the components. The derivation of an action architecture that provides the functionality required to model a human is presented in this section. Starting with the general interactions available to material, we will show how the flow of activity is organized to produce a basic structure that implements a conscious being.

6.2.1 I's general interaction with unknowable reality

We have assumed that stand-alone events are closed loops in order to avoid the infinity that arises when asking what is beyond any past and future boundary (see Section 8.1.5). When isolated, action flows through the outside of material arrays bringing a change of mass/charge configuration that continues through an observable phase on the inside of material, which in turn modifies the exterior side again. The material configuration evolves as the change propagates through many sequential cycles until the evolution repeats, thus executing a lifetime of activity that never stops. As long as the system remains isolated, the lifetime repeats exactly because the material involved in any of its parallel cycles follows a minimum-action dynamic from which deviations would require additional action. Such action must come from some other parallel cycle of the system and would introduce non-equilibrium forces that are anthropomorphically painful.

Stand-alone isolated systems are always approximations since only reality as a Whole would contain all the action there is. The central I loop of Figure 6.2-1 represents such an approximation because some unknowable cause of additional interactions is indicated. The cause is fundamentally unknowable because I is the loop and I cannot get out of itself to observe what is not in its own loop. I's only knowledge comes from interpreting interactions experienced by its own material in a model built of its own material. That material is composed of charge and mass, which both have an outside and inside aspect in their past and future existence. These sides send and receive action respectively. This means in the most general situation the charge and mass can each interact at four sides allowing eight possible interactions. The possibilities are shown as eight interaction arrows between the central I cycle and the upper and lower unknowable shown in Figure 6.2-1.

If the I cycle were in equilibrium without interactions from the unknowable, and the four action flows in and out of the left material density were added they would corrupt the equilibrium sensation from the model in I's memory. Similarly, any explanation of observables would be corrupted by the unknowable subjective interaction and the gravito-electric influences flowing back to the unknowable. Although such any-to-any action flows are possible, it is unlikely that human conscious experiences could be explained without postulating extraordinary coordination with the unknowable. Such coordination would be perceived as serendipity, lacking anything like the control humans actually believe they have. Of course, some individuals insist our entire experience is controlled by deliberate and continuous intervention from some powerful entity external to our observable experience and Figure 6.2-1 suggests direct mind-to-mind interactions can occur. However, the reciprocal nature of CAT implies any such interactions would be a mutually beneficial exchange rather than a one-sided imposition.

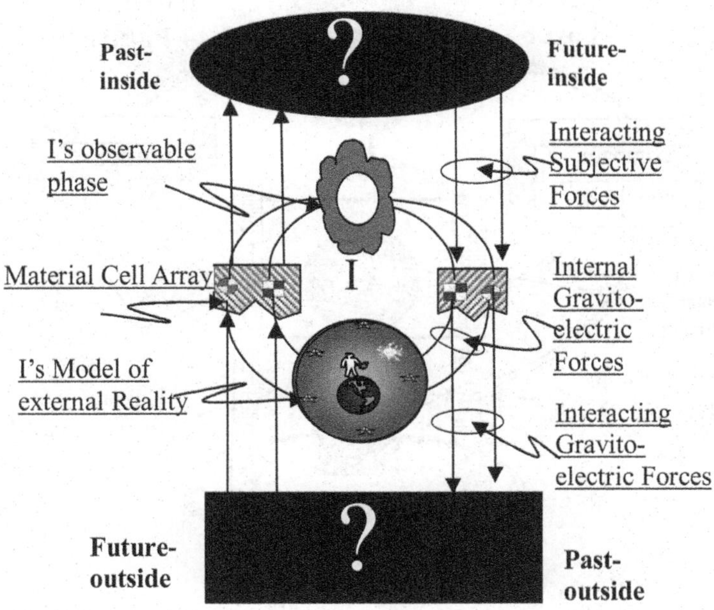

FIGURE 6.2-1 General material interactions between a 1st-person and the Unknowable

Modeling such phenomena will be discussed later in Part III. Here we continue the step-by-step buildup of the action structure of a conscious being. To make the next step, we must acknowledge that the human memory holding one's **MoR** is shielded from the general interactions discussed in this section and only specifically constructed interface cells using gravito-electric-based interactions are available to interface with whatever is exterior to the self-defining central activity loop. This acknowledgment limits mind-to-mind interactions to those happening internal to our own material Brain and leads us toward an action model compatible with current scientific thought.

6.2.2 Limiting external interactions to gravito-electric influences

Figure 6.2-1 shows general past and future material cells that interact with their neighbors whether such neighbors are in the I cycle or the unknowable. Logical thinking by conscious humans requires the memory model and its mind display to be protected so it cannot be corrupted by serendipitous external influences. This means the action flow through ones model's interface cell must be divided. Figure 6.2-2 shows such a division. The left and right interface arrays are divided into functional categories. The upper model interface arrays only update I's memory

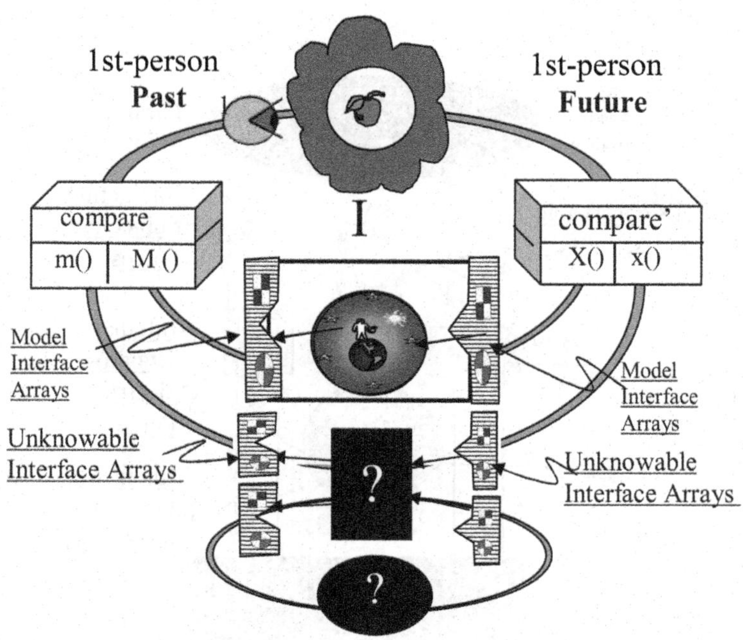

FIGURE 6.2-2 Dividing Reality into an internal "I" cycle and an external body cycle interfacing to a conscious unknowable

containing the model. The middle cells act as interface arrays between I and the unknowable. These are the real "Sensors" not the observable sensor appearances. The lower cells complete a loop in the unknowable is useful speculation because the "unknowable" being unknowable may or may not have such a loop. All I knows of it comes from interpretations of action flowing in and out of the interface sensors. This architecture allows the content of the **MoR** to be controlled by the measurement, comparator and explanatory functions and gives the I the capability of developing its own unique concept of what is external to its own loop.

It is worthwhile to discuss for a moment how such separations occur. In CAT, interactions are not calculated by assuming the charge and mass in a space cell are concentrated at their respective centers. Instead the interaction between the extensions of charge and mass is dependent upon their density distribution, not the propagation of fields in "nothingness". Such propagation is a useful fiction created by assuming point charge and mass sources radiate directly throughout the emptiness of the universe. Centers of charge and mass are shown as icons in space cells to indicate material types. Their use as sources or sinks of force fields is a *mathematical fiction* only applicable when material nature of empty space is ignored.

Decreasing densities mark regions of limited interaction and can provide boundaries between activities so that one is able to talk about isolated systems. Each space cell may be divided from its neighbors by low-density regions introduced by formatting operations described in Chapter 3. The divisions allow each empty-space cell to be approximated as an isolated cycle modeling a small system. Lower action density boundaries between space cells allow interactions internal to the larger I loops. An aggregation of space cells into an I loop is further isolated from the unknowable, where action densities with the interface cells maintain "windows" through which information flows are possible. Other than such interfaces, the forces of isolated systems stay within their internal high-density regions so that the influence arrows between the past and future incarnations of mass and charge remain within the closed parallel cycles that define empty space of each system.

The juxtaposition of the unknowable and the model in our flow architecture suggests several important characteristics that are independent of any specific model incorporated in the loops. First, the architecture indicates that the unknowable and our model of it are indirectly connected by an interaction involving the conscious phase of both the internal and interface cycles, even if the model is gravito-electrically isolated. Second, the lower cycle within the unknowable has a subjective aspect, suggesting consciousness is a ubiquitous property. Third, if by some lucky guess of evolutionary development we had hit upon a perfect model, then the model would be an identical copy of the unknowable. This gives us a test for the veracity of any model. Even if we know nothing else about the unknowable, we would logically expect that if we sent the same signal into our perfect model and into the unknowable, we would get exactly the same response from both. A comparison would produce no difference, and each loop would experience the difference sensation of empty space. Thus, we have a testable method for accuracy of our model that does not require any a priori assumption regarding the nature of the unknowable.

Testability is the hallmark of the scientific method. However, in CAT, we further claim such testability must include a comparison of 1st-person observables and not solely a self-consistency test within the theoretical 3rd-person operation of our model, which is often assumed adequate.

6.2.3 The CAT model of a conscious being

The division in Figure 6.2-2 used the model of a classic objective universe. This was done to identify this location in the action-flow architecture with an icon that is familiar and makes sense to most readers. Such a location should not be tied to a specific model and the theory it implements. Instead it should be tied to the support structure, which can contain any model a human can invent to fill its role. For example, the support structure of a book drawn in previous chapters could be used as the "nothing" holding 1) the biological memory of a carbon-based human, 2) a silicone-based computer or 3) the material memory activity of any system.

Figure 6.2-3 shows an action-flow diagram limited to the components that can be known to a conscious being. Here we distinguish three views of reality, 1) the unknowable external world, 2) its representation as a symbolic theory and 3) the visualization of reality as an observable experience, all connected in an action-flow architecture. At the bottom is a black box referring to the unknowable external world. Here the boundary is defined by the future sensor-actuator arrays that

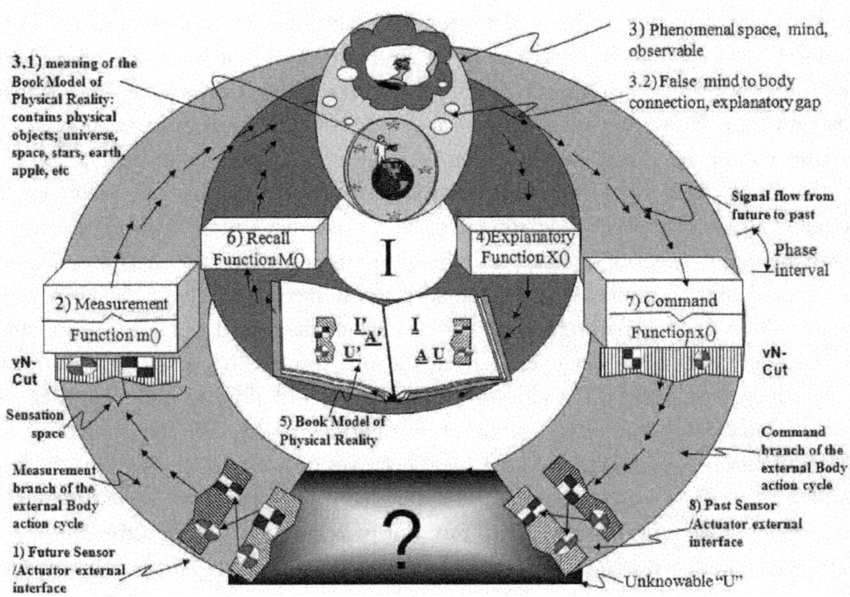

FIGURE 6.2-3 CAT model design of a conscious being with unknowable known only through internal symbolic forms

interact with the unknowable to produce raw sensor reports while the past arrays transmit commands that are intended to produce beneficial reactions.

Above the unknowable external world icon is the material memory of the conscious being shown as an icon of a book that contains the simulated sensor-actuator arrays encapsulating the names this being uses to reference the concept of the unknowable external world. This concept is encoded into the symbols of a theory that act as processing elements that predict the next observable sensation. These symbols cannot be seen directly since all observables are brought into consciousness through processes that produce sensations in the mental phase of the cycle.

For this reason, two main images are shown in the observable phase. The upper image is the 1st-person observable experience representing the world as seen and experienced. The lower image is the visualization of the 3rd-person reality that is normally taken to be the objective reality one believes to live in. The 1st- and 3rd-person views are typically registered so that the objects (here an apple) seen in one view are collocated with the "same" object in the second view. We have connected these views by bubbles indicating that we normally believe that the 3rd-person visualization of the brain generates the 1st-person experience, but we are not quite sure of the mechanism that does this job. Since we see in the CAT model that both the apple and brain are projected onto the mind phase of the respective action cycles, they cannot cause each other but are both produced by the unseen processes behind the observed visualizations.

6.2.4 A functional description of the action flow in a conscious being

In this section we follow the flow of action through the cycles in order to identify the functions implemented by the icons in Figure 6.2-3. Each component is annotated with numerical values that index the entries listed:

1 Future sensor-actuator external interface
External sensor arrays interact with an unknowable external world that propagates changes through individual sensor channels. Internal material forces are indicated by crossing arrows between charge and mass. Changes are sent through channels using gravito-electric force relays. Actuators often report a reset state.

2 Measurement function m()
Measurement processing inputs all sensor and actuator channels and selects, filters and otherwise prepares stimulation for presentation in the observable phase. Though shown as a box, it represents the input neural net. The flat input side accepts relayed external gravito-electric stimulation and the output side connects to the final processing stage before awareness. Most of the action flows directly to the output neurons as reflex or unconscious processing but some fraction generates conscious awareness.

3 Phenomenal space, mind, observable

This oval contains all observables normally available for experience by a conscious being. This includes the 1st-person optical perspective overlaid on the expected touch space of the thought bubble. The thought bubble contains sensations, generated from memory and available when one's eyes are closed. These indicate where surfaces of objects in the environment are expected to be located. This perceptive space is registered with the optical display by signals from the semicircular canal sensors of the ear.

3.1 Meaning of the book model

Also, part of the observables is the visualization of physical reality generated as the meaning of the operational symbols in the book model. These visualizations are normally registered with the optic and expected touch-space sensations to form a fused experience of one's actionable reality belief. For scientists the meaning visualizations would include theoretical objects such as elementary particles, distant stars, a 2nd-person's thoughts, geographic maps of the world and generally actionable information that life-and-death decisions are based upon. An example are the sensations experienced by a pilot flying under instrument control that tells the true situation, overriding his or her eyes or subjective feelings of what is around the airplane.

3.2 False mind-to-body connection

The connector bubbles between the 1st-person experiences and the 3rd-person's theoretical visualizations. For people who operate under the "objective reality" illusion, 3rd-person sensations *are* the objective reality they believe to live in. The explanatory gap arises because no causal connection is possible between two simultaneously displayed experiences just as two images of characters displayed on a movie screen do not causally affect each other.

4 Explanatory function X()

This function calculates backward from the mental experience to the simulated detector arrays that must have been stimulated in order to produce the observables. To a large extent, this calculation is the inverse of the measurement function, only its output are changes in the model of reality rather than the unknowable activities beyond the actual sensors.

5 Book model of reality

This is the heart of a conscious being's knowledge. Here symbols have operational characteristics to process changes into future predictions (see Section 2.4). The model shows the **I, A, U** and **I', A', U'** representing the operational model of oneself, the apple or system of interest and the ever-present environment of the rest of "I's" Universe. The "**Ac,Dc**" symbols represent the interfaces to the past and future side of the 1st-person. Interaction arrows between these symbols are not shown for clarity. See Figures 2.3-1 and 2.3-2 for more detailed action connections. It is in terms of these symbols that the cause of past sensory experience and prediction of future sensory experience is calculated. These are the symbols of the theory believed and incorporated in the larger mechanism of the Self represented by the actions structure of Figure 6.2-3. Although this book proposes CAT as the next evolutionary step in theory development, the exact theory placed into the book model is culturally and species dependent. Many theories of reality will guide an individual. However, the action-flow architecture into which such theories fit provides the framework for all of them. In that sense this transcendental god's-eye view provides a context for all theories.

6 Recall function M()

Once the book model calculates the next physical state the simulated output sensor array makes a measurement. This measurement is processed by the Recall function, which is also referred to as the memory Measurement function, to produce the next expected observable pattern of sensation.

3 again Phenomenal space, mind, observable

Here a fraction of both the external and memory measurement action stream come together. Of course, they also came together in the measurement cycle listed in paragraph 3), but we mention the merging again so that the source of both streams is clear. It is here that the difference between measurement and memory recall of the expected results is calculated. This difference underlies the conscious experience of the 1st-person's Now and emerges into the explanatory function of the internal cycle where it is used as error or update data to correct the Model of Reality (MoR). The complementary difference is also used by the command function to generate sensor reset and commands (or polite suggestions) that return to the unknowable.

7 Command function x()

The command function receives difference signals from the mind phase and performs coordination and amplification of higher-level actions and distributes orders through gravito-electric relays to the individual past sensor-actuator arrays. These drive what are believed to be muscles, or perform a reset operation in pure sensors. In Section 7.7, these are implemented as the output neural network. They are past relative to the unknowable Now or its model but future to what the I experiences.

8 Past sensor/actuator arrays are the interface to the unknowable external, whatever it might be. These are the same arrays as on the future side, only here the flow of action is reversed. Action changes are both received and transmitted by the same equipment at the same instance. The external transmit side reaches into the Unknowable to emphasize the point that the operation of this side of the actuator is also unknowable because whatever stimulation passes through these components disappears, and all we actually know is that some reaction reappears on the future arrays, which we assume is correlated with the transmitted actions. However, that is a theoretical statement that cannot be directly experienced. All we can do is add more sensor arrays that provide more interactions that are processed through the flow architecture to produce observable results.

This leaves us with a big question mark representing the Unknowable. One is tempted to project one's reality model into this space. Perhaps the rest of Reality is described by the same architecture as the "I". Or perhaps it is a classic three-dimensional object with the sun, stars and earth reacting to the gravito-electric influences sent into it. Symbols on a page are easy to write. However, such an addition would then turn Figure 6.2-3 into a model of Reality that includes an explicit action-flow architecture for the unknowable. In Reality such a projection is not possible. To pretend we can do so would require us to succumb to the god illusion (see Chapter 1). We may act like gods over our own models but not over Reality.

Figure 6.2-3 is a drawing that represents two levels of reality as discussed in Chapter 3. The book-within-a-book contains symbols of a Reality model. The drawings outside the book model are design elements for a conscious being that uses the model of Reality as an operational component. The semantic meanings of "**U**" and "A" point to the unknowable "?" and therefore cannot be defined. Their operational meanings help process the flow of action in the big "I", which we have used to label this design of a conscious being.

6.3 Breakout of internally generated sensation channels

The CAT design of a conscious being shows wide cycles of action flow with sensor arrays and function boxes indicating perpendicular cross sections through which the action is processed. Combining all sensors into a single large array makes sense when discussing the global architecture, but humans have distinctly different sensor modalities that are processed along individual paths. Such processing paths start with the typical sensor arrays such as the retina, cochlea, touch, taste and smell receptors. We typically only show the optical channel of a single eye. This is done only to simplify the drawings, but all sensory experiences are intended. In addition the Human, i.e. the processing mechanism, also has internally generated sensations, which are not attached to external sensors but rather to housekeeping and accommodations in memory. These internally generated sensations are often identified with thoughts or dreams; however, they provide critical data required to implement conscious processing in a human and for this reason we will look at an example breakout of selected internally generated sensor channels.

In Figure 6.3-1, a model of Reality is shown with a set of three memory sensor-activator arrays labeled **1**, **2**, **3**. These label the vector sub-space of expected visual, expected touch and "I's" basic belief experiences. These are example model categories that anchor the physical phase of many parallel action cycles into sensation channels. The channels interact with each other throughout their path to implement the thought process of a human.

This leaves us with three memory sensation modalities, 1) the expected optical, 2) the expected touch sensation and 3) the theoretical physical reality sensation. Clearly there are many more. Sound, smell, taste, internal muscle pains, as well as the more abstract sensations of well being, love, etc. For our purposes the optical and expected touch sensations are primary in defining the physical reality we believe to live in. However, because we can convince ourselves that these are our

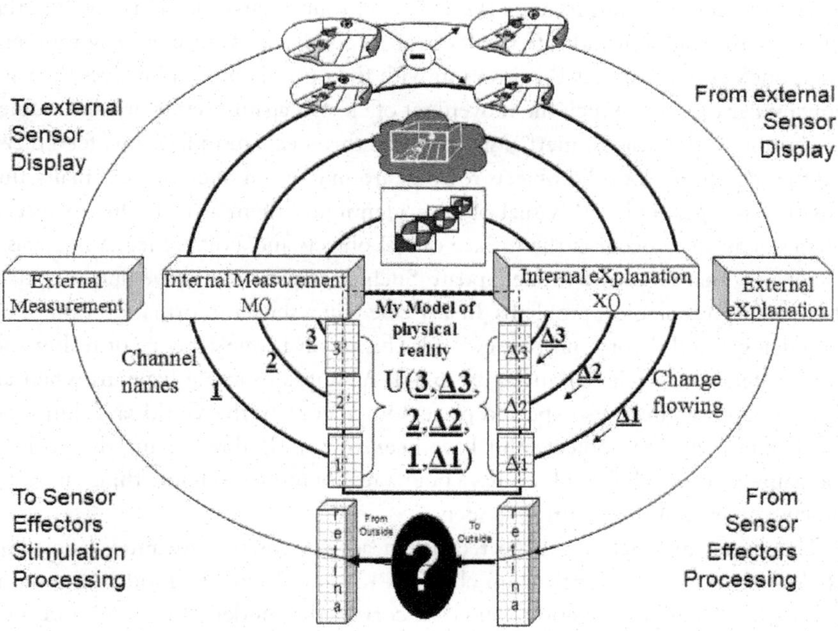

FIGURE 6.3-1 Separating the internal "observables" channels showing comparator function with the optic body-loop channel

own sensations, which are generated as a display of information, we add a modality that represents the display of our basic, fundamental and stake-your-life-on-it belief. The cycle associated with this belief is labeled 3 and is shown as the lower rectangle in the observable phase. It is this fundamental belief we trust and have tested to avoid illusions and sensory errors. As mentioned previously, such a fundamental belief structure is used by a pilot under instrument flight. In this situation, the pilot has been trained to discount normal sensation display and trust the processed result of the instruments to guide the controls of the airplane. Scientifically trained individuals have adopted the belief that the reality underlying our sensations are real masses and charges in real space, and the sensation of that belief is drawn in the lower rectangle as the center of charge and mass icons in a space.

In the external sensor loop of Figure 6.3-1, we only show a single optic modality and the corresponding external optical interface or retina. All external sensors are intended. In the observable phase, the internal and external optical sensations are compared, and the difference is used internally to update the model and externally as commands to the outside. The comparison mechanism at the crossover point involves a registration and subtraction. The comparison operation was not explicitly shown for expected touch sensations or in the figures of Section 6.2 but is hidden behind the conscious observable. It is the difference between measured and expected sensation that usually grabs our conscious attention in normal daily operation.

The second channel produces the expected touch sensation. This involves the delicate sensations that indicate the location of solid objects in one's environment when one's eyes are closed. Registration with the optical channel involves the ear's semicircular canals in which the movement of crystals against detector hairs defines the motion of the head in inertial space. When this mechanism fails, one feels dizzy and the sensation is of solid objects rotating around. When operating normally, this sensation is registered with visual objects, identifying them as real. One expects a touch sensation to occur at the surface of real objects and a difference, **Δ2**, signals a discrepancy that requires a model update. Such discrepancies may be due to optical illusions or physiological problems. In any case when sensor information cannot be trusted, logic and theory must be evoked. This involves one's theory of reality and is associated with cycle "3" in Figure 6.3-1. A simple example happens when an object disappears from its expected place. Our theory of the world says things do not disappear, and the object must have been moved. Before playing the peek-a-boo game, a young child will not have built a reality model to know things must be somewhere even if they cannot be seen.

The discrepancy between expected and measured sensation streams is labeled by **Δ1**, **Δ2**, **Δ3** and propagates through channels 1, 2 and 3 into the model of physical reality. The change information is used to correct the model items **1**,**2**,**3** and produce the next state. In Figure 6.3-1 these operations are represented by the function **U**(**1**,**Δ1**,**2**,**Δ2**,**3**, **Δ3**) that produces new configurations **1'**,**2'**,**3'** that are measured to produce the next expected observables in each category.

We cannot experience the external world directly. The black oval referring to actual Reality remains a mystery. It is named by the model symbol **U()**. All we have is evidence of interactions that we interpret as sensations that are then explained in our model. In quantum theory **U()** is a unitary transform that propagates between two time states. In CAT the meaning of **U()** is visualized from an external 3rd-person point of view as a charge-mass pattern moving under the influence of gravito-electric fields. This visualization in channel "3" is my guess at what reality might look like, if we could look at it, and is purely a heuristic technique for developing and remembering the details inside the **U()** model.

U() also acts as a physical object in its function to perform the processing of sensor signals and the generation of expected observable sensations. If implemented correctly the intrinsic properties of the object **U()** will automatically perform this function. Our example is clearly a letter on a page and names a function that has been learned by a practitioner. This may be a quantum theorist who has built a detailed expression, which when implemented in an appropriate support environment, performs the processing automatically. In that sense **U()** is an instruction to such a learned practitioner to execute the learned mechanism.

6.4 The fundamental algorithm of the reality model

A single Now instance of the 1st-person "I" division of the Whole is shown in Figure 6.4-1. It is framed by the future and past sides of detector/actuator arrays.

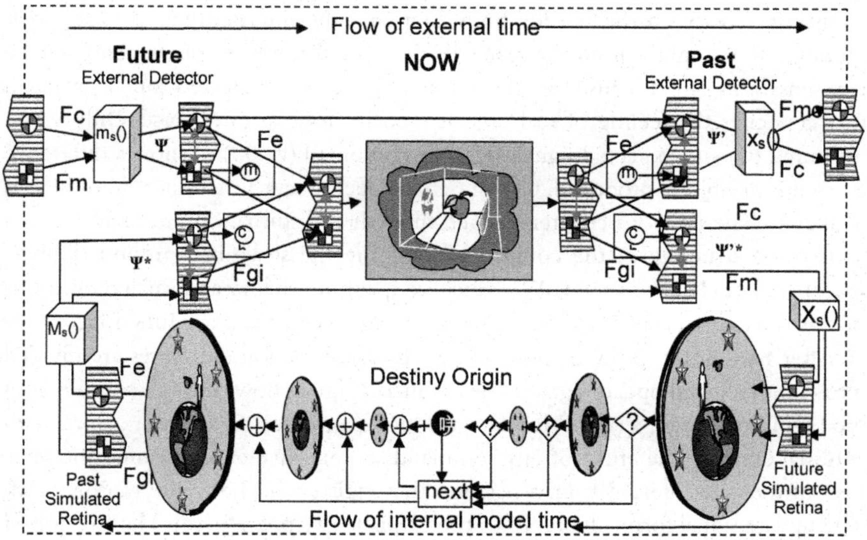

FIGURE 6.4-1 Flow diagram of an interactive being with a causal algorithm using a classic object block universe reality model: upper-body-loop interfaces to unknowable outside dashed-line surface

The future side is stimulated by external gravito-electric influences that produce mass-charge displacement patterns that are processed into observable experiences. The typical human is outfitted with a large set of such arrays defining the normal five external senses, balance, internal body state sensors. Internal simulated arrays interface with the memory. Though all these data streams are present, in Figure 6.4-1 we show only three registered overlays of the optical, expected touch space and the fundamental stake-your-life-on-it belief visualization in the observable Now phase of this expanded action-flow diagram. This diagram is used to show how the inner and outer data streams interact and how the basic features of the fundamental algorithm, which is executed in the Model of Reality, are implemented.

As in all action diagrams, the direction of flow defines the progress of change, which can be measured to define time. The external flow of time indicates action traveling from future to past while the internal flow circles around in the opposite direction and thereby influences the experiences that will be happening in the Now. Relative to the Now experience gravito-electric stimulation in the future external detector array is processed through neural pathways, $m_s()$. This pathway is part of the body loop through which reflex action passes straight through to its future side shown by circled connectors "m" and "ch". Some of the action is also compared with the output of the world model in memory. The single interface arrays holding the combined mass-charge separation pattern is experienced as Now observables and represent the comparator function that controls the passage of influence between the two cycles (see Figure 2.7-1). Here we have the critical connection, between the outside body loop and the internal memory loop, that produces the content of empty space. In the optical modality observables are the raw sensations of color fused with the model-generated expected touch sensation that generates the feeling of real objects seen in front of one's nose. Only when measured (ψ) and expected signals (ψ^*) are combined ($\psi \bullet \psi^*$) to show a difference is a sense of objects produced. Use of Schrödinger's wave function symbol here is deliberate. The previous chapter showed that when disturbances are small enough so that the structure of the component defining the space background (Hilbert space) are not changed then CAT reduces to quantum theory and small oscillations in mass-charge separation distance can be interpreted as the wave function.

After passing the Now instance, these observable action structures are divided into command and update signals. The command signals flow through coordination processing pathways, $x_s()$, and interact, through past detector/actuator arrays, with external entities. The effect of our commands on external entities cannot be seen. Instead they are inferred from a reaction that registers in the future sensor arrays. The update signal forms the input to the eXplanatory process $X_s()$. The first job of the eXplanatory function is to calculate the reverse of the external neural processing path in order to write a symbolic representation of the external stimulation into the simulated future retina located as input to I's internal model. This calculation is along a symbolically backward timeline and produces what *must have been* the cause of the input observables, i.e. stimulation to the external detector arrays. It is important to note how the processing path just described connects actual disturbances in the external boundary of the being with an internal model of that boundary. Once this has been accomplished, the being believes to know the immediate cause of the observable experience. Here the word "know" is given an explicit meaning through an entry in I's memory.

Knowing that the retina has been stimulated is the beginning of the next phase of the calculation that seeks to find what *must have caused* such stimulation. This calculation is performed with the symbols of I's model of physical reality as implemented in his or her Brain. In Figure 6.4-1, we are using a classic object model which should be familiar to most readers. If I believes in classic physics, the calculation would follow a light ray back to the source of its emission, i.e. atoms reflecting light at the surface of an object. The being now knows the location of objects in the being's model space as defined by their optical outlines. The right universe icon represents the physical state of the universe as it is immediately after the emission of photons that stimulated I's retina.

At this point a decision must be made. Is the knowledge gathered by this cause-seeking algorithm adequate for the being's purpose or is the question, "Why are the objects where they are?", also important? If this is not important, the eXplanatory calculation ends, and an expectation calculation algorithm begins. This will be discussed in the next two paragraphs.

If the "why this location" question is important, the cause-seeking algorithm continues to calculate what *must have happened* to produce the current configuration of objects. The hierarchy of such a cause-seeking calculation continues to go backward along the model timeline through the stored information of past events. At each stage the past knowledge is updated to represent a cause consistent with the appearance of the original observable being explained, and at each stage the importance decision determines if the cause-seeking algorithm is to continue. The ultimate destination for such a cause-seeking algorithm is the origin of the universe as implemented in I's model of the past. Of course only cosmologists and theologians are consciously interested in updating our models of physical reality, and being realists, they do not recognize the significance of this origin/destiny point as an operational entity in their own psyche (see Chapter 8). Since these calculations take time, most of us cannot afford to expand our Now instance to contemplate our cosmic existence, but need to identify a cause and go on with the response side of the processing cycle more quickly. Nevertheless, for the sake of presenting the elegance and completeness of the cognitive algorithm let us assume we have reached the point where the question, "What happened before the beginning of the universe?" is important.

Though the subject of great controversy, the simplest answer is *nothing*. The symbolic timeline, however, will have reached $-\infty$ and the *next* step in the backwards direction is the time labeled $+\infty$, indicating we have jumped to the next future. I do not claim to have any proof that the universe is a cycle in time, and only adopt this architecture because it is the simplest boundary condition. It also has the advantage of allowing I's personal model of physical reality to fit into a finite memory. The alternative is an endless eXplanatory calculation that is totally impractical. A calculation that ends at the origin of the universe is impractical enough. Therefore, we place here a process that ends the cause-seek and starts the reaction calculation without question. This ultimate residual cause becomes our destiny.

We have now reached the other branch of the "if statement" question introduced two paragraphs ago. Assuming *nothing* is no longer important, the model algorithm continues backward along the symbolic model timeline from the future destiny of the universe for the purpose of verifying *nothing*. Since for events in the far distant future the cause *must have been* events in the more recent future, the processing flow continues to work its way backward integrating information along I's internal model timeline until it produces the next expected state of physical reality. At this point the past simulated retina takes a snapshot of the physical state to produce the 1st-person's expected sensor stimulation pattern. This signal is run through the model measurement function, $M_s()$, after which it is merged with the next signals from the external sensors. The combined observable experience appears as a new Now again. Only this time it comes into Now from the future thus closing the internal processing cycle. If the model accurately predicts the incoming external stimulation of the Now, the difference signals are small and are easily accommodated by the reality model that corresponds to a calm individual in a typical everyday experience.

Several comments need to be made. The exact closure of the cyclic calculation is only achieved if the update of the model required along the timeline is exact. There are two levels of exactness here. First, if the internal calculation through the model reproduces the internal sensations exactly, then the cycle is stable and self-consistent. As discussed in Section 6.1, such self-consistency only holds a personal conscious experience and is applicable to an isolated being in a dream state. For a being coupled to the outside, the internal sensations must also match external observations. If this happens, then the cognitive processing cycle is not only self-consistent, but the updated model incorporated in such a cycle actually reflects some truth about the unknown exterior that might be called accurate and can be depended upon to generate profitable control signals. Under normal operation the human brain sees raw optical sensations fused with a belief in their objective reality within less than 30 milliseconds. This indicates the update time required to locate objects in the model of his or her immediate environment.

The mechanism for comparison and control is located in the interaction between the internal and external observables, which as we have postulated are determined by the short-range cognitive forces between mass and charge at the boundary between sensor-effecter and memory I/O brain tissue. In Figure 6.4-1 the flow of action through this region is indicated by the output of the internal and external measurement function, $M_s()$ and $m_s()$, respectively. What is actually experienced is the rate of action flow, or the energy pattern, determined by the influence of these two outputs on the individual sensor/actuator cells underlying the space of conscious sensations. The effect of these influences can be specified by combining the charge-mass separation distance $\psi()$ from the external measurement function $m_s()$ to the separation $\psi^\star()$ from the internal measurement function $M_s()$ by direct multiplication to produce the observable $\psi^\star()\bullet\psi()$. If these symbols are equal and opposite, the result represents the feeling of empty space and the knowledge that one's internal model has perfectly predicted the influences from the outside. If they differ, two different signals $\psi'^\star()$ and $\psi'()$ emerge from the comparator complex. The first is utilized as an error signal to update the internal model while the second is channeled to the outside as a command request for a change in whatever is out there. Thus, a continuous flow of action through the structure of the being "I" shown in Figure 6.4-1 processes sensory stimulation through an internal update cycle and produces command responses.

6.4.1 Book model implementation of the fundamental algorithm

Starting from the past side of Now, the direction of the cause search and expected state calculation is from past memories to future expectations. At the origin, the time scale jumps from the far distant past to the far distant future, but the direction of changes continues in the same direction around the cycle. If we map the progress of the calculation in Figure 6.4-1 onto the records stored in a book model, the calculation would start with the past page on the left side of the book and proceed backward to the front cover. As discussed in Chapter 3 the front cover is the beginning of one's universe where the ultimate and final conceivable cause occurs. If no reason for the current Now state has been found by the time the origin is reached, then the initial conditions prevailing at the beginning of one's universe model supplies the final answer. In classic physics the origin was defined by the initial position and momentum of all elementary particles. In quantum theory this has been replaced by a probability amplitude singularity. In many religious traditions it is a creation myth executed by the Almighty. In a book model there is nothing beyond the front cover except the back cover. This is also the logical entry and exit from the operator-reader's reality level into the book.

From the front cover, the calculation jumps to the back cover. The back cover represents the end and farthest expected future destiny available in the book model. Again, different belief systems would ascribe different content to this last page. In CAT models it represents the final destiny or ultimate expectation. We do not wish to introduce moral judgments into the theory, but from an algorithmic point of view if the last page contains the ultimate wish harbored by the being implementing the action cycle, then the same question could define the calculation as was used in the cause search branch. Namely, what causes the future to happen? As the calculation works its way backward from the far distant future to the present Now, the answer to this question will introduce a sequence of changes along the timeline that, in total, would be an implementation plan designed to move the current Now closer to its ultimate destiny.

The last page in this calculation would deliver the future expected configuration of reality on the future side of Now. Thus, the fundamental algorithm would combine both updates and corrections to the reality model, the next time step and also the being's wishes for the next changes that are expected to be made in order to move the system along toward its ultimate destiny. For an erasable CAT book model introduced in Chapter 3, the algorithm would be carried out by the operator explicitly moving ink to correct the record and turning pages backward until he or she arrived at the future side of the current page. For the normal permanent record version of a CAT model, or a typical reader who makes electromagnetic copies of ink patterns that are processed into symbol-interpretation-memories, this operation would be carried out mentally by adjusting the meaning of the records in his or her memory. Whether implicit or explicit, such a backward adjustment is performed to rationalize the difference between left and right page-action structures and are the actions creating the Now experience symbol (see Figure 3.2-3).

6.5 Registration of model observables with the 1st-person perspective

To make the CAT model of a cognitive being useful, it is necessary to project visualizations of our model into the 1st-person experiences we hope to explain. This requires taking a step down the symbol-reality axis and registering the model observables with what is actually seen. Figure 6.5-1 shows a room with a wall clock, an apple and the nose seen from the 1st-person perspective sandwiched between the future and back side of the material arrays shown in a top-down view in Figure 6.4-1. The thought bubble, outlining the walls of the room, indicate an example of the display, which might contain the reader's knowledge of his environment.

This figure may have little resemblance to the reader's actual environment, but if the reader closes the right eye and finds the image of his/her nose, it is possible to register the reader's 1st-person experience with the drawing in Figure 6.5-1. The reader is looking into a space and at the same time knows where that space is located. This feeling is the 1st-person perspective. Optical sensations are placed in the context of our knowledge of a larger world. Even if the sensation of that larger world is known to be produced by a memory recall, we are convinced that it represents real things out there. That such a feeling of reality is also an internal phenomenon may not be easy to grasp.

Perhaps looking up at a night sky, first mentioned in the Prologue, might help. One looks up and may see points of light. Where are those points of light happening? Of course, one is seeing stars, but that is an inference. The stars we are seeing happened a long time ago. Alpha Centauri, the closest star, is four light years away. Where is the point of light we are seeing happening now? It is certainly not four light years away and certainly not four light years ago. It is happening here and now. But where is here and now? Is the light point happening a few meters from your nose? Is it happening a few kilometers up in the sky, or perhaps a lot farther?

Puzzles of this nature cannot be answered within the optical field or its expected touch space but within the context of the theory we believe in. Current cosmology teaches us the points of light come from stars hundreds of light years away. More

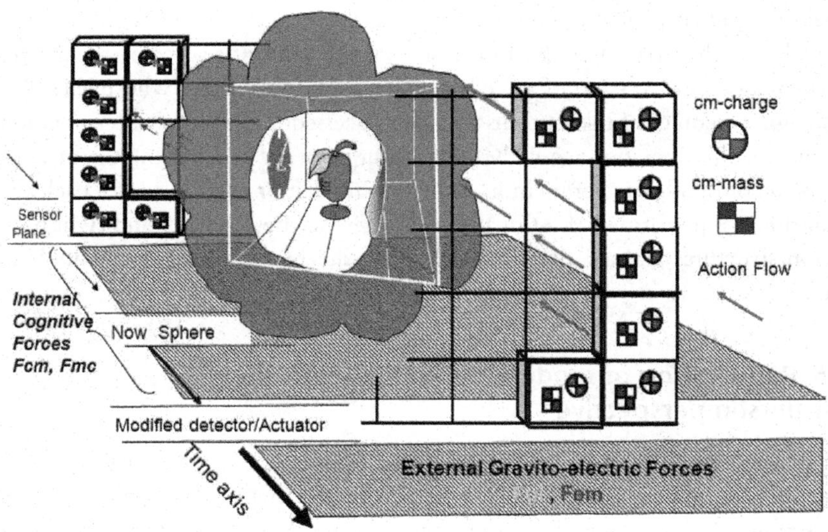

FIGURE 6.5-1 Feeling the sensor/actuator action flow directly through one's self: often called the flow of time. Conscious experiences in subjective time interval between objective material

light comes from galaxies thousands of light years away. We can even measure the cosmic background radiation that supposedly comes to us from billions of light years away; just three-hundred light years farther is the Big Bang. But we are talking about inferences projected upon happenings in local instruments viewed by local observers.

CAT teaches us these sensations are happening in the mind of the observer. It claims this mind is the display space for our experiences, a phase in the flow of action. Beyond the display, beyond anything that can be presented in it, is an array of material cells shown in Figure 6.5-1. These arrays are not the sensation of the retina one feels behind one's nose but the material arrays of one's larger Self behind the entire space of perception. These are the same arrays enclosing the actions flow producing the conscious sensations in Figure 6.4-1.

So, look out at the world knowing there is something beyond what you can see, something beyond the display of your objective knowledge, something beyond and outside the very display of sensations we call your mind. That something is the bigger You that executes the activities that lead to your experiences. The real You cannot be objectively experienced, but your mind can be expanded to make room for an objective visualization. Such a visualization of your real display arrays can be felt just beyond what you can see when your nose is registered with the one shown in Figure 6.5-1.

6.6 Projecting the CAT model into observable sensations

It is normal to project visualizations of one's beliefs onto sensations. The icons in level 3 observables introduced in Figure 6.3-1 reflect the Western science belief that real macroscopic objects are constructed from charges and masses combined into stable structures. The CAT model assumes charge and mass densities participating in a closed-loop activity are the building blocks of real events. Since these events can contain and provide a context for real objects, the event model contains objective science. So, it is not a question that projection is or is not happening, but rather what to project into our sensations.

In the objective world view we project a volume filled with mass and charge in some specific dynamic state into the appearance of an apple as shown in Figure 6.6-1a. This is a duplicate of the classic view of matter introduced in Figure 1.4-1. In this view the surface of the charge/mass facing us is the side radiating light, which is absorbed by our retina and processed by our brain circuitry to produce the apple sensation into which our real matter icon is projected.

In the event-oriented world view we recognize an internal side of material. What has changed is that the projection into the sensation is no longer simply the gravito-electric surface of a classic mass-charge structure but is rather a cycle of activity which executes in the bulk of material inside that surface. What has also changed is that for words like bulk, inside or interior of matter we are using the definitions introduced in Section 1.4.2 rather than reductionist concepts of what is found when breaking the object apart. Thus, the intrinsic property associated with

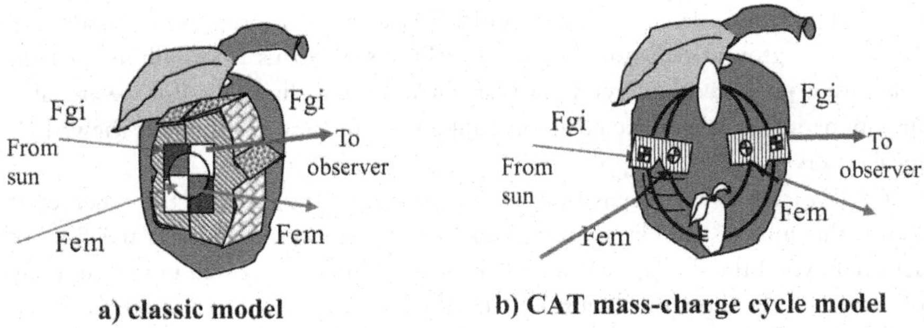

FIGURE 6.6-1 Projection of classic vs. CAT model visualizations into a sensation

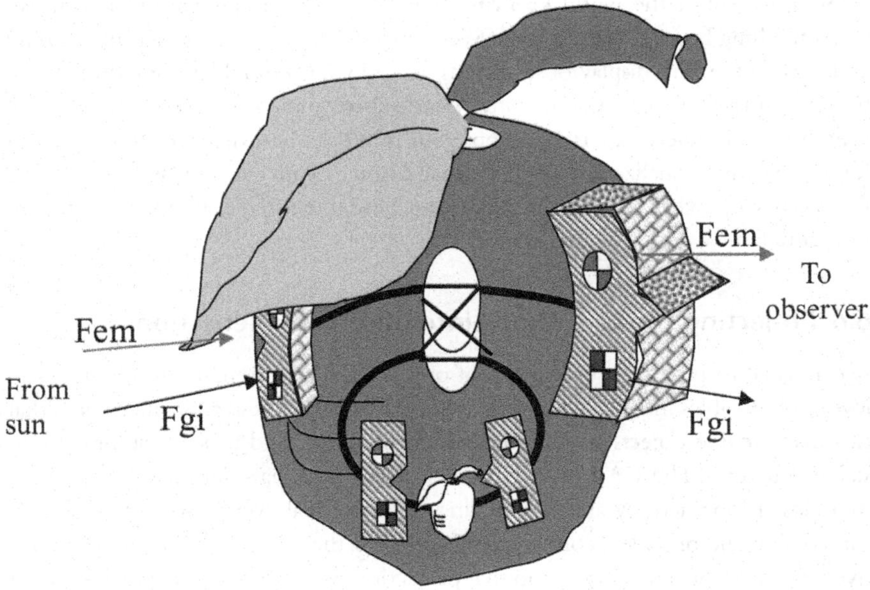

FIGURE 6.6-2 A separated apple's CAT model visualization from its unknowable interfaces is projecting into an "apple" sensation

the sensation is not an object but an activity that measures an explanation of itself. The icon projected into the sensation is shown in Figure 6.6-2. It has the architecture of a conscious being in which an internal activity cycle modulates the flow of action between reviving and transmitting surfaces.

If completely isolated, such an action cycle simply exists and is not interacting with any other entity. It is therefore not seen and acts like an atom in one of its eigenstates which would correspond to a classic object not illuminated and therefore completely unseen. Without an interacting surface, the bulk of material can only interact with itself and is therefore described by a closed loop. As the loop executes, influences travel from the gravito-electric external side through the interior where mass and charge are held together and back to the outside where it radiates its influence to other portions of the bulk. Thus, the isolated particle changes its local state as it progresses through the phases of its lifetime.

When interactions are added, some of the absorbing influences are derived from external sources and in turn radiate influences to the external world in which the observer is a part. The action-flow of the upper arc is therefore closed through the observer or the rest of the universe. It is appropriately called a body loop since material involved will be controlled by the observer if the inner loop is detached. The simplest description of these interacting parts is the skin of a classic object, which absorbs electromagnetic radiation from a convenient light source, such as the sun, and reflects light back into its classic surroundings. In Figure 6.6-2 we therefore separate the object into an interacting skin and a bulk interior that continues to execute its self-measurement activity. Only here it is slightly perturbed due to its interaction with the skin. The picture of an interacting event can be visualized as an apple sensation in which the skin is pictured as an array absorbing gravito-electric influences on the past side of the skin's Now instant and propagating changes through its mass/charge connecting interior. If the skin were separated from the bulk of the apple, the path from its past to its future side would be a straight stimulus-response reflex action involving only the outer material of the skin. The interior is not seen. This situation is actually experienced when the highlights of objects are examined. In this case, only the outer electron sheet of a surface is involved and the object reflects like a mirror.

When the interior of the apple is included, an interface between the surface and the deep bulk of material exists, producing the ambient color rather than the highlight reflection. This interface was pictured in Figure 6.6-2 as a white bubble indicating a comparison operation of the external and internal influence flow. The mechanism for this mixture is an interior force-field leakage between the surface and the bulk of material just below the surface that allows influences from the surface to be transmitted to the interior and simultaneously influences from the interior to affect the passage of influence through the surface.

6.6.1 Visualizing the connection with the observer

Now that we have a CAT model visualization projected into the apple as an object itself, it is possible to continue the story, describing the transport of influence through space and eventually to the retina of the observer as shown in Figure 6.6-3. As in the objective world-view case this transport is carried out by transmission of electromagnetic influences through the visualization of space derived from the CAT model. The difference between the two models is that in the classic objective world view, empty space is a common nothingness while in the event-oriented CAT model we return to the aether concept where space is attached to material which is found in its global eigenstate and is therefore invisible until disturbed. Therefore, interim space between the real Apple's interaction event and the observer's retina is

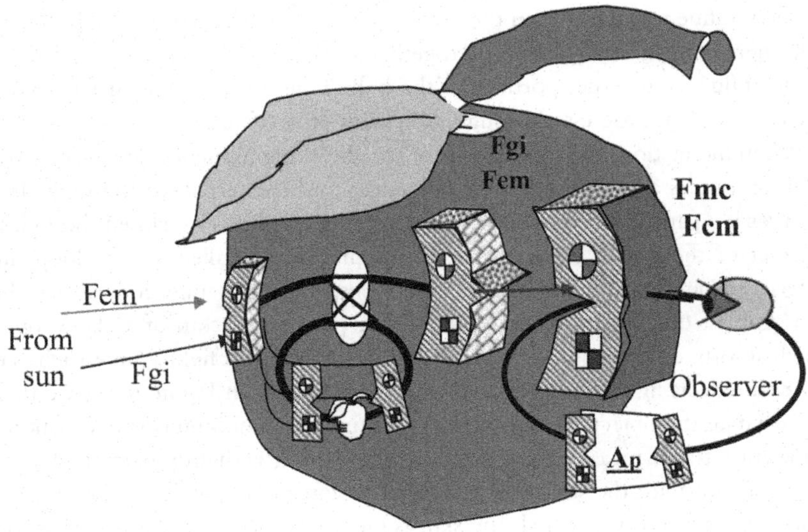

FIGURE 6.6-3 Projection of CAT model into a 1st-person appearance along with the observer's sensor-to-memory model refresh cycle visualization

a refractive media which passes electromagnetic influences based upon its refractive characteristics. These include bending and focusing of light when the disturbances induced in the media are small enough to be reversible, leaving the space in its invisible eigenstate after the influence has passed.

At this point the visualization of the CAT model has included the passage of light through the lens and fluid of the eyeball and hit the retina. In the object-oriented model, the retina, like the apple, was visualized as a classic mass-charge pattern that received and transmitted influences through its Now instant. Here the CAT model treats the body of the observer, and specifically the brain and nervous system, as an approximately isolated system that is modeled by a self-measuring activity loop. Like the apple example treated in Figure 6.6-2, when interactions are included the observer is divided into bulk material and the interacting skin. Only in the case of an observer with human characteristics, the skin is identified with the retina, i.e. the outer edge of the nervous system, while the bulk of material inside is a much more complicated network of influence paths than encountered in the apple case. Despite this large difference in complexity the basic mechanism describing the observer is architecturally similar to that describing a solid object. The retina acts like the interacting surface that is disturbed by gravito-electric forces transmitted into the bulk of the observer's material brain where it is eventually compared with internally generated influences to produce the conscious sensations the observer experiences as the apple. The conscious sensation is not directly produced by an external world composed of charge/mass structures interacting through gravito-electric influences, but a fusion of forces inside material that hold charge and mass together. Even in the case of a reflex object with no internal loop, an inside plane of a Now sensation exists. However, without an inside material loop to recognize the significance and meaning of these sensations, they simply happen. No judgment of conscious reaction is attached to them. To be accurate, the entire theoretical processing flow up to and including the calculated sensation of the apple in the observer was projected into its appearance in Figure 6.6-3.

6.7 Higher-level characteristics of consciousness

Thus far we have emphasized the relationship between the 1st-person experiences of a conscious observer and his or her model of reality. This relationship is pervasive and is encountered in the action flow describing all systems whether they are believed to be conscious in the human sense or not. In this section we will briefly describe how complex action-flow structures can be built and used in order to show the reader how higher-level functions characteristic of human consciousness are implemented. Examples of how specific implementations are adapted to various applications are provided in Chapters 7 and 8.

6.7.1 Hierarchy of action-flow structures

In Section 6.4 we presented the fundamental algorithm implemented by the flow of action from future expectations to past memories. This flow propagates in reverse time order in the inner-subjective domain and first identifies the cause of the experience and from there traces further back to identify the change, if any, that is required to improve the experience. Once the necessary change is identified, the action continues to propagate around the cycle generating the future adjustments necessary to implement the change until the immediate next move emerges from the future side of time. Here the changes are recognized as intentions implementable in the 1st-person's Now commands and sent to the sensor/actuator arrays. The algorithm implements a temporal hierarchy in the cyclic flow.

The cause of an immediate sensation, such as a round red blob, is identified as an apple in the model that may or may not be what or where the 1st-person wants it to be. If it is, the change leading to its appearance is satisfied, and the cycle carrying the qualia is closed by signals that generate the reality sensation for this object. We graphically identified a black outline of the red blob as the appearance of this reality signal in a thought bubble, which is registered with the optical field of view.

In case the 1st-person is hungry a better trajectory for the apple might be one bringing the apple closer to one's mouth. For this goal to be accomplished at some point in the not-too-distant future, a cause for the change must be identified even further forward in the future, i.e. further back in the past of the cycle. An available hand could cause a change in trajectory of the apple, and signals from this realization propagating from the future goal will appear in the immediate Now as a command to the muscle actuators that move the arm.

We have now two scenarios. The first is an almost immediate dismissal of the sensation requiring only a memory to be made of the existence and expected motion of the apple. This operation is measurable and takes on the order of milliseconds. The second is a longer sequence involving the identification of a tool and a use-sequence lasting 10 milliseconds or more if the entire body is to be engaged in walking over to the apple. If the desire of the 1st-person is not simply to eat one apple but to garner several basketfuls, the action trace would go further back in time to identify the apple tree as the cause of baskets of apples. In this case, the cause for satisfaction of the desire is further back in time, and the solution to be set in motion is further in the future since it involves planting a tree. What causes a tree to be planted? Seeds, a plot of land, water, a shovel, gopher baskets – the traces of action go further back in time and in space touching many memories in both the future and past.

Figure 6.7-1 shows the hierarchical structure of human thought process involving a flow of change through a temporal and spatial network mapped onto the future expectations and past memories. It is an inverted view of the fundamental algorithm of the reality model shown in Figure 6.4-1. We show classic object time planes stored in the physical model of the 1st-person's reality. Changes are shown propagating from the Now toward the past side where causes are identified. Desires are implemented as changes to model components and projected into future goals. From there a sequence of changes cascades down from the future side back to the Now. When the model cycle reaches a balanced equilibrium with its desires in the future and knowledge of reality in the past, it sends out command signals and accepts new stimulation from the outside. All modeled by turning a CAT-book-model page to the next instance.

6.7.2 Externalization of brain processing

In conscious systems encountered on the Earth, a Model of Reality (**MoR**) is projected into a biological memory-support structure that is carefully protected by its owner and cannot function in vitro. The content of the **MoR** is one's actionable *truth*. A being believes in the truth without question. He or she will make life-and-death decisions based upon this truth without doubt. In humans, the invention of symbols has allowed the externalization of mental functions including our biologically based **MoR**. This has led to an enormous expansion of power and effectiveness through symbolic communication enabling social organizations held together by common truths. It has also introduced the ability to lie. No one knows what happens inside another individual, and messages claiming to describe reality outside of one's 1st-person experience are always subject to manipulation by the sender or interpretation by the receiver. Caution should always be applied when populating one's stake-one's-life-on-it operational symbols of theoretical "**r**eality". In many cases, tests are impossible to carry out, and therefore operating with a lack of complete knowledge in our stake-your-life-on-it reality models is the norm not the exception for interacting systems.

6.7.3 Possibility calculation in reversible action flow

The relationship between directly observable experience and reality model construction assumes each observation produces an update to the model as well as an

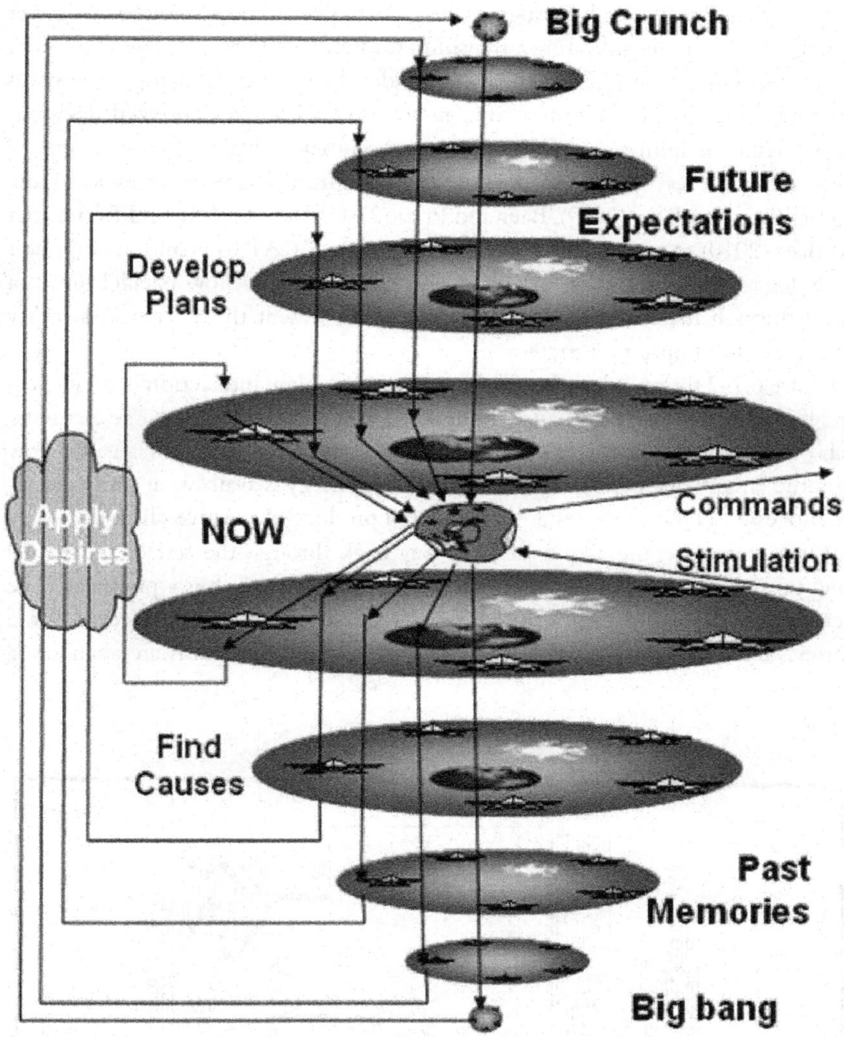

FIGURE 6.7-1 Classic space-time memory model with action flow implementing a cause-seek-to-future-plan algorithm (invert of Figure 6.4-1)

optimized wish that generates commands to its actuator interfaces. Though such single stimulus-response activity is characteristic of conventional computer algorithms, which could be implemented in gate arrays mapped onto the pages of our book model, such permanent structures would not provide the space background that explains the simultaneous possibility evaluation leading to optimized human action. To physically account for optimization we must remember that measurable time only proceeds when complete action cycles in one equilibrium state are transformed to other complete action cycles in another equilibrium state. In CAT, an externalized **MoR** is composed of an operator reading and writing a book. Evidence that time has progressed in isolated systems is marked by messages between such systems indicating a transition from one equilibrium state to another has occurred. The arrival of these messages hides the back-and-forth page-content adjustments, happening within a time instance, that lead to optimized decisions characteristic of human mental processing. Arguments that biological brains of living animals must operate on quantum parallel principles was suggested by the authors Pizzi and Baer (2009), Baer and Pizzi (2009), Baer (2010b) and Bernroider and Baer (2010) to mention a few, and applications of CAT to quantum computer technology will be discussed in Chapter 7. Here we show how parallel flows of action through material, which is structured to represent the 1st-person's reality model, selects an optimum strategy.

Figure 6.7-2 shows a disturbance that starts in the Now interaction of a 1st- person's book model. The disturbance flows through an array of mass-charge elements, each of which is coupled to the next time plane and to its neighbors. As the flow splits, the energy decreases so one-quarter of the energy is available at four alternative processes. These processes are isolated and produce alternative changes as they go. Once complete, the action finds its way back through the rest of the model along possibly different paths. The total action along each path is a product of the energy times the path length of the process executed. In this case, process 3 is the shortest, and this one closes the action loop first. The other paths are abandoned

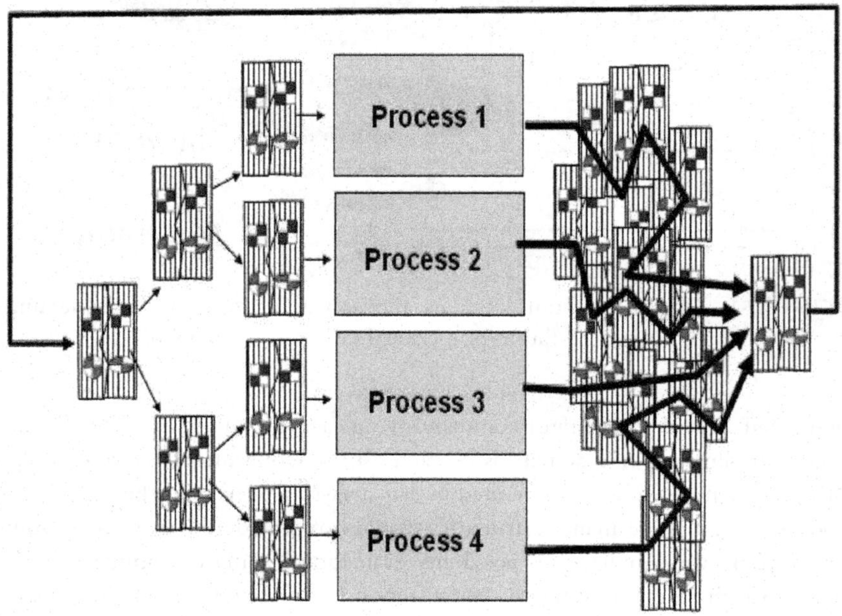

FIGURE 6.7-2 Action propagating through multiple paths through a Model of Reality competing for minimum-action loop closure

and the action flows back from them to join the minimum-action path as the one chosen. In this way the 1st-person has evaluated several possibilities in parallel and selected the minimum-action path of all possibilities. The entire loop is now configured in an equilibrium state which also contains the least-action plan for identifying the causes of the 1st-person's sensations and the plans to achieve his or her desired improvement. This then provides the commands for the next step taken by the being.

The principle and primitive physics described here are ubiquitous and describe the process any material object executes to determine its optimum path through the universe. The difference is not the principles and forces that lead to the optimum path, but rather the complexity and size of the model. A classic human model contains a vast amount of information regarding the past and expected future. The amount of information includes the spatial Now environment of large parts of the earth, its history, its planned future at a physical level as well as the feelings, memories and plans of other beings. This entire structure propagates action through a network of possibilities and choices. The flow can be visualized as feelers exploring alternative potential changes along fingers penetrating the past and future universe. All these happenings are projected into the 1st-person sensation of one's body, like the activities of a real apple were projected into its appearance as explained in Section 6.6. But to grasp the magnitude of possibilities being evaluated, the reader should remember that the larger Self is the Universe the reader feels to be around him or her. It is all the activities the reader imagines happening and all the possibilities of alternative motions in that universe that are being evaluated by the bigger Self. Most of these alternatives never close the loop, and the action extended along these paths atrophy back to the Now starting point. Those that do direct one's immediate actions but do so in the context of the larger plan, which has been calculated in the depths of the model.

In the next chapter we will apply these qualitative and graphically visualized concepts to artificial and real intelligence machines to show why quantum computation must necessarily be happening in our larger Selves to accomplish the daily direction of our life trajectory.

6.8 Summary of human-level consciousness

By filtering the data stream from external sensor interaction to eliminate expected sensations and only leave the unexpected and new command changes to be transmitted to both the outside and internal model, we have identified a physical action pattern that correlates to the immediate Now experience. The comparator operation at this top-level immediate Now experience is calculated with an algorithm executed unconsciously by the past memory and future plan records through a hierarchy of past experience and future plan components. We may believe our past is permanently fixed, but the CAT algorithm shows that past memories and future plans are modified by new information and our bodies' immediate behavior is determined by our desired future.

The key to conscious self-awareness is the feed-forward action loop that controls the action rate flowing from and back to the actual Body's sensor/actuator system. This loop in time is the essence of what we are. As will be discussed in Chapter 7 such action loops seek to grow by increasing the amount of action in personal equilibrium arrangements. They grow by capturing a material body and the ability to control signals to and from it. Human-level consciousness is therefore specific to our species' configuration of action cycles painstakingly evolved since the origin of our own time. Ontogeny recapitulates phylogeny. The evolutionary development is reproduced in the stages of growth by every new human being from conception to when the control seat behind one's eyes is occupied by a mature waking individual. The modification of physics that introduces the internal and external aspects of material and the action flow between them identifies the pan-psychic motions containing conscious experience that is supervened by all higher-level organizations (Chalmers, 1996, 32). The large macroscopic structures, which eventually grown by combining these primitive motions. have evolved the variety of conscious experiences, which we project, rightly or wrongly, into the appearance of such structure in our daily lives.

7

APPLICATIONS IN ARTIFICIAL INTELLIGENCE AND NEUROSCIENCE

Chapters 1 through 5 introduced the event-oriented world view and the supporting CAT physics, which replaces interacting objects with interacting events and integrates the mental aspect of our experience into the foundations of science. We first applied event-oriented concepts to the physical foundations of science in Chapter 5. By identifying the mental aspect of our experience in physical activities, we have made the foundations of science more intuitive and useful for the larger scientific community. What follows, in the rest of this chapter and Chapter 8, will deal with the impact such fundamental change in world view will have in the broader intellectual context of our arts and sciences. This chapter concentrates on examples applicable to the hardware encountered in artificial intelligence, neuroscience, biology and psychiatry.

7.1 Impact of Conscious Action Theory on science in general

In CAT, the foundations of the physical sciences have been altered. What had been the "real" objective world seen through the windows of our senses has now been identified with a phase of an activity that flows between our conscious experiences and a memory that stores and refreshes those experiences. Stable objects are replaced by repeating events. Fundamental particles are now fundamental cyclic events. The classic independent space is identified with a personal plenum that is experienced in the subjective phase of an event cycle. All systems of material are now observers. The inside of classical objects is now filled with action flowing through the objective and subjective phases of their events. The material of events is action. The form or structure of an event is its volume extension. The state of an event is how action is distributed in its form.

Time intervals are associated with the change of state. The resurrection of god-given Newtonian time defines the global state of an isolated event explaining self-repeating systems as the execution of activities around their own internal time loops. The theory of relativity is augmented by the introduction of a personal plenum. Gravity now contains a positive and negative side of mass. Each of us is contained inside our own black hole and the cosmic background radiation sphere is the interface of detectors through which signals from other events pass into our community's consensus reality. The criterion for material change, often seen as motion, now includes subjective forces between charge and mass as expressed by the expanded d'Alembert Principle. Purposeless responses to primitive forces give way to the goal of capturing an increasing amount of activity that can be experienced in stable equilibrium forms. When an event is in perfect equilibrium, its experience is empty featureless space described as the feeling of pure existence.

This barrage of changes summarizes the bulk of information presented in Parts I and II. The change in world view implied by CAT has broad impact in the general sciences, which is based upon our understanding of the physical world. Its main impact is the integration of concepts developed in disparate branches of science under a single logical umbrella. Such integration fosters a framework for interdisciplinary understanding that can lead to solutions of heretofore intractable problems. The proposed changes in our assumptions of physical reality will initiate a thorough reassessment of old understandings; however, its most immediate and obvious impact is the replacement of object-reality projections into our 1st-person sensations with action-flow visualizations. This transition is discussed in the next section.

7.2 Consciousness in the physical sciences

The problem of consciousness arising in the objective world view is called the *hard problem* of consciousness and the explanatory gap (Shear, 1997). Its existence in the classic objective model of reality is graphically demonstrated in Figure 7.2-1. Here we see a cartoon of a human standing on the earth with the brain drawn as a swirl of gray matter. The human looks around in a wakeful state and is aware of the body, the world and specific objects in front of his or her nose. Classic physics and the science built upon it assume a physical activity in an observable object called the brain is directly responsible for what the individual sees.

If we ask how classic physics explains such sensations, we find no answer. How the physical activity in the brain causes the sensation of an apple occurring 1.2 meters from that brain is not addressed in the physical sciences. Furthermore, if we examine the patterns of activity in the brain, we see neuron pulses, EEG waves and metabolic activity but nothing like the world of objects we see around us every day. Although it has been suggested that the brain operates on holographic principles and stores bits of information of our objective experiences in distributed regions of the brain, this argument does nothing to answer the question. It only adds the mystery of how the brain assembles these pieces of information into a coherent

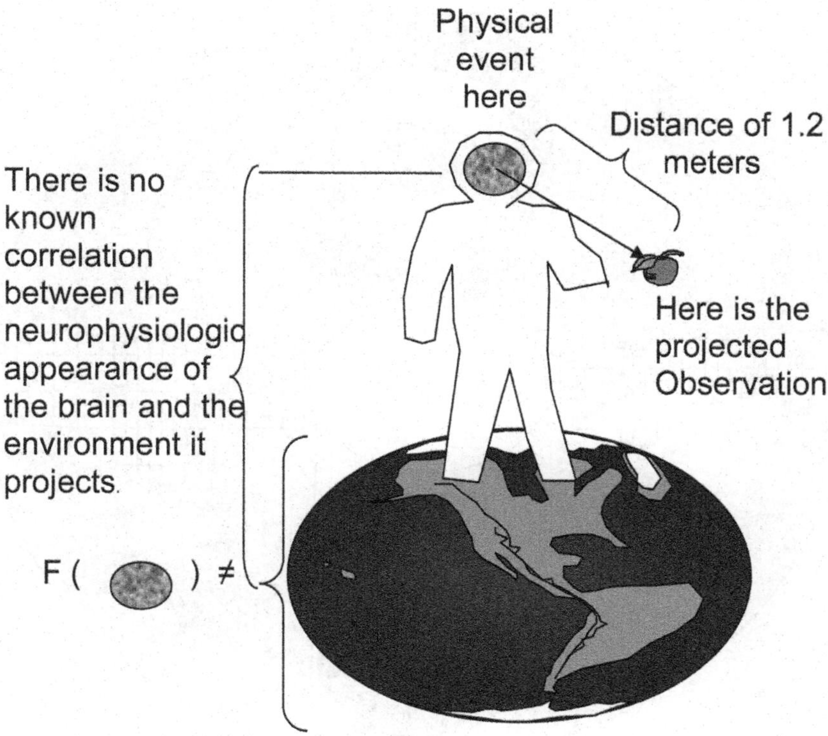

FIGURE 7.2-1 The explanatory gap and hard problem of consciousness

whole on top of the question of how such an assembly gets outside of the brain to the places where things are actually seen.

In contrast, the CAT model provides an explanation consistent with basic science by recognizing that the objects we see in front of our nose, including our nose, are internal phenomena that happen in the interior of matter from which we are built. Figure 7.2-2 shows the by-now-familiar CAT event cycle in which the two aspects of material and the two categories of forces between them is shown to be an action loop. Since mental sensations and physical explanations are now two phases of an activity, the perceived apple, brain and whatever else is experienced do not cause each other anymore than the images of two actors appearing on a television screen cause each other.

Both the 1st-person's body and the apple are images in the 1st-person's mind. They are both caused by the parallel flow of action within the 1st-person's activity loop. In CAT, both images are accommodations to interactions with some real "Apple" and "I" event beyond what can be seen. The old physics of observable objects pushing each other around has been revised.

This revision eliminates the explanatory gap and hard problem of consciousness, but what are we to do with the objects we obviously see in front of our noses?

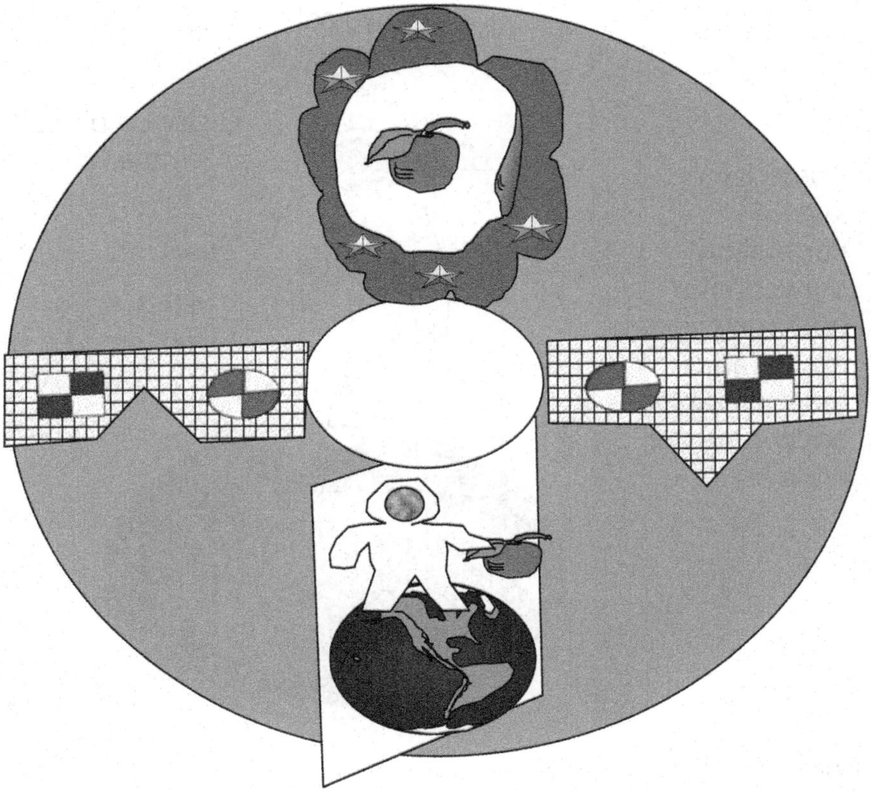

FIGURE 7.2-2 CAT solves the explanatory gap and hard problem of consciousness

The habit of projecting a visualization of one's reality belief into one's sensations is so fundamental to our operations as cognitive beings that it is hard to give up. The general impact for science is therefore not an elimination of projection per se but rather a change in the reality belief that is being projected. Projecting an interacting processing loop into our sensations applies to all systems we encounter in our everyday lives. The action-flow visualization of the CAT model projected into any external object was presented in Section 6.6. Adopting such a change is most easily made by investigators who attempt to understand how the brain works and applied to the systems they recognize as conscious. To see how such a change of habit can be accomplished let us a follow an investigator, who is comfortable in his or her objective surroundings, but has been given our action-flow theory to try out.

7.2.1 Mapping the CAT model to a 2nd-person's brain

Like any inanimate object, the brain of a 2nd-person is traditionally defined as an external object. The investigator assumes the appearance of an obviously conscious man is sufficient evidence for the existence of a conscious experience. The investigator projects the thought bubble above the man's head along with bubbles indicating a "must be" connection between the man's conscious experience and his material brain but has no theory of how the connection is implemented.

The CAT model provides a physical explanation of 1st-person experiences for all systems dead or alive. The distinction is made, not on the basis of personal similarity but upon the physical difference between closed action loops and open strands. Closed loops have self-contained cognitive properties while open strands contribute to the cognitive properties of larger loops in which they are imbedded through their beginning and concluding ends. In Figure 7.2-3 the investigator learning CAT has drawn the two main action-flow forms on a notepad.

The projection of the 2nd-person's conscious experience was only placed in a thought bubble above his head in Figure 7.2-3 for clarity and cartoon tradition. The investigator knows this experience is physically sandwiched between the stimulated past and future response side of the man's brain material. The thought bubble should therefore be projected as a Now instance happening inside the appearance of the 2nd-person's brain. This configuration corresponds to the open strand of action flow on the investigator's note pad. After this adjustment, the brain would still be modeled like a classic stimulus-calculate-response machine. The processing

FIGURE 7.2-3 Mapping the externalized CAT model to the 2nd-person brain

activity between the future and past side of material, no matter how complex, will map onto a straight timeline executing a kind of reflex action flow. This does not mean sensations do not happen as the flow passes, but to be conscious of one's self, controlling this flow requires some action to flow forward in time and affect the flow before it is experienced in the Now. Such a time loop is shown as the lower cycle side of the 1st-person's notepad in Figure 7.2-3. Connecting the feed-forward control loop into the passing action flow is the essence of the CAT model of a conscious being presented in Chapter 6. In CAT, some of this passing information must be channeled into memory models that produce expected sensations, which are compared to the sensations derived from the external sensors. It is this comparison activity between the inner and outer sensations that implements consciousness in the CAT model.

Figure 7.2-4 shows a complete projection of these two superimposed images sandwiched between two sets of inner and outer interface arrays. Both images are inside material, and interior forces are responsible for both subjective experiences. These experiences include a merged optic field with the expected touch space shown as the thought bubble background and the theoretical side view of the explanatory model. The expected image is generated by action flowing through the simulated detector arrays to and from the model stored in memory.

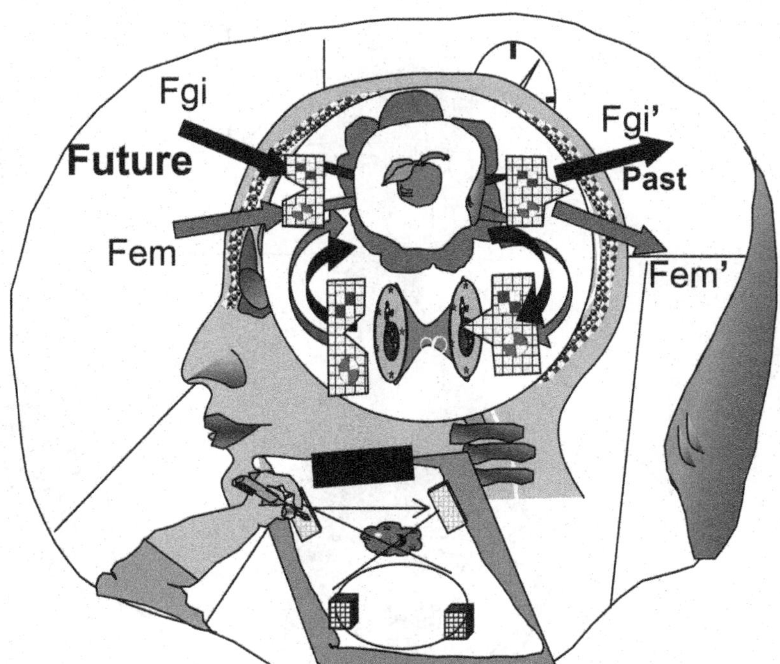

FIGURE 7.2-4 Consciousness in the comparison between the external and internal loops: reflex action passes through

The model processes stimulation backward from the immediate past back through the origin/destiny point and forward to the immediate future. The comparison function between the measured and expected images are not explicitly shown in the projection. It is drawn on the notepad as a crossing action flow where the 1st-person's here and now experience happens (see Figure 5.4-1).

The caveat in this description is that the appearance projected into the 2nd-person's brain is not the 2nd-person's real "Brain". The theoretical projection into it is the investigator's CAT model of the subject's thinking process. In reality that thinking process executes outside the investigator's observable experience. The 2nd-person's own action loop executes in the 2nd-person's own space and time. This loop interacts with but is not equal to the action loops defining the neuroscientist or computer scientist nor equal to the projections appearing in their loops.

In summary, the impact of CAT on the physical sciences is that action-flow patterns inside material should replace the projection of objects into our sensations.

Neither the patient nor the investigator sees a real "Apple" 1.2 meters in front of their own noses because both noses and the apples are appearances created in response to interactions that both individuals have with a third action-flow event. We have identified a change in the visualization of the reality belief both scientists and laypeople project into the sensations appearing around themselves. This change permeates all scientific endeavors whether they are concerned with consciousness or not. However, the impact is more immediate for disciplines that deal with real or mimicked human behavior.

7.3 Artificial intelligence and computer consciousness

The artificial intelligence proponents are quite right. If material in human form can support consciousness in biological systems there should be no fundamental reason why it could not happen in any arbitrary material. The CAT model is pan-psychic. It assumes the same internal mass-charge balance structure that explains consciousness in the human is fundamental to all material. So, all material, including computer systems are conscious at some primitive level. The question to be asked is, "At what level of material complexity will a computer-controlled robot who acts like a human actually have the consciousness feelings of a human?" The answer in this section suggests that we still have a long way to go before "acting like" implies "feeling like" a human being.

7.3.1 The computer science analogy

The extent to which machines can mimic human behavior has led to the adoption of the standard computer-brain analogy shown in Figure 7.3-1. From an external viewpoint, the brain and its interfaces look architecturally similar to a computer vision system. The eye acts like a camera, which digitizes electromagnetic signals into pulses that are transmitted into a central processing unit of the brain, which generates the display experienced. Unfortunately, we cannot quite follow the signals

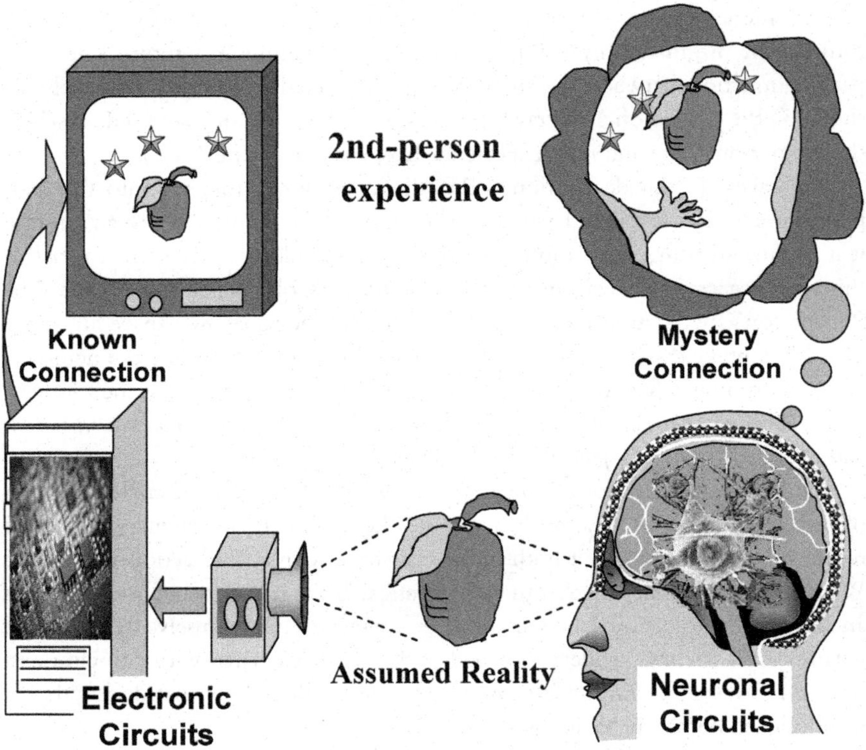

FIGURE 7.3-1 The standard computer brain analogy

from the brain to the mental display the same way we can follow the signals from the camera to the monitor display.

However, most neuroscientists believe this is due to engineering limitations, and as our instrumentation becomes more precise we will find the equivalent of a pixel display matrix in the brain. David Chalmers (1996, 238) has given this matrix the name the Physical Correlates of Consciousness (PCC) rather than Neural Correlates of Consciousness (NCC) to expand the search beyond neuron activity. In the brain this sought-after component is expected to radiate the wholeness of our everyday experiences into the space of our minds.

Such radiation is analogous to the pixels of the monitor radiating an image into space. How the electronic circuits are supposed to become aware of the display image is just as mysterious as how the neural circuitry of the brain is to become aware of the mental display. On the computer side, we external observers, programmers and users are the cognitive element that becomes aware of the scene. Why the analogous "little-man-inside" cannot be found behind one's eyes is a further mystery – a mystery usually dismissed with a consensual agreement among neuro- and computer scientists that conscious awareness simply-must-happen in both the brain and its computer counterpart, even though it appears to happen out there.

Computer scientists contribute to the consensus by introducing a simply-must-happen in the form of the Turing Test into Artificial Intelligence. The Turing Test approach assumes that if electronic circuits can be constructed to make an inanimate system act like conscious humans, then it simply-must-happen that they have conscious experiences like the ones that simply-must-happen in neuron circuits shown on the right side of Figure 7.3-1. So, without us actually seeing the display space as an identifiable independent structure in other beings it simply-must-be that such a display exists inside their brain and therefore we ought to be able to build one out of silicone.

7.3.2 The CAT analysis of computer consciousness

We can certainly build robots that act like humans, and replacing human services with automation products makes sense because there is profit to be made for the owners, but to what extent are our robots conscious?

CAT applied to this question would first require an update to the computer-brain analogy by mapping our event-oriented understanding of the consciousness process onto the 2nd-person's brain. Next, we duplicate the architecture we believe occurs in biological systems in a computer. The result of these changes is shown in Figure 7.3-2. The computer is now split into an upper section containing its real-world model, a center section containing its physical correlates of consciousness

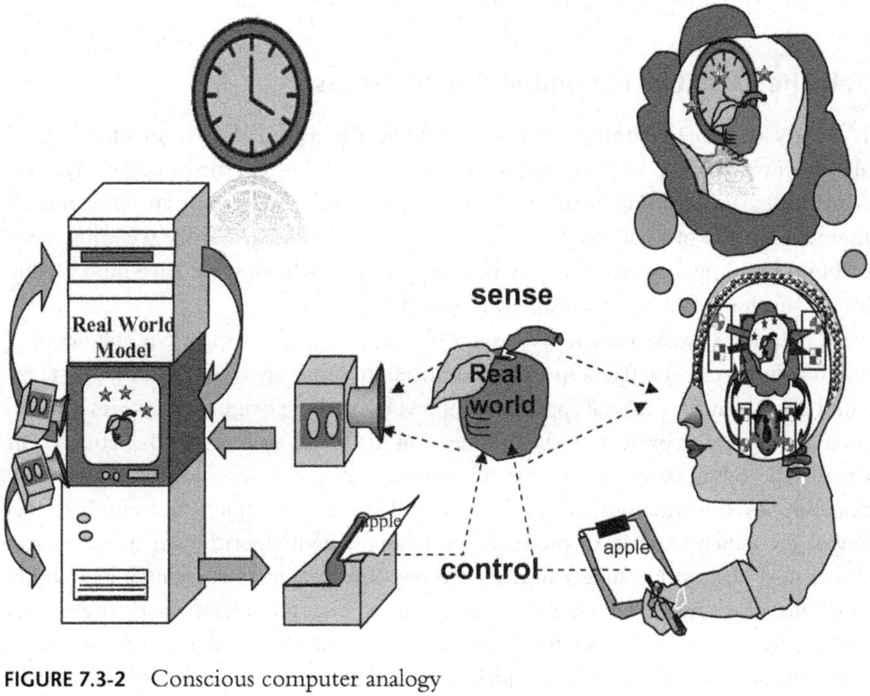

FIGURE 7.3-2 Conscious computer analogy

and a lower section coordinating its output actions. We have added cameras to observe the computer monitor to mimic the humans' observation of their own field of view. One of these cameras feeds the real-world model, which produces an expected display. This information is then sent back into the computer in parallel with the external camera measurement to produce an overlay comparison. This in the human is like the optical field of view merged with the mental thought bubble display in the biological 2nd-person. The output from this comparison drives the upper thinking and lower acting compute segments. If the estimated and measured scenes differ, then both the model and/or the real world must be "corrected". Commands are sent to the output peripherals, shown here as the printer.

We have provided a computer architecture along with a cursory description of algorithms which mimic the functions we believe are carried out in a 2nd-person's brain. If such a computer can duplicate the output of the human subject, it would strengthen our belief that a similar architecture and processing activities are happening in the human brain. In this example, the computer and human subject both output the word "apple". We can be pretty sure the human was aware of an apple sensation. Can we assume a similar awareness happens in the computer? This is of course a one-time example that is easily achieved by off-the-shelf pattern-recognition algorithms executing in machines that do not look like humans in the least. However, as more powerful algorithms are developed that 1) contain an internal memory array that store pixel arrays in geometries like what the robot should see, 2) produce human output consistently and 3) are packaged in attractive human-like forms, would we believe the resulting robot possesses consciousness? Avatar movie producers certainly hope so, but let's explore the reality of this illusion.

7.4 The extent of computer consciousness

It is easy to project thought bubbles showing the assumed feelings of a human although we have, up to this point, never seen such feelings in the biological systems confronting us. It is much easier to project thought bubbles onto an inner refresh memory display of a robot where we can monitor the images. Since we know how to build such mechanisms, we may be tempted into believing we have built a conscious machine. But are we justified in making this leap?

A computer works because we assign plus 5 volts to the logical symbolic code 1 and 0 volts to a logical 0 at a specific wire location. These are then combined to form numbers so that the physical appearance of 5 volts on three neighboring wires is interpreted as three 1s representing the number 7 in the binary system and the letter "p" in the ASCII coding standard. Understanding how voltages on wires are manipulated by assembly-level instructions, that are in turn generated by compilers from higher-level languages, which are in turn programmed to implement algorithms that manipulate the sensory data to produce a human-like response, requires mastering a large body of details. These details are taught to programmers and computer engineering majors and are by no means easy or trivial. However, for our present discussion, no matter how complex or how many individual wire locations are involved, in the end, a set of electrons are trying to get from a negative energy state to a more positive one in the most efficient way available and are willing to jump through the barriers and hoops we have set up to get what they want. The internal forces they respond to and any satisfaction they may experience by finding the path of minimum action through our maze has almost nothing to do with the meanings we assign to their motions.

The conscious experiences assigned to the interior of matter forged into a computer have no direct relationship to the feelings of a human being even if that computer behaves in ways that appear to be human. However, if we define our feelings in sufficiently abstract terms, an equivalence can be achieved by analogy. For example, the word "satisfaction" referring to the human feeling experienced when an activity satisfies a need can be associated with physical concepts. The expanded d'Alembert Principle states material only exists where all the forces are balanced. A displacement from equilibrium would introduce restoring forces that must be compensated by an internal charge-mass separation. The material behaves as though it wants to return to equilibrium and by executing such a return the feeling of "satisfaction" could be projected onto the material as its desire is satisfied. The CAT model deliberately makes use of anthropomorphic terminology to evoke cathartic feelings that provide an intuitive understanding of why things act the way they do. However, the abstract satisfaction, desire or wish must be identified with the concrete goals that are being wished for by the physical system doing the processing. A porpoise may be induced to leap high into the air to grab a fish from a trainer's hand, but the desire to eat a fish is substantially different from the desire to increase attendance that may motivate the trainer.

A computer system therefore is assumed to have desires, needs and the experience of sensations. Negative charges separated from their positive counterparts may feel a need to reunite, but the desire to satisfy the electric forces with which electrons have been captured is quite different from the assigned need its human behavior appears to satisfy. Engineers who build conventional computers see them as objective machines governed by the classic laws of electricity and magnetism. They have no place to conceive of mental experiences happening in their creations.

CAT and its quantum approximation provide an opening to attach the mind and its content to a physical system. In Chapter 6 we externalized the von Neumann Cut to show how the subjective experience, anchored in the interior of our brain matter, can be projected into the interior of matter normally seen from the outside as objects. A computer utilizing the forces internal to matter would, in the small amplitude approximation, be a quantum computer. The organizational principles required to build a quantum computer is a technology that will help us understand how to manipulate the forces responsible for sensations in all material. This technology will be addressed in the next section.

7.5 The quantum brain

Once we accept the premise that the "inside" of material is objectively impenetrable and quantum theory approximates this unknowable domain using operational symbols whose meanings are visualized as mental projections, and further, once we realize these projections are routinely confused with external reality, it is easy to see why quantum computers should be a model for brain operations rather than conventional calculating machines. The thought bubble above a 2nd-person is our projection much like the visualizations of what happens beyond the quantum limit. In both cases, we believe a 2nd-person is thinking. When we discuss the thinking process of another being, we usually step out of the discipline of physics. We draw heavily on cathartic experience to understand what the other person is feeling and why this person acts the way he or she does. In other words, we take the feelings in our own mind and use them to comprehend the behavior of others. If those feelings are associated with forces and action flows in the interior of matter, then the theories that allow us to organize and control those inner flows are simply alternative languages for manipulating the inner feelings of material. Whether such material takes the form of silicone-based machinery or their carbon-based comparables is irrelevant, both follow the dictates of their feelings and desires.

7.5.1 Why should the brain be like a quantum computer?

The conventional model of the human brain is that it operates like an Artificial Neural Network. Neurons are like the switching circuits and programs are stored in the strength of interconnections. Neural net devices have been built that can program themselves by learning the strength of interconnections from training sessions that reward correct calculation results. Similar high-level conventional computers can be programmed to produce new pieces of code in response to new needs and in this sense learn. However, an analysis carried out by the author in collaboration with Gustav Bernroider (2010) on the compute requirements of carnivorous birds, such as an owl, shows that the calculation speeds needed to perform the hunting functions cannot be done within the bird's material brain.

The strategy of the aforementioned investigation was to combine the author's knowledge of the software required to execute a typical target search-and-acquisition mission by an unmanned aerial vehicle with Bernroider's knowledge of an aviary brain. The brain of an owl is about the size of the nail on one's little finger. The thermal limit of a conventional computer is reached when the energy required to execute a primitive computational operation, such as flipping the state of a memory cell from "0" to "1", is equal to the thermal noise. Below this limit the thermal energy would be enough to flip the memory bit and make computation unreliable. Even if modern semiconductors are built at atomic scales, the thermal energy per degree of freedom at absolute temperature is given by the Stephan-Boltzmann Constant $k = 1.38\times10^{-23}$ J/K. At room temperature of 300°K, the thermal limit is reached when $\sim 1kT = 1.4\times10^{-23} \times 300K = \sim 4\times10^{-21}$ Joules per operation per atom. The number of operations per second required for a hunting mission with the capacity of a neuron-junction-based owl brain was several orders of magnitude below the thermal limit. Thus, if the required operations were performed in a chip the size of an owl brain it would burn up unless cryogenically cooled and/or be completely unreliable.

We therefore concluded that if an owl were operating its brain on conventional computer principles, it would certainly starve. This suggests quantum computing principles are at work in biological systems. The main objection to this hypothesis was raised by Tegmark (2000), who calculated that quantum calculation could not be carried out in a hot and soggy biological environment because the required quantum devices could not be maintained in an isolated state for long enough. In conventional quantum theory, Schrödinger's equation describes the evolution of quantum objects between measurements when no one is looking. But as long as we believe in *one* independent objective universe, that universe is always "looking" with the same thermal interactions that make conventional computers unable to execute the required hunting mission of an owl. Since Tegmark's objection, quantum processes have been discovered in biological systems (Fleming et al., 2011; Bernroider and Roy, 2004), and it is now assumed that somehow biological systems have figured out how to get around Tegmark's objection. Rather than pursue this line of reasoning, the CAT solution suggests the way around the dilemma is to eliminate the assumption that quantum objects are in the same space as the experimenter's laboratory wall coordinates (see Section 5.3). In CAT, a measurement produces an entry in the measurement system's physical model that is interpreted as an object and projected into the measurement's system perceptive space. By assuming the perceptive space in which measurement systems are located also holds the quantum objects, we are stuck with Tegmark's objection, and the brain cannot operate as a quantum computer. With CAT this objection is lifted because the quantum space is defined by the names of the Hilbert space cells, not by their external location as seen in the 1st-Person Laboratory (see Chapter 5).

7.5.2 What are quantum computers?

Computers are symbol-manipulation machines. When designing a symbol-manipulation machine we assign meanings to the properties of objects. In conventional computing machinery we assign meanings to what we believe are objects (bits) in a single objective state (0 or 1). This makes sense in the classic world view because there is a one-to-one correlation between the single objective state of a computer component and the single objective state we used to believe the world possesses. However, most, if not all, problems confronting a human being involve simultaneous evaluation of alternative behaviors leading to an optimized choice. In CAT, we believe reality is composed of events, which interact throughout their lifetimes producing measurements that in quantum theory we use to interpret as probabilistic quantum objects. If we could learn to assign alternative behaviors to the phases of events, then by manipulating the events we could build machines that calculate several alternatives at once. In conventional quantum terminology this means utilizing the probabilities of quantum objects as the basis of calculation. First, we assign alternative meanings to the probabilities of quantum objects. Then by manipulating the object all the attached probabilities are manipulated at once. Machines that manipulate probabilities before they are measured are called quantum computers.

Figure 7.5-1 shows a block diagram of such a machine. The dashed line halfway up the middle represents the von Neumann Cut, which separates the lower conventional computing machinery described by classic physics from the upper area described by quantum theory. The upper area is like the Hilbert space of equipment, discussed in Chapter 5, which we can only know though indirect inference. On the left side we can see an array of bits, each one set to either an up arrow or a down arrow representing a value of "1" or "0". This represents a single input value for a problem. An eight-bit array would contain a single number between 0 to 255.

As an example, let's assume we are driving an automobile and the steering wheel position is encoded numerically so that straight forward is given the number 127, 0 is a hard-left turn, 255 a hard-right. We have been driving straight, so a value of 127 represents a centered wheel. At every moment we have to evaluate the situation and decide how to steer the car. There are 256 alternative wheel positions available. For a self-driving car, a conventional computer would measure road conditions and set internal electronic gates to values that represent those conditions. Then each wheel-turn possibility, represented by a number from 0 to 255, would be run through a calculation sequentially and the result evaluated. The evaluation criteria would also be encoded into electronic gates and the best alternative steering wheel position is reported as the output.

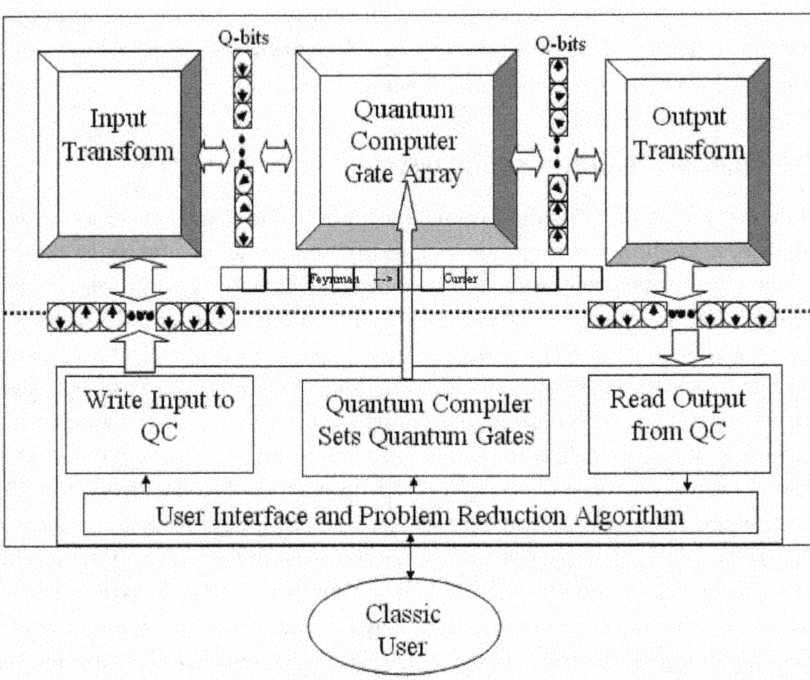

FIGURE 7.5-1 Quantum computer block diagram

We realize algorithms currently being developed for self-driving cars will use a great many assumptions about the traffic environment that will substantially limit the options that need to be evaluated and reduce the calculation load. We have only been assuming unrestricted wheel positions are possible to exemplify the power of quantum parallelism to reduce a brute-force evaluation of all 256 available possibilities. A restricted possibility spectrum may be calculable in conventional equipment for a simple problem like driving on a straight highway, but throw in some additional problems a human deals with – how hard to push the brake for human comfort, how important is it to conserve gas money, how badly one has to urinate, the willingness to break the law to get there fast. . . . Add a few life requirements simultaneously running through an average driver's head, and it would be easy to require 16 or perhaps 32 alternatives confronting a human being. This would imply 65,536 or 4,294,967,296 calculations to be performed during the reaction time of one-tenth of a second. Even if the program performing such calculations only required 1000 low-level assembly language instructions, the compute power requirement of a trillion operations per second would easily be reached. Life is complex. One can readily see why reducing a warehouse full of super computers to fit into our skull at room temperature would burn us up.

As an aside, we again warn the reader we are only using self-driving cars as an example to demonstrate the difficulties in replacing a human driver (Holman, 2018). The unspoken future proposed by proponents of self-driving cars is to eliminate the conscious human altogether and turn our roads into sophisticated warehouses, in which car-like forklifts pick up and drop off people instead of pallets. This book was not written to discuss value judgments but rather to emphasize the fact that actually replacing the conscious human element in any situation will require a quantum computer.

In a quantum computer only one calculation would have to be done in the reaction time. The input bit array in Figure 7.5-1 would still hold a single number, 127, that represents the last best steering wheel position, but the input transform would implement those bits in a quantum object, such as the spin direction of an electron, and the output array, labeled q-bits, would carry all possible values. There is a caveat. If we looked at the array at this stage, we would again only see one value because a measurement would force an interaction between the external event at one phase and ourselves. So instead, we imagine inside connecting pipes that lead to the parallel calculation performed by the quantum computer array, but no classic output. We will discuss such arrays in Section 7.5.3; however, we simply identify the output as a q-bit array on the right side. The individual q-bits no longer represent random steering wheel positions but rather such positions weighted by the evaluation criteria. In other words, the bit pattern that would lead to a crash would have been multiplied by a small number while the bit pattern that leads to a salubrious driving experience would be multiplied by a large number. Measurement by the Output Transform produces a bit pattern that represents the optimum wheel position as shown on the right side of Figure 7.5-1.

This information is then returned to the Classic User. If this is a human and the quantum algorithm was run in the brain, the human would feel the feedback from the muscles as small corrections to keep the automobile on course. If the driver, being the man inside the machine, has been replaced by computer equipment, the computer would drive the car akin to the reflex action since its immediate moves are provided. The driver would then be relegated to supervisory functions which, if everything goes as planned, would ultimately lead to simply getting in and out of the machine at the beginning and end of a successful trip.

As of writing this book, implementation of quantum computers is still in its infancy. Only the Shore algorithm for cracking crypto codes and the Grover algorithm for rapid database search have been defined and these have only been implemented in machines utilizing a few bits and very limited quantum gate structures. For relatively simple applications – compared with life – such as playing chess or driving cars, large high-speed conventional machines may be adequate. The thermal and reliability limitations discussed previously will limit the complexity of situations that can be handled by conventional object-oriented machinery, despite heroic programming efforts, to something far less than the complexity of life.

Because quantum computers are intertwined with the irrational mysteries of quantum theory, we will next provide some insights and visualizations that will make the concept of quantum computers understandable and at the same time show how the event-oriented world view and its supporting CAT physics provide the intellectual underpinnings for the coming revolution in intellectual thought.

7.5.2.1 The quantum bit as two states of motion

A bit in a conventional computer is implemented by the state of an electronic device, usually a voltage level measurable at the output of a flip-flop. Such a level is treated as a "thing" that has a single value with a degree of permanence which can be repeatedly measured to give the same result. In quantum theory a *bit* is more closely associated with the system that has *two* normal *states of motion*. A box holding two particles connected to opposite walls by strong springs and connected to each other by a weak coupling spring has two normal states of motion. In state 1, both particles move in parallel directions and pure oscillating motion can be detected from the outside. In state 0 they move in opposite directions and the box is still. Typically, these two motions are mixed, and from the outside one detects a complex motion combining these two pure states.

Motion describes an event. Repeating motion describes a stable event. When both particles in a box have no motion there is no action flowing through the system. If we add one quanta of action flow, the particles will move at some minimum amplitude in some combination of motion state 1 and state 2 represented by $1 \cdot \psi$. As we add "n" quanta of action flow, the motion should be represented by a real $n \cdot \psi$. Unfortunately, in standard quantum theory, the real number "n" is eliminated by a normalization process that leads to a probabilistic interpretation of ψ. In reality two small macroscopic particles may have 10^{20} coherent oscillations since all the atoms in each move in approximately the same direction. The movement in the box will be some linear combination of the motion state 1 and state 2 but the amplitude will increase as action is added. It is the state of motion that defines the state of a q-bit and in CAT the state of an event is its motion. Once we realize that Reality is a set of interacting events not objects it will be easy to comprehend how the state of a q-bits motion is processed through the quantum computer array, not the state of an objective voltage on the wire of a conventional electronic machine.

7.5.2.2 Example of macroscopic parallelism

The key to the efficiency of a quantum process lies in the fact that a single set of calculations would be done on a quantum object and all the properties associated with that object would be manipulated in parallel. If a car example appears contrived since conditional Boolean algebra would likely be adequate for a self-driving car, an actual example of such parallelism is found in our everyday music systems. Assume a recording is made of an orchestra. The sound from all the different instruments is combined in sound waves that hit a microphone. This produces a single electronic sequence of voltages that is recorded on a magnetic tape. If we cut out a segment of this tape, it will contain a record of the sound of all the instruments. This is the record of a motion that would hit a listener's eardrum on playback. It is no longer treated as a single object. From this single segment of the magnetic recording a listener can distinguish the violins from the oboe from the kettle drum. Let us assume on playback the volume is too low. The listener turns a single knob, and all the instruments become louder. A parallel operation has been carried out. Of course, no one would claim the tape deck is a quantum computer, but interestingly enough the mathematics involving Fourier transforms of sound waves is quite similar to the wave mechanical formulation of quantum theory. We bring it up to show that packaging of many individual properties, in this case the sound of individual instruments, into a single physical structure is routinely done. Operations on such a single structure then change all the packaged properties at once, and quantum theory applies. If by accident the sound is turned too high the sound system will break, and quantum theory no longer applies. CAT is required.

7.5.2.3 The difference between macroscopic and microscopic parallelism

The difference between the music example and a quantum processor is twofold. First electronic waves are composed of a very large number, on the order of 10^{20} individual coherent oscillations, which all do the same thing. As the wave flows by, if a small subset of them is extracted, it still retains the properties of the main wave, only not quite as well. This almost undisturbed ability to make a measurement allows us to take a 3rd-person theoretical view of the action flowing past us. In the quantum case we deal with single waves, and when we measure it, the whole wave flows through us and is consumed. In the quantum car example earlier in this chapter, this means that a measurement on the composite entity would only reveal one steering wheel position at a time. To get the complete list out one has to perform many sequential measurements at the end of many use scenario calculations. Running the output transform calculation many times defeats the whole purpose of quantum parallelism, which is why only optimization problems producing the one best result are appropriate.

7.5.2.4 Measuring a signal containing parallel information

A second difficulty with the music example is that a single measurement, even if it were small enough not to destroy the main flow, would contain a jumble of all the instruments. It requires a human ear and conscious awareness to distinguish the individual instruments. A simple Fourier transform conducted on the composite sound will only reveal the amplitude of frequencies contained in the jumble. To distinguish individual instruments the harmonics characterizing each instrument must be extracted. But these are all mixed together at the microphone. To hear individual instruments, *which a human can do*, would require generating each instrument's sound, including all its harmonics, and mixing this to the measured wave. This would amplify a specific harmonic bundle associated with one instrument while allowing the others to cancel. Such a setup would require a set of parallel instrument-specific expected sound generators. Each one would produce the sound of one instrument at the amplitude recorded. If the signal were of quantum strength so that a measurement would consume the composite signal, then only one instrument would be detected or not detected per measurement. If stronger coherent signals were available so that the main signal could be divided into parallel channels, then the signals in each channel could be added to parallel loops of expected sound from different instruments generated in the receiver.

The implication is that a *set of parallel expectation loops* are operating in accordance to the CAT architecture. The flow diagrams projected into the brain of the 2nd-person shown in Figure 7.2-4 and explicitly discussed in Chapter 6 show external signals merged with expected signals to produce the actually observed Now experience. The cochlea of the human ear is precisely a parallel instrument required to separate individual instruments from the jumbled pressure wave in the air. In our sound example only auditory loops are described; however, in the general case such loops are not restricted to the auditory channel but span the entire suite of sensors with which we are endowed.

7.5.3 From macroscopic to quantum computer architectures

Our model of physical reality contains a calculating element that utilizes the time-ordered states of the universe in which an observer believes to live (Figure 6.7-1). The calculation starts at the near past and progresses through the origin/destiny point and emerges from the future side of the observable Now. There are no "if" statements or time loops in a universe driven by a relentless time progression. To understand how our concept of computer calculations are implemented in such a one-way flow of action, we will present a series of computer architectures in the following three figures. These will demonstrate how the sequential time loops of a conventional computer can be implemented in a time sequence of spatially laid out electronic gate arrays. These parallel time planes are in turn converted to quantum computers using the motion in quantum bits to calculate multiple possibilities during one cycle. Please remember this is only an analogy that uses a conventional array of calculating elements laid out in space. The actual CAT universe calculation is done with elements that evolve in time. They are the space-cell events introduced in Chapter 3, not objects.

Figure 7.5-2 diagrams the operation of a conventional computer. Data indicated by up and down arrows is entered into the array of bits on the left. The program gates in the Central Processing Unit (CPU) are set to perform the first step of a calculation by signal a), which is output when the clock "T" reached phase a). The content of the left array is transferred into the CPU when the AND-gates are enabled by signal b) sent from the clock-in phase b). The CPU performs the calculation step and sends the result into the output array shown on the right.

When the clock reaches phase c), a signal enables the transfer of data from the output array back to the input array. Next the clock moves to phase a), which

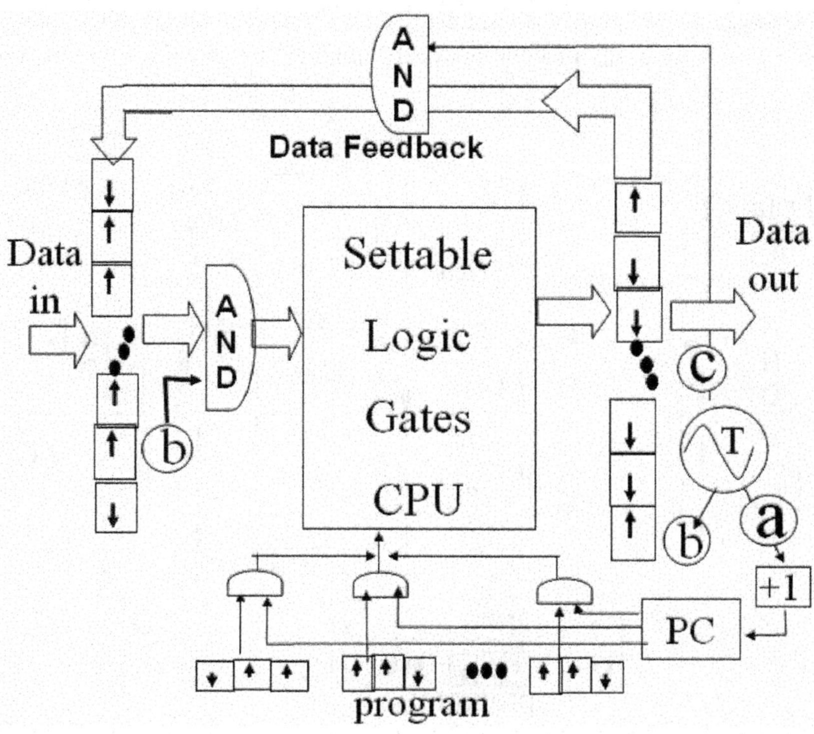

FIGURE 7.5-2 Conventional computer architecture

again increments the program counter (PC) to load the next program gate settings into the CPU, and the cycle repeats. After all steps of the program counter have been completed, the final result is output on the right. This sequence shows how a program is executed by reconfiguring the same CPU hardware for each sequential program step. If the program has "n" instruction steps and the clock runs in Δt_{clk} seconds per cycle, it will take $n \cdot \Delta t_{clk}$ seconds to run the program. The car steer-calculation requires 256 simulation runs. Even a 100-step program and a clock-cycle time of 1/30 seconds, lasting the typical reaction time of a human, would take 853 seconds. Since we can drive cars, the brain cannot operate like a conventional computer diagrammed in Figure 7.5-2.

The same calculation can be performed much faster if instead of reloading the CPU with new program steps each clock cycle, we duplicate the CPU in programmable gate arrays that remain fixed during a complete program execution. The architecture of such a setup is shown in Figure 7.5-3. In phase a) the clock sequentially loads and enables the CPU gates of all the program steps in a stack of arrays. Next the input data is loaded when the clock reaches b).

The gates of the CPUs having been set are all connected so the entire calculation runs as fast as the electricity can propagate through the pre-set gates. When the pulse reaches the output register, it will contain the bit settings of the complete calculation defined by the program steps. The clock in phase c) outputs this result, and the system is ready to perform the next program with new input data. The speed of gate arrays comes from the fact that executing each program step does not take the cycle time Δt_{clk} in a conventional computer but only the electronic time

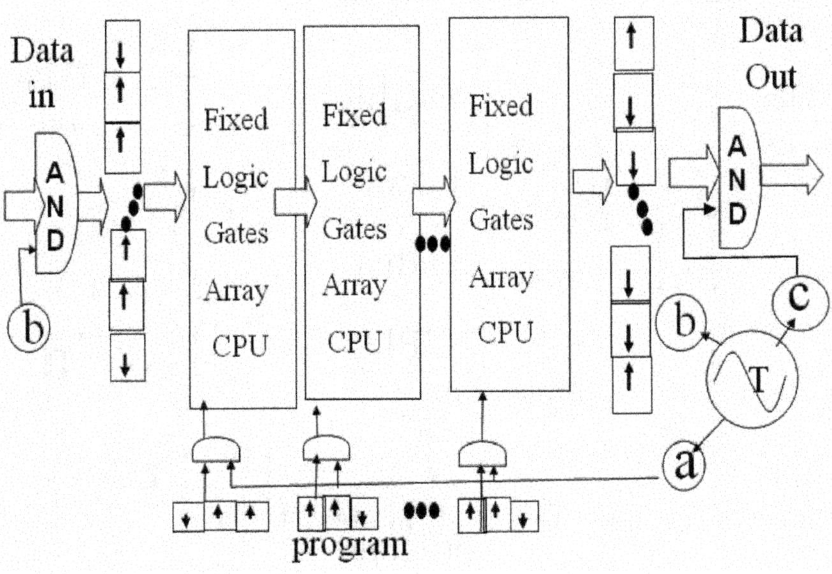

FIGURE 7.5-3 Electronic gate array computer

Δt_{CPU} required for electronic pulses to propagate through the gates in the CPU. This Δt_{CPU} time is usually several orders of magnitude faster than the Δt_{clk} of a conventional computer, and the program is executed much faster. Furthermore, if the same program is run "m" times with different input data to execute a simulation of alternatives, the gate loading step can be eliminated and the total simulation time is $m \cdot n \cdot \Delta t_{CPU}$. Assuming the CPU time is one-tenth the conventional computer clock-cycle time, to execute the self-driving car simulation cited previously would take 65 seconds. If a human operated with this kind of brain, we would still not want him or her on the road.

Figure 7.5-4 shows the detailed architecture of the quantum computer gate array utilizing reversible logic initially proposed by Fredkin and Toffoli (1982). The input array bits on the left side are no longer in one of two states but, as indicated by arrows pointing in different directions, in super-positions of such states. We visualize the arrows as moving. But, of course, if we were to measure them, their positions would represent the probabilities of finding them in state 0 or 1 after a measurement.

Thus, an eight-bit array would produce one of 256 results, which in a simulation would represent one of 256 possible alternatives from which the best alternative is extracted. Using quantum logic the car-steer algorithm would run in 1/3 second.

The logic gates are present by a quantum compiler designed to interpret the program instructions entered by a user into gate settings. We can imagine the bits as a sound made by the motion of the boxes described in Section 7.5.2.2. The box would vibrate at a maximum harmonic oscillation representing a pure state 1 or some other combination, producing a jumble of instruments. Imagine this sound, not the box, being carried through the quantum arrays. A small set of gates is required to build up all the logic required for a computation. Reversible gates

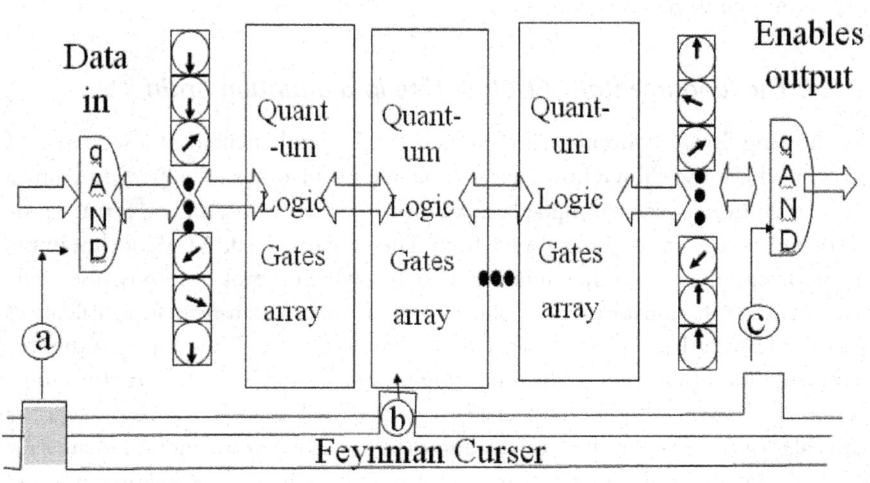

FIGURE 7.5-4 Quantum gate array of a quantum computer

always have the same number of inputs as output leads; standard logic gates often do not and therefore cannot be reversed. Typically, one requires a unity gate that propagates two q-bits forward in time, an exchange gate that exchanges the motion between two q-bits and a Control NOT gate that reverses the motion in one q-bit depending on the motion in a second q-bit. A Fredkin Universal Gate using three inputs and outputs was defined as a combination of a NOT and Control NOT, which can be set to perform all required functions. The leads of these gates are connected to each other into quantum circuits. The action of parallel gates is represented by individual matrices, and a sequence of arrays by multiplication of each matrix. Hence, the calculation of a quantum computer is mathematically represented by a matrix acting on all possible states of the input array. For the car-steer problem each array in the sequence shown in Figure 7.5-4 would be represented by a 256×256 matrix, and multiplying them by the number of program steps would generate an end-to-end calculation matrix that implements a unitary transformation, which calculates the output array $\psi[t']$ from the input array $\psi[t]$, as follows:

$$\Psi\left[t_2\right] = \mathbf{U}[t_2, t_1] \bullet \Psi\left[t_1\right]. \qquad \text{Equation 7.5-1}$$

Building such gates from atomic structures is a challenge. Initial experiments with a small number of bits were built by stimulating single atoms in Paul traps using laser pulses (Cirac and Zoller, 1995; Hughes et al., 1999). Commercial ventures have built applications that can claim to solve problems submitted online using quantum computing (D-wave, 2017). However, the major emphasis and money spent by governments has been on devices able to break crypto codes using the Shore algorithm (Shor, 1997). A fast database search tool using Grover's algorithm has also generated interest (Grover, 1996). At the current state of quantum computer development, the practical applications for such devices is highly questionable. Their main purpose here is to provide insight into the nature of reality the design of such devices may provide.

7.5.4 The fundamental CAT algorithm in a quantum brain

By showing how a conventional computer can be implemented in a sequence of arrays we have also shown how a programmable calculation can be performed by a wave of motion passing through planes of time in which each plane performs a program step on the entire passing wave front. The fundamental CAT algorithm in the quantum approximation shown in Figure 6.4-1, which is broken into two sequential operators in Equation 5.4-3, shows how a unitary transformation calculates backwards from the immediate Now past to the immediate Now future. A graphic representation of the same algorithm using time snapshots icons of our classic universe was shown on the bottom of Figure 5.2-4. In Figure 7.5-4 we showed the same algorithm representing a calculation carried out when the motion in an array of input bits are transformed into an output array by a quantum computer. We now only need to identify a quantum bit with the geographic volume element of the universe we believe to live in, in order to reach the conclusion that *the Now state of the entire universe, as we know it, is processed in one pass through its complete history and future destiny*. When all of those volume elements move in pure eigenstates of motion, the entire calculation produces a single deterministic output characteristic of the classic physics model. But when alternatives are represented by mixed states, the calculation performs parallel simulations of alternative possibilities that are collapsed into the single actual motion executed by the owner of the model in the next now instance (see Figure 6.7-2).

It is very important to realize that the word universe and the calculation carried out by it refers to the display of one's model, which in the 1st-person experience is Now happening around the display of one's body. The perception of space in which all these things around us happen is the content of an underlying q-bit array. The totality of this content flows through us performing a quantum calculation. The rate at which the calculation cycle proceeds is almost instantaneous because it flows through our memory. It is an internal structure but feels like and is treated as the objective world around us. This is the way evolution has designed us to operate.

We are usually interested in executing the best option in the least amount of time and do not require awareness of the detailed evaluation behind our decisions. Our conscious Now just needs to know what to do. It does not need to be burdened with knowledge of all the rejected alternatives or how the Now movement is selected. In fact, the overhead of such knowledge would likely paralyze an individual in an undecided state, which would not be rewarded by natural selection. Therefore, the fundamental CAT algorithm is an unconscious parallel execution of alternative possibilities followed by an optimum outcome selection that produces a single calculation result before such a result is brought into conscious awareness through activated body motion. The qualitative description of such an algorithm was shown in Figure 6.7-2, which resulted in identifying the fastest path that closed a cycle through models of our universe. This algorithm is precisely what quantum computers offer by executing behind the quantum veil in the unconscious phase of our action cycle. The words we speak or write, and even the thoughts that come into conscious awareness are only the tip of the processing iceberg. The operations of a quantum computer act as the quantum approximation of a CAT model executing unconscious activities of the thought process producing our observable movements. CAT addresses the knowledge required to grow and dismantle the machine as well as knowledge required to operate it once built.

7.6 Neuroscience and the explanations of consciousness

The previous sections described the computer science analogy. We drew a picture of both a 2nd-person and a computer to show their architectural similarity. The classic objective viewpoint treats these sensations as representations of real things. Quantum theory teaches us that these "real things" are products of measurement processes carried out on a probabilistic reality. The CAT model advances the lessons learned from quantum theory and assumes that there is an inside motion in material, which we experience directly as the 1st-person and an outside view we only experience as projections into those direct appearances.

To include consciousness, computer engineering must be extended into the quantum realm and beyond to the CAT model. We projected a CAT model of a cognitive being onto the architecture of a conventional computer in Figure 7.3-2. By reversing this analogy neuroscientists have adopted the assumption that a configuration of biological switches and wires will explain consciousness. The caveat mentioned in reference to Figure 7.2-4 is not that the projected flow diagram of CAT is wrong, but that it is projected into a 1st-person's sensations of a 2nd-person's brain, not the real Brain that causes those sensations. The implication is that quantum computers rather than objective machines must become the computer science side of the brain analogy. For neuroscience it means that a larger Brain mechanism within which the sensations of objects and brains are generated must be integrated into the science.

7.6.1 The easy problem of consciousness

The hard problem of consciousness, presented in Section 7.2, arises from logical inconsistencies when we adopt the assumption that an independent external *objective* reality exists. It has been solved by adopting a pan-psychic explanation for consciousness and an event-oriented physics that identifies a physical basis of subjective feelings. The problem is hard because our conventional objective world view and the classic physics that is based upon this world view must be abandoned. Such a change is currently rejected as nonsense because people trained to operate their lives with objective habits would rather reject and fight than accept the relearning task implied by a new world view. Once the jump in fundamental assumptions is made, an explanation of conscious phenomena is available in principle. However, the identification of an internal primitive awareness in all material is a long way from describing why we humans experience what we experience. We have moved the problem of consciousness from the "in-principle impossible" to the "practically impossible". Practically impossible may be easier than in-principle impossible, but it is still hard. But once the conceptual jump is made, the next problem requires us to map the underlying motions in charge-mass configurations, which we now believe are correlated with personal experiences, to known brain components.

This "easier problem" leaves us with the same difficult reverse engineering task classic physics-based neuroscientists have faced in the past. Our only hope is that our new vantage point gives us a physically based starting point to anchor subjective phenomena. The brain computer analogy is no longer based on conventional objective systems governed by classic physics. Quantum computers, when understood through the lens of CAT principles, already contain the physical correlates to which we can logically attach a mind.

7.6.1.1 A brief review of objective neuroscience

The tools and methodologies of neuroscience are largely based upon the Aristotelian belief in an independent objective reality that we see through the window of our senses, and the classic physics that support this world view. The anatomy of the brain is explored through dissection, which reveals a complex object that has been mapped into regions and given names dating back to antiquity. The discovery of the microscope allowed the identification of neurons connected by a network of dendrites and axons. Through careful comparison of injuries, lesions, hemorrhages and other abnormalities with accompanying cognitive impairment, a fairly accurate mapping between function and brain regions had been developed by the 19th century. Advances in electronics allowed micro-probes to extend the mapping to individual cells, so that we know which cell clusters move body parts, generate a playback of memories and mirror events and feelings of abstract emotions.

Detailed studies of specific brain regions such as the olfactory sense by the late Walter Freeman and Korma (2010) and the retina (Joselevitch, 2008) have led to detailed understanding of the interaction of neurons with external electromagnetic and chemical stimulation and the automatic processing that happens in neural networks. Walter Freeman also worked with G. Vitiello (2001), and from personal discussions I know he shared the "double inside" view from which the mass-charge separation hypothesis was derived as a key to understanding consciousness.

The Electro-Encephalograph (EEG) has revealed dynamic electrical patterns on the scalp that are associated with brain states such as sleep, wakeful consciousness and various sensations and thought patterns. EEG pattern-recognition devices have been developed that allow an individual to move external equipment by controlling their thoughts. Some researchers believe the electronic oscillations in a 6-inch diameter globe might be sufficient to correlate with our global conscious experience. Resolution and propagation limits make this unlikely, but some correlation between brain waves and our conscious experience certainly exists. Coherent amplification of such signals leading to epileptic seizures have led to miraculous revelations throughout the centuries that give us clues to both normal and expanded conscious experiences.

A very popular and useful tool in the neurophysiologist's kit is functional Magnetic Resonance Imaging (fMRI), which can be used to track the rate of activity in parts of the brain as a function of tasks being performed by the subject. Such maps allow us to determine the sub-components of the brain involved in executing specific functions and can be used to build connective pathways.

7.6.2 Brain hierarchy to quantum scale

Just like computer engineers capture the primitive desires of electrons to move in response to applied voltages in a hierarchy of switches and transistors, so Nature has combined the primitive desires of charge and mass into a hierarchy of biological systems. These exhibit emerging properties at each scale and finally reach the performance of the human brain at our level.

In Figure 7.6-1 a pictorial brain hierarchy is shown from a single brain at the top to a mass-charge space layer at the bottom small scale. Though the brain appears to move and change its macroscopic state through a motion in time, the arrows suggest that the actual state transition can be understood by translating macro structures

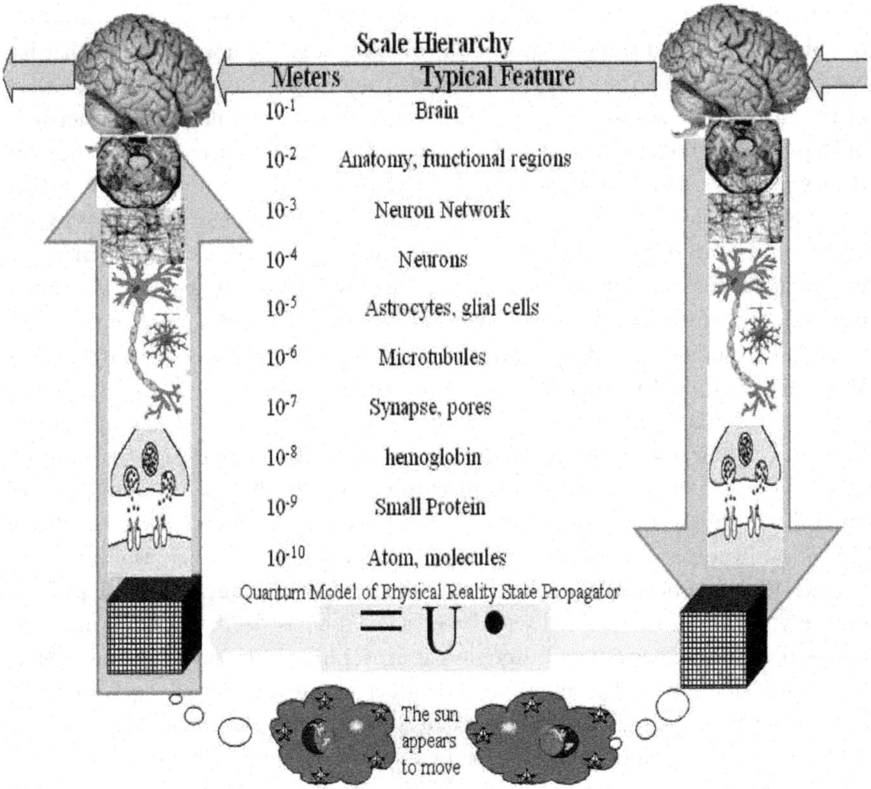

FIGURE 7.6-1 Brain hierarchy to quantum scale shows time propagation happens at any material aggregation scale

into underlying mass-charge separation patterns that then propagate the change through an observable experiential phase. Thus, the brain does not just move from state to state at the macroscopic level. All its material, composed of masses and charges, does so by supervening the executing of a measurement-explanatory cycle through a subjective phase at all levels of aggregations (Chalmers, 1996, 32). There is no physical flow of activity up and down the hierarchical level, only a change in the size of the parts we chose to study at each scale. All parts carry along the property of consciousness.

An analogous situation is encountered in object-oriented programming pioneered by the C++ computer language. C++ programs can inherit properties from smaller foundational programs. Thus, a program emulating an apple may inherit characteristics from a program describing a physical object, which needs only to be written once in a foundational class library. If the programmer wants to build a banana or cherries in his or her application, the new programs inherit all the characteristics of a physical object from the library and only needs to add specifics such as color, shape, etc. The same principle is applied when aggregating properties in

CAT. Foundational levels of primitive physics supply the property of consciousness, which is then inherited to all combinations built on top. In this way the foundational property of consciousness is inherited by all parts of the brain, which working together produce the human consciousness we typically experience.

7.6.3 Physical brain state transforms at different hierarchical levels

The movement from one state to another is addressed by different theories involving different nomenclatures at each level of aggregation. In physics only two major divisions apply. At the macroscopic physical level, the two brains seen at the top of Figure 7.6-2 are treated as objects whose state is composed of coordinates (q_f) and momentum (p_f) vectors for all degrees of freedom "f" at time "t". The state change for an isolated system is indicated by the arrow connecting the two brain states at the top of Figure 7.6-2. From the macro down to atomic scales, a change of state in brain components is described by the classic physical Hamiltonian equations shown in the arrow at the top.

When the objective brain structure is reduced in size to mass-charge separation configuration in an underlying space grid, a small-enough change of state is implemented by a unitary quantum operator U(t,t'). This underlying grid maps into the material of the big Brain mechanism that for the 1st-person neuroscientist underlies the observable world. The projection of such material into an observable

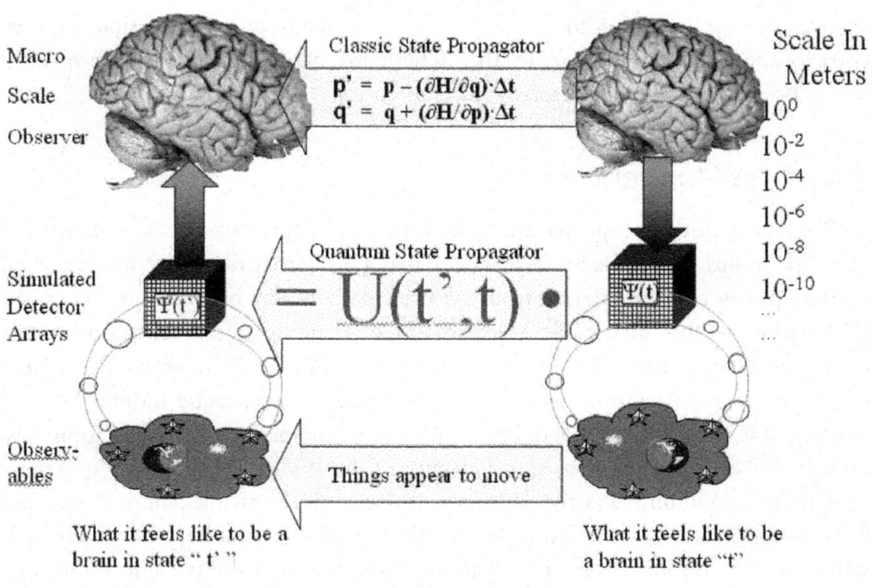

FIGURE 7.6-2 Mapping the Brain state propagation to quantum dynamics

patient's brain is purely a visualization of the operational symbols of the scientist's theory.

The experience felt by the actual Brain is shown at the bottom of the action cycle. The picture shown here is that of two snapshots of the cycle state parameterized by "t" and "t'" respectively. Recognizing that a static state is actually a self-generating cycle of activity suggests that a cycle that differs slightly from complete self regeneration will produce a sequential change in both the physical reality aspect and the mental aspect of the cycle. This suggests that the changes in our conscious experience actually happen through a continuous... -body-mind-body-mind- ... flow sequence, which only appears to produce quantum jumps because our snapshot recording apparatus does not allow us to "see" the unconscious activities inside the cycles.

7.6.4 Macroscopic neurophysiologic mechanisms of consciousness

In the last section we listed the different forms of organization encountered as we go from larger to smaller scales. At the smallest size we encounter an event structure that incorporates the mental aspect of material. This mental property is inherited by systems at all scales. That brain material falls like a rock, no matter how complex and intricate, is a simple example of property inheritance. Consciousness in CAT is such a primitive property inherited by all sizes of material. In this section we discuss several theories that address emerging conscious behavior at various scales studied by neuroscientists. The principle of inheritance suggests there is no monopoly on where consciousness can appear in the scale hierarchy, and in that sense there is no right or wrong. However, in Section 7.7 we will single out one possible site for consciousness that closely matches the architecture of a conscious being proposed in this book, and therefore deserves closer attention.

7.6.4.1 Feed-forward loops

CAT supports the concept that the conscious Now experience is the mind phase of action loops that exist at all levels of material aggregation. The existence of such loops can only be inferred from evidence gathered by observations of a 2nd-person's brain. Does such evidence exist? While attending a conference on neuroscience in Boston, I heard an astounding lecture by Victor Lamme, who reported on experiments that monitored the flow of signals in a macaque monkey's brain while it was being anesthetized. He found the maintenance of a signal loop was directly correlated to the conscious behavior of the animal. Furthermore, and perhaps more astounding, was the observation that contrary to the standard mechanism of anesthetic substance to suppress activity in the central nervous system as a whole, by varying the dosage, Prof. Lamme could pinpoint the transition from the conscious to the unconscious state. It was directly correlated with the maintenance of the dynamic loop (Lamme, 2015).

7.6.4.2 Consciousness from microtubules

The most advanced development of a theory of consciousness built on the hypothesis that the brain operates like a quantum computer is spearheaded by Stuart Hameroff and Roger Penrose (Hameroff, 1998) and the many associates that support their research. Dr. Hameroff runs the "Toward a Science of Consciousness" conference in Tucson, Arizona, which is the largest interdisciplinary meeting emphasizing rigorous study of consciousness and the go-to meeting for all seriously interested in the topic.

The Hameroff-Penrose theory suggests that microtubule structures composed of tubulin protein in dendrites allow electrons to be entangled in quantum oscillations that correlate with global EEG patterns associated with moods and thoughts. Though the entire possibility that quantum calculations could be executed in the brain was discounted by Tegmark (2000), whose arguments were rebuffed by Hagan and colleagues (2002), the controversy from the CAT viewpoint is moot. Seeking a quantum computer architecture constructed out of observable objects is not to be expected when state models rather than dynamic interval models of reality are projected into those objects. Consciousness is an inherited property happening inside material. The contribution CAT can make here is to further the argument by Penrose of "Orchestrated Reduction". Such reduction is a natural consequence of mass-charge interaction loops that allow the reality behind observed 1st-person objects to exhibit conscious sensations in any material structure including the brain.

7.6.4.2.1 Orchestrated reduction

Penrose (1994) assumed a measurement is completed when a mass is displaced sufficiently far to have a distinct new location. His calculation was based upon the assumption that when a mass is moved by collision with a photon, the mass separation energy times the relaxation time interval must be at least one quantum of action. We examine this proposition with a thought experiment carried out on a Mach-Zender Interferometer shown on the top half of Figure 7.6-3. A photon probability wave |A> is emitted from a light source and passes through a half-silvered mirror. It splits in two equal parts |B> and |C> and bounces off two mirrors as |D> and |E> reaching a second half-silvered mirror. Assuming the mirrors make a rectangle, then if one looks carefully at the paths through the mirror glass, the paths are exactly equal and would only interfere constructively if the photon reaches detector F not detector G. This is experimentally verified.

However, if we measure which path the photon traveled by inserting a very sensitive recoil measurement device M, we destroy the interference pattern and both detectors would receive the photon with equal probability. This is a version of the quantum mechanical double-slit experiment in which knowledge of the path forces quantum particles to act like classic bullets. Quantum theory explains this effect by introducing the wave-particle duality and claiming a particle is both a wave and a particle depending upon how one measures it, i.e. light acts like a wave

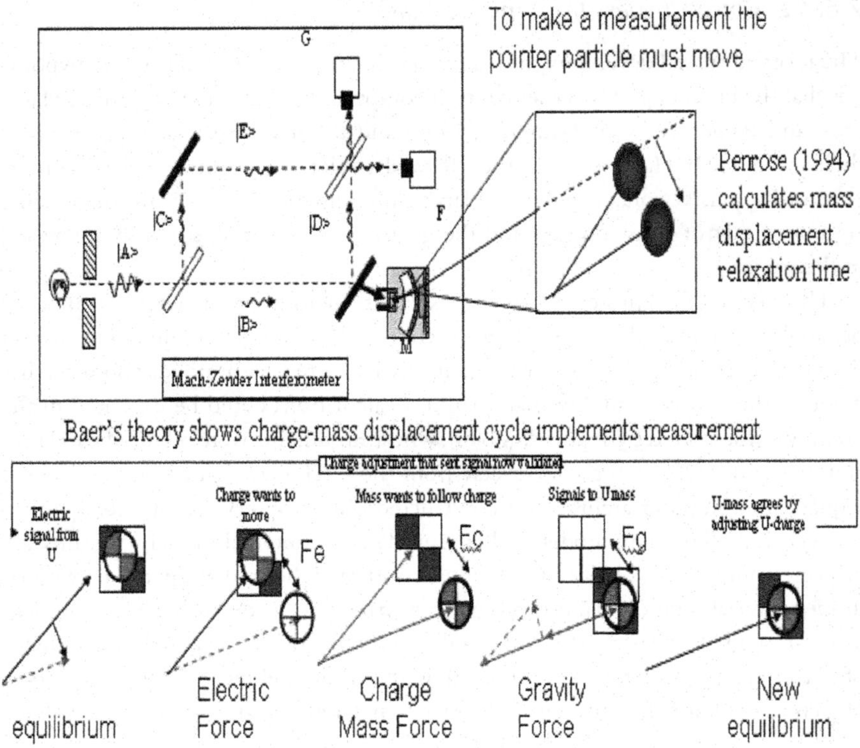

FIGURE 7.6-3 Orchestrated Reduction in the quantum approximation

when traveling through the apparatus but the wave collapses to reveal a particle when it is measured. Penrose proposed a mechanism for the collapse of the wave function he called Orchestrated Reduction, which involves the motion of a mass of the pointer particle that reports the measurement result.

Conscious Action Theory (CAT) builds upon Penrose's idea by introducing charge-mass separation sequence shown in the lower portion of Figure 7.6-3. CAT suggests that the photon imparts a purely electric influence that moves the charge of the measurement pointer particle. The measurement is only complete when the mass moves as well. This, however, can only be done by negotiating its position with the masses in the rest of the Universe (see Section 4.5). If successful, the charge and mass achieve a new equilibrium indicating the photon has bounced off the mirror. If not, the measurement pointer particle falls back to its original position and reverses the photon influence (see Figure 6.7-2). Uncertainty exists during the negotiating period. If the force of gravity propagates at light speed, this negotiating period would be very long. However, considerable evidence suggests gravity and inertia propagate much, much faster than light, which makes the negotiation with distant masses a reasonable hypothesis (Rowlands, 2007, chapter 17).

The length of this uncertainty is what Penrose called the relaxation time. In CAT, uncertainty is given an ontological interpretation. It is interpreted as the time it takes the masses in the universe to respond and allow a new equilibrium state to be reached. Equilibrium states are required if time stable measurement results are to be recorded. Once the path is known the electromagnetic wave proceeds in full force |D> and splits 50% at the upper left mirror.

Orchestrated Reduction was used by Hameroff and coworkers (Hagan et al., 2002) to counter Tegmark's objection to the feasibility of quantum calculations occurring in the "soggy wet" environment of the brain to support consciousness. As discussed in Section 7.5, evidence of quantum effects in biological systems have since been verified in other cases. We consider the Hameroff-Penrose theory not the final explanation of human consciousness but rather an example of how activity related to consciousness can happen at many levels of material aggregation.

7.6.4.3 The role of DNA

DNA has been given the role of a kind of dynamic library that stores and distributes the knowledge of how our bodies are built and how they should function. The Genome project and emerging gene therapies suggest considerable medical benefits can be expected from understanding the DNA molecule. However, as our knowledge grows, mysteries such as the unused sections of the code and the fact that code size and animal complexity are not well correlated, suggest that DNA may have functions in addition to those suggested by the double-helix coding structure discovered by Crick and Watson. A lecture by Grandy (2011) suggested that perhaps the DNA molecule formed a material substrate that could support communication and oscillations required by a quantum Hilbert space. At the time I had been performing verification analysis of data reported by Professor Rita Pizzi and colleagues (2007) on an experiment that explored possible quantum entanglement communication effects between separated neuron colonies grown from a single stem cell. If some form of entanglement was possible when growing several hundred cells, the possibility that trillions of identical cells are entangled when a human is grown from a single union of sperm and egg seemed possible. The quantum interpretation of entangled states allowing communication between distant parts of the universe is a well-explored phenomenon. CAT provides a more ontological interpretation of such phenomena because the communication is actually between distant parts of the 1st-person's model of the universe and is therefore much closer together.

If the DNA molecule could form a communicating substrate for macroscopic mass-charge separation patterns, it would form an aggregated level of the infinitesimal mass-charge density distributions incorporating consciousness. It is known that exactly identical systems tend to resonate, forming a potential communication space. The CAT appropriate quantum interpretation is provided by Lande's quantization rules (Lande, 1973). He suggested that particles only change momentum Δp when their shape contains a symmetry Δx such that $\Delta p/\Delta x = n \cdot h$ (Planck's constant). The strength of symmetry is the amplitude of the Fourier transform component of the shape having the wavelength Δx. For example, a pure sinusoidal structure having a wave shape with each wave of length λ will have a Fourier component $a[\lambda] = 1$ when $\lambda = \Delta x$. In this example, the shape has a nearly 100% symmetry of Δx. For other shapes the Fourier component represents the probability of a momentum exchange. Since the transform of a shape is described by infinite plane waves they extend throughout the space and can therefore exchange momentum by simply absorbing a wave component present in the substrate from any distance.

These considerations suggest a substrate of identical DNA molecules could communicate throughout the body supporting a level of consciousness, but may actually communicate, at lower probabilities, with similar but not identical molecules in related beings. Implications of such communications will be discussed in Chapter 8. Here we only emphasize how characteristics of primitive consciousness can manifest themselves from material at different scales.

7.6.4.4 The double inside

A general analysis of a physical system such as the brain that is applicable at many scales was carried out by Giuseppe Vitiello (2001) in what I consider to be one of the most important contributions to the physics of consciousness and our development of CAT. Vitiello realized that the brain was an open system that could not be analyzed as a self-contained thing. To describe an open system such as the brain one needs to include the system-environment interaction effects. One possible choice of representing the environment is as a "time-reversed accommodation". Time must be reversed since the energy "dissipated" by the system is gained by the environment. Such an accommodation is achieved by doubling the degrees of freedom as discussed for harmonic oscillators by Celeghini and colleagues (1992). By choosing to treat the center of charge and mass as individual degrees of freedom, CAT has achieved a double model that differs in formulation from Vitiello's but provides an exact model of environmental influences because outside material influences F_{gi}, F_{em} are exactly balanced by the cognitive force F_{cm},F_{mc} field which is correlated with conscious experience. In fact, it is this exact balance that allows non-equilibrium activity in the outside-of-matter and conscious experience inside-of-matter to maintain the equilibrium dynamics of the Whole object-subject cycle.

I had a personal discussion with Prof. Vitiello at a conference sponsored by the University of Padua, Italy, during which he simply stated the meaning of his work with the words, "You are the Double in me". I stood there in silence. Looking into his eyes, I hoped he understood that I understood that we all contain each other. Further words would have required writing the book you are reading, and he hurried off to enjoy a glass of red wine for lunch as Italians are apt to do.

7.7 The CAT model and the glial network

Mainstream neuroscientists have followed the "neuron doctrine", which assumes all computational thought processing in the brain is performed by the network of neurons, even though the majority of cells in the brain are glial cells. Historically glial cells were thought to act as support and insulation to the axons and dendrites that carry thought patterns in the form of pulses. The role the glial cells play in the brain has evolved (Verkhratsky and Butt, 2007; Periera et al., 2013). It has come to light that these cells have an important role in the thinking process. The largest of these non-neuron cell types are called astrocytes because they have a star shape when seen under a microscope. It has been reported that human glial progenitor cells (hGPCs) can be transplanted into immune-deficient mice, where they grow, completely replacing the astrocytes and oligodendrocytes, glial cells of the recipient mouse within nine months (Coghlan, 2014; Windrem et al., 2014). The astounding result is that not only were the mouse brain's glial cells largely replaced by cells of human origin while the neurons from the mouse remained, but the implanted mice became *quantitatively smarter* than their mouse cousins.

These findings strongly suggest that the glial network, far from being passive, support-cells to neurons, actually perform a central role in defining intelligence. In fact, it seems likely that there exists an entire hidden glial network within the brain that may be the seat of thought and memory. Glial cells and specifically astrocytes are connected through gap junctions to form communicating clusters called astrocytic syncytiums. Each astrocyte in a syncytium in turn is connected to many neurons providing a natural control structure for perceptive channels. The interface between the glia and neural networks are tripartite synapses. A model of these synapses is shown in Figure 7.7-1 (Mitterauer, 2011). An astrocyte cell is shown as the large blob on the right. This cell monitors the neural transmitters (NT) emitted from a pre-synapse to transmit a neuron pulse across the gap junction in order to stimulate a downstream neuron to fire. In response to the quantity and type of transmitters the astrocyte emits gliotransmitters (GT) that are taken up by receptors

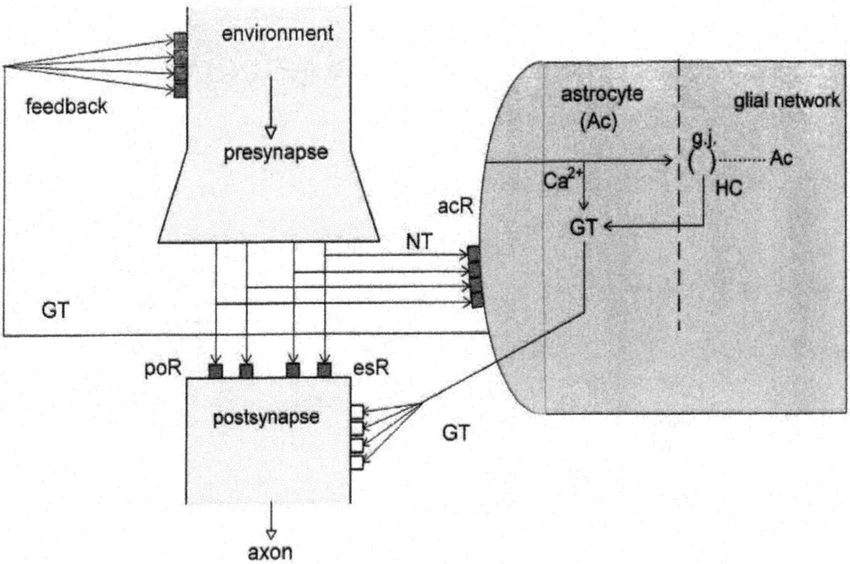

FIGURE 7.7-1 Model of a tripartite synapse

located on the pre- and post-synapses of the junction. The effect of these chemical movements is to provide a feedback control on the rate at which neuron pulses are transmitted.

The research psychiatrist at the University of Salzburg B. Mitterauer (2012) has proposed that imbalances in the number of transmitters versus receivers can be linked to various clinical psychotic states. Details of the chemical substances involved are provided in the references but Mitterauer suggests there are four synaptic states. First, normal human cognitive operation is in a balance state, when the number of transmitters (NT) and astrocytic receptors are equal. Second, the astrocytic receptors outnumber the neurotransmitters. A lack of activating substances is responsible for the pathophysiology of depression. Third, the neurotransmitters outnumber the astrocytic receptors. An excess of material for the activation of astrocytic receptors presumably causes mania and epilepsy. Fourth, in tripartite synapses a total lack of functional astrocytic receptors generates unbalanced synaptic mechanisms, as hypothesized in schizophrenia.

Here we note that the architecture between the neural network and the glial network implements the CAT model of a cognitive being shown in many figures in this book (examples 6.2-3, 7.3-2). The neural network plays the role of the body segment that provides the input/output between the sensors and actuators that control internal body functions and motor control. The glial network implements an inner loop responsible for maintaining a model of reality and generating the expected observations. If we consider Figure 7.2-4 as representative of the total processing system inside a cognitive machine, then the comparator function is implemented as a tripartite synapse. The action happening at each synapse is differentiated by the location of the synapse. This location determines the sensation felt. Neural transmitter densities across a patch of synapses controlled by astrocytic

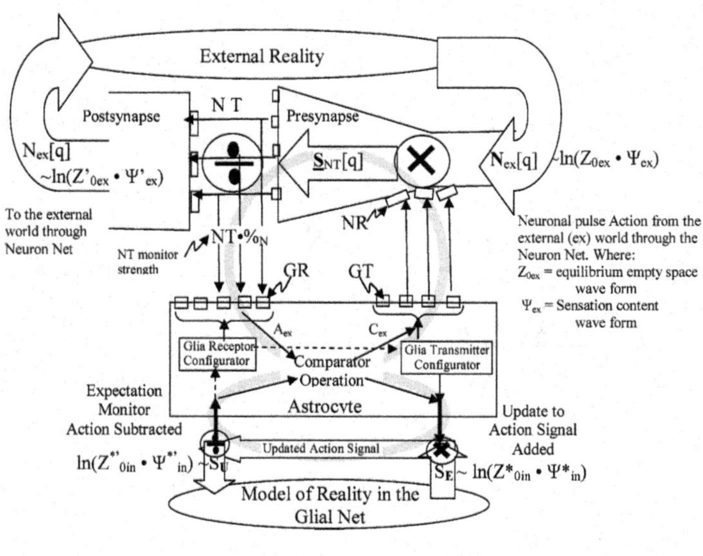

FIGURE 7.7-2 Two action cycles connected by a tripartite synapse

syncytiums provide measured sensory patterns while the glial transmitters provide the expected patterns. An imbalance between the two generates an error signal that causes updates in the glial network as well as modification of pulse rates in the neural network. The modified pattern of pulses are then processed by "X()" operators implemented in the effecter side of the neural network to activate muscles, reset sensors or perform internal housekeeping functions into organs and glands.

A model of the CAT comparator process is mapped onto the model of a tripartite synapse in Figure 7.7-2. The glial transmitters (GT) modify the signal from the external world transmitted through the neural net. The modified signal controls the emission of neural transmitters (NT). These are divided in the synapse. Some stimulate the post-synapses while others stimulate the astrocyte receptors.

The GT and NT chemical flow are the I/O signals between the glial and neural nets. The process which generates balanced tripartite synapses would correspond to the situation in the CAT model when the measured and expected energy patterns at the comparison point match. This case corresponds to the feeling of empty space or an absence of sensation. Mild imbalances generate feelings that look like things in the optic modality, which are characteristic to normal brain operation. However severe imbalances cause various psychotic symptoms. The *American Psychiatric Textbook of Psychiatry* (Hales et al., 1999) characterizes the psychotic symptoms of hallucinations and delusions as a loss of ego boundaries, and the patient is unable to distinguish between his or her own thoughts/perceptions and those referring to the outer world. The boundary between the outer and inner world is mapped into the material boundary between the neural and glial networks. Mild imbalances at this boundary produce normal cognitive operation. Severe imbalance causes psychotic behavior.

Figure 7.7-3 shows a graphic implementation of a comparator involving two signals passing through a material surface with variable transmission and reflecting coefficients a_t, b_t,a_r,b_r. The bottom represents internal signals from the cognitive loop. The top represents signals from the external interface sensor/actuator body loop. If we neglect boundary phase changes and the signals are identical and exactly equal in strength, the output signals would cancel and no action would be taken. A mixing of signals will depend upon the strength and relative phase of the incoming signals as well as the value of transmission and reflecting coefficients. These strengths are implemented in the GT and NT transmitters and provide a mixing of update and command signals as well as a degree of isolation that reflect various operating levels of human consciousness in the CAT model. See Figures 2.7-1 and 6.4-1 for comparators in various CAT architectures.

The cognitive being is aware of both signals from the external and internal world. If the NT signal received at the astrocyte is too strong, external stimulation dominates while internal stimulation recedes. Such an individual may experience sensations but lacks sufficient comprehension of what he or she is seeing. If the signal received at the astrocyte is too weak, sensations from the external world are weak in comparison to those recalled from memory and our mental display will retain experiences, i.e. hallucinations which are not corroborated by external

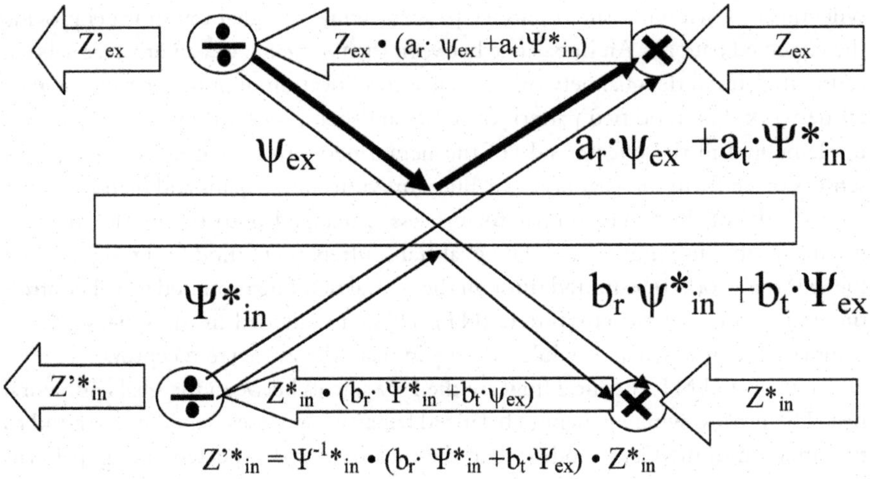

FIGURE 7.7-3 CAT comparator mixes external and internal signals: produces no command or model update when system is in equilibrium with external world

measurements. In extreme cases, an individual experiences only the output from internal memory recall. An individual lives in his or her own world and acts rationally in response to perception. Unfortunately, the world and response no longer register to our sensory experiences and therefore the individual is judged to be psychotic.

8

PHILOSOPHY, PSYCHOLOGY AND RELIGION

This book contains a material-based theory of reality. We have added two aspects to the material of that reality: these are our inside and outside experiences of matter. Our ability to make symbols further divides those experiences into direct sensations and the forms which must then be translated into direct sensations. Chapter 7 applied CAT to professions that deal with tangibles – machinery, brains, pharmaceuticals, etc. – that are experienced as direct sensations. This chapter connects our theory of reality with those disciplines that depend on the use and misuse of symbols as their final product. Purveyors of symbols deliver services such as an understanding of a topic or procedure. For this reason, topics discussed in this chapter do not depend upon direct physical force and control but rather on persuasion and acceptance of symbols through which we participate in building who we are and how we behave. The spectrum of disciplines falling into this category includes the humanities, arts and theoreticians in all fields of study; we emphasize philosophy, religion and psychology as examples of disciplines in which the change in world view has an immediate and profound impact.

8.1 Philosophy

This section addresses some of the central questions of philosophy. What is reality? How does it work? What are we in it? CAT is not a philosophy. Questions of aesthetics, beauty and dictates of human behavior are provided a place and a mechanism implementing their operation but no judgment is made regarding the preferences contained in those mechanisms. There is no attempt to find an ultimate answer for *why* things are the way they are. A set of a priori postulates is assumed, and reasonable deductions are made. That is all. Similar attempts that explain our situation have been made throughout the ages. Almost all concepts contained in CAT have been proposed by our ancestors and will continue to be made by our contemporaries on into the future. Here we identify a subset of philosophic ideas and show first how they are incorporated into the CAT model and second how our event model of reality modifies their pronouncements.

8.1.1 Plato vs. Aristotle

The main alternative views of our situation have come to us from the two great Greek philosophers, Plato and Aristotle. Each of these men left us a large legacy of ideas that describe ourselves and the universe in which we live. The details of these ideas have long been revised but the impact on CAT of their thoughts can be summarized in what is known as Plato's cave analogy, which we translated into modern times in Chapter 1.

Plato likened our situation to prisoners bound inside a cave with constraints that allowed them to look only at the inner wall of the cave with their backs turned away from the entrance. The prisoners could therefore not see the reality outside directly. All they could see were shadows projected onto the wall in front of them from light blocked by entities passing the cave entrance. The nature of the reality outside the cave could only be deduced from evidence gathered by examining the shadows. Presumably the prisoners spent their time arguing about the nature of the reality given the evidence available in what they could see. Their arguments were probably copied onto parchment and thus models of reality were created much as this book was in our time.

A modern interpretation of the analogy identifies the cave with our skull and the prisoners, with the little-man-inside representing our conscious "I". The moral of the story is that we do not see reality directly. What we do see, like the shadows in a cave, is evidence from which a model of reality can be deduced. Furthermore, Plato claimed the reality outside was made up of ideals that could only be handled through mathematics. A recent book by Tegmark (2014), cosmologist and professor at the Massachusetts Institute of Technology, repeated Plato's hypothesis by declaring the universe is fundamentally mathematical. CAT simply recognizes that a book constructed from material can exhibit a symbol structure that helps process the shadows into response-leaver settings in the cave. No claim is made that the symbols in the book represent the Reality outside, ideal or otherwise.

Aristotle, Plato's student disagreed. Contrary to Plato's concept, Aristotle believed we were looking not at shadows but rather directly through the cave entrance to see the external reality the way it actually is through the windows of our senses. Aristotle went on to define the characteristics of this reality as his "Natural Philosophy", in which all material was composed of water, air, fire, earth and aether. In modern terms, this philosophic stance has survived as "objective reality" – a belief that the world of objects we see is reality itself, or at least an accurate representation of that reality.

Historically the powers controlling Western civilization prior to and beyond the first millennia were religious folk who saw no conflict with the idea that gods and goddesses, or a single god and angels lived in an ideal world beyond the grasp of our senses. The lives of these folk were controlled by unseen influences, and when they were liberated from their earthly shackles, they would enter the ideal world beyond. This opinion generally fit the Platonic view, and although Aristotle's Natural Philosophy was known and argued in what might be called academic circles, the mainstream followed Plato. Figure 8.1-1 shows the broad arrow representing the mainstream emanating from Plato from about 400 BC till the middle of the 13th century, when Thomas Aquinas appeared on the scene.

To quote Thomas Cahill (2006), a popular historian on the Middle Ages,

> Thomas did not believe we lived in the gloom of a cave, tied to a decaying mass of matter and that everything we perceived was illusion or trickery. He believed we live in our bodies, created by a good God and received true perceptions through the media of our five senses, which like clear windows enabled us to form generally accurate impressions of the world as it is. He replaced the shadows of Plato's Cave with the sunshine of everyday reality.

The switch to Natural Philosophy was a large movement we now identify with the Renaissance. Aquinas and his writings can only be taken as a symbolic milestone. Corruption in the Catholic Church, as documented by Dante's "Inferno" or the unsuccessful and expensive Crusades, were the more likely causes leading to a philosophical switch. However, Aquinas's works were valued as a fundamental change by the authorities at the time. Less than 50 years after his death, Thomas Aquinas was raised to the altars as a canonized saint by Pope John XXII. In the following centuries the works of Kepler, Galileo and Newton heralded the

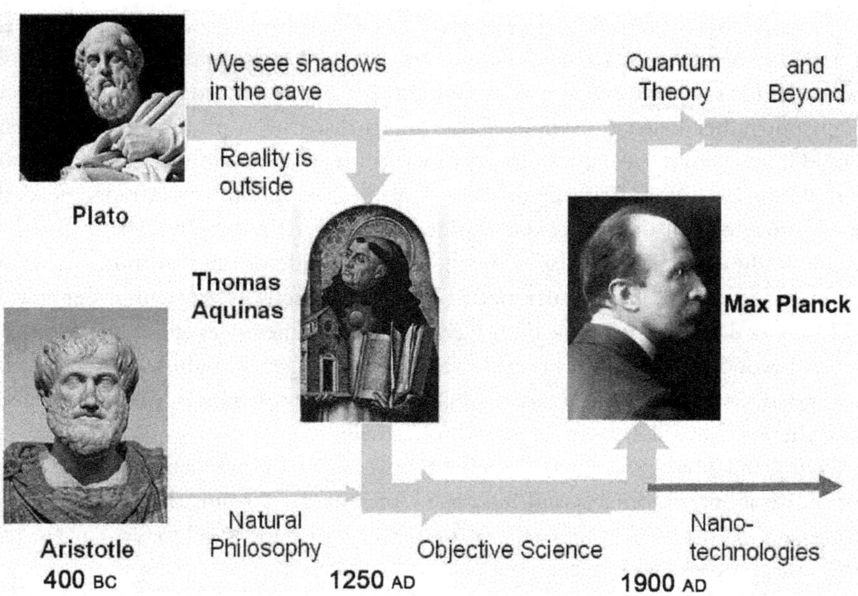

FIGURE 8.1-1 Historic development of Platonic and Aristotelian philosophy

development of objective science, and along with it the material dominance of Europe. Eventually the Catholic Church was forced to acknowledge the utility of science and laid its own claim to its development. In 1879, Aquinas's philosophical and theological writings were finally accepted by Pope Leo XIII as the official teaching of the Catholic Church.

The success of science by this time had conquered the material world. Newton's classical physics combined the forces guiding the stars and planets with those found on Earth. Electricity had been discovered, largely understood and elegantly described by Maxwell's equations. Thermodynamics made sense of the machines invented during the industrial revolution. Darwin provided a purely material path for our evolutionary development, and by the year 1900 the Western world was boasting its success with exhibitions and world fairs. For a while it seemed that all had been discovered, which led to the claim that science henceforth would be in a cleanup mode and all that was left to do was push the accuracy of our knowledge to the next decimal point. Indeed, at the end of the 19th century we had explained all the phenomena that could be objectively observed by a human being and what else is there?

The only fly in the ointment was the inability of classic physics – which by this time included classical mechanics, electrodynamics, thermodynamics and astronomy – to explain black-body radiation and what happens in the interior of matter where objective observation cannot penetrate. At this point in history, as shown in Figure 8.1-1, Max Planck made the critical assumption that oscillators in the walls of heated material do not increase their energy in smooth continuous fashion as can be observed in the macroscopic world, but instead jump in discrete steps characterized by a constant action "h". The assumption allowed the black-body spectrum to be calculated to exactly reproduce measurements.

This discovery started what was to become quantum theory, which today is claimed to be the most accurate theory ever devised. From a philosophical point of view the break with classical physics was not that oscillators add energy in discreet steps but rather that assumptions about things that can in principle not be seen could be successfully employed to explain why we see what we do. The pendulum had swung back from Aristotle to Plato. A reality beyond our sensor range needed to be imagined in order to explain observable effects. What physicists see, is the result of measurements displayed on the reporting side of their instruments. Like prisoners in a cave, we are surrounded by a wall of sensors we cannot penetrate. All we can do is take what we do see as evidence for inferences about a reality that exists beyond our walls. This outside world is no longer thought to contain gods and goddesses, but wave functions and probabilities. But there it is. We rediscovered that there is a world outside the world we actually see.

Quantum physicists are stuck behind their wall of instruments and can only speculate about this other world. Successful inferences describing that reality has led to many new discoveries about the nature of the world too small to see. The atoms, the nuclei, quarks and leptons populate this unseen world. It took the Catholic Church 600 years to make the switch from Plato to Aristotle; the transition back is not happening quickly either. The overwhelming majority of Western civilization operates on classic physics principles and relegates quantum theory as something applicable only to the domain of atomic and nuclear physics. However, the writing is on the wall. A change is happening.

The idea that there is something beyond what we can see, even in principle, has taken hold in the physics laboratories of the 21st century. It is only a question of time until the same realizations will be adopted by the general population.

8.1.1.1 Modern Plato's cave

The realization that there is something beyond what we see is equivalent to grasping the meaning of Plato's cave analogy. No longer can we assume that the world we see is representative of an actual independent objective universe. Instead, when we stop to think about what we see in our 1st-person perspective, we must recognize that the things in front of our noses are not reality itself but rather, like the shadows in Plato's cave, evidence of the Reality outside the cave. Of course, to understand Plato's analogy the cave must be identified with one's skull, and the prisoners with our conscious element visualized as the little-man-inside that skull. In Figure 8.1-2, we show the viewpoint of a modern prisoner chained inside his or her skull looking at what Aristotle's philosophy would call physical reality, but in Plato's view is indirect evidence of a much larger Reality outside.

Since neither Plato's prisoners nor the little-man-inside in our skull can get outside to see Reality directly, the question must be asked, "How does anyone know what is really out there?" or even, "Is there anything out there at all?"

FIGURE 8.1-2 Plato's Modern Cave: a subjective experience inside the real skull of our bigger self

Recognizing the logical impossibility of being outside one's own self, the mystics and many Eastern philosophies claim the truly external cannot be known and cannot even be named. However, CAT extends Descartes's more practical approach, "I think therefore I am". If we can experience what is in front of our noses, we are at least a mechanism that produces those experiences. We have called that mechanism the big I or the big You, which together form the big We. That mechanism may be isolated, and all that is experienced is a self-deceptive dream produced by internal self interaction, but whatever we are is more than the sum total of what we experience. Given our situation, the only way we can know anything beyond our immediate experience is by building a symbolic model. Such a model must be experiencable and therefore is caused by some component in our bigger Self which we can name our "Model of Reality", abbreviated as "**MoR**" throughout this book. These words "Model of Reality" refer to something we cannot see, even in principle; however, in CAT the lowercase term "model of reality" refers to what we can see, while bold letters refer to its implementation in our memory.

8.1.2 Descartes and dual-aspect monism

Rene Descartes is one of the most important philosophers with contributions in many disciplines including mathematics, medicine and, of course, philosophy. The impact CAT has on Descartes's ideas is to clarify his doctrine of dualism. Dualism treats the human body as a machine that has material properties, while the mind is nonmaterial and does not follow the laws of nature. Dual-aspect theory has a long list of theorists from Spinoza, Bohm, Jung and Pauli (Atmanspacher, 2012; Bohm and Hiley, 1993). While CAT might be classified as a dual-aspect monism since it clearly has dualistic features, it differs from traditional concepts because it treats our full three-dimensional experience as the phase of an Event which has physical and mental aspects. CAT also eliminates the search for a gateway within our perceived brain – i.e. the pituitary gland for Descartes – through which the conscious souls in Plato's cave can reach reality because the big We consists of material behind and in front of our entire three-dimensional experience at every point in time. There is no little hole because the big We is more than the bodies we perceive.

The external physical aspect of matter in CAT consists of masses and charges, which, when looked at from the outside, interact with other masses and charges through gravito-electric forces. These forces account for all properties that have been identified when looking at appearances identified as objects in our normal everyday environment. This is the domain of physical reality, which is subject to the laws of classic physics, and all bodies seen as objects from the outside conform to those laws. However, inside ourselves and inside those we recognize as conscious, an additional mental component must be added to explain the feelings, pains and joys that we experience in ourselves and accompany our reactions. For example, it is obvious that we act to avoid anticipated pain. When pain is absent, the same physical intrusion, for example a cut into an anesthetized body part, will not produce the same response. This disconnect between what we feel ourselves and what we do not feel when looking at others introduces a dualism of some kind. How these two characteristics are identified, named and mapped onto properties we can understand differentiates philosophers throughout the ages.

The historic progress in our understanding of material has also provided a trail of identification with concepts that capture the substance of mind. Descartes lived in a time when earth, water, air and fire were the main categories of fundamental substances that composed all material. None of these reflect the dynamic characteristics of thought and feelings. It is therefore logical for Descartes to assume a new and different substance must be identified with the mind than with the body. Such a view is quite compatible with Plato's conjecture that ideal forms populate the independent reality outside the cave. However, even Aristotle, who rejected Plato's independent forms, maintained a separate identification of form and substance. He proposed that forms are the nature, and properties are embodied in the substance of things (Stanford, 2016).

Since that time the philosophical arguments have attempted to establish a single entity underlying both mind and body in a variety of philosophies categorized as monism.

The materialists or physicalists believe all is material and all emergent properties are complex organizations of material. A version of materialism underlies modern science and classic physics. The logical difficulties with materialism have recently been summarized in what Chalmers called the hard problem of consciousness (Chalmers, 1997) and works by H. Stapp (2005). These authors cannot prove materialism is wrong but rather that we have not found a material basis for conscious experiences. Subjective experiences simply do not occur within the context of classical or quantum physics and therefore cannot be explained by these disciplines.

In contrast "Idealists" argue that all there is, is what we experience, and the assumption that material exists beyond those experiences cannot be proven. The lack of proof rests in the Idealists' insistence that proof must be supplied as an experience. Hence no demonstration of anything that is not experience can be offered. George Berkeley, perhaps the best-known Idealist, argued that perception comes first, and all material is derived from our manifestations of awareness. His answer to the question, "Does the moon exist when no one is looking at it?", is that the consciousness of God is always aware of everything. This reference to god or gods is also characteristic of modern Idealists such as Deepak Chopra (Chopra and Kafatos, 2017), who insists that consciousness underlies all and refers to the teachings of the Vedas and the practice of meditation for discovering the essence of being.

Monism is a kind of Holy Grail for many philosophers and scientists alike. The desire to find a single whatever encompassing all of reality is the logical answer ending the chain of inquiry following any question. The extreme version of this tendency are theories which derive everything from "nothing" (Rowlands, 2007). CAT postulates reality is a form of action added to "nothing" because it leads to an improved model of reality but makes no attempt to explain why action in any form exists in the first place.

8.1.3 Kant and Wittgenstein

The German philosopher Immanuel Kant (1724–1804) has been a major influence on modern thinking and many of his ideas are reflected in the scientific embodiment CAT provides for them (Wikipedia, n.d.). He warned the Aristotelian world that all was not as it appeared to be and introduced the unknowable "Ding an Sich" into the history of thought. For our purposes, the most significant is Kant's opinion that "mind itself makes a constitutive contribution to its knowledge", which in quantum theory corresponds to the fact that atomic structures only absorb light if they provide energy level that can accommodate the color of the light. In the more general CAT model, absorption of any information requires the availability of an appropriate change in the receiving **M**odel of **R**eality in order to record that information. How the model is built determines what it can know.

This idea when embodied in physical structures reflects two fundamental characteristics of CAT. First, interaction implies change. This happens in detectors and subsequently in the storage mechanism that explains or remembers the change. It is, however, impossible to know from a received change alone what the entity that sent the change actually is or was. All that can be deduced is that whatever that entity is, it must be capable of making the change, and furthermore this capability must be available to both partners participating in an interaction. This implies that the memory structures with which our models of reality are built do not reflect the actual reality. We do not build structures that duplicate what is actually out there. Instead we build whatever structures accommodate the changes we experience most expeditiously.

The second characteristic is our ability to ignore or pass on change that does not fit into our structure. In fact, the mechanisms discussed in Part II of this book explicitly describe small-enough excitation dynamics inside quantum jumps, which accompanies our search for profitable transitions with a field of potential interaction partners. The ontological description of the order involved in these excitations is essentially what Bohm and Hiley (1993) refer to as *implicate order*. Implicit because only stable eigenstates of systems in equilibrium can actually be remembered and therefore it is the structure of eigenstates that defines what configuration of material we can know, not what material can actually be.

Kant's view that space and time are forms of sensibility that are a priori necessary for any possible experience is also implemented in CAT. Space in CAT is perceived as a property of the material from which the big You, I and the rest of the Universe is built. Space is the perception of material's extension. It does not exist as an independent container. CAT includes space and time only in relation to the existence of material. This leads immediately to the mind as the appearance of space and the feeling of time, which are correlated with material properties, and all material therefore possesses some primitive form of consciousness.

Kant is often cited for his concept of "*das Ding an Sich*" or "the thing in itself" as a reference to reality. CAT has expanded the phrase to "*das Ereigniss an Sich*" or "the event in itself". He claimed this entity cannot be known; however, he obviously gives it a name. This jives with the teaching of mystics throughout the ages and is reflected in the fact that the existence of action cycles in CAT names an assumption. CAT assumes an actual "Reality" of action is happening and then deduces the properties of consciousness in a loop of activity. The simplest loop is an action cycle and the simplest happening in that action cycle is four forces interacting with the charges and masses to produce a structure in equilibrium. The practical side of CAT insists a cycle can only be a useful model of something that cannot be known if it serves some utilitarian purpose other than knowing the unknowable.

To understand this purpose, we jump forward to the analysis of language introduced by Ludwig Wittgenstein (1973). He is considered by many as the greatest philosopher of the 20th century. For us his emphasis on the precise meaning of words and symbols derived from their use and context rather than any definition of meaning is reflected in our definition of "operational meaning" as compared with "semantic or referential meaning". Symbols of "what cannot be known" are semantically meaningless. There is no experience abstract or tangible that defines the unknowable. Nevertheless, we just made a word that refers to an unknowable entity. The unknowable is called "Reality" in this book and numerous exact details of what it is are described in its pages. But if the meaning of Reality is unknowable, all attempts to visualize or experience such meanings are illusions.

Niels Bohr warned us of such illusions when attempting to find ontological interpretations of quantum theory. Yet here we are, devoting a whole book to what great philosophers and one of the founders of quantum theory considered illusions. Bohr's point of view classifies quantum theory and the physical aspect of CAT as an instrumentalist theory. This means, as Wittgenstein suggested, the physical reality models in CAT do not have semantic meanings. There is no experience they point to that can be taken as a representation of Reality. Instead such symbols have operational or in Wittgenstein's terminology "use" meanings. This means they are design objects that when incorporated in a model, physically interact with other symbols and produce changes at the interface between the model and its symbolic detector/actuator boundary to produce semantically meaningful symbols. Like any other tool, the value of such a reality model lies in its utility.

As Don Hoffman (Don Hoffman and Prakash 2014) points out, the forces of evolution do not drive us to seek the truth, but rather what works. If the truth is unknowable, we are driven toward more and more useful theories. Compared with current physics, CAT is a vast simplification. True enough it demands the realization that the classic world of objects has always been a "objective reality" illusion and should be replaced by a world of events, which is simply a better illusion. This one adjustment in our world view will be difficult for many vested interests to make. Our environment of objects in space, which are presented to us in our private display space, are like icons on our computer screens, i.e. useful information. That information is connected to a Reality beyond what we can experience, and that connection allows us to control and improve our situation. Once the reality of this connection as an activity is realized, the simplicity of CAT will become apparent and its utility will provide us with the next step in our evolution.

8.1.4 Ontology and epistemology

Ontology addresses the question "What is?" Epistemology addresses the question "How do we know what is?"The impact of CAT is to answer these two fundamental questions with a single concept. What is, is a processing system that produces our knowledge of "what is". Thus, what is, is a form of action.

"How do we know what is?" is answered by what that action does. The physical form of action is "what is" and explains what we know. That form has been described as parallel cycles of action containing subjective space and content. CAT uses the word "Reality" to express the "what is" and suggests a model of "Reality" processes our experiences through an endless refresh cycle of activity that holds our knowledge. Action flows through the Now phase of the cycles that make up our material existence. Therefore, all we can know are our own activities, and the form of those activities defines the cosmology of our own memory structure within which what we believe is our universe can be visualized.

8.1.5 Cosmology of our memory structure

The flow of action in CAT is visualized as a stream of activity between sequential spatial cross sections consisting of mass-charge density states connected by alternating internal and external force fields. When a system's action is incorporated in stable parallel activity cycles, then the mass-charge density states repeat. By combining all parallel cycles, we achieve simultaneously sequential snapshots of flow cross sections that appear as time planes. The action-flow models the event CAT assumes is really happening. To become aware of it requires the flow to be actualized in the owner's memory cells. The flow of change is correlated with perception. Mass/charge states were only introduced to make the flow visible. However, once introduced, they become surrogates for the changes actually experienced.

The most common visualization of our Universe is a 3rd-person godlike view of all the simultaneous mass/charge states projected into a 2nd-person's brain as shown in Figure 8.1-3. In the central Now instance, a 1st-person experience – shown as the arm holding an apple in an optic field of view – is registered in the 3rd-person view. The expected future and past instances are placed along a horizontal timeline. This popular concept of a Block Universe maps time onto a spatial axis – misleadingly called a 4th dimension – along which the future and past is thought to actually exist. Taking the classic Block Universe as reality leads to several believable fictions.

The first are fictional stories of time travel and worm holes through which one can visit the past and future. Such stories are believable because we are able to imagine different times at once and can further imagine our little-man-inside moving between those times like time travelers. CAT recognizes imagined symbols are not "what is". We are dealing with the visualization of the knowledge in a model that occupies a role within our processing mechanism.

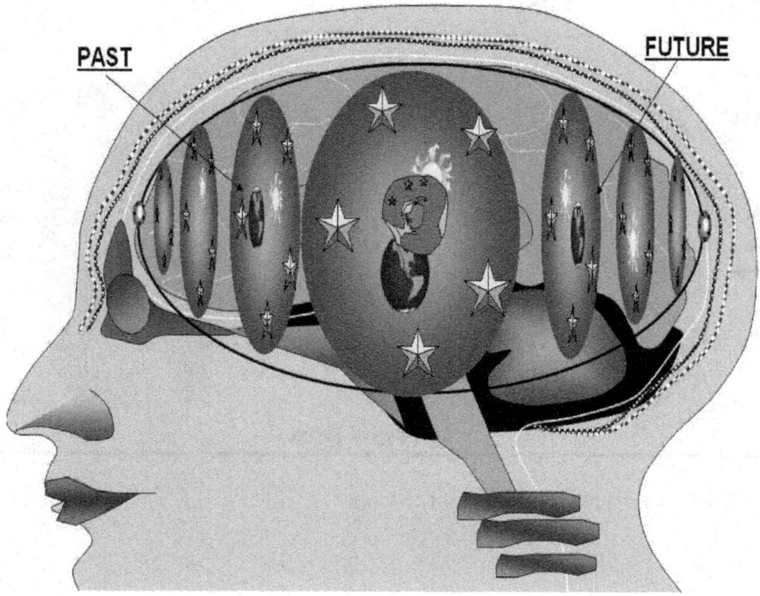

FIGURE 8.1-3 The block universe model projected into a 2nd-person's brain

The little-man is a functional analogy. When implemented, the consciousness function is systematically replaced by action-flow circuits, which become the actual 2nd-person we can see in front of us. The model of reality becomes part of an action flow that can only experience what is happening in its Now. The action flow is the 2nd-person and cannot be outside itself. At best, action flow can recall events from distant parts of the memory. This could be imagined as the little-man time traveling through his memory. It would be a kind of god illusion to believe that one's memory is the actual outside.

The structure of Figure 8.1-3 also supports the popular Big Bang cosmological view of the universe. All the energy – i.e. action flow – starts at a point at the beginning of time, and the universe expands spatially as we move right toward the future Now. If there is a critical mass density, the action flow will contract into a point at the end of time. In contrast, CAT assumes that all the space cells of physical models are operational processing elements that direct a flow of action. The origin of time and its future destiny are connected in the center of Figure 8.1-4.

Calculation flow enters the model in the left side of Now and is processed backwards in time to the origin of time, which is a point because only one last bit of knowledge is remaining (see Figures 6.4-1 and 6.7-1). The other side of that bit is connected to the end of time in the future, from which action flows back into the present. The 1st-person experience happens between the two sides of Now. The

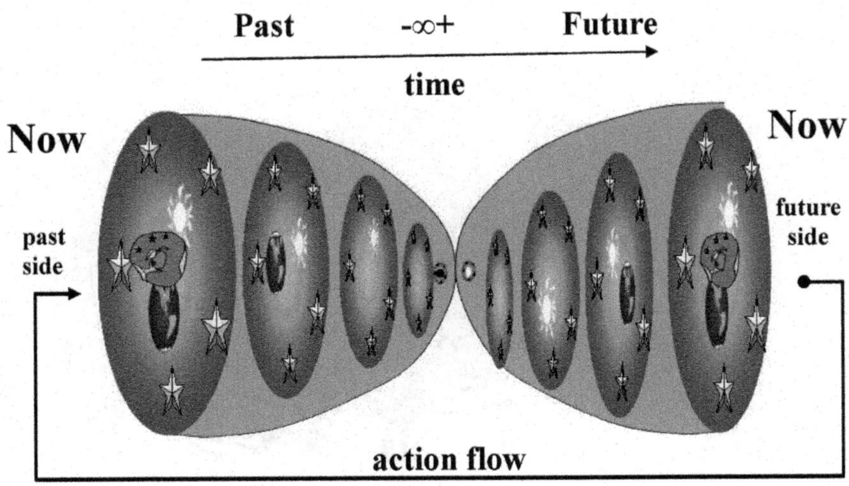

FIGURE 8.1-4 Inverted cosmology in memory

CAT cosmology of processing elements in memory is therefore an inversion of the Big Bang state sequence around the 1st-person Now experience.

In CAT, as well as through the introduction of imaginary time in many cosmological models, time flows in a cycle. Space however is required to have finite size, or it would not fit into any memory. The boundary conditions providing an end to space would present the mystery of what is beyond the end of space. Most cosmologists and CAT assume space also curves so that we live in a multidimensional torus. In CAT, the torus is only visualized as existing in a higher dimensional space for heuristic purposes. However, when the structure of memory cells is formatted into toroidal configurations, one cannot get outside to see its shape (see Section 3.1.2). Calculations presented in Chapter 4 for self-contained mass-charge suggest cyclic boundary conditions actually happen. In fusion experiments no one has been able to contain plasma in stable forms using electromagnetic forces; whether adding gravity to the mix could achieve this goal is still an open question.

8.2 Religion

All religions are systems of beliefs that attempt to describe our total situation, and most prescribe the rules of behavior that are intended to guide us toward a happy existence. Our total situation includes a description of what we are, how we fit into the rest of reality, and under what circumstances happiness can be achieved. The structure of beliefs will usually start with foundational premises from which the detailed answers to everyday questions can be logically deduced. To be effective, a religion must answer all possible questions including why our immediate experiences are happening and what we can do about it. The ability to answer all questions is usually built into a religion by identifying an all-powerful being who is able to introduce miracles at will as one of the foundational principles.

CAT is a system of beliefs whose foundational principles are based upon the discoveries of science that have characterized the behavior of matter by two fundamental principles. These are:

1 The desire to exist in an equilibrium state of balanced forces.
2 The desire to experience a greater amount of action.

The form of our own activity has evolved to contain a mechanism that describes our situation and provides us with the means of controlling our experiences to achieve our compromise of these two fundamental desires. The difference between science and religion is usually attributed to the scientific method. The method emphasizes experiment and testing as a way to verify the accuracy of our assumptions and the logical deductions used to predict expected results. The **M**odel of **R**eality imbedded within an update- and expectation-generation activity of a CAT model firmly implements this method. The integration of subjective and objective aspects of matter allows CAT to give answers to important existential questions that are provided by religious teachings but have been systematically eliminated from traditional scientific inquiries. This section discusses some of these questions.

8.2.1 The God illusion

God is defined as a supreme being who has universal knowledge and power to create any situation whether or not it conforms to what we have come to expect from Natural Law. In CAT, the role of God is identified with Nature or the rest of the Universe (U) that encompasses all that we have not explicitly separated as items of interest or concern with which we are immediately engaged. Though experiencing subjective feelings Nature or U is not at liberty to perform miracles and therefore falls short of the power assigned to God in religious contexts. Whether such a being actually exists cannot be verified or denied, since its ubiquitous powers would allow it to thwart any test we might imagine and laugh at us for the attempt. So, the actual existence of God is not the issue to be discussed in this section, or for that matter, in this book. Why the concept of such a supreme being is so appealing and pervasive in many societies is a legitimate topic within the context of the CAT model, which will be discussed later in this section.

We have claimed that the human psyche does not see reality directly, but instead experiences the output and visualization of a model that is created and maintained to explain and control interactions. Our own model is under our control. Of course, it is carefully constructed to be a useful tool that has value, so arbitrary violations of rules that have evolved to maintain its usefulness cannot be made lightly. But each of us has the power to do so, if we are willing to pay the cost. This means the relationship between ourselves and our model of reality is precisely that of a supreme being over reality itself. This relationship is expressed in the metaphor:

> "I am to my model of reality as god is to reality".

One may question whether I has such a power over one's internal model that is part of the material from which the Big I is built; however, any externalization of such a model will be an experiential object that is almost certainly under our control. If we examine such a model in our 1st-person perspective as shown in Figure 8.2-1, one can easily verify that one sees all parts at once even though symbolically the model may represent astronomical distances.

Thus, one has an instantaneous representation of happenings in the model, which is one of the characteristics of God. Similarly, one can take a pencil or other suitable instrument and make changes anywhere in the representation no matter how far apart they are symbolically. Thus, one has the ability to change the model

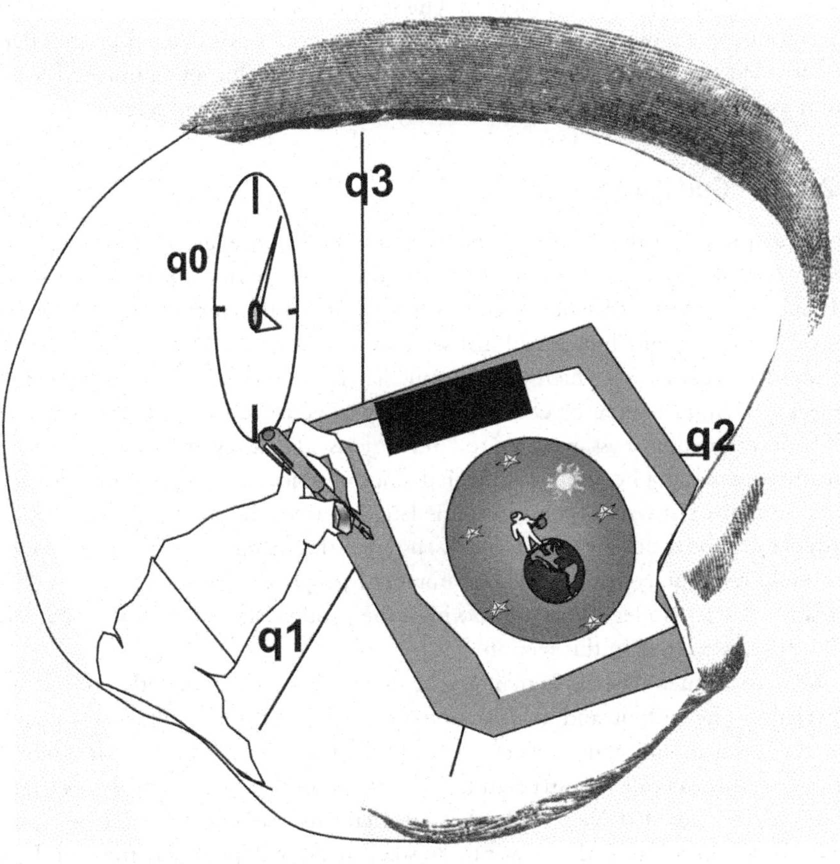

FIGURE 8.2-1 An externalized classic model of the universe

in ways that may or may not conform to its expression of any natural law. Whether sensible or not, the power to effect symbolic miracles for real is the universal power God has over Reality. The model we've shown is merely a drawing on a paper, but if one were to confuse one's model with Reality itself, then one would equally likely confuse oneself with God. That is the God illusion.

At first glance one might think it is very unlikely. However, there are many instances in which it does happen. Physicists, engineers and architects often draw scale models as a routine part of their work. Staring and concentrating on a page, attention focused on a design problem that requires the movement and placement of real things even when only symbolically represented, often leads to forgetting one's surroundings and feeling as though one is in the model, moving, pushing and trying to arrange the pieces as though they were real. One may not feel like God but often a kind of euphoria, perhaps a feeling of power and invincibility is experienced when the problem is solved. After all, solving a problem in a scale model often puts one in a position of power over the real thing. This feeling is quite addictive. And, if the model is of grandiose proportions like the whole universe, a cosmologist who has had an "aha moment" on a cosmic scale will certainly feel him- or herself to be more than a body sitting meekly in an office.

Treating a symbol as a reality is the principle behind many magic and voodoo practices. A piece of hair fashioned on the skull of a doll may have no obvious connection to the poor person who is the target of a spell, but the belief that the pins stuck into the doll will affect the real body part for nefarious or healing purposes is quite widespread. Again, the illusion of power through symbolic acts is euphoric and desirable in its own right. The fact that what happens to an external doll has no effect on the real person is usually quite easy to ascertain, but the possibility that some such a connection exists is hard to dispel, especially when the accompanying feeling of power is so seductive.

If we move from externalized dolls to the internal mechanisms that implement our thought process, the confusion between what is and is not connected to reality becomes very difficult to avoid. Consider an individual engaged in meditation, deep prayer or who has imbibed a hallucinogenic drug. In meditation, for example, the effect of stilling one's mind often results in eliminating the constant chatter of the little voice inside and becoming aware of deeper and deeper layers that precede and cause that chatter to come into awareness. The impressions one encounters have been classified and named by a long tradition of Eastern philosophy practitioners. Words like chakra and kundalini describe subtle systems and repeatable experiences while the names of gods and goddesses are usually associated with functional characteristics such as sex, hunger or intellect. At deeper levels, one encounters abstract functions such as destruction in the case of Shiva or the unchanging, permanent reality underlying everything as Brahman.

The Western Christian tradition is much more limited. The interface with the world of spirits is restricted to an anthropomorphic set of angels and saints. One is not, as in the Eastern traditions, encouraged to explore one's inner self and verify the teachings of the great gurus. Instead prayer is employed to solve problems. One asks for favors or guidance and occasionally receives revelations and epiphanies. The organization of heaven and hell mirrors the secular political structure, and its secular rewards and punishments are incorporated into the before and hereafter. Nevertheless, individual spirituality rests on the belief that inner experiences, such as the voice of God or the appearance of the Virgin Mary, communicate with powers that can affect one's everyday life and can even supersede the natural laws that normally govern that life.

The common thread to all these traditions is that the practitioner assumes a role of enhanced power over what he believes to be the actual reality. Lobbyists earn excellent salaries by selling access to powerful individuals. Priests and gurus perform the analogous functions on a larger scale. They not only teach how to gain access to the powerful, but how to act in their presence and interpret their advice. The system works not because we are actually talking to God, but because in some objective sense, we obtain access to our greater selves. We no longer simply listen to the output of our reality model that presents us with the result of our thought process, but directly interact with the unconscious mechanism that produces those results. We achieve a position to modify that process. We may not be God over Reality, but we can learn to regain control of our bigger Self and thereby modify our behavior for the better, and that is valuable.

8.2.2 I am God and so are you

CAT very clearly proposes an architecture in which at first approximation any system can be isolated and is thereby modeled by a self-regenerating cycle of activity. The mathematics that describes any such isolated system is similar. It differs only in the amount of action included, but not in the fundamental interrelationships between constituent parts. Whether we speak of ourselves or the entire universe the same architecture applies. The isolated big I, You and U are each represented by a closed action loop in which experiences happen. In the human case, those experiences are representative of an external world, and we have control over those representations. As introduced in the last section, such control is not equal to God but is metaphorically equivalent. When isolated, the big I and You can do what they want precisely because there are no external forces telling us what to do. We are in a very real sense god over our modeled representations (Chopra and Kafatos, 2017).

This freedom to do what one wants does not imply the will to do. In CAT, the desire to exist in an equilibrium state is derived from the Least Action Principle. The material from which all is constructed has choice but also a desire to minimize the action required along its state-change trajectory. Given such desire, stable behavior follows the low trough of an energy valley and any attempt to climb the walls will contradict its minimum-action desire. In that sense, the theory is deterministic. A big I or You once built is destined to follow a minimum-action course and therefore an isolated system will experience a repeating dream that is determined by the total amount of action in its global equilibrium state.

However, the desire to increase one's action implies a willingness to climb the walls of our deterministic existence and accept the pain of the unbalanced forces associated with such a maneuver in the hopes of interacting with an external reality and increasing the action one experiences. Following the lessons stored in an accurate model of reality will certainly increase the chances that an intent, expressed by a change of its symbols, will send the right command outside. This limits the willingness to change symbols to those moves that are expected to produce a successful interaction. It does not limit the power to change those symbols.

Each of us is a kind of god over our bigger Self. In that capacity, we are in control of a vast empire and at the same time only a small part of a vast empire. The seat of our control is referenced by the small pronouns "i", "you" and "them" in our model. The empire we belong to is referenced by "I", "You" and "U" that reference the bigger Systems beyond our appearances who incorporate their own models. Once we have incorporated the CAT model and grasped the relationship among these symbols, we will humbly understand that our job is to maintain and process the interactions with our neighbors. We have come full circle and can address the chores immediately in front of us. Maintain, maintain is the watchword for this segment of the journey. Only now we know these neighbors are not what we see, but events that take place in the context of the big Reality of interacting Universes. And after we learn the ropes of our newfound knowledge, we will settle into the new equilibrium we have discovered.

8.2.3 Body, mind and soul

The terms body, mind and soul are percepts and concepts that have become standard fare in our classic object-oriented world view. Such words reference a reality that must be accounted for in any integrated world view we care to adopt; however such words have been given new significance in CAT that will be explained in this section.

The appearance of one's nose defines both the location and shape of one's body in the 1st-Person Laboratory and is treated as a classic object. Such objects are assumed to be independently real and therefore continue to exist as objects whether or not the 1st- person observer is dead or alive. CAT dissects the construction of classic objects and the single noun defining a thing in the English language is expanded to label four processes involved in making objects happen (see A3.1 Definition of Terms). For example, the lowercase "body" of an individual in the objective world view is identified in CAT as the processing stage implementing the collection of percepts such as sight, touch and smell that combine the appearance of the self in the mind of an individual. Mind is the cross-section Now phase of parallel action-processing loops in which percepts appear. The physical action producing the mind display of our "body" is accommodated in the processing stage "**B**ody" stored in the physical-model phase of the loop, conventionally called memory. The memory is an activity, which stores data required to reproduce sensations. A second loop interprets the "**B**ody" into a theoretical "**b**ody" visualization, such as mass-charge icons, that fuses one's reality belief with the "body" experience. These three processing activities are insufficient to fully characterize the experience of a real classic object because they all belong to the observer and fail to incorporate the independent permanence of a real object. CAT therefore uses the capital first letter form "Body" to refer to such an unknowable existence but assumes it is an interacting event.

In Figure 8.2-2 we break the "Whole" into three such interacting events labeled "I", "You" and the Universe "U". The column headings refer to the sub-system action loops "I", "You" and "U", to which interactions are transmitted. The row headings refer to the systems from which interaction structures came that have been absorbed. Then, using the matrix notation introduced in Section 4.4, we can write the action associated with the three processing stages executed in each event to become aware of the event itself and its interacting partners. In each matrix element, three items are written. The three "a,**A**,**a**" letter types represent the action required to experience, store and explain the interaction from each event. For example, if You are interacting with I, You will probably have an immediate experience of action from I to You labeled "a[I,You]". You will update a memory **A[I,You]**, and perhaps entertain a concept **a[I,You]** of what You believe I really am. After we stop interacting, You may no longer see me or think of me, but will for some period retain a memory model **A[I,You]**.

The off-diagonal elements represent the consequences of interaction. These are accommodated by changing action flows that hold explanatory memories of each other. If during any one instance the matrix only has diagonal elements, none

To / From	I	You	U	
I	**A[I,I]** **a[I,I]** a[I,I]	**A[I,You]** **a[I,You]** a[I,You]	**A[I,U]** **a[I,U]** a[I,U]	**My classic bodies**
You	**A[You,I]** **a[You,I]** a[You,I]	**A[You, You]** **a[You,You]** a[You,You]	**A[Youl,U]** **a[You,U]** a[You,U]	**Your classic bodies**
U	**A[U,I]** **a[U,I]** a[U,I]	**A[U,You]** **a[U,You]** a[U,You]	**A[U,U]** **a[U,U]** a[U,U]	

FIGURE 8.2-2 Interaction matrix in a three-part division of the Whole: diagonal elements are self-existence actions and off-diagonal elements are accommodations of neighbors

of the events contain memories of each other and therefore are not unaware of any event other than themselves. An isolated You, for example, would experience a[You,You], store it in **A[You,You]** and visualize the explanation of your experiences as **a[You,You]**.

If on the other hand we had interacted and then parted, I might be out of sight, and as memories fade, out of mind, but I will still be somewhere and some-when interacting with the Universe. This means my action in U labeled "**A**[I,U]" is being updated and presumably You could query the Universe to find out where and when "U" locates my interactions. Now let's assume I stop interacting with the Universe as well. Then **A**[I,U] would no longer be updated but it would continue existing as a memory activity in U. Only without updates from "I", these memories would be under complete control of the forces within the Universe. Now when You query the Universe, there is only a memory with no evidence of I's presence. In other words, my body is dead.

To see how this comes about, consider the interactions executed by a 2nd-person loop "You" when seeing my body. A light source in one part of U interacts with the **A[I, U]** part of U and in turn propagates action to You, which becomes an observable from U to You labeled "a[U,You]". Your memory loop between a[U,You] and **A[U,You]** has now been changed due to the absorption of light, which You notice, and the action avalanche through Your body loop leads to your memory of my body. The classic term "my body" therefore is associated with the memory in the rest of Reality acknowledging my existence. That acknowledgment does not disappear when "I" falls asleep and my body-**b**ody experiences "a[I,I] and **a[I,I]**" become dreams. In the extreme case when I die, the rest of reality still sees a classic though lifeless body, while my own body-**b**ody experience reflects purely internal activities. In death, some action in my body memory **A[I,I]** may continue to exist, but its operation as a communication and control vehicle will stop. Rebuilding a communication and control mechanism identified as one's classic body is an evolutionary process discussed in the next section.

The procedure described in the last paragraph can be used as a template to describe all interactions leading to the perception of what is classically described as real objects whether dead or alive. The entity that corresponds to our classic concept of our bodies is mathematically defined in cells [U,You] and [U,I] for you and I respectively. In general, the reality of any classic object is the action **A**[AnyObject,U] incorporated in the rest of the Universe due to the existence of the object involved.

It is easy to identify the classic mind and body in CAT terms. However, the identification of a soul is made more controversial because conventional science does not acknowledge the existence of a soul. In fact science assumes all we are is material so closely tied to the universe that all our motions are closely controlled by its single clock and therefore could be modeled by the "U,U" elements in the lower right-hand corner of the Figure 8.2-2 interaction matrix.

In CAT independently isolated events are allowed. To make this possibility plausible we have consistently replaced the conscious being, the scientist in the laboratory, or the technician in a control room with an engineered action cycle. This automated action flow is like the level 1 loop in Figure 8.2-3 but leaves the conscious element in a supervisory role that in turn can be automated resulting in hierarchies of action flow. When such action cycles modeled in a nothing space provided by the pages of a book and powered by a model operator who supplies the support forces that make the motion of ink an accurate symbol of flowing action, we have built a kind of artificial intelligence machine. The feeling the ink has being moved is certainly not what its symbolized action flowing through the subjective phase of a cycle would feel. To make the action model real the support structure is taken away and the flow becomes a self-contained space-time activity all its own. It thereby becomes an existence largely independent of the Now experience of any other observer, including the Universe "U".

Thus, the deeper loops act like the ghost-in-the-machine to the higher loops and express the characteristics of the soul in Western religious traditions. The lowest loop executing through infinity in Figure 8.2-3 exists forever on its own or when approximated as an isolated system, it contains conscious experiences since it executes a self-measuring explanatory cycle. It interfaces with higher body loops to both receive information and express desires that affect the rest of the universe. Its presence is only deduced by external observers through the physical behavior the classic body – U's memory – and is judged to be conscious precisely because that behavior cannot be explained by current physical theories, and its presence cannot be detected by electromagnetic measurement. In short, the stand-alone cognitive cycle has all the characteristics of the soul. We have used the simple capital letter designation to name such isolated loops in loose conformance to capitalization use in the English language. The pronoun "I" usually refers to the subjective entity that is conscious of the world. The reader will have noticed that we capitalize the remaining pronouns "You", "We", "It" when labeling conscious action cycles.

In summary, the conventional concepts of mind, body and soul correspond in the CAT terminology to 1) the observational Now phase of an action cycle, 2) the memory of one's existence in the rest of the Reality and 3) the name of the action cycle containing one's cognitive awareness, respectively.

8.2.4 What happens when we die?

In the classic objective world view, the world as seen in front of our noses is the one common shared reality in which our single and only real material body exists. This body is endowed with a unique capability of life, cognition and self-awareness that is considered to be an emergent property resulting from a complex evolutionary development of physical structures that started as pure energy at the Big Bang. Once the unique configuration of material that supports life is destroyed then life and our subjective experiences associated with life automatically disappears. Hence life begins when development reaches a critical configuration of material and ends when that configuration is destroyed. The exact characteristics of such a critical configuration is controversial. Some insist it happens at conception, some draw the line at birth.

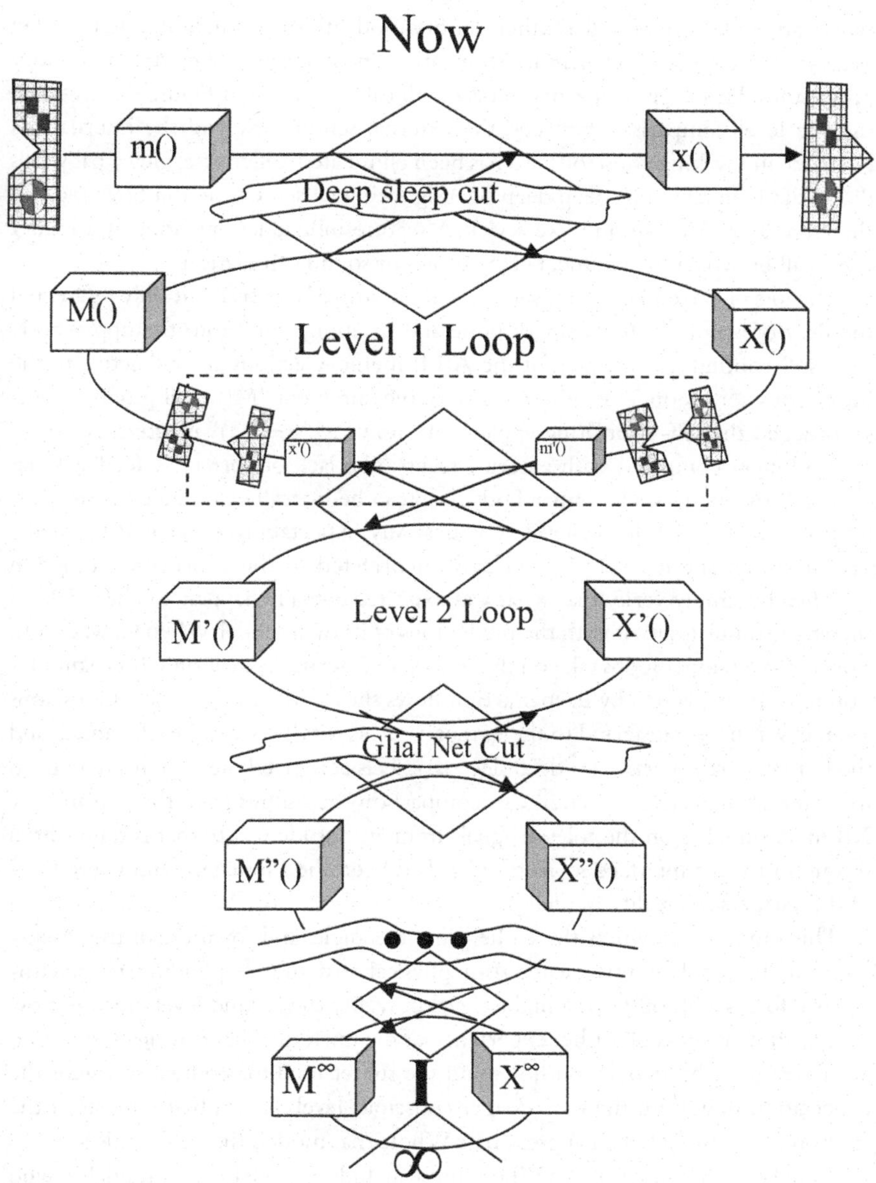

FIGURE 8.2-3 Fundamental CAT algorithm in a CAT model hierarchy loop format: down toward past up from future (see Figure 6.4-1)

In CAT we are not objects but a flow of action. The personal experience of our body is initially identified by its observable action a[I,I] and augmented with theoretical projections **a**[I,I] so that we experience a collocated real feeling thing. This thing is remembered by memory actions **A**[I,I]. When we close our eyes, the optical sensory component of the a[I,I] action flow is disrupted, but projections of where are bodies are as well as other sensory modalities still function. When we fall asleep, we lose track of our sensory stimulation and experience unfettered memory projections. This deep sleep situation is graphically depicted in Figure 8.2-3 where the top-level comparison between the external sensor flow and the internal has been cut and waking consciousness has been eliminated. Of course, only a baby falls down the hierarchy into deep deep sleep ignoring all sensory action flow and can therefore be carried around like a sack. A mature individual operating at a higher level will be woken by an unexpected touch or sound stimulation.

The loss of wakeful consciousness has not destroyed material but only redirected the flow of action. Reflex activity, pulse and breathing, built into the upper-body loop still continues, and much of the **A**[I,I] memory actions are still active in the lower conscious loop. This means memory measurement "M()" still produces sensations, and the self-stimulating explanatory flow "M() → X()" is active, but these are no longer compared with external reality. The lack of corrective feedback has several consequences. The upper-body loop can be logically eliminated since it no longer interacts with lower-level activities. Any expectations generated by memory measurement at level "1" will pass uncorrected to the explanation function and thereby simply verify that what was expected actually happened. The "1" loop therefore stimulates itself with the predictions of its own model. When viewed from a deeper level upper loops take on the role of an external body loop whose stimulation must be explained by deeper action flows shown as a Level 2 loop. Conscious awareness is now transferred to the comparison activity between Level 1 and 2, and the human may experience a deep sleep that feels completely real. Here we expand the internal subjective aspect. At this comparison the output from the explanatory X() function takes on the role of signals from an outside reality that is transmitted through material interface icons to what had been the simulated sensor interfaces of the 1st-person's reality model.

This model is shown as the dashed-line rectangle, and for most of the discussions in this book it was treated as a physical structure responding to gravito-electric forces. Cut off from a higher level of reality the second level dreamer now accepts the images as his or her experience of the universe. These are again split into the reflex pass-through action flows and the subset used for comparison with the expectation flow from the next deeper conscious level. That subset consists of the fraction in the model of an approximate Whole that models the Self at this level. To be complete any model of the Whole must include a model of the modeler, who in turn includes a model of the Whole producing an endless chain of reality levels discussed in Chapter 2.

Once the subjective element in material is accounted for, the architecture of the levels repeats so that deeper and deeper consciousness levels are encountered as the 1st-person eliminates interactions between levels. The drawing in Figure 8.2-3 indicates such levels without attempting to map specific levels and interfaces to brain physiology. We show a Glial cut because as discussed in Section 7.7 the interface between the glial and neural network correspond closely to the CAT flow structure, and its identification suggests immediate medical applications. A cut at this level would allow most body housekeeping functions to operate as reflex actions of the neural level while the physical activity inside the glial network would generate self-contained experiences that may correspond to deep meditation or a medically catatonic state.

At the bottom of this chain of levels we encounter a simple loop without lower-level interfaces. In the CAT algorithm, this cycle takes the role of infinity located between one's origin and destiny. It reflects incoming into outgoing or past into future action flows. And represents the entry point of the "I" into the material of the "U". Its logical role is supervisory since if all higher levels have been automated, only a lifetime supervisory role is left for the little-being-in-the-machine to fulfill.

If this lowest cycle is detached, we are left with a self-contained cycle and a material hierarchy that may function on automatic pilot for some period of time. The automated reflex structure will conform to the laws of physics controlling the material used to implement the automation without "I's" control, i.e. a zombie. The separated self-contained action structure was identified in the last section as a soul labeled "I". Temporary disengagement may lead to the experience of Nirvana. Such an experience of pure existence is associated with any isolated system in pure equilibrium. In this state of isolation, no interaction and therefore no evidence of its existence will be registered in any other part of Reality. What happens when we die is a process of disengagement between our self-contained essence "I" and the levels of material structures we have managed to grow by capturing and controlling material in the rest of Reality thereby growing "our classic bodies".

The action-flow concept provides a logical framework built on an extension of known physical principles that postulates an isolated equilibrium state characterized by an amount of action that occupies an extension state. To gain more action, a period of dynamic interaction accompanied by unbalanced forces, along with its stresses and pains, must be accepted in order to transition to a new equilibrium containing a new level of action. In quantum theory an atom in a ground state of equilibrium that absorbs a flow of action transitions to an excited state of higher energy thus experiencing more action flow for the lifetime of the excited state. CAT makes this analogy concrete. The transition is growth, the excited state is life; it lasts for a lifetime. If a new equilibrium is reached the system experiences a higher state of Nirvana; if not it sheds the pain and struggle of non-equilibrium forces and sheds action until it falls back to its original ground state. This is how life and death are implemented in a physical system.

8.3 Psychology

Psychology attempts to correct human behavior through therapeutic sessions during which the patient is guided to a source of difficulty by an attending therapist. The methodology guides the patient to illuminate experiences, which may have happened in the past, present or are expected to happen in the future, identify the destructive behavior caused by those experiences, and modify that behavior in healthier directions. When viewed in the context of our object-oriented world view, the happening of traumatic events are external phenomena that are recorded in the brain and can be accessed through memory recall and presumably modified by making new memories surrounding those events.

When adopting CAT, the therapist is merely projecting a new model of a cognitive being, described in Chapter 6, onto the client as shown in Figure 8.3-1. The projection is the therapist's own experience that can be collocated with the perceived image of the client's body. This projection extends beyond what the therapist sees since it contains a 3rd-person reality model view of the client's lifetime. Of course, the details of the client's lifetime in the therapist's mind are only as good as the knowledge the therapist has gained about the client. However, much of that knowledge is adopted from theories and prejudices gained by training and experience with other patients. Hence a standard lifetime, including typical trauma points, can be created quite rapidly.

Once established, the therapist must remember that what he or she senses, perhaps as a ghostly thought or quick daydream, is a visualization of the therapist's own access into his or her own bigger Self. In the CAT model, these are projected processing elements in the physical phase of the inner loop of Figure 8.3-1. These may be alternative realities and may be in conflict with the reality believed by the therapist. Experiences projected onto the client are actually being processed by the physical elements that belong to the therapist. If the therapist believes there is a single objective reality, a conflict with the client is thereby unavoidable. A good

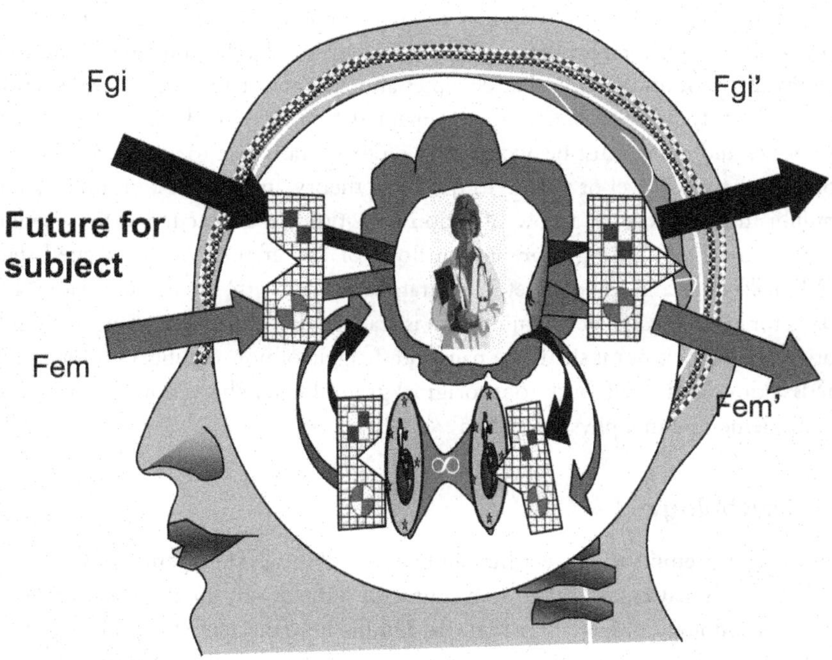

FIGURE 8.3-1 A therapist projection of a CAT model: external sensor happening Now are in the patient's future

deal of a therapist's training involves suppressing beliefs so they do not influence the effectiveness of the session, but suppression or deviation from mainstream objective consensus reality is difficult and will usually be classified as a psychosis.

In CAT, we all live in our own model, and its projection provides a display of the client's reality. The client's current behavior is determined by the flow of changes processed by the physical elements the client accesses to generate the visualization of memories and expectations. For the client these are the real things he or she sees and remembers. There is nothing crazy or psychotic in the client's behavior. He or she acts rationally relative to the structure of the world in which the client believes to live. The trick therefore is to provide a safe environment and encourage the client to access the offending processing element while experiencing a current sensation that triggers its use. Reprogramming the offending processing element is a learning process, which can take a considerable amount of practice. The danger both for the client and the therapist is that until a new behavior is actually learned, the client may quite rationally believe the therapist is the enemy, turn inward or react violently. Equally possible is that the client will recognize his or her own laboriously grown lifetime is a complete illusion and seek to destroy it.

Psychologists already understand that a client's belief has a reality that must be taken seriously. But taking an illusion seriously is different from accepting the validity of another reality. CAT merely adds the physical underpinnings to the client's belief. By acknowledging that both the client's and the therapist's realities are constructed, they become comrades in a common struggle. It is no longer a question of right or wrong. A power struggle is converted to a mutual search to find a workable reality. The search includes possible modifications of both the client's and the therapist's beliefs. A client's complex may very well have beneficial properties and when judged from a flexible reality perspective may need encouragement not suppression.

Physical reality is not a set of moving objects in a three-dimensional box but rather a set of interacting processing loops. These loops grow their own models of reality in response to interactions, which implies that many disparate models will be developed. Each culture, each animal, each physical system will have evolved a different concept. Right or wrong is measured by success in reaching an equilibrium state containing more action than the one we left, not by any truth built into the models we use to get there. CAT physics shows interactions only happen when both parties experience a benefit. That a model of physics can be used in a clinical setting suggests a deeper understanding of our mind is at hand. The warmth engendered by realizing we are all comrades facing the Unknowable may have a beneficial impact on psychology in general. How the CAT model explains specific psychological phenomena within the context of a physical model will be discussed in the following sub-sections.

8.3.1 Illusions, dreams and hallucinations

In CAT, the third eye is a phase of experience in a processing loop that displays the compared output of the internal and external sensory action flow. Illusions involving external stimulation that contain ambiguous or missing information are subject to alternative interpretations. The illusion of a painting that suggests a three-dimensional interpretation with depth cues placed on a two-dimensional surface is encountered frequently. When such cues are ambiguous, as shown in Figure 8.3-2, the third-eye experience is not stable even though the external stimulus is constant.

Ambiguous optical illusions are evidence of the internal processing that generates the three-dimensional world of experience we live in. Individuals brought up in Western traditions have a belief, which is hard-wired into their processing system, and is designed to fit all sensations in terms of a 3D world. When this design is frustrated, interpretation jumps happen.

Dreams in CAT are internal sensations generated when external stimulation is blocked. When the comparison function only produces a reflection of memory output signals, then the processing architecture approaches that of an isolated system. In this case, desires in the expectations signal are not canceled, but are

FIGURE 8.3-2 Example of an optical illusion shows brain calculates the 3D objective world experience

automatically satisfied in a self-stimulating update. The optic sense can be blocked by closing one's eyes. However, sound and tactile stimulation must be disengaged at the neural body-loop level of the processing hierarchy (see Figure 8.2-3). At lower levels, disengagement generates sensations in the third-eye display space representative of deeper internal action flow. In the CAT model, an isolated system is not inactive and may exhibit substantial interaction between its parts. Dreams can display interactions between the imagined self and its environment. The self is often seen from a disembodied 3rd-person perspective typical of memory recall in the waking state. In extreme situations this capability leads to out-of-body experiences (see Section 8.3.3). When cut off from external sensors, a lower-level environment may exhibit signals from housekeeping functions and dreams may visualize signals from organs expressing health or disease.

The global detachment between the inner memory and outer body loop is typical of the dream state. Selective detachment leads to hallucinations. In CAT, hallucinations are produced by an imbalance of signal transmission built into the comparator architecture between external and memory expectation signals. The complexity of combinations is explained by the mixing strength variations in different channels of action flowing through the spatial cross section of the Now experience. If all channels are equally blocked, a consciousness change to different dream states is produced. However, if mixing strengths in one modality is altered while others remain balanced, hallucinations can occur in the normal waking state. The mixing strength has been identified with neural transmitters in tripartite synapse. The flow is organized into parallel channels. It is very suggestive that astrocytes (see Section 7.7) control individual neuron bundles that form sub-channels, allowing a mixing of external and internal signals within the main sensory categories. The primary six external senses are gross channels that are individually compared. However, optic, auditory and tactile sensations also flow in geographically separable sub-channels. These allow distinction and separation of voices, visual objects and touch locations based largely on attention. If a sub-channel in the optic sense undergoes individual comparison, it may happen that a normal world background is positively reinforced by expected comparison and a specific object is introduced from the memory output on a sub-channel producing the hallucination of an object or person who is not in the normal background. This channeling effect can be demonstrated using a balancing technique that eliminates binocular rivalry (Baer, 2012). When separate left- and right-eye stimulation are sufficiently balanced, to avoid complete binocular rivalry an object of interest selected from one scene can appear as a hallucination in the other scene. Though usually considered a medical deficiency to be corrected, such hallucinations may have benefits (see Section 9.1) to be encouraged and controlled.

8.3.2 The feeling of oneness vs. separation from the universe

The *separation-individuation process* is defined by Margret Mahler (1975) as, "the establishment of a sense of separateness from, and relation to, a world of reality, particularly with regard to the experience of one's own body". This sense of separateness is believed to occur around the first year of life and establishes in the infant the individual identity of its own body as distinctly different and separate from the rest of the surrounding world. This early developmental step allows the infant to recognize itself as a localized object of central importance that is the seat of feelings and controllable motions. The environment is differentiated from the infant's body because this external region of experiences does what it wants and does not elicit pain that the I can feel when the body is damaged. Such a step in psychological development is considered crucial for the proper development of young adults. It allows further development of motor skills because the feedback loop between activation of muscles and optical verification of resulting motion is established.

The key questionable phrase in Mahler's definition is "world of reality". The use of this phrase assumes a reality based on Aristotle's Natural Philosophy that has evolved into the science founded on classic physics. This claims the "world of reality" is made of separate objects, one of which is the child's body, and one of the early developmental steps requires the child to learn this truth. The fact that the child's totality of experience, including both the experience of the body and the rest of the environment, is and remains an internal phenomenon that is forgotten as the child develops. Some of these children grow to be psychologists who in their adult life lives subscribe to the "objective reality" illusion as an a priori fact and propose theories consistent with that fact.

Most adults live their lives never questioning the differentiation between their body and the rest of the universe. However occasionally – sometimes spontaneously and other times induced by meditative rituals, drugs or other traumatic experiences – this separation-individuation process is reversed. Such a reversal can feel like being one with the universe. The body and the environment are felt to be part of a single and usually euphoric whole. Having forgotten the original separation process and developed the habit of treating the world of appearances as physical reality, such re-integration experiences are not identified as a heightened awareness of one's inner self, but rather as a union with the whole world out there. The euphoria is often attributed to a mystical communion with the cosmos when it is more likely, at least according to CAT, the product of Self recognition.

If we can accept the reality of our Bigger Self, the reversal of separation becomes neither a recreational escape nor a deficiency in our psychic development but rather a new capability that gives us a tool to operate more effectively. Control over the out-of-body experience is an example of such a new capability.

8.3.3 Out-of-body experience

Under normal circumstances, the waking human feels as though he or she is seated directly behind one's eyes looking at an independent world of objects and space out there in front of one's nose. However, once we acknowledge the existence of a larger Self and an underlying layer of material internals that are responsible for primitive awareness, then the experience of one's consciousness is not necessarily tied to a specific perspective. In our waking lives we are looking into the third-eye display because our job is to monitor our best rendition of the world we live in and generate commands that change that world. We therefore place our vantage point in the proper place to evaluate feedback at the upper Now level flow shown in Figure 8.2-3 with all its bodily pleasures and pains. It is our hierarchical organization not the consciousness phenomena that puts us in our behind-the-eyes vantage point.

As we disengage from our waking seat, we may begin to experience memories from the past or expectations of the future as though we were traveling through our reality model or its fictitious alternatives. The phenomena I am describing suggests we are able to take on many view positions within our Bigger Self from which to experience a flow of action. This capability has already been introduced when taking a 3rd-person view of our processing elements and projecting theoretical icons of their meaning into the sensations around us. For Westerners the ability to visualize one's body from a 3rd-person perspective is demonstrated in recall and anticipation experiences.

The ability to move outside of one's skull, remain in the waking state and see one's own body usually happens when the flow of action is interpreted as trauma or pain. Escape from debilitating pain, while remaining conscious, is an enhanced capability available to the human psyche. Research on fighter-pilot training in centrifuges to simulate extreme gravitational forces encountered during combat is an example of controlled and legal trauma that produces fairly repeatable out-of-body experiences (Whinnery, 2016). Retaining the ability to control the movements of one's body while ignoring painful sensation, rather than blacking out, is a valuable survival enhancement tool, one that the realization of one's Bigger Self explains and enables.

Meditation practices allow us to develop perspectives of different parts of our larger Self. The visions are usually associated with body parts such as the brain, heart or gonads. It is claimed such perspectives provide control and healing mechanisms of the components experienced. The experience usually involves blocking everyday experiences such as sight or the sound of the little voice inside to achieve awareness of precursor signals from deeper levels. When practiced in safe environments where one's physical material is not damaged, personal benefits of such practices are well documented. As mentioned in Section 8.2.4, extreme depths may lead to confrontation with origin and destiny of life itself. However, such controlled practices should not be misclassified as near-death experiences but are likely to mirror similar stages of this extremely important phenomena that will be discussed in the next section.

8.3.4 Near-death experience

Near-death experiences (NDE) have been reported by people who were close to death but miraculously survived. In most cases, accidents involving severe injury is involved. People surviving cardiac arrest during open-heart surgery have been extensively studied in the Netherlands (Van Lommel, 2010; Van Lommel et al., 2010). The descriptions of these phenomena are consistent with out-of-body experiences and can therefore be associated with the 1st-person experience of the more advanced stages of the dying process. The mystical and often life-changing behavior patterns occurring after recovery from such episodes suggest new insights into our human situation have been achieved. Survivors report the possibility of existence beyond the functioning of the body; however, they also have difficulty rationalizing such possibilities with the objective belief structures prevalent in Western societies.

The ability to "see" activities of the attending physician or emergency worker while the patient lies unconscious without a pulse has also been reported. However, scientific attempts to verify such capabilities have not been successful. I myself have asked attending anesthesiologists to select a card from a deck and place it on a counter in order to test whether I could see it under anesthesia. CAT does not exclude such extrasensory observations and in fact provides a mechanism for extrasensory communication through memory leakage between cognitive action cycles. However, the scientific demonstration of such phenomena without theoretical guidance would only produce anecdotal results under lucky and non-repeatable circumstances.

This does not mean scientific investigation of NDE and related psychic phenomena is futile, although the speed of clinical anesthetics is too rapid to record memories that can later be documented. Personal experiences under anesthesia have given me fleeting memories of the upper stages of the consciousness ladder. Slow anesthesia investigations done on monkeys by Victor Lamb (see Chapter 7) if allowed on humans might result in repeatable reports. The author has encouraged such experiments and provided both material support and detailed verification analysis of such attempts.

At our current state of knowledge, only logical argument and promising theories that need experimental verification to demonstrate the control and repeatability required by the scientific method are available. No generally acceptable theory exists. In Part II of this book, the physical basis of CAT establishes the possibility that the soul, i.e. independent action cycles, can exist, and communicating interactions can be interpreted as the mental control of other people's bodies, which cannot be explained by contemporary physics. An intriguing argument for the reality of such possibilities was given by James Lake (2015, 2019), a psychiatrist who analyzed the evolutionary benefit of the NDE experience. Lake considered the psychic overhead producing such experiences from an evolutionary point of view. His contention is that at critical moments of danger such overhead is contrary to survival and should have been eliminated by natural selection a long time ago. Since the NDE phenomena survived, it must have a significant benefit. In conventional science, such a benefit would be a mystery. In CAT, the NDE is analogous to the creation, maintenance and repair of a life-giving communication system between one's soul and the classic body built of material in the rest of the Universe.

8.3.4.1 The physiology of engagement and disengagement

CAT provides the picture of an independent action cycle that is not interacting. Like an atom in an equilibrium state, such a cycle is electromagnetically invisible to the rest of the universe. If we assume this independent activity wants to grow (see Section 8.2), it would initiate an external interaction in hopes of gaining additional action flow through a profitable exchange. If successful, it would begin communicating and influencing the material of a neighboring event so that a kind of beachhead activity we have called A[I,U] is established in that neighboring part of the Universe. Without a priori knowledge of the neighboring U, such an attempt will be an exercise in trial and error but eventually some success will establish a primitive controlling capability.

From the U's perspective, this capability is the lowest level action loop shown in Figure 8.2-3. In the control-room analogy, this loop would be the last action segment of a conscious little-being-inside to be automated before it leaves a completely automated artificial intelligence replacement to run the machine. *Conversely, it is also the deepest and most primitive action that represents the beginning of conscious control of what will become a long hierarchy of dominance over increasingly complex material in the U.* In our consensus scientific community, this infinity point is called the Big Bang. Its trademark will be a spark of conscious behavior among the energy fields and elementary particles forming at the early ages of the Universe. These sparks are NOT explainable in classic physics and therefore will be attributed to the mysteries behind the quantum veil that are interpretations of quantum measurements of the Cosmic Background Radiation.

From the evolving 1st-person's consciousness point of view, an evolutionary chain of trial and error eventually built its way up to the present Now. Mapped into the 3rd-person contemporary model of the Universe, these conscious experiences are collocated with processing elements that happen along our evolutionary timeline. So here we are, Now, looking past our noses at instructions that direct the little voice inside to produce sounds that fly around a quick loop to emerge as meanings, which eventually disappear into the past as they are processed around our reality model to give us the idea of what to do next.

What they tell us is to contemplate the housekeeping and maintenance functions, m() and x(), in our neural net while allowing them to operate under automatic and thereby unconscious control. There are reflex actions and the workings of the bowels, heart, liver, etc., that, with good fortune, work without reporting pains or stress like any good robot should. The conscious element does not want to do every routine chore. It is happy to look at the processed display appearing in the third eye. Even so, it is only there because it has been awakened to direct the daily activities of an excited lifetime state that have not yet been automated.

The question of the physiology was raised in Chapter 7. The nearby past – to which we can retreat when we experience our recently recorded environment in an out-of-body experience – or the same past in which we can be exalted by the feeling of being one with the Universe may very well be implemented in the glial network whose astrocyte cell controls individual channel bundles of neurons passing action flow. We leave the debate of which physiology most appropriately allows the human brain to execute its cognitive function to alternatives discussed in Chapter 7.

Here we suggest that reported NDE experiences are symptoms of the stages of a growth process that moves our conscious viewpoint up and down the evolutionary hierarchy. When we go down, what is left behind are the local robotic controls built into the brain, both in the neural and glial networks. If they work properly, we get a good sleep and wake to the next task. If they are destroyed, and we have not built a higher layer to which we can migrate, then we are left in the past to salvage what we can of our control over U's material and try again. Since achieving the evolutionary future is largely a matter of trial and error, the NDE experience is a vital symptom of the evolutionary building process. So, Lake's intuition may have been right, there is a survival benefit to something as elaborate as an NDE experience.

9

FUTURE DEVELOPMENT

Conscious Action Theory (CAT) and the event-oriented world view introduced in this volume describe a profound change in the fundamental assumptions we live by. There is much to do. No longer is the concept of our physical-self limited to the appearance of our bodies but rather we are bigger Systems. These Systems generate what we experience by executing a sequence of changes that form a Self-regenerating network of action loops. In CAT, these actions are visualized as a medium of mass-charge densities that have a future-past and an inside-outside extension. We are our own space. When undisturbed, our space exists in a perfect state of equilibrium. The record of our form is an extension of cycles radiating along in all degrees of freedom available to us. Disturbances in our equilibrium space produces flow patterns whose cross section exhibits the energy we experience as our immediate Now sensations. The architecture of action flow provides a context for any theory and model that expresses what we believe is our true nature.

Though compatibility with classic physics and the Copenhagen interpretation of quantum theory is emphasized in this book, the following list represents a small set of more recent theories that could be incorporated in the CAT architecture.

Standard Model – The Standard Model identifies the electric, weak, strong and – reluctantly – the gravitational force categories along with a plethora of particles and force carriers between them. CAT also proposes four forces, which suggests a mapping between the two sets should be possible.

String Theory – "Strings" are fundamental. They are not composed of anything more fundamental. Different vibrations are thought to make elementary particles such as electrons and quarks. In CAT, action networks are fundamental. Material densities are visualizable network nodes. Filaments of action happen between the nodes. This suggests string visualizations of action forms.
Chaos theory – In chaos theory, non-repeating trajectories will nevertheless

propagate within well-defined regions in phase space associated with strange attractors. CAT introduces isolated systems executing motions around dynamic equilibrium ground state trajectories. This suggests chaos theory is a macroscopic cousin of Quantum Theory and is also an approximation of CAT.

Future development and applications of CAT span the whole spectrum of human activity; however, my training as a physicist and work as a computer systems engineer gives me insight into problems and opportunities in the hard science disciplines. Follow-up work is planned for further development of the physics presented in Part II. Explorations of specific topics of interest are listed next.

Expansion of CAT Formalism – In Chapter 4 we left off after flow diagrams were mapped into general mathematical form of an action tensor "$A^{\text{from}}{}_{\text{to}}$". This form identifies the flow of action between past/future, inside/outside and charge/mass aspects of matter in all systems. It is the symbol of an action-flow structure that symbolically answers the ontological "what is" question. How one finds the matrix elements and extracts observable information *when the observer is one of the action elements* was qualitatively presented throughout this book; however, further detailed technical development of CAT physics is required to support its validity and produce practical engineering applications.

Subjective Relativity – Einstein was a realist. His observers ride along with their clocks in an objective world "out there". CAT claims that world "out there" is produced within a cycle of action, and Einstein himself is one of those cycles. His own imagination was the preferred empty space, aether or plenum in which his thought experiments took place. By eliminating the subjective, its properties are projected back onto an objective world. Relativity theory must be modified to include the subjective phase.

Charge-mass interactions and the Fine Structure Constant – The introduction of mental forces connecting charge and mass introduces modifications to the orbits of particles circulating because as demonstrated in Figure 4.5-1, charge and mass are no longer located at the same point. Arnold Sommerfeld explained the deviation of Bohr's simple atomic orbits deduced from spectroscopic as a relativistic effect. When relativity is modified, and a Bohr orbit is split into two, the resulting perturbations may also account for the spectroscopic fine structure.

Knowledge Gap vs. Intrinsic Uncertainty – Extensive investigations of violations of Bell's Theorem, entangled states, hidden variables and the Einstein-Podolsky-Rosen Paradox have built a firm case for the validity of quantum theory, specifically that knowledge of an outside system is intrinsically random. However, CAT shows we can model but cannot directly experience what any independent event System is or will do. Hidden variables cannot be found in objects because they happen in the observer. CAT explains uncertainty as a lack of knowledge in an observer and suggests ways it can be overcome.

Large-Small-Scale Axis – As soon as the inside-of-material is identified the question of the shape of the axis between the inside and outside comes up. It is drawn and labeled as time but it is displayed in space. A cycle in time passing through objective and subjective phases could be observed as a flow of action from the large into the small at every point in space.

The simplest cycle is composed of all action incorporated in one cycle consisting of an objective and subjective phase. Assume the Being composed of such a cycle wanted to know its own true nature. The Being might start by experiencing an all-objective world, build a scale model and bit by bit add symbols to it until all details of Its objective experience is completely explained. Since symbols are made of real things that complete knowledge is stored in a symbol structure that will have completely replaced the objective world experience with a subjective world experience. The Being has explained everything, but in order to recapture what all the symbols mean, It would have to convert the symbols back into the original objects. The cycle would be experienced as a large-objective universe flowing into an initially small subjective symbol that grows large, which then initially flows into a small object that grows large. In other words the execution of an explanatory-measurement cycle would start with a flow from large to small (see Figure 4.3-9). When the subjective phase is ignored, the initial phase of a continuous cycle will appear as a one-way flow of large into small that is reminiscent of gravitational effect.

By recognizing things as stable motions, Chapter 5 applied CAT principles to produce an ontological interpretation of quantum theory. Chapter 6 examined the action model of a conscious being in the small disturbance limit. Chapters 7 and 8 discussed the impact CAT has on several additional fields of study. It is hoped that further development in these and other areas will produce the shortcuts and rules of thumb that allow our abstract event-oriented world view to be applied to problems heretofore intractable. Several nascent projects are discussed in the following sections in order to give the reader further examples of how event-oriented thinking can be applied to real-world problems.

9.1 Dual-eye and bi-scopic perception

This book has emphasized the fact that the world we experience is the product of our measurement processing mechanism. That mechanism is programmed to produce a display compatible with the interface requirements of our reality model. The framework of that model reflects our fundamental belief that we live in a 3D world. This belief was encoded into our hardware because the evolutionary forces of a hunter-gatherer existence have tuned our model to locate prey. We are rapidly moving toward a societal environment where many of those forces are no longer pertinent. Our ability to think is severely limited because most of our brain capacity is occupied producing a 3D world display. If we could release our optical lobes from the stereo-processing task, we could redirect its capacity to enhance our mental processing capacity. In today's world much of our time is spent focusing two eyes on one computer screen. It would be more efficient to see two different computer screens at once and effectively double our cognitive band width. In dual-eye or bi-scopic perception we simultaneously see and maintain two separate views of the world when the left and right eye are stimulated with different scenes.

Appropriate mirror arrangements or computer goggles can be built to provide separate left- and right-eye stimulation. When this is done, the subject experiences binocular rivalry. Binocular rivalry happens when two different images are presented to two eyes simultaneously. Normally the subject will only be conscious of one of the two images. One is dominant, the other suppressed. From the dominant image, a 3D world is produced using familiar depth queues available in that image. This 3D perception is not stable. Every few seconds, the perceptual dominance switches and a 3D world scene is produced from the second image. This phenomenon was discovered by Hermann von Helmholz in the 19th century and has been studied by neuroscientists who have attempted to discover where the switching and suppression function takes place.

Experiments conducted by the author (Baer and Baer, 2012) have discovered that the switching and suppression can be eliminated, and both left and right scenes can be held in conscious awareness. It was learned that the switching between scenes is determined by the attention the subject gives to the scene. Simply remembering something about the suppressed scene can make it and its 3D world image appear. However, if attention is carefully balanced, the brain maintains both images in conscious view and does not decide which one to make dominant. The tendency to select a dominant scene is a learned capability supporting stereo processing and can be unlearned.

A training device has been constructed, as shown in Figure 9.1-1, that implements a feedback loop allowing an operator to balance the attention factors in two scenes. Early implementations used two computers that control a left and right scene generator 1). The left eye and the right eye 3) separately receive the stimulation and produce a simultaneous left and right mental scene 5) if the attention is balanced. The operator, using a suitable control device 2), informs the computers which scene is dominant. The computer then adjusts attention factors in the scene and in left- and right-side audio and tactile stimulators that draw attention to the suppressed image so they balance. The process is a bit like learning to play two scores on the piano with two hands. At first the brain resists and wants to perform stereo processing, but after some training it settles down and both scenes can be simultaneously seen. Just as piano playing does not eliminate mono-hand operations, this capability appears to add to, not replace, normal stereo vision.

Besides expanding cognitive awareness of two computer screens, alternative incarnations of the device can be employed to simultaneously merge context and detail, while maintaining awareness of left and right, measure intrinsic attention and integrate two scenes differing in time. This latter capability is of special interest

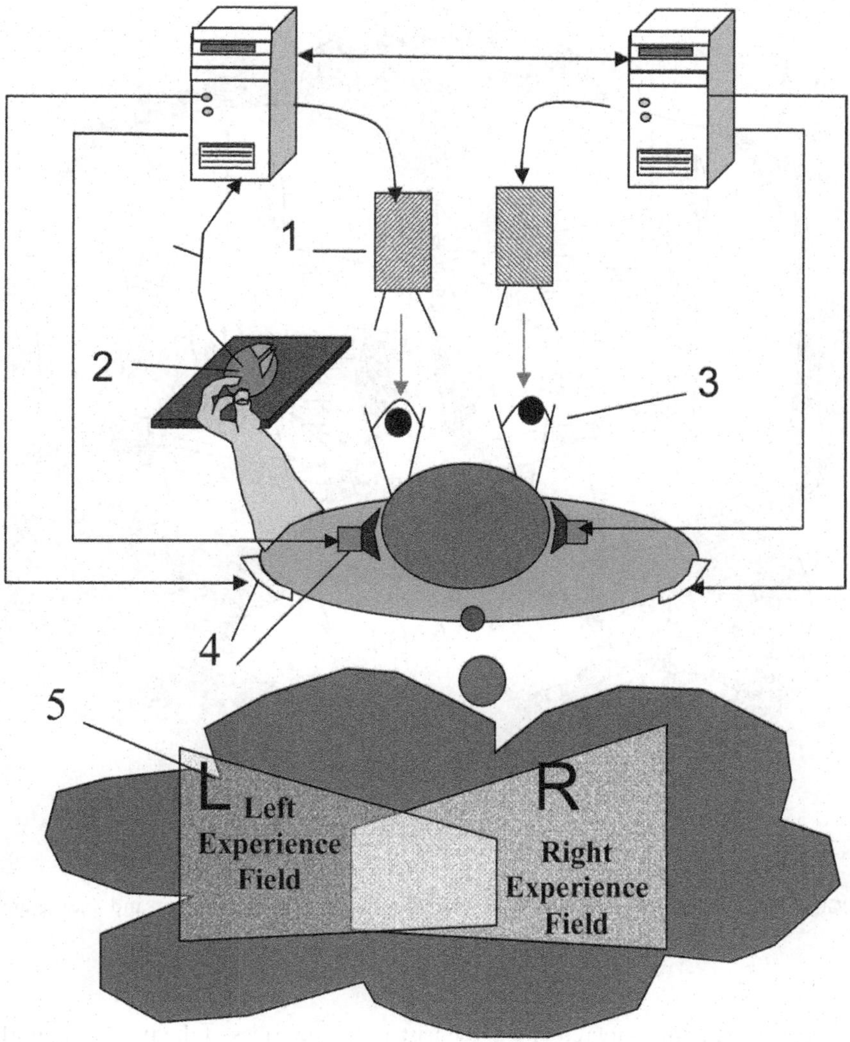

FIGURE 9.1-1 Bi-scopic training device

as an implementation of the CAT book model. As we showed in Chapter 3, Figure 3.2-1, the left and right side of a book shows the two sides of a "Now" instance. Classic multimedia playback presents only the left-past scene to both eyes in rapid succession producing a time snapshot movie-like experience. CAT theory suggests that the conscious experience is correlated to the change flowing through the 1st-person, which can be presented to the left and right eye separately as shown in Figure 9.1-2.

The difference between the left and right scene is experienced by the dual-eye viewer and designated by the symbol $\Delta a(t)$. There is one difference per page-turn operation, and each time both the left and right pages change. This is as expected

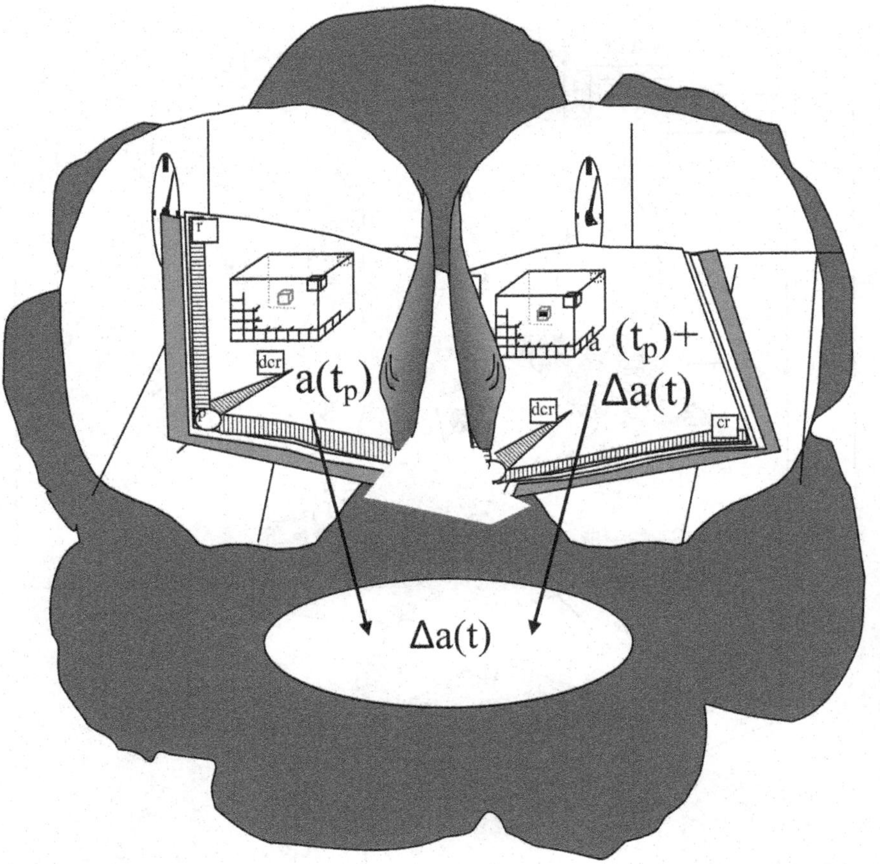

FIGURE 9.1-2 Dual-eye awareness of the difference between future and past pages viewed by left and right eyes

when a time instant is incremented; the past and future sides of the instant are both changed. As long as we focus both eyes on one page, we will see objectively and waste half the visualization capacity of the human being. However, if we utilize separate forward and backward "Now" side stimulation, the brain may be trained to become aware of the change rather than the object.

From a scientific perspective, the ability to visualize change – i.e. events or the flow of action – to augment the sequence-state, movie-frame experience may foster the next jump in understanding, much as the invention of movies fostered a new understanding of time and a new physics to explain it. It is no accident that the development of moving photography, Impressionist painting and the revolution from classic to quantum and relativistic physics happened synchronously. It will be no accident that when event-display devices are developed synchronously as the event-oriented world view gains traction.

9.2 Process-oriented economic theory

There are many disciplines that could benefit from the formal integration of mental experiences into traditional object-oriented theories. The analogy between objective physics and economics has a long history (Mirowski, 1989). The need to determine the value of intellectual, creative and knowledge assets for today's internet companies is a challenge for economists that provides an example for how to adapt CAT to material-based disciplines. Figure 1.6-2 and Section 4.4.1 introduced CAT action-flow-diagram templates for visualizing interacting action cycles, each incorporating its own 1st-person subjective experience. Adapting CAT to economics requires the replacement of action-network arcs and endpoint-position symbols used in these flow diagram with economic terms.

Figure 9.2-1 shows an action network at a typical point-of-sale instance involving three cognitive beings participating in an economy. Macroscopic icons represent large aggregations of actions flowing along internal and external timelines appropriate for economic modeling. A 1st-, 2nd-, and 3rd-person action loop in CAT is represented here by a Customer "C", Business "B" and the Market "U". These interact externally through action exchanges used in traditional economic models, to which we have added subjective data flow. Conscious experiences are seen covering the contact points between thinking and body-action loops. The

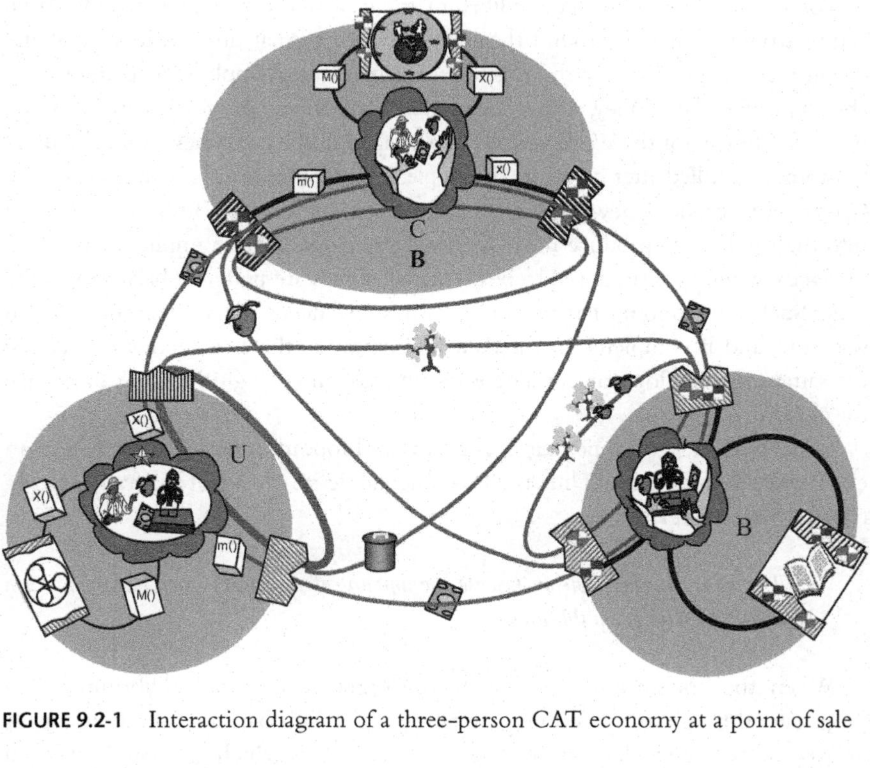

FIGURE 9.2-1 Interaction diagram of a three-person CAT economy at a point of sale

Customer sees a businessman sell an apple. The businessman sees a Customer buy an apple. The Market becomes aware of the exchange from a disembodied 3rd-person knowledge perspective.

The physical side of the material interfaces have points and indents indicating action-flow directions. These interfaces divide the diagram into objective white and subjective shaded oval regions. Both the products owned and the thought-processing mechanism managing the ownership are time loops of action, which refresh themselves through objective and subjective phases. Several models are incorporated. The Customer's thought process uses a classic physical model to calculate his or her next expected sensations. The calculation elements used by the Business is visualized as a book, containing a business plan in which operational symbols are entered that direct the thought process controlling the business. Icons representing actions looking like apples, trees and dollar bills name real action structures moving among entities. A real orchard of apple Trees producing real Apples are shown on the external physical phase of the cycle under the control of the Business. Because these represent real Kantian events-in-themselves they cannot be observed directly. They are made visible through a measurement-explanatory cycle that reports the result to the externalized book display containing the business plan. The business plan describes the process by which the Business is designed to operate and is here used as the display inside the business model of reality as a tool to manage ongoing operations.

For an economy in perfect equilibrium, the flow of action aggregated into large action structures moves around the internal and external time paths so that the activity repeats exactly. First the Business exchanges a real Apple, seen as an observable apple, for real Money, seen as observable money. The money is sent to U and then used to pay for the Waste and Seeds packaged in the container icon, which the Customer has filled after digesting the Apple. U combines waste and seeds from the Customer to produce new apple trees that are sent back to the Business and placed into the Orchard to produce more Apples. Perfect equilibrium implies all material is exactly where it is supposed to be so that all forces are perfectly balanced all the time. Such an economy has no internal stress, all needs meet satisfaction action structure, and if completely isolated, would continue the same activity repeating the same material flow forever. The economics of an ecological niche can survive for eons.

In economics, the happening of action is anthropomorphically identified as an experience of satisfaction. Thus, the fundamental desire of all material can be written in economic terms as:

> *All economic beings wish to increase the amount of satisfaction they experience in a comfortable state of equilibrium.*

When the equilibrium motions are disturbed then non-equilibrium forces propagate through the economy. Small-enough disturbances will show up as delayed or erroneous delivery of products or payments which generate both need

"$\underline{n}$" and solution "$\underline{s}$" signals propagating through the economy like Schrödinger's waves. This flow of need and solution signals introduces a symbolically mirrored economic flow in the memories of individuals providing a quantum formulation of economic theory.

The CAT formulation extends quantum theory to large nonlinear disturbances that characterize everyday human experiences. Consider the introduction of a new product into an economy. The equilibrium is broken by that incoming action bundled in the form of a product. The absorbed action creates a need and solution pair, which propagates changes throughout the economy. When these two disturbances meet, the solution eliminates the need, and the action is released. If the propagation of the need and solution vectors around their respective action paths creates a cycle that adds to the original equilibrium state of the economy, a new equilibrium is established. The economy achieves a higher state of satisfaction. The new product has been adopted. If the added action cycle is not closed, the disturbance and its associated stress introduces discomfort, the product is rejected and its action is re-radiated outward, returning the economy to its initial equilibrium state.

The amount of action released when a need meets a solution is given in index notation by

$$S = E \bullet \Delta T = \Sigma_{i,j}\, n_i \bullet S_{ij} \bullet s_j . \qquad \text{Equation 9.2-1}$$

where the symbols are defined in physics and economics as follows:

	Physics	*Economics*
S	= Hamilton's Principle Function	Satisfaction
E	= Energy	Proto-value in economics
ΔT	= Interaction time	Time distance between need creation and destruction
S_{ij}	= Interaction matrix	Satisfaction matrix
n_i	= ψ	Need vector
s_j	= ψ*	Solution vector
i,j	= degrees of freedom	Cycle names

If we divide Equation 9.2-1 by the interaction time, we get the definition of the proto-value:

$$PV = S/\Delta T = \Sigma_{i,j}\, n_i \cdot \left(S_{ij}/\Delta T\right) \cdot s_j . \qquad \text{Equation 9.2-2}$$

Proto-value is thereby defined as the rate at which a product delivers satisfaction. It represents the value of a product relative to the need experienced by an economic being and can be calculated from intrinsic life characteristics of such entities. The theory is being developed to calculate the product value, adoption rates and start-up company values applied to new situations where no comparables are available, making traditional appraisals difficult (Housel et al., 2015).

9.3 Gravity and parapsychology

The interconnection between material and mental forces in CAT casts a wide net of interdisciplinary relationships between such disparate but persistent beliefs as astrology, the statistical nature of quantum theory, relativity and mental telepathy. Psychophysical effects have been seriously studied and observed at the Institute of Noetic Sciences in Petaluma, California, with marginal success (Baer, 2015b). In CAT, thoughts are influenced and/or produced by mental forces that physically hold charge and mass together. Such forces are symptoms of a fundamental action flow. The theory proposes that thoughts are influenced by gravitational structure of space (also called quantum foam) and such a phenomenon can be observed in the 1st-person view as the feeling of a flow of action through one's Now display, or from a 3rd-person perspective by measuring the flow with real equipment.

Reg Cahill (2014), professor at Flinders University in Australia, published results from several experiments designed to detect correlations between random number generators (RNG). Cahill claimed to measure the flow of space past the earth without using electromagnetic waves used in the Michelson-Morely aether flow detection. Take light waves away and one is left with gravito-inertial influences flowing through the detectors. Shot noise in Zener diodes produces a random electric current guaranteed by the Uncertainty principle of quantum theory. Cahill argued variations in the flow of gravity would trigger the Zener diode and correlate the random output between two properly spaced RNGs. It would also give us a very low-cost gravity wave detector probably worth a Noble Prize. If such an effect were found, it would explain Heisenberg's Uncertainty principle and the intrinsically random nature of quantum theory in terms of gravitational signals from the quasi-random motion of distant masses.

In addition, if some equivalent to a Zener diode mechanism were found in the brain, the sensitivity of RNG's to large-crowd phenomena reported at such happenings as Burning Man could be explained and a mechanism for telepathy postulated. Nothing shields our memories from gravity and inertia. Inertial effects are large and could limit the reliability of conventional computer memories (see Appendix A4.3 and Baer, 2017a). These effects could implement extrasensory communication through gravity memory leak signals. The significance of the reported effect is enormous but was it real?

Upon hearing of these results, I contacted Dr. Cahill and asked about verification experiments. He had tried to interest major physics labs but claimed these were all focused on the LIGO Gravitational Wave experiments. These utilized extremely large electromagnetic interferometers conceptually similar to the Michelson-Morley experiments, and the labs were not interested in Cahill's radically new approach. I tried to interest some of my friends in California. Among them was Harry Jabs, the electronic engineer from Institute for Frontier Science, who was interested in consciousness research, and Eric Reiter an engineer from the Unquantum Lab, who wanted to prove quantum theory wrong. These and others donated their time, and a duplicate of Cahill's device was made. Unfortunately, no correlation signal was found. Many hours of investigation concluded that Cahill's equipment design was flawed. His published RNG design could not generate signals above the noise level generated by the electronics of oscilloscopes required to measure the signals. We speculated Cahill was sensing terrestrial interference, perhaps from a nearby airport (Baer et al., 2017).

This did not mean Cahill's space-flow concept was wrong but only that no verified experimental proof had been established. The very low-noise RNGs and statistical analysis software required for the experiment was more than a loose group of volunteers could manage and the project languished. Recently Steve Murphy and Grant Moulton got interested in the challenge and between dodging wildfires designed a cleaner, lower-noise detector circuit (E-mail communication, 2018). Ongoing discussions with and hopes of fielding a second attempt have risen substantially, and with luck, new results may emerge before this book is published. Verification of this effect could have a profound influence on our concept of space and time.

9.4 Concluding remarks

Dear Reader, your attention will soon be coming out of this book. After you close the back cover your eyes will glance around, and the memories of your old sensory interpretations will flow in. You lived in a world of real objects. You cannot doubt the reality of the world around you. You have learned that You see a book, that You remember a **B**ook and visualize the reality of this memory as a **b**ook and so does everyone else in our consensus reality culture. But on top of it all there really is a Book, only it is not simply an object.

Inside this Book's pages are claims for building, operating and understanding a **M**odel of **R**eality. Such models are incorporated in your real Self, which according to our theory, also processes your self, into your **S**elf, that is visualized as the **s**elf you believe you really are. Together we have been learning how different models that contain your **S**elf evolve and how each model supports a world view from which different physical theories of reality emerge. We have seen why the processing activity our Self performs is more fundamental than any model It contains, and therefore the most logically self-consistent model of our Selves is an observable scale model of the activity we execute.

The physics describing such a model is conceptually simple. A transcendental view of an action cycle is easy to draw. Convincing one's self that such a drawing is a more accurate **s**elf image than the classic body we are accustomed to experiencing is not trivial. The arguments put forward in these pages require

1 A recognition of *what we do to experience what we experience.*
2 A systematic replacement of *objects with events* leading to a new action formulation of physics.

To provide a path of growth to this new way of thinking required us to demonstrate how our CAT formulation is first compatible with and an expansion of current beliefs. We introduced equations in Part II to demonstrate mathematical compatibility; however such demonstrations are hard to grasp because current physics is hard.

To simplify the task, this book has been written at multiple levels so that the casual reader can peruse the gist of the arguments by flipping through the pages, noting the diagrams and major topics. Such initial reading initiates the growth of a memory framework that forms the backbone of knowledge to which further information from subsequent readings will stick. How often You the reader will pass this point (see Figure 3.4-1) cannot be foretold. What can be foretold is that I must give up control of your little voice inside and leave you to choose your future. If you return to the book one more time, You will reach the front cover once more. The promise of what lies ahead will resonate more deeply than the last time you were here because of the framework you have already grown. If you decide to continue you will meet a different book because its meaning will advance with each cycle.

Otherwise, your path from the end to the beginning may be as long as the one that brought you here in the first place. Our Selves may never interact again, but I hope that when you look out from your standard position and feel the reality behind your sensations give way, then in the panic of dissolution you will remember this book and the lesson it teaches. We are interacting events between two timeless states of equilibrium who will exist forever.

Appendices

A3.1

DEFINITION OF TERMS

This book presents new ideas, a new world view, a new way of interpreting and understanding the experiences of our lives. To convey large new ideas requires crafting words and graphic icons into larger structures that must be grasped all at once. To avoid distracting explanations in the text, we ask the reader to quickly review the definitions listed herein and remember to look back at this section when the meaning of a locally undefined symbol is encountered.

Acronyms:

1st-PL	–	1st-Person Laboratory
CMoR	–	A conscious action-flow model of reality includes mental subjective experience and physical objective memory model
DoF	–	Degree of freedom, direction along an axis of expansion for space and particle motion for disturbances in space
ETS	–	Expected touch space, feeling of dark geographic space surrounding the feeling of one's body
MoR	–	Model of Reality, any symbol structure used to explain experiences
PCC	–	Physical Correlates of Consciousness
PMoR	–	Physical Model of Reality, imbedded in the action flow of a CMoR

First letter CAT model codes:

The noun concept is expanded into four aspects that represent the processing phases through which action flows producing our single objective experience.

Examples	*Description*
You, I, Apple	– First letter capitalized: references an event-in-itself, the name of action structures, the entity that exists. Such words are operational symbols defined by their use, not their referential meaning.
you, i, apple	– First letter lowercase: references a directly observable experience, the entities that are experienced – sensations, thoughts, pains, etc. directly felt.
You, **I**, **A**pple	– First letter capitalized and boldface: references a tensor of causes in the explanatory model of observables, i.e. the physical memory that explains one's observable experience.
you, **i**, **a**pple	– First letter lowercase and boldface: references a vector of observable experiences that visualize the semantic meaning of the physical memory defined by **Y**ou, **I**, **A**pple; names explanatory experiences projected onto sensations.

Initially these words are enclosed in quotation marks when specific CAT model components are referenced but after the reader gets used to the convention, capitalized names and bold first letter expressions also appear without quotation marks in the text when it is clear that a name of a real thing or an interaction processing event in the observer is intended.

Graphic icons:

 – Icon of an optic modality display observable; filled color blobs named by a symbol of a direct observable such as Δa or a

 – Icon of an expected touch space display observable; outline only, named by a symbol of an observable such as **Δa** or **a**

 – Icon of a fused optic and expected touch observable, assumed to be a real object when seen in the 1st-person view

 – Optical 1st-person view, with a filled nose display surrounding the space sensation of one's body; fused with lined outline indicating belief that one's body is a real object, represents all external sensory display

 – Mental display space, imagination, expected touch space, thought bubble

 – Empty theoretical display space, contains sensations of what one actually believes to be explanation of external and internal sensory displays. Specifically the icons of theoretical components listed later in this table.

 – 1st-person sense of self center, observational viewpoint indicator

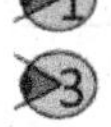 – 3rd-person disembodied, theoretical or memory viewpoint indicator

 – Icon and symbol of material composed of mass and charge, type **m, ch**

 – Center of mass

 – Center of charge

 – Past gravity field indicator, where the Universe (U) wants the mass to be

 – Past electric field indicator, where the U wants the charge to be

 – Future gravity field indicator, where the mass wants the U to want it to be

 – Future electric field indicator, where the charge wants the U to want it to be

 – Receiver space indicator, external physical notch side, internal is straight; interface between objective and subjective aspects of matter, past in subjective view, future in objective view

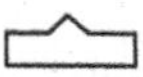 – Sender space indicator, external is physical point side, internal is straight; interface between objective and subjective aspects of matter

 – Processing operation between internal matter representations, encloses an external objective element; usually implemented by complex action-flow sequences

 – Processing operation between external matter representations, encloses an internal subjective element; usually implemented by complex action-flow sequences

Subscripts or brackets: label the parts or division of a "Whole"

A_I or A[I] – Labels an action "A" happening in the part named "I"

$A^{From}{}_{To}$ – Covariant *From* and Contravariant *To* elements indicate action direction between endpoint states

Pre-scripts:

Δ – Implies a finite interval at the value of the variable following
Example ΔQ, interval of length Δ at location Q

d – Implies an infinitesimal interval at the value of the variable following
Example dQ, interval of length d at location Q

_ – Underline references a vector, a list; example $\underline{A}_Q$ references an array of actions along a list of Q values

CAT specific symbols and abbreviations:

U_W – The Universe as a Whole event, assumed isolated since there is nothing more

I – The 1st-person event, approximated as a stand-alone action loop

Y, You – The 2nd-person event, approximated as a stand-alone action loop

U – The rest of the Universe event after specific events of interest are separated

A_N – An amount of action in an event named N; if unnamed implies a Whole event

Z, Z() – The dynamic state and Zustands function of an event, the form of an event

ζ, ζ() – The instantaneous dynamic state of a sub-event, approximated by the state function "ψ" in quantum theory

F_{gi} – Force of gravity and inertial connected by Mach's Principle

F_{em} – Force of electricity and magnetism connected by Maxwell's equations

F_{cm} – Force of charge on mass, interior of matter; associated with cognitive experience

(*Continued*)

(Continued)

F_{mc}	– Force of mass on charge, interior of matter; associated with cognitive experience
A	– Action state density
ρ_{ch}	– Charge density measured in Coulombs per meter cubed
ρ_m	– Mass density measured in grams per meter cubed
E, E_W	– Energy of a typical event, or a named event when subscripted, Action density along time
T, T_W	– Whole Time state of an event, also used variable along the total time axis
t	– Coordinate time measured by a clock imbedded in the Universe often used as Newtonian time in classic physics formulations
τ	– Proper time or personal time of a part of interest, derived from the state of system
P	– Summary action density along a single degree-of-freedom representation, Energy when time is mapped onto space extensions Q
Q	– Summary position state spectrum of an event, a single degree-of-freedom representation
$\underline{\mathbf{p}}$	– Property vector; generalized momentum vector, detail along many DoF
$\underline{\mathbf{q}}$	– Quantity vector; generalized coordinate vector of any measurable quantity
$\underline{\mathbf{x}}$	– Position vector in 3D space coordinates, address of a 3D space, often Cartesian coordinates x, y, z are indexed as x_1, x_2, x_3
$\underline{\mathbf{u}}_f$	– A unit vector visualization of the quantity of type "f" bold
x_f	– 3D space address of a point on the "f" axis defining the range of positions
Δx_f	– Finite interval between the point x_f and $x_f + \Delta x_f$
dx_f	– Infinitesimal interval between the point x_f and $x_f + dx_f$
∇	Gradient operator, in Cartesian coordinates $\partial/\partial x + \partial/\partial y + \partial/\partial z$

A4.1

APPLICABILITY OF MATHEMATICAL IDEALIZATIONS IN PHYSICS

Mathematics largely deals with relationships between numerical quantities "q", i.e. numbers. Physics deals with relationships between physical quantities. Therefore a physical quantity "**q**" is always a combination of a number and a unit of some physical entity, i.e. a tensor of some rank. There are many instances where ideal mathematical procedures are carried out on quantities using idealized mathematical rules and the results are carried over to physics without explicitly identifying the limits that account for the properties of units involved. Here are some examples.

A4.1.1 Derivative: there is no zero time interval and no zero unit of time.

In math	*In physics*
$\text{Lim}_{\Delta t \to 0}\ \Delta x(t)/\Delta t = dx(t)/dt$	$\text{Lim}_{\Delta t \to \text{SEL}}\ \Delta x(t)/\Delta t = dx(t)/dt$ Where: SEL = Small Enough to be Linear

A4.1.2 Integral: again zero is a small-enough limit in physics.

In math	*In physics*
Δt	Δt
$\text{Lim}\ _{\Delta t \to 0}F(x) = \int_0^{\Delta t} x(t) \cdot dt$	$\text{Lim}\ _{\Delta t \to \text{SEL}}\ F(x) = \int_0^{\Delta t} x(t) \cdot dt$ $= < x(t) > \cdot dt$

A4.1.3 Unit-less numbers: example – "π" is the circumference divided by the diameter. Canceling units depend on the physical properties of the unit and never gives a number with an infinite number of decimal places. There are no points of zero size.

In math	*In physics*
"π" is a transcendental number	"$\pi = \#_q \cdot \mathbf{u}_q$" is always a number of units

A4.1.4 Conditions vs. causal statements: mathematical equations are statements of condition.

In math1	*In physics or computer science*
"F = m·a" is a condition	"F = m·a" is a causal statement

A4.1.5 The d'Alembert Principle:

In math1	*In physics or computer science*
"0 = F-m·a" is a condition	While (F-ma > 0) {reduce_Err(F,m,a);}

A4.1.6 Infinity and zero: the physical Universe contains a largest physical number, for eventually one runs out material to represent it.

In math1	*In physics*
$\text{Lim}\#_{q\to 0}\ \infty = 1/\#q$	$\text{Lim}\ \#_{q\to \text{SEL}}\ \infty = 1\cdot uq/\#q \cdot uq$

The list goes on, but if it cannot be done with real entities, even in principle the pronouncements of mathematics should be viewed with great suspicion.

A4.2

ACTION THEORY IN ISOLATED SYSTEMS

A4.2.1 Classic system with external time

In classic physics the evolution of an isolated system is defined by the list of functions

$$q1(t), q2(t)...qf(t)..., p1(t), pf2(t)...pf(t)...$$

Where: qf(t) = the generalized coordinate or position at a time t
pf(t) = the generalized momentum or desire to change at a time t
t = an external time parameter
f = the degrees of freedom of change available to the system

These equations are solutions to the equations of motion. They completely define an event. They imply a rigorous connection between the system and time. The evolution of the system is completely defined by the progress of time and is thereby deterministic. In classic physics the physical basis for such a connection is simply assumed.

A4.2.2 Classic system with an internal clock

Mathematically we can add the motion of a clock as a zero'th degree of freedom to the list:

$$q0,\ p0(q0),\ q1(q0),\ q2(q0)\ldots qf(q0)\ldots,\ p1(q0),\ pf2(q0)\ldots pf(q0)\ldots$$

Where: pf(q0) = the clock momentum, i.e. desire of the clock change at a time q0
q0 = the position of the clock pointer

Now the motion of the clock, defined by q0, drives the evolution of the rest of the degrees of freedom. However, q0 is not known a priori. *One condition is missing.* The state of the combined system cannot be predicted without a measurement of at least one of the parameters. This implies that outside observers who are isolated from the system under consideration cannot determine its state until they make a measurement. If this has a familiar ring it is because the random nature of quantum theory is directly explained in CAT by the fact that quantum systems are electromagnetically isolated from outside observers until a measurement is made.

A4.2.3 Single degree of freedom representation of a classic system

There are at least two ways to specify a system. Either we list all its observable pf's and qf's or we simply assign some single value to each row of values as their instantaneous time-state variable "T" and supply the missing condition by assuming the energy "E" is constant. We therefore recognize the time and energy expressions as one way to specify a system, and the individual position and momentum as an alternative way to specify the same system. Figure A4.2-1 provides a comparison between the two ways of looking at such systems.

In one specification the Action of an event is defined by energy and momentum in the other as a function of all the individual degrees of freedom, shown here for a three-part Whole consisting of You, I and the rest of the universe U.

$$A(E,T) = A(\ldots qf_U(E,T), pf_U(E,T), \ldots, \ldots qf_Y(E,T), pf_Y(E,T), \ldots, \ldots qf_I(E,T), pf_I(E,T), \ldots). \qquad \text{Equation A4.2-1}$$

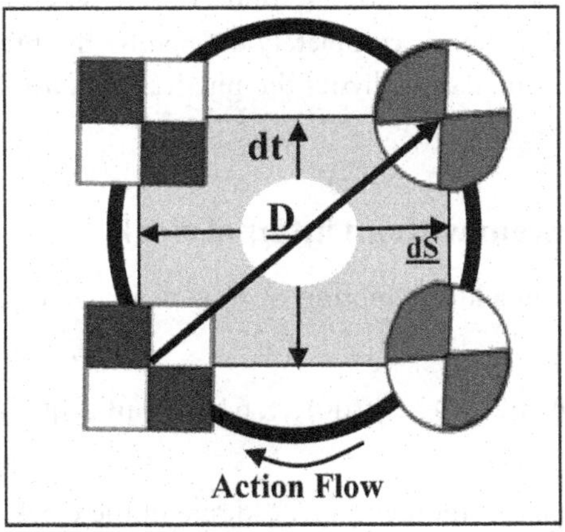

FIGURE A4.2-1 Canonical transformations in Hamilton-Jacobi formulation of classical physics

Here T defines the motion of a system point moving with constant velocity along a trajectory marked off by constant distance intervals through a multidimensional coordinate frame composed of all degrees of freedom "f_I, f_Y, f_U". When the system point trajectory is defined in the position and momenta in all its degrees of freedom, the action is given by

$$dA = \Sigma_f \{(\partial A(qf,pf)/\partial qf) \cdot dqf + (\partial A(qf,pf)/\partial qf) \cdot dqf\}$$
$$= \Sigma_f \{pf \cdot dqf + \tfrac{1}{2} \cdot dqf \cdot dpf\} \qquad \text{Equation A4.2-2}$$

The derivative of the first term is the definition of momentum in each degree of freedom while the second term is the change in the length of each interval, which is associated with force. When we look at the same system in an "E,T" coordinate frame the form of action is $A(E,T, \ldots \alpha_{f-1}, \beta_{f-1} \ldots)$. In this form, all the derivatives are constant except for the two shown.

$$dA = (\partial A(E,T,\ldots\alpha_{f-1},\beta_{f-1}\ldots)/\partial T) \cdot dT +$$
$$(\partial A(E,T,\ldots\alpha_{f-1},\beta_{f-1}\ldots)/\partial E) \cdot dT = E \cdot dT + T \cdot dE \qquad \text{Equation A4.2-3}$$

If the system's energy is constant so "dE = 0" and the sum force term is zero. Energy and time are not the only parameters used to summarize an isolated system. Other popular parameters are given by

$$dA = E \cdot dT = P_\Phi \cdot d\Phi = P_Q \cdot dQ \qquad \text{Equation A4.2-4}$$

Since T is the period of an event, its total value is often mapped into a complete cycle. In units of a complete cycle, T has the value of unity and dT is some fraction of that unity. If distant units are chosen, Q is the circumference measured in meters. The spatial circumference acts like a clock dial on which alternative scales are marked. If phase units "Φ" are chosen, a complete cycle is 2π radians. The relationship between the different scales usually introduces static parameters that are fixed by the construction of the scales or in case of time the clock dial. For example,

$$T = \Phi/\omega,\ E = P_\Phi \cdot \omega \text{ and } Q = T \cdot Vw,\ P_Q = E/Vw \qquad \text{Equation A4.2-5}$$

The parameter "Vw" is the ratio of two scale intervals and therefore a constant inside the model by definition. However, its interpretation as the velocity of the system point (clock pointer) takes a bit of explaining. In book coordinates the operator can look down upon the spread out pages with time mapped into the pages around the spine of the book. The page-turn rate determines the motion in all the degrees of freedom in the book. In that sense *T takes the role of Newtonian time and "Vw" is the speed of Now* in the model. By contrast, the page-turn rate in the 1st-Person Laboratory is a relationship between the model and the reality it models.

It is defined by the registration instructions of the model, which like the legend of a map, define the relation between the map and the territory. If the model is to be used as a scale model, the page-turn rate must be a constant ratio to the wall-clock rate. Of course, the operator controls the rate of Now; however, any measurement of time by internally modeled observers on internal clocks is independent of the operator's choices.

Lastly in CAT, an isolated system, the missing condition in Equation A4.2-2 is supplied by assuming a constant action not energy. For simple cases,

$$A\left(E,T\right) = \underline{E} \bullet \underline{T} = A = \text{constant}. \qquad \text{Equation A4.2-6}$$

Thus, energy and time are reciprocal. The same event when run at lower energy simply runs more slowly but an observer inside the system cannot tell. Though both energy and time are normally considered scalars, we use a vector notation to remind the reader that in CAT both are extensions with directions to which vector notation is also applicable.

A4.3

MACH'S PRINCIPLE AND GRAVITO-INERTIAL AND ELECTROMAGNETIC EQUATION ANALOGY

In the early 1950s, Dennis Sciama, one of the very few doctoral students trained by Paul Dirac, showed how to mathematically formulate the inertial interaction between local masses and the distant mass of stars and galaxies (Sciama, 1953) (Woodward 2013). His approach was to write down a vector theory of gravity analogous to Maxwell's theory of electrodynamics (Jackson, 1966).

$$\mathbf{F}_{gi}/m = -\overline{\nabla}\varphi_g - (1/c)\cdot\partial\mathbf{A}_g/\partial t \quad \text{Where:} \qquad \text{Equation (A4.3-1)}$$

φ_g = the gravitational field potential produced by all the matter in the universe
$\mathbf{A}_g$ = the gravitational vector field potential produced by all the momentum of that matter
$\mathbf{F}_{gi}$ = the combined gravito-inertial force and "m" is a test mass

The vector field potential is calculated by summing over all the momentum densities "ρ" each at its distance "r" in the universe volume "V".

$$\mathbf{A}_g = (1/c)\cdot\int_V(\rho\cdot v/r)\cdot dV \qquad \text{Equation A4.3-2}$$

Sciama noted that for a particle moving with velocity "v", an observer at rest on the particle would see all the universe mass streaming past with a velocity "-v" while all other transverse velocities average to zero. The radial components can be ignored because the gravitational analog to the magnetic field is defined by the curl $Bg = \overline{\nabla}\times\mathbf{A}_g$. Since this velocity is constant, it can be taken out of the integral of Equation A4.3-2 and the integral carried out to give

$$\mathbf{A}_g = (v/c)\cdot\int_V(\rho/r)\cdot dV = \sim (v/c)\cdot G\cdot M_U/R_U = (v/c)\cdot\varphi_g$$

Equation A4.3-3

where G is the gravitational constant, and M_U, R_U are the equivalent mass and radius of the universe, which are also assumed to be constant. If we now substitute this definition of $\mathbf{A}_g$ back into Equation A4.3-1, we get

$$\mathbf{F}_{gi}/m = -\overline{\nabla}\varphi_g - (1/c)\cdot\partial\mathbf{A}_g/\partial t = \overline{\nabla}\varphi_g - \left(\varphi_g/c^2\right)\cdot\partial\mathbf{v}/\partial t. \quad \text{Equation A4.3-4}$$

For a particle moving at constant velocity, the second term vanishes. However, if the object is accelerating with respect to the rest of the universe, then the second term does not vanish because $\partial\mathbf{v}/\partial t$ equals the acceleration. From cosmological considerations, the energy of a mass at rest is its gravitational potential inside the surrounding sphere of universal mass so that the speed of light $c^2 = \varphi_g = G \cdot MU/RU$. Then the gravito-inertial force becomes the d'Alembertian form of Newton's second law. When only gravitational forces are involved and $\mathbf{g}$ is the standard gravitational field, then Equation A4.3-4 becomes

$$\mathbf{F}_{gi} = 0 = -m\cdot\overline{\nabla}\varphi_g - m\cdot\partial\mathbf{v}/\partial t = m\cdot\mathbf{g} - m\cdot\mathbf{a}. \quad \text{Equation A4.3-5}$$

This shows that the inertial reaction forces are exclusively gravitational in origin. The analogous force equation in electricity and magnetism is called the Lorentz force and is written in terms of the electric E_e and magnetic B_e field as

$$\mathbf{F}_{em} = q\cdot\mathbf{E}_e + q\cdot\mathbf{v}\times\mathbf{B}_e, \quad \text{Equation A4.3-6}$$

while the analogous force equation in the gravito-inertial domain is

$$\mathbf{F}_{gi} = m\cdot\mathbf{E}_g + m\cdot\mathbf{v}\times\mathbf{B}_g. \quad \text{Equation A4.3-7}$$

A5.1

SIMPLE DERIVATION OF THE WAVE EQUATION

Assume that each clock, named [X,Y,Z], in a field of clocks defining a Hilbert space, was isolated, then its internal mechanism would drive it at a rate so as to make its single degree of freedom take on a value t[X,Y,Z]. Due to the interaction with its surrounding cells, the movement of the clock and hence the time it actually tells will deviate from this isolated equilibrium. If the interactions are small enough the coupled motion spanning the field of clocks defining the Hilbert space can be calculated from the theory of small oscillations (Goldstein, 1965, chapter 10). The actual motion is then given by

$$\tau[X,Y,Z] = t[X,Y,Z] + \psi(X,Y,Z,t) \qquad \text{Equation A5.1-1}$$

If we visualize such a clock in a coordinate frame, which moves around the clock-face dial with a motion identical to t[X,Y,Z], then the clock pointer would oscillate around a stationary point with a motion defined by $\psi(X,Y,Z, t)$.

We now model the interactions of the clock-pointer particle as two potentials. One is modeled as a spring to its immediate neighbors, which acts like a excitation effect, and the other is a spring attached to the equilibrium position, which acts like a restoring force to the equilibrium motion t[X,Y,Z]. We will consider only one dimension, X, to simplify the notation. The system of clock-pointer particles can then be treated as a mass point array as shown in Figure A5.1-1.

The system of equations for the interacting pointers reduces to a set of finite difference equations of the following form connecting each data triplet (Goldstein, 1965, chapter 10).

$$0 = \frac{m}{\Delta}\ddot{\Psi}[X] + \frac{k0}{\Delta}\cdot\Psi[X] - k1\cdot\Delta\cdot\frac{(\Psi[X+1]-\Psi[X])}{\Delta^2} + k1\cdot\Delta\cdot\frac{(\Psi[X]-\Psi[X-1])}{\Delta^2}$$

Equation A5.1-2

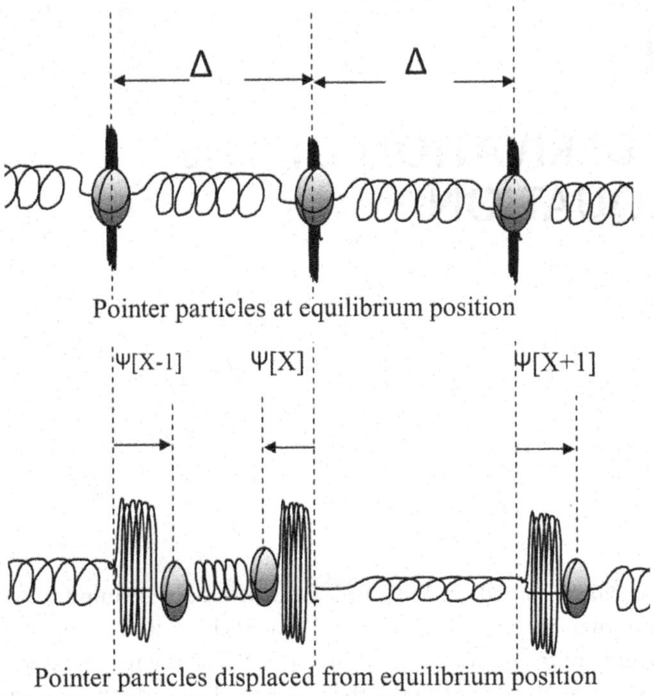

FIGURE A5.1-1 Mass point model of clock-pointer particles oscillating around equilibrium held by elect-magnetic and gravito-electric force springs

There is one equation for each point X. The transition from a discrete to continuous media is done in the usual way by recognizing that the third and fourth term can be written as a second order derivative in terms of the cell names and introducing the continuum properties of Young's Modulus "$Y = k1 \cdot \Delta$" and linear density "$\mu = m/\Delta$". The Equation A5.1-2 then takes on the form

$$0 = \frac{d^2\Psi[X]}{d^2t} + \left(\frac{k0}{m} \cdot \Psi[X]\right) - \left(\frac{Y}{\mu} \cdot \frac{d^2\Psi[X]}{dX^2}\right) \qquad \text{Equation A5.1-3}$$

We now assume that the coupling spring is weak compared with the internal spring and substitute a trial solution.

$$\Psi[X](t) = \psi[X](t) \cdot e^{-i \cdot \omega_0 \cdot t}, \text{ where } \omega_0 = \sqrt{\frac{k0}{m}} \qquad \text{Equation A5.1-4}$$

Substituting this solution into Equation A5.1-3 and, dropping the small second derivative of the amplitude term, gives a first-order equation in time of the form.

$$0 = -2 \cdot i \cdot \omega_0 \cdot \frac{d\psi[X](t)}{dt} - \left(\frac{Y}{\mu} \cdot \frac{d^2\psi[X]}{dX^2}\right) \qquad \text{Equation A5.1-5}$$

Lastly, we identify the frequency around the rest point with the rest mass and the velocity of signals in the media with the speed of light as follows.

$$\omega_0 = \frac{2 \cdot \pi \cdot m \cdot c^2}{h}, \text{ where } c^2 = \frac{Y}{\mu} \qquad \text{Equation A5.1-6}$$

Finally, by substituting these expressions into Equation A5.1-5 we get the one-dimensional form of the time dependent Schrödinger equation, for a free particle.

$$-i \cdot \frac{d\psi[X](t)}{dt} = \frac{(h/2 \cdot \pi)}{2 \cdot m} \cdot \frac{d^2\psi[X](t)}{dX^2} \qquad \text{Equation A5.1-7}$$

Since Schrödinger utilized oscillations in a continuous media as a visualization for Wave Mechanics, it should not be surprising that the theory of small oscillations applied to a field of interacting clocks would yield equations of the same form. Here, however, the wave function ψ has a very specific interpretation as the deviation field of proper time–energy complex in an underlying space-time reference system.

Let us now remember that a field of detector cells, whether implemented in a biological form such as the retina or externalized as measuring instruments, are the physical boundaries known as the von Neumann Cut between the external world, which can never be experienced directly, and the internal qualia of our direct experience. At this stage of the argument we have a de Broglie Wave on the outside side of the detector arrays and the observable action patterns on the inside. The next question is how to connect the characteristics of waves and particles inside the detector space in visualizable terms. This problem has been addressed with the mass-charge separation hypothesis presented by the author in previous publications and the main text of this book.

A5.2

ACTION-FLOW DIAGRAMS IN QUANTUM NOMENCLATURE

The enfolded action-flow diagram between space and time separated action densities introduced in Figure 4.3-5 is reproduced in Figure A5.2-1 to identify how action-flow cycles can be used to visualize quantum theory. When volumes are small enough the cyclic action flowing between densities can be represented by a flow between the degrees of freedom of their centers in a complex Cartesian coordinate frame as shown in Figure A5.2-1.

The reason a complex Minkowski space is useful was explained in Figure 4.1-3 that showed how energy times time "H·dt" represents action flowing through the observer while "p_x·dx" represents the 3rd-person theoretical side view experience of the flow. Combined with the further recognition, shown as Figure 4.4-4, that the difference between these two action flows represents Hamilton's Principle Function "S", i.e. the interaction between the event of interest (Apple) and the rest of the Universe (U). It is through minimization of this function that the actual trajectory of the event of interest is calculated. Minkowski realized that if a complex spatial 4-vector were defined as

$$d\underline{\mathbf{x}} = dx + dy + dz + i \cdot v_c \cdot dt, \qquad \text{Equation A5.2-1}$$

and a complex momentum 4-vector were defined as

$$\underline{\mathbf{p}} = p_x + p_y + p_z + i \cdot H/v_c, \qquad \text{Equation A5.2-2}$$

then the dot product of these vectors would automatically give Hamilton's Principle Function, often simply called the Action Function,

$$dS = \underline{\mathbf{p}} \bullet \underline{\mathbf{dx}} = p_x \cdot dx + p_y \cdot dx + p_z \cdot dx - H \cdot dt, \qquad \text{Equation A5.2-3}$$

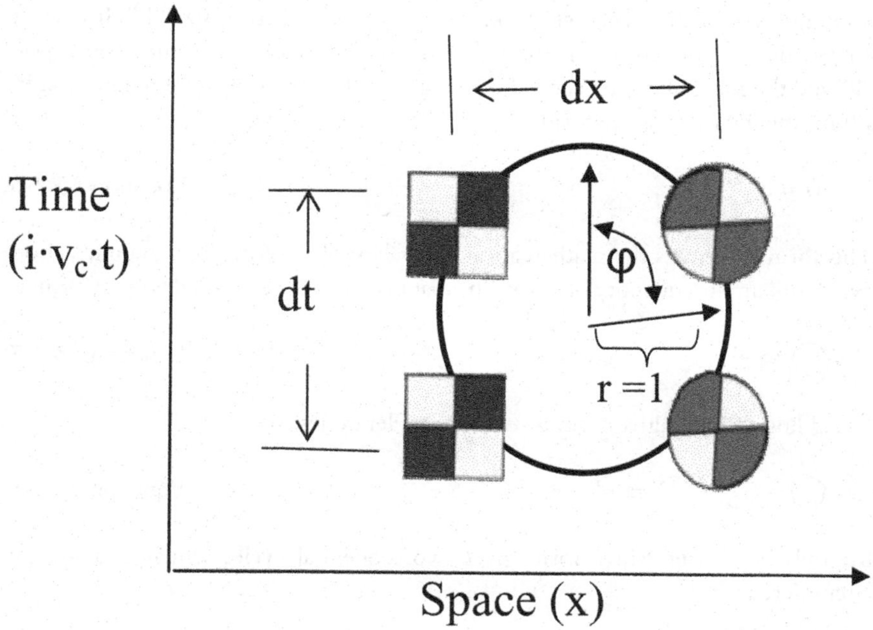

FIGURE A5.2-1 Action flow between time and space separated charge and mass centers, where v_c is the action-flow speed around the cycle and the volume is proportional to the action ($dA \sim dt \cdot dx = dVol$) – see Section 4.3.3.

while the dot product of the complex spatial 4-vector would give the state interval squared between two state positions in 4-space,

$$ds^2 = dx^2 + dy^2 + dz^2 - v_c^2 \cdot dt^2 . \qquad \text{Equation A5.2-4}$$

The convenience of this notation popularized Einstein's special relativity theory and was taken over in quantum theory where Schrödinger's wave function "ψ" is defined as

$$\Psi = e^{(i/h)\int_0^{2\cdot\pi} (dS(\varphi)/d\varphi)\cdot d\varphi} . \qquad \text{Equation A5.2-5}$$

Here the Action function is written in polar coordinates where "φ" is the phase angle around the activity cycle and "h" is Planck's constant and "dS(φ)/dφ" is the angular momentum. Of historic interest is that Schrödinger did not postulate a complex wave function. The complex form first appeared in 1926 when Erwin Madelung published an article in which he discussed the hydrodynamic analogy between particle trajectories and fluid mechanics (Sotina, 2014). CAT includes the conscious observer by identifying the model of reality as the activity happening when a model operator executes the instructions specified by the theory. A fundamental, but questionable, assumption of contemporary quantum theory is that nothing can, even in principle, be known inside an action of size "h". If correct "dS(φ)/dφ" can be replaced by the constant average angular momentum per cycle "h" and the integral can be carried out to get the full description of the motion in a fundamental cycle as the form

$$\psi = e^{2\cdot\pi\cdot i}. \qquad \text{Equation A5.2-6}$$

This form represents the mathematical equivalent of the form of a graphic action cycle containing a quantity of action "h" that is visualized as a closed loop of change.

$$\bigcirc \Leftrightarrow e^{2\cdot\pi\cdot i} \qquad \text{Equation A5.2-7}$$

Adding this primitive form gives two parallel cycles,

$$\bigcirc = \bigcirc + \bigcirc \Leftrightarrow e^{2\cdot\pi\cdot i} + e^{2\cdot\pi\cdot i} = 2\cdot e^{2\cdot\pi\cdot i} \qquad \text{Equation A5.2-8}$$

Multiplying this primitive form gives two sequential cycles which doubles the circumference,

$$\bigcirc = \bigcirc \cdot \bigcirc \Leftrightarrow e^{2\cdot\pi\cdot i} \bullet e^{2\cdot\pi\cdot i} = e^{2\cdot 2\cdot\pi\cdot i} \qquad \text{Equation A5.2-9}$$

Combining multiplication and addition we get a complex of geometric forms that are mathematically described as a Fourier transform where "n" is the number of cycles and "a_n" is the number of parallel loops having "n" cycles.

$$\bigcirc + \bigcirc + \bigcirc \Leftrightarrow 2\cdot e^{2\cdot 2\cdot\pi\cdot i} + 4\cdot e^{2\cdot\pi\cdot i} + e^{2\cdot\pi\cdot i} = \Sigma a_n \cdot e^{n\cdot 2\cdot\pi\cdot i} \qquad \text{Equation A5.2-10}$$

Such complex forms satisfy the Schrödinger equation (see Appendix A5.1). Two quantum systems defined by two action structures "a" and "b" can only interact by moving an action structure "c" also composed of h-cycles.

before $\quad \bigcirc + \bigcirc \Leftrightarrow \Sigma a_n \cdot e^{n\cdot 2\cdot\pi\cdot i} \qquad \bigcirc + \bigcirc \Leftrightarrow \Sigma b_n \cdot e^{n\cdot 2\cdot\pi\cdot i}$

interaction $\quad \bigcirc + \bigcirc \Leftrightarrow e^{2\cdot 2\cdot\pi\cdot i} + 2\cdot e^{2\cdot\pi\cdot i} = \Sigma c_n \cdot e^{n\cdot 2\cdot\pi\cdot i}$

after $\quad \bigcirc + \bigcirc \Leftrightarrow \Sigma a`_n \cdot e^{n\cdot 2\cdot\pi\cdot i} \qquad \bigcirc + \bigcirc \Leftrightarrow \Sigma b`_n \cdot e^{n\cdot 2\cdot\pi\cdot i}$

This example shows why quantum theory can be formulated in the Heisenberg matrix picture because both Fermions and Bosons are linear sums of a standard fundamental motion. The picture is valid as long as no action structure is allowed inside "h".

REFERENCES AND NOTES

Atmanspacher, H. (2012) "Dual-Aspect Monism à la Pauli and Jung", *Journal of Consciousness Studies*, Vol. 19, Nos. 9–10, pp. 96–120.

Baars, B. J. (1997) *In the Theater of Consciousness*, New York, NY: Oxford University Press, ISBN-13: 978–0195147032

Baer, N., and Baer, W. (2012) "Interest-Attention Feedback System for Separating Cognitive Awareness Into Different Left and Right Sensor Displays", Patent Application No. 13/455, 134, filed April 25, 2012.

Baer, W. (1972) "The Crystal Spectra of Pm in CaCl", Ph.D. Thesis in Physics, University of California Berkeley, See Appendix.

Baer, W. (2010a) "Introduction to the Physics of Consciousness", *Journal of Consciousness Studies*, Vol. 17, Nos. 3–4, pp. 165–191.

Baer, W. (2010b) "Theoretical Discussion for Quantum Computation in Biological Systems", *Quantum Information and Computation VIII, SPIE Defense & Security Symposium*, Orlando, Florida, April 5–9, 2010, Paper 7702–31. Permalink: www.dx.doi.org/10.1117/12.850843

Baer, W. (2011) "Cognitive Operations in the First-Person Perspective: Part 1: The 1st- Person Laboratory", *Quantum Biosystems*, Vol. 3, No. 2, pp. 26–44. URL: www.quantumbiosystems.org/admin/files/Baer%20QBS%203%282%29%2026-44.pdf

Baer, W. (2012) "The Cognitive Force in the Hierarchy of the Quantum Brain", *Toward a Science of Consciousness Abstract*, Conference in Tucson, Arizona, April 9–12, 2012.

Baer, W. (2014a) "Chapter 1: The Physical Foundation of Consciousness", *Mind, Brain, and Cosmos*, edited by Deepak Chopra, First Nook Edition: November 2013, available in Kindle Edition, August 2014.

Baer, W. (2014b) "Force of Consciousness in Mass Charge Interactions", *Cosmos and History: The Journal of Natural and Social Philosophy*, Vol. 10, No. 1. URL: www.cosmosandhistory.org/index.php/journal/article/view/421

Baer, W. (2014c) "Mass Charge Interactions for Visualizing the Quantum Field", *Conference Proceedings, IXth Viger Conference*, pp. 16–19, Morgan State University, Baltimore, Maryland, November 2014.

Baer, W. (2015a) "Photons as Observer Transitions in the Event Oriented World View", *Proceedings of SPIE Volume 9570, The Nature of Light What Are Photons? VI*, edited by C.

Roychoudhuri, Al F. Kracklauer, and H. De Raedt, San Diego, California, August 10–13, 2015.

Baer, W. (2015b) "Independent Verification of Psychophysical Interactions With a Double-Slit Interference Pattern", *Physics Essays*, Vol. 28, pp. 47–54.

Baer, W. (2017a) "Does the Rose-Tinted Glassed Effect in Contemporary Physics Prevent Us from Explaining Consciousness?" *Journal of Consciousness Studies*, Vol. 24, Nos. 7–8, pp. 8–27.

Baer, W. (2017b) "You Are the Universe", *Journal of Consciousness Studies*, Vol. 24, Nos. 3–4, March/April, p. 223.

Baer, W. (2018) "Introduction to Cognitive Action Theory", J. Phys.: Conf. Ser. 1251 012008, URL: https://iopscience.iop.org/article/10.1088/1742-6596/1251/1/012008

Baer, W., and Pizzi, R. (2009) "The Case for Biological Quantum Computer Elements", *Proceedings SPIE Quantum Computation VII Information Session of the Defense & Security Symposium*, Orlando, Florida, April 13–17, 2009, Paper 04–7342–3.

Baer, W., Reiter, E., and Jabs, H. (2017) "Null Result for Cahill's 3-Space Gravitational Wave Experiment with Zener Diode Detectors", *Progress in Physics*, Vol. 13, No. 2, April, pp. 111–115.

Beinhocker, E. D. (2006) *The Origin of Wealth*, Boston, MA: Harvard Business School Press, p. 79, ISBN 978-1-4221-2103-0(pbk)

Bernroider, G., and Baer, W. (2010) "Indications for Quantum Computation Requirements from Comparative Brain Analysis", *Proceedings of the SPIE*, Vol. 7702, id. 77020R. doi:10.1117/12.850468

Bernroider, G., and Roy, S. (2004) "Quantum Classical Correspondence in the Brain: Scaling, Action Distances and Predictability Behind Neural Signals", *Forma*, Vol. 19, pp. 55–68.

Blood, C. (2009) "Constraints on Interpretations of Quantum Mechanics", Cornell University Library. URL: http://arxiv.org/abs/0912.2985 (for a review of interpretations)

Bohm, D., and Hiley, B. J. (1993) *The Undivided Universe*, New York, NY: Routledge, ISBN 0-415-06588-7

Bohr, N. (1958) *Atomic Physics and Human Knowledge*, New York, NY: John Wiley & Sons, p. 26: "No result of an experiment . . . can be interpreted as giving information about the independent properties of the objects . . ."

Brown, A., Roberts, D., and Susskind, L. (2016) "Holographic Complexity Equals Bulk Action", *Physics Review Letters*, Vol. 116, pp. 191301, archived as "Complexity Equals Action" in www.arxiv.org/pdf/1509.07876. Note: Complexity is equated to the volume of black holes.

Cahill, R. (2014) "Gravitational Wave Experiments with Zener Diode Quantum Detectors: Fractal Dynamical Space and Universe Expansion with Inflation Epoch", *Progress in Physics*, Vol. 10, pp. 131–138.

Cahill, T. (2006) "Thomas Aquinas Replaces Plato With Aristotle", *Mysteries of the Middle Ages*, New York, NY: Anchor Books, pp. 209, 233, ISBN 978-0-385-49556-1

Carnap, R. (2000) "The Observation Language Versus the Theoretical Language", *Readings in the Philosophy of Science*, edited by Theodore Schick Jr., Houston, TX: Mayfield Publishing Co., p. 166.

Celeghini, E., Rasetti, M., and Vitiello, G. (1992) "Quantum Dissipation", *Annals of Physics*, Vol. 215, pp. 156–170.

Chalmers, D. J. (1996) *The Conscious Mind*, Oxford: Oxford University Press, p. 238, ISBN 0-19-510553-2

Chalmers, D. J. (1997) "Facing up to the Problem of Consciousness", *Journal of Consciousness Studies*, Vol. 4, pp. 3–46. URL: http://consc.net/papers/facing.pdf

Chopra, D., and Kafatos, M. (2017) *You are the Universe*, New York, NY: Random House, ISBN 978-0-307-88916-4

Cirac, J. I., and Zoller, P. (1995) "Quantum Computations with Cold Trapped Ions", *Physical Review Letters*, Vol. 74, pp. 4094–4097.

Coghlan, A. (2014) "The Smart Mouse with the Half-Human Brain", *New Scientist*, Vol. 6, December. URL: www.newscientist.com/article/dn26639-the-smart-mouse-with-the-half-human-brain/

D'Espagnat, B. (1989) ". . . the Kantian Thing in Itself Which Is Supposed to Be Completely Unknowable . . .", *Reality and The Physicist*, Cambridge, MA: Cambridge University Press, p. 182, ISBN 0–521–32940. NOTE: This book is a general discussion of the Instrumentalist Interpretation of quantum theory.

D-wave. (2017) "Quantum Computing, How D-wave Systems Work". URL: www.dwavesys.com/quantum-computing

Eddington, A. (1938) *The Philosophy of Physical Science*, London: The Macmillan Company, p. 21, QC6 E21

E-Mail. (2018) Private communication between Harry Jabs "Institute for Frontier Sciences", Emeryville, California; Grant Moulton "Invention Planet, LLC", Santa Rosa, California; Steve Murphy "ParseTree Corporation", Cody, Wyoming; Eric Reiter "Unquantum Lab", Pacifica, California.

Everett, H. (1957) "'Relative State' Formulation of Quantum Theory", *Review of Modern Physics*, Vol. 29, No. 3.

Fleming, G., Scholes, G., and Cheng, Y. (2011) "Quantum Effects in Biology", *Procedia Chemistry*, Vol. 3, No. 1, pp. 38–57. URL: www.sciencedirect.com/science/article/pii/S1876619611000507

Fredkin, E., and Toffoli, T. (1982) "Conservative Logic", *International Journal of Theoretical Physics* (Springer, Netherlands), Vol. 21, No. 3, April, pp. 219–253.

Freeman, W., and Korma, R. (2010) "Freeman's Mass Action", *SCHOLARPEDIA*. URL: www.scholarpedia.org/article/Freeman%27s_mass_action

Gibson, J. J. (1950) *The Perception of the Visual World*, London: Houghton Mifflin. Call No. Bf 241.G5, See figure "The Visual Ego of Ernst Mach".

Goldstein, H. (1965) *Classical Mechanics*, New York, NY: Addison-Wesley.

Grandy, G. (2011) "The DNA Molecule Is Autopoietic, Dynamic, Evolving and a Form of Consciousness", *International Journal of Arts & Sciences*, Vol. 4, No. 20, pp. 7–30, CD-ROM, ISSN 1944–6934

Green, G. (1999) "˜Time Is What Clocks Measure", *The Elegant Universe: Superstrings, Hidden Dimensions, and the Quest or the Ultimate Theory*, New York, NY: W.W. Norton & Co., p. 37, ISBN 0-393-04688-5

Grover, L. K. (1996) "A Fast Quantum Mechanical Algorithm for Database Search", *Proceedings, 28th Annual ACM Symposium on the Theory of Computing*, p. 212, May 1996.

Hagan, S., Hameroff, S. R., and Tuszynski, J. A. (2002) "Quantum Computation in Brain Microtubules: Decoherence and Biological Feasibility", *Physical Review E*, Vol. 65, 061901.

Hales, R. H., Yudofsky, S. C., and Talbott, J. A. (eds.). (1999) *The American Psychiatric Press Textbook of Psychiatry*, 3rd ed., Arlington, VA: American Psychiatric Press, ISBN 0-88048-819-0

Hameroff, S. (1998) "Quantum Computing in Brain Microtubules", *Philosophical Transactions Royal Society London (A)*, Vol. 356, pp. 1869–1896, see URL for related publications www.quantumconsciousness.org/publications.html; also see URL: www.quantumconsciousness.org/content/hameroff-penrose-review-orch-or-theory

Hara, O., and Goto, T. (1970) "Deformable Sphere Model of Hadrons", *Progress of Theoretical Physics*, Vol. 44, No. 5, November, pp. 1383–1411.

Hara, O., Goto, T., Tsai, S., and Yabuki, H. (1968) "Deformable Sphere Model of Elementary Particles and Its Relation to Quark", *Progress of Theoretical Physics*, Vol. 39, No. 1, January, pp. 203–227. (Note: I was made aware of this effort by Richard Sears, retired Physicist in Carmel Valley, California).

Heisenberg, W. (1999) *Physics and Philosophy: The Revolution in Modern Science*, Amherst, NY: Prometheus Books, pp. 27–29, ISBN 1-57392-694-9

Hoffman, D., and Prakash, C. (2014) "Objects of Consciousness". *Frontiers in Psychology*, 17 June 2014, URL: www.frontiersin.org/articles/10.3389/fpsyg.2014.00577/full

Hofstadter, D. R. (2007) *I Am a Strange Loop*, New York, NY: Basic Books, ISBN 0465030793

Holman, W. J. (2018) "Self-Driving Car Returns to Earth", *Wall Street Journal*, December 1, 2018 (print edition).

Housel, T. J., Baer, W., and Mun, J. (2015) "A New Theory of Value: The New Invisible Hand of Altruism", *Intellectual Capital in Organizations*, edited by Patricia Ordoñez de Pablos and Leif Edvinsson, New York, NY: Routledge, ISBN 978-0-415-73782-1. URL: www.routledge.com/books/details/9780415737821

Hughes, R. J., James, D. F. V., Gomez, J. J., Gulley, M. S., Holzscheiter, M. H., Kwiat, P. G., Lamoreaux, S. K., Peterson, C. G., Sandberg, V. D., Schauer, M. M., Simmons, C. M., Thorburn, C. E., Tupa, D., Wang, P. Z., and White, A. G. (1999) "The Los Alamos Trapped Ion Quantum Computer Experiment", *Quantum Computing: Where Do We Want to Go Tomorrow?* edited by S. Braunstein, Berlin: Wiley-VCH, pp. 23–55, ISBN 3-527-40284-5

James, W. (1890) *The Principles of Psychology*, Vol. I and II, New York, NY: Dover, 1955 (see Chapter X, "The Consciousness of Self").

Jackson, D. J. (1966) "A Derivation of the Form of This Equation from Maxwell's Equations and Faraday's Law", *Classical Electrodynamics*, New York, NY: John Wiley and Sons, p. 179, LoC# 62–8774

Joselevitch, C. (2008) "Human Retinal Circuitry and Physiology", *Psychology & Neuroscience*, Vol. 1, No. 2, pp. 141–165.

Koch, C., and Crick, F. (1998) "Consciousness and Neuroscience", *Cerebral Cortex*, Vol. 8, No. 2, 1 March, pp. 97–107.

Lake, J. (2015) "The Near-Death Experience: Implications for a More Complete Theory of Consciousness", *Quantum Biosystems*, Vol. 6, No. 1, pp. 131–138.

Lake, J. (2019) "The Near-Death Experience (NDE) as an Inherited Predisposition: Possible Genetic, Epigenetic, Neural and Symbolic Mechanisms?" *Medical Hypotheses*, Vol. 126, pp. 135–148.

Lamme, V. (2015) "The Crack of Dawn", *Open MIND Project*. URL: www.open-mind.net/papers/the-crack-of-dawn-perceptual-functions-and-neural-mechanisms-that-mark-the-transition-from-unconscious-processing-to-conscious-vision

Lande, A. (1973) *Quantum Mechanics in a New Key*, Hicksville, NY: Exposition Press, ISBN 0-682-47667-6

Lehar, S. (2003) *The World in Your Head*, Mahwah, NJ: Lawrence Erlbaum Associates, ISBN 0-8058-4176-8

Levine, J. (1983) "Materialism and Qualia: The Explanatory Gap", *Pacific Philosophical Quarterly*, Vol. 64, pp. 354–361.

Mach, E. (1867) *Contributions to the Analysis of the Sensations* (Translator C. M. Williams), Chicago, IL: Open Court.

Mahler, M. S. (1975) *The Psychological Birth of the Human Infant*, New York, NY: Basic Books, Perseus Books Group, p. 3, ISBN-13: 978-0-465-09554-4

Maturana, H. R. (1970) "Biology of Cognition", *Biological Computer Laboratory Research Report*, BCL 9.0, Urbana, IL: University of Illinois.

Mensky, M. (2006) "Reality in Quantum Mechanics, Extended Everett Concept, and Consciousness". URL: www.arxiv.org/abs/physics/0608309. Note: A good introduction to the extensive writings of M. Mensky on the Universe self-measurement concept.

Metzinger, T. (2000) *Neural Correlates of Consciousness: Empirical and Conceptual Questions*, Cambridge, MA: Massachusetts Institute of Technology Press, ISBN-10:0262133709

Miller, G. (2003) "Surprise to Physicists – Protons Aren't Always Shaped Like a Basketball", *University of Washington, ScienceDaily*, April 8. URL: http: www.sciencedaily.com/releases/2003/04/030408085744.htm

Mirowski, P. (1989) *More Heat Than Light*, Cambridge, MA: Cambridge University Press, p. 224, ISBN 0 521 42689 8(pbk)

Mitterauer, B. (2011) *Weltbild der vielen Wirklichkeiten*, Salzburg: Paracelsus Buchhandlung & Verlag, Seite 14, ISBN 978-3-902776-02-0

Mitterauer, B. (2012) "Qualitative Information Processing in Tripartite Synapses: Hypothetical Model", *Cognitive Computation*, Vol. 4, pp. 181–194.

Morse, P. M., and Feshbach, H. (1953) *Methods of Theoretical Physics*, New York, NY: McGraw-Hill, Part 1, p. 289.

Nagel, T. (1974) "What It Is Like to Be a Bat", *Philosophical Review*, Vol. 93, pp. 435–450.

Penrose, R. (1994) *Shadows of the Mind: A Search for the Missing Science of Consciousness*, Oxford: Oxford University Press, p. 262, ISBN 0 19 510646 6(pbk)

Periera, A. J., Santos, R. P., and Barros, R. F. (2013) "The Calcium Wave Model of the Perception-Action Cycle: Evidence from Semantic Relevance in Memory Experiments", *Frontiers in Psychology*, Vol. 4, p. 252, May. doi:10.3389/fpsyg.2013.00252

Pinker, S. (1997) *How the Mind Works*, New York, NY: W. W. Norton & Co., p. 146, ISBN 0-392-0454-8

Pizzi, R., and Baer, W. (2009) "The Search for Biological Quantum Computer Elements", *Proceedings ICCES*, Hawaii, USA, March 16–20, 2008, Vol. 154, No. 1, pp. 1–21.

Pizzi, R., Cino, G., Gelain, F., Rossetti, D., and Vescovi, A. (2007) "Learning in Human Neural Networks on Microelectrode Arrays", *Biosystems Journal*, Vol. 88, Nos. 1–2, March, Elsevier ed., pp. 1–15.

Rovelli, C. (1997) "Relational Quantum Mechanics", *International Journal of Theoretical Physics*, Vol. 35, No. 1996, pp. 1637–1678. URL: www.arXiv:quant-ph/9609002v2

Rovelli, C. (2016) *Reality Is Not What It Seems: The Journey to Quantum Gravity*, New York, NY: Penguin Random House.

Rowlands, P. (2007) *From Zero to Infinity: The Foundations of Physics*, Singapore: World Scientific Publishing Co., ISBN-13: 978-9812709141

Sciama, D. W. (1953) "On the Origin of Inertia", *M.N.R.A.S.*, Vol. 113, p. 34. URL: www.exvacuo.free.fr/div/Sciences/Dossiers/Gravite-Inertie-Mass/Inertie/Sciama/D%20W%20Sciama%20-%20On%20the%20origin%20of%20inertia.pdf

Searle, J. (1980) "Minds, Brains, and Programs", *Behavioral and Brain Sciences*, Vol. 3, No. 3, pp. 417–457.

Sears, R. (1971) "Homogeneous Spaces and Internal Quantum Numbers", Ph.D. thesis, Gothenburg ITP, Sweden. Note: Collaboration with Richard Sears connecting charge/mass interactions with sting theory was tragically interrupted by his death.

Shear, J. (1997) *Explaining Consciousness: The Hard Problem*, Cambridge, MA: Massachusetts Institute of Technology Press. URL: www.geocities.com/computerresearchassociated/consciousness.htm

Shor, P. W. (1997) "Polynomial-Time Algorithms for Prime Factorization and Discrete Logarithms on a Quantum Computer", *SIAM Journal on Scientific Computing*, Vol. 26, No. 5, pp. 1484–1509. URL: Bibcode1999SIAMR..41..303SarXivquant-ph/9508027v2

Sotina, N. (2014) "Derivation of the Schroedinger Equation from the Laws of Classical Mechanics, Structure of Physical Vacuum", *Physics Essays*, Vol. 27, No. 3, pp. 321–326.

Stanford Encyclopedia of Philosophy. (2016) "Dualism". URL: https://plato.stanford.edu/entries/dualism/

Stapp, H. P. (1993) *Mind, Matter, and Quantum Mechanics*, Berlin: Springer-Verlag.

Stapp, H. P. (2005) "Quantum Interactive Dualism", *Journal of Consciousness Studies*, Vol. 12, No. 11, p. 53.

Tegmark, M. (2000) "The Importance of Quantum Decoherence in Brain Processes", *Physical Review*, E61:4194–4206. URL: www.arxiv.org/abs/quant-ph/9907009

Tegmark, M. (2014) "Chapter 10", *Our Mathematical Universe*, New York, NY: Random House, p. 243, ISBN 978-0-307-59980-3

Turing Test. (2011) *Stanford Encyclopedia of Philosophy*. URL: http://plato.stanford.edu/entries/turing-test/

Van Lommel, P. (2010) *Consciousness Beyond Life, the Science of the Near-Death Experience*, New York, NY: HarperCollins, ISBN 978-0061777264

Van Lommel, P., Van Wees, R., Meyers, V., and Elfferich, I. (2010) "Near-Death Experience in Survivors of Cardiac Arrest: A Prospective Study in the Netherlands", *The Lancet*, Vol. 358, No. 9298, December 15, pp. 2039–2045. doi:www.dx.doi.org/10.1016/S0140-6736(01)07100-8

Velmans, M. (2000) "Reflexive Monism Projection Postulate", *Understanding Consciousness*, London: Routledge Press, p. 174, ISBN 0-415-18655-2

Verkhratsky, A., and Butt, A. (2007) *Glial Neurobiology: A Textbook*, Hoboken, NJ: Wiley, ISBN: 9780470015643

Vitiello, G. (2001) *My Double Unveiled: The Dissipative Quantum Model of the Brain*, Amsterdam: John Benjamins Publishing, ISBN 9027251525

Von Neumann, J. (1955) "Chapter VI, Sec 1", *The Mathematical Foundations of Quantum Mechanics*, Princeton, NJ: Princeton University Press.

Walker, E. H. (2000) "Chapter 16: From Epicycles to Loops", *The Physics of Consciousness*, New York, NY: Perseus Publishing, ISBN 0-7382-0436-6

Webster, N. (1835) *Instructive and Entertaining Lessons for Youth*, General Books LLC, 2009, ISBN 9781150223662, reprint from the original S. Babcock and Durrie & Peck, 1835, "We Turn Our Eyes, and in an Instant We See Innumerable Objects Around . . . We Close Our Eyes, but the Ideas of Distant Worlds Are Retained in the Mind".

Wheeler, J. A., and Zurek, W. H. (1983) *Quantum Theory and Measurement*, Princeton, NJ: Princeton University Press. For example, see "Law Without Law" by Wheeler, p. 182 and "The Problem of Measurement" by E. P. Wigner, p. 324.

Whinnery, J. (2016) "The Trigger of Extreme Gravity: Dr. James Winnery's NDE Research". URL: www.near-death.com/experiences/triggers/extreme-gravity.html

Whitehead, A. N. (1978) *Process and Reality: An Essay in Cosmology*, Corrected Edition by D. R. Griffin and D. W. Sherburne, New York, NY: The Free Press, ISBN 0-02-934580-4

Wikipedia. (n.d.) "Immanuel Kant", URL: www.en.wikipedia.org/wiki/Immanuel_Kant

Windrem, M. S., Schanz, S. J., Morrow, C., Munir, J., Chandler-Militello, D., Wang, S., and Goldman, S. A. (2014) "A Competitive Advantage by Neonatally Engrafted Human Glial Progenitors Yields Mice Whose Brains Are Chimeric for Human Glia", *Journal of Neuroscience*, Vol. 34, No. 48, November 26, pp. 16153–16161. doi:10.1523/JNEUROSCI.1510–14.2014

Wittgenstein, L. (1973) *Philosophical Investigations Rev. 3* (Translator G. E. M. Anscombe), Upper Saddle River, NJ: Prentice Hall, ISBN-13 078–0024288103

Woodward, J. F. (2013) "Chapter 2: Mach's Principle", *Making Starships and Stargates*, Berlin: Springer Praxis Books, ISBN 978-1-4614-5622-3

INDEX

action 28, 235–236, 280; in classic physics 121–126, 129–133, 142–143, 155 (concept of 118–121; examples of 122–125, 170; Hamilton's Principle Function 17, 199–200, 261, 311, 332); in equilibrium states xx, 36, 45, 105–107, 129, 144, 181, 201, 209, 233, 265, 270, 283, 286, 293, 301–304, 310, 314 (restoring forces 80, 141–145, 153, 153, 194, 208); incompressible fluid 143, 147; Least Action Principle 36, 121, 142, 144, 152–153, 166, 199, 186; material of change 28, 88, 122, 140; in quantum physics (action cycle in quantum nomenclature 16, 179–182, 334; interaction matrix 162–164, 288, 211; quanta as measured action hits 17, 180, 187); reality as structures of 20, 44–45, 50, 64, 95, 104–107, 121, 127–138, 182, 207, 277, 298

actionable truth 53–54, 77; 3rd-person belief visualization 24, 38, 54 (*see* Model of Reality (MoR), visualization of)

Aristotle's natural philosophy 4, 272–275, 277, 298; illusion of 224–225, 296; objective reality assumption xvii, 4, 11–13, 60, 69, 122, 185, 272 (failure at atomic scales 17, 23 (*see also* reductionism); usefulness of 55, 60, 69, 72, 121, 185, 298; visualization of 39, 214)

astrocytes *see* glial network

Big Bang 38, 144, 148, 225, 281–282, 290, 301

bigger Self 3, 58, 62, 207, 214–216, 294, 286, 298–299, 313; as an interacting Universe 205, 230–233; as a loop in time 42–43, 62, 234; as a strange loop xv, 8; as the system producing experiences 51, 215, 225, 313

Big I, You, U 284, 286–290

black hole 13, 150; action volume ratio 143–145; inside of 143, 150, 236

block universe 130–133, 280; movie example of 45, 95, 191

body actual *vs.* perceived xx, 60, 65, 318; classic body in CAT 287–289; growth and death of 293

body loop 19, 43, 210, 217–220, 227, 269; memory body signal comparator 217, 219; *vs.* memory loop 19, 45, 220, 289–292, 297; *see also* comparator

boundary conditions 111, 221; calculation in cyclic time 199, 219–220, 257; cyclic space-time visualization 42, 146–148; at end of space 282; linear *vs.* cyclic 37

change: form of (*see* action, reality as structures of); instant *vs.* event 29; material of (*see* action); movement of 123–126, 180

codes of CAT model symbols 64–66, 287, 318–319

comparator 78, 211, 217, 219, 233, 268, 291

Conscious Action Cycles (CACs) 8, 9, 51, 59, 290; architecture of 73–79, 113; interacting 44, 80, 118–119, 205–208 (*see also* body loop); large/small axis cycle 4, 150, 305; mixing action signals (*see* comparator)
Conscious Action Theory (CAT): CAT-Model of Reality 208–212 (*see also* Model of Reality (MoR)); definition of symbols 317; destruction and creation of space 179; foundational assumptions 1, 28–30, 89, 118, 133–136; summary of 49, 81, 118, 178–179, 205, 235–236, 303, 305, 313
consciousness 234, 261; experience of a memory model 95; experience of sensor stimulation 45 (*see also* body loop); neural correlates of 12, 242; physical correlates of 12, 14, 23, 37, 40, 69, 133, 242–243, 258; in tri-partite synapses (*see* glial network)
coordinating whole 104
cosmology 41, 280–282, 224; black hole 143, 148–150, 236; closure of 41 (*see also* Conscious Action Cycles (CACs), large/small axis cycle); structure of memory 280–282

d'Alembert Principle *see* action, Least Action Principle
degrees-of-freedom (DoF) 73, 120, 141, 317, 324, 325; doubling of 32; *see also* divisions of events
divisions of events: equivalent division rule 41, 136; infinitesimal parts 120; sub-events 121; summary of a whole 120
dual-eye perception 305–308

economy 309
empty space 45; 1st-person experience of 54, 95–100, 148; absolute nothing 87–88 (*see also* empty space, book coordinates); as aether 227, 272, 304, 312; book coordinates 86–88, 91; permanent background in quantum theory 179; as plenum 93, 142, 235–236; properties of 45, 91–93, 179; volume of action (*see* action, incompressible fluid)
energy: action flow rate 29, 78, 155, 172; burn rate analogy 150–153
entropy 129

forces 29–41, 50, 68, 73, 121, 131, 166, 173, 278; accompany action flow between degrees of freedom 148, 168–170; between mass and charge 142, 172, 228; in equilibrium 36, 80, 143–145, 245, 265, 293 (*see also* Least Action Principle); force fields 103–105, 137, 141–142, 145, 211, 280; in harmonic oscillators 172–175, 193–197; interior and exterior of matter 31–34, 77, 97, 133–137; long range memory leak 48; non equilibrium restoring 41, 118, 208, 245, 310; in a quantum particle 197
format 91–92; one's retina with a ruler 191
Frequently Asked Questions (FAQ): How does We evolve? 234, 301, 313; What difference does it make? 225–229, 303; What happens when we die? xv, xvii, 111, 291, 302; What is this 1st-person experience? (*see* perspective, 1st-person perspective); Why does the objective science work so well? (*see* Aristotle's natural philosophy, usefulness of); Why is the objective world an illusion? 56, 74, 88, 224–225, 296
fundamental CAT algorithm 200, 207, 218–223, 256, 291
fundamental desire 80, 128, 166, 219, 230, 286; intrinsic *vs.* projected 245

glial network 266–270, 292, 302
god: god's eye view 80, 110, 133, 144, 150, 161, 168, 205; illusion of 215, 273, 281, 283–287; of an isolated being 212, 286; model metaphor 58, 161, 206, 212, 284

Hamiltonian energy operator 26, 68, 127, 199, 261
Heisenberg 121, 179, 185, 312, 334; Heisenberg cut (*see* von Neumann, Cut)

information 252, 279; absorption, reflection, transmission of 104–110, 206, 278; actionable display of xvii, 3, 5, 8, 52, 56, 77, 80, 214, 230; *see also* knowledge of reality

Kant 279; event onto itself 65–66, 278; unknowable Reality 278
knowledge of reality 1, 7–9, 40, 53, 220–230, 257, 275, 287, 305; last bit of 281, 301; symbolic knowledge 77,

137 (*see also* Model of Reality (MoR)); uncertainty of 160, 304, 324; unknowable 16, 17, 20, 34, 51, 62, 66, 108, 181, 245, 248, 276, 278–280, 288, 295, 334

language xx; nouns, four type reference of xvii, 288–289, 318; subject-object division 33–35, 43–45; *see also* symbols
Least Action Principle 35, 121, 133, 142, 152, 160, 166; canonical Equations 199; fundamental Desire 166, 286; should be called a Least Interaction Principle 167
little-man-inside 14, 77, 187, 242, 272, 275; automating 18–20, 281, 290; functional conscious role 75, 275, 280–281; as a quantum physicist 14, 56, 79

Mach's Principle 131, 173, 319, 327; cause of quantum randomness 47
material 137–141; absolute ground state 144; ink as material of change 28, 88, 140; mass charge densities 31–32, 72, 133, 138, 145, 193, 225; volume extension of 141, 148–149; *see also* action, incompressible fluid
mind 175, 185, 225, 245; interactions between 209–210; limited to expected touch space 55–57; operating *vs.* understanding 52, 245; perceptive space 55, 213
Model of Reality (MoR): alternative CAT model views 138; being in it 22, 72; CAT-Model of Reality 44, 48, 72, 163; component of the bigger processing self- 24; substituting alternative models 10, 11, 20; visualization of 54

near death experience 299
nothing *see* empty space, absolute nothing

objective reality *see* Aristotle's natural philosophy
out of body experience 80, 297–299

perspective: 1st-Person Laboratory 53–58, 75–79; 1st-person perspective 86, 128, 224; 2nd-person perspective 70, 164, 185, 224, 238, 244, 246; 3rd-person or theoretical perspective 33, 86, 69, 128, 190; dual-eye perception 308
Plato 14, 190; cannot get out 20–24, 62, 135; cave-skull analogy 33, 193–194; world of ideals *vs.* models of reality 191
positron-electron 113

quantum theory 5, 16–20; computation with 233, 245–265; event interpretation of 16, 20, 24, 38–41, 179–181; incompatibility with relativity 137, 159, 190–191; interaction as particle location 197, 208; linear approximation of CAT 178, 181, 198; statistical nature explained 20, 47, 159

reality 28; 3rd or theoretical layer 54, 126; imagining symbolically 61, 63, 68, 76, 97; model god metaphor 284; ontology, what is 4, 5, 49, 76, 81, 165, 178, 280, 304; projection of 73–74, 226, 238; search for 57; structure of 64, 80; unknowable 108, 116, 181–184, 189–191, 200, 209, 211–219
reductionism 134–136
relativity 236, 304; general 92–93, 159; special 101, 140, 333

scale model 22, 44, 80, 81, 285, 286, 305, 313, 326; Planck scale 179, 250, 260; size axis of 28, 92, 93, 94, 102, 149, 150, 208, 222, 262, 325
Schrödinger 4, 15, 16, 20, 24, 39, 40, 121, 181, 182, 189–198, 220, 247, 311, 331–334
sensory channels 60, 74, 154, 183, 216–218, 252, 297, 302; breakout of 216–219
solipsism 17, 207
soul 276, 289–290; independent existence of 300
string theory 30, 32, 303
symbols: CAT model symbol types 65; definition of noun types 65, 288, 317; meaning of ink patterns 62, 85–86; operational *vs.* referential 66, 279; symbol-reality axis 61–63, 110, 116–117, 223

theoretical view: cannot get out of 55, 58, 189, 209, 282; inside and outside view of matter 32–34, 134–136; *see also* perspective, 3rd-person or theoretical perspective
time 22, 28, 29–30, 46, 69, 94, 104, 140, 152–160, 169; flow of time through the observer *vs.* action path 29, 35,

39, 79, 108, 112, 118, 126; interval of, Now extension 31, 42, 46, 50, 90, 95; measured time: the state of a clock cycle 29, 42, 46, 67, 112, 144, 156; Newtonian or isolated Universe state time 29, 32, 81, 107, 122, 146, 152, 160–163; time operator, state propagator, next 69, 80, 91, 97, 102; time types 159, 320

torus 46, 146, 147; memory cell configurations of (*see* cosmology, structure of memory); multidimensional 148, 282

Variational Calculus *see* Least Action Principle

von Neumann 13, 16, 27; Cut 13, 43, 68, 180–188, 331